Cell Biology
of Cancer

Cell Biology of Cancer

Edited by

David Glover, Alan Hall and Nick Hastie

SUPPLEMENT 18   1994

JOURNAL OF CELL SCIENCE

Published by THE COMPANY OF BIOLOGISTS LIMITED, Cambridge

The Company of Biologists Limited is a non-profit-making organization whose directors are active professional biologists. The Company, which was founded in 1925, is the owner and publisher of this and *The Journal of Experimental Biology* and *Development* (formerly *Journal of Embryology and Experimental Morphology*).

Journal of Cell Science is devoted to the study of cell organization. Papers will be published dealing with the structure and function of plant and animal cells and their extracellular products, and with such topics as cell growth and division, cell movements and interactions, and cell genetics. Accounts of advances in the relevant techniques will also be published. Contributions concerned with morphogenesis at the cellular and sub-cellular level will be acceptable, as will studies of micro-organisms and viruses, in so far as they are relevant to an understanding of cell organization. Theoretical articles and occasional review articles will be published.

Subscriptions

Journal of Cell Science is published monthly and in 1995 will have 12 normal issues and 1 casebound supplement. The 12 normal issues will be in the form of 1 volume (108). In 1995 the Supplement will be 'Organization of the Cell Nucleus' edited by Ron Laskey, Tony Kouzarides and Colin Dingwall.
Supplements may be purchased individually – prices on application to The Company of Biologists Ltd.

Subscription rates 1995 (for volume 108 plus Supplement 19)

USA, Canada and Mexico: Institutional US$1125; Individual US$185.
Rest of the World: Institutional £645; Individual £105.
(All prices include post and packaging. Airmail delivery is available at an extra cost of £125 (US$220).)

Orders

Orders for 1995, which can be in £ Sterling/Dollars or using Access/Visa credit cards, should be sent to Subscription Administrator, The Company of Biologists Ltd, Bidder Building, 140 Cowley Road, Cambridge CB4 4DL, UK (telephone 01223 426164; 24 hour ordering by Fax 01223 423353) or to your normal agent or bookseller. Individual rates apply only when payment is made by personal cheque or credit card and is sent direct to the Company, not by way of an agent.
Orders must be accompanied by payment. Please contact the above address for prices of back volumes.

Back numbers

Back numbers of the *Journal of Cell Science* may be ordered through The Company of Biologists Ltd. This journal is the successor to the *Quarterly Journal of Microscopical Science*, back numbers of which are obtainable from Messers William Dawson & Sons, Cannon House, Park Farm Road, Folkestone, Kent CT19 5EE, UK.

Journal of Cell Science
Supplement 18
December 1994

Typeset, Printed and Published by
THE COMPANY OF BIOLOGISTS LIMITED
Bidder Building, 140 Cowley Road, Cambridge CB4 4DL, UK
© The Company of Biologists Limited 1994

ISBN: 0 948601 42 6

Preface

This collection of papers reflects three areas of cancer cell biology. The first, cancer and development, is a field that for hundreds of years has intrigued pathologists. The relationship is illustrated most dramatically in the paediatric tumours such as Wilms' tumour of the kidney and retinoblastoma. Through studying these tumours we hope to gain insights into the processes of normal development; conversely, we will never understand the malignancies without a grasp of the mechanisms governing normal development. Now we are beginning to identify the genes that play essential roles in normal differentiation and which when mutated lead to malignancy. In particular, a number of so-called tumour suppressor genes can be categorised in this manner. Hence, both the retinoblastoma and Wilms' tumour genes are essential for normal development and tumours arise through inherited or somatic mutations of these genes. Developmental tumours do not just arise through loss of function of tumour suppressor genes. Hence dominant mutations in the Ret proto oncogene (a tyrosine kinase receptor), the Pax genes (developmental transcription factors) or Bcl2 (an anti-apoptotic gene) can all lead to cancer. It is now clear that the daughters of dividing stem cells can adopt several alternative fates - to continue in cycle, to differentiate, or to die (usually through apoptosis). Developmental cancers can arise through genetic disruptions that alter these fates. Thus we now know that mutations in the retinoblastoma (Rb) gene affect the balance between the cell cycle, differentiation and apoptosis. Furthermore, in order to understand human cancer it is necessary to have recourse to animal model systems. Hence, one of the themes covered by contributors to this book is the creation of mouse strains with specific mutations in genes associated with development and cancer. However, we must not forget that *Drosophila* is still a classic system for studying developmental cascades. At least fifty different genetic loci in *Drosophila* are associated with inherited predisposition to cancers. Already seven of these genes have been cloned and shown to constitute *Drosophila* tumour-suppressor genes. The functions of several of these genes in signalling pathways are discussed as well as their possible relevance to human cancer.

Signalling pathways play an essential role during development, but their characterisation has been driven by studies on a variety of biological systems largely utilising cultured cells. Recent years have seen much attention upon the so-called MAP kinase signalling cascade. The ras signalling pathway exemplifies the extent to which this system has been conserved. Protein-protein interactions mediated through SH2 and SH3 domains play a crucial role in linking the EGF tyrosine kinase receptor to sos, the exchange factor for ras. The specificity of these interactions appears to be determined by individual SH2 domain sequences. The role of the MAP kinase cascade in maturation of *Xenopus* oocytes exemplifies how this pathway might not only be used to signal G_1 events in cell proliferation, but also G_2-M events that can regulate microtubule behaviour. The relationship, and in some cases parallel behaviour of MAPK and cdc2 kinase in oocyte maturation, is intriguing.

Several articles in this book also look at cell surface receptors in their own right. Mutagenesis of the major autophosphorylation site of the CSF receptor, for example, prevents cells from expressing myc and from entering mitosis in response to CSF-1. However, other responses, fos and jun expression do take place. Links with cell cycle events are explored through the effect of TGF-β receptors as negative regulators. TGF-β results in the induction of p27 protein, one of the rapidly expanding members of cyclin dependent kinase inhibitors, which forms an inhibitory complex with cyclin E/cdc2.

This theme is revisited in the final part of the book - devoted to cell cycle regulation - which considers properties of another cdk inhibitor, p21. p21 expression is induced by p53 whose properties in normal and tumour cells are discussed. The diversity of the cdk and cyclin family members is also addressed in this section. It seems that consequent to this diversion is a need for several forms of the activating phosphatase cdc25. The mammalian cdc25 appears to be specifically required at G_1-S to activate G_1-specific cyclin-cdk complexes. Although this book focuses on cancer and the cell cycle, the role of yeast in establishing key aspects of cell cycle control is not overlooked. We see how studies with fission yeast have identified a gene, rum1, which appears to encode another cyclin dependent kinase inhibitor protein that serves to regulate the dependency of the fission yeast cell cycle on START, the point at which it becomes committed to the next cycle. Of several checkpoint controls monitoring the completion of DNA replication, the role of the fission yeast gene *cdc5* in the replication checkpoint is discussed.

This book can only be expected to cover but a fraction of the ongoing research in this rapidly moving field and therefore is just a snapshot of the field at a particular point in time. Nevertheless, we hope they provide a useful opportunity to survey recent developments in a broad context. We wish to thank all of the contributors and hope that its readers will find it stimulating.

David Glover
Dundee

Alan Hall
London

Nick Hastie
Edinburgh

Contents

Supplement 18   1994

Journal of Cell Science, Supplement 18, 1-5 (1994)
Printed in Great Britain © The Company of Biologists Limited 1994

Wilms' tumour - a case of disrupted development

Kiyoshi Miyagawa, Jill Kent, Andreas Schedl, Veronica van Heyningen and Nicholas D. Hastie

MRC Human Genetics Unit, Western General Hospital, Edinburgh, UK

SUMMARY

Wilms' tumour is a paediatric kidney malignancy that arises through aberrant differentiation of nephric stem cells. We are studying the role of one Wilms' tumour predisposition gene, WT1. This is a tumour suppressor gene whose function is required for normal development of the genitourinary system. WT1 encodes a putative transcriptional repressor of the zinc finger family. Here we discuss how one of the normal functions of WT1 may be to suppress myogenesis during kidney development. Furthermore, we describe how we are proposing to use YAC (yeast artificial chromosome) transgenesis to analyse WT1 regulation and function in mice. We also discuss the evolution of the WT1 gene amongst different vertebrate classes and how this may provide insights into genitourinary evolution.

Key words: Wilms' tumour, WTI, transcriptional repression, tumour suppression, zinc finger

INTRODUCTION

Wilms' tumour (nephroblastoma) has long been considered a wonderful example of the way in which tumours can arise through abnormal development (van Heyningen and Hastie, 1992; Haber and Housman, 1992; Hastie, 1993). These tumours arise from mesenchymal stem cells, which usually differentiate into the epithelial components of the nephron. Normally during kidney development the mesenchyme condenses around the ureteric buds and in response to inductive signals from the bud differentiates into epithelial cells, which go on to form the proximal and distal tubules and the glomerulus of the nephron (Fig. 1). The tumours appear to arise from aberrant rests of stem cells, which persist into early childhood. Normally such rests are transient structures that would disappear by 36 weeks of gestation.

The majority of tumours consist of a combination of blastemal stem cells, stromal cells and epithelial structures that often look like tubules and incomplete glomeruli of the nephron. However, a minority of tumours contain ectopic tissues of mesodermal origin including skeletal muscle, bone and cartilage. We are keen to explore the molecular basis for the production of these ectopic tissues in the tumour.

By studying these tumours we hope to gain insight into normal kidney development. Conversely we will not understand tumorigenesis without an appreciation of the mechanisms controlling normal nephrogenesis.

Unlike the situation for the other well known paediatric tumour, retinoblastoma, there appear to be several different Wilms' tumour predisposition genes (van Heyningen and Hastie, 1992; Haber and Housman, 1992; Hastie, 1993). We are studying one of these, the WT1 gene, which is located on chromosome 11p13 (Call et al., 1990; Gessler et al., 1990). The WT1 gene is a tumour suppressor gene that encodes a protein with four zinc fingers of the Kruppel type. The last three zinc fingers of WT1 share strong homology with those found in the known transcription factors SP1, EGR1 (krox24) and EGR2 (krox20). Unlike these other zinc finger proteins four different isoforms of WT1 are produced through two alternative splices, one leading to the insertion of 17 amino acids upstream of the zinc fingers, the other inserting three amino acids (KTS) between zinc fingers 3 and 4 (Haber et al., 1991). It has been shown that WT1 proteins bind to G-rich target DNA sequences, three nucleotides to each finger (Rauscher et al., 1990; Bickmore et al., 1992). Also the products that differ by the insertion of the KTS have different DNA binding site preferences and may therefore bind to different target genes (Drummond et al., 1994).

The WT1 gene is expressed in a limited set of tissues during development, chief among those being the kidney, the gonads, the spleen and the mesothelium (Pritchard-Jones et al., 1990; Armstrong et al., 1992). All these tissues are of mesodermal origin and all experience a mesenchymal to epithelial transition when WT1 is being expressed. We have proposed that WT1 plays a role in switching cells from a mesenchymal to an epithelial fate. In the kidney expression of WT1 is very low in the uninduced mesenchyme but then increases dramatically during the induction process within the condensed blastema (Fig. 1). Expression then becomes restricted to the posterior part of the newly formed epithelium and is eventually limited to the epithelial layer of the glomerulus. Genetic evidence suggests that WT1 may have different functions at three different stages of nephrogenesis (Fig. 1).

Children who inherit heterozygous deletions of the WT1 gene often develop kidney tumours during the first five years of life but may also suffer from mild abnormalities of the genital system. The tumours arise when the second copy of the gene is also mutated, consistent with Knudson's two-hit hypothesis for tumour suppressor genes. However, children who inherit heterozygous mutations (usually missense mutations) restricted to the zinc finger region of the protein can develop very much more extreme anomalies including severe glomerular nephropa-

LOOSE MESENCHYME

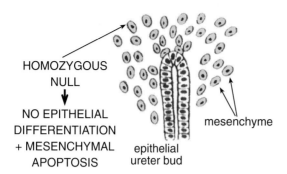

HOMOZYGOUS
NULL

↓

NO EPITHELIAL
DIFFERENTIATION
+ MESENCHYMAL
APOPTOSIS

mesenchyme

epithelial
ureter bud

CONDENSATION

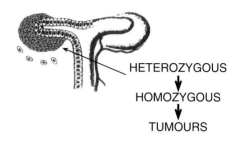

HETEROZYGOUS

↓

HOMOZYGOUS

↓

TUMOURS

COMMA-SHAPE

S-SHAPE

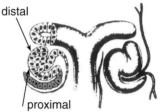

distal

proximal

TUBULE ELONGATION

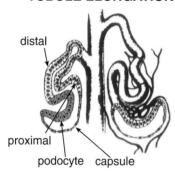

distal

proximal

podocyte   capsule

PODOCYTE FOLDING

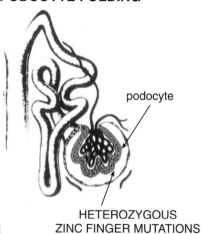

podocyte

HETEROZYGOUS
ZINC FINGER MUTATIONS

↓

GLOMERULAR SCLEROSIS

Fig. 1. The expression of WT1 during nephrogenesis and the 3 different phenotypes arising through WT1 mutation. The shaded cells are those expressing WT1: low in the loose mesenchyme; high in the condensed mesenchyme and the podocyte layer of the glomerulus.

thy, gonadal dysgenesis and Wilms' tumour (Pelletier et al., 1991; Bruening et al., 1992; Baird et al., 1992; Little et al., 1993). Hence it has been proposed that these mutant proteins are acting in a dominant negative fashion; perhaps the mutant form partially inactivates the wild-type protein encoded by the normal allele by forming a heterodimer. Children with the zinc finger mutations and severe genitourinary abnormalities have the Denys-Drash syndrome (DDS).

Proof that the WT1 gene is essential for the development of the genitourinary system has come from the analysis of homozygous null mice (Kreidberg et al., 1993). WT1 null mice completely lack gonads and kidneys and the mesothelium is abnormal. In these mice the mesenchyme of the kidney fails to differentiate into epithelium and is subject to apoptosis.

It is now apparent that mutations in the WT1 gene are only found in 10-15% of Wilms' tumours. So far there have been no clues to suggest that tumours arising through WT1 mutation have different pathological features from those arising in the absence of WT1 mutation. If such differences could be defined they could provide significant insights into WT1 function.

WT1 always behaves in transient transfection assays as a repressor of gene expression (Madden et al., 1991). Hence we can envisage that the normal function of WT1 is to shut off the expression of genes required to maintain kidney stem cells in cycle. When WT1 function is lost stem cells keep in cycle and fail to differentiate. Compelling candidate target genes for regulation by WT1 include the insulin-like growth factor 2 gene (IGF2) and the insulin-like growth factor 1 and 2 receptor

(IGF1/2 receptor) (Drummond et al., 1992; Werner et al., 1993). Both of these genes can be expressed at high levels in Wilms' tumours and are normally expressed at maximum level in undifferentiated kidney mesenchyme. Furthermore it has been shown that WT1 can bind to the promoters of these genes and repress reporter expression from these promoters in transient transfection systems. However, there is no proof as yet to support the idea that these are true physiological targets of WT1 during development.

Our experiments are now directed towards understanding the function of the WT1 gene during development: can WT1 exert a mesenchyme-epithelial transition when expressed ectopically? What are the physiological target genes regulated by WT1 during the development of these mesodermal tissues? Also as the genitourinary system is one that has evolved during vertebrate development we are characterising the WT1 gene from all the major vertebrate classes, with the hope that this might provide insights into the function of WT1 as well as into the evolution of the genitourinary system.

ACTIVATION OF THE MYOGENIC PROGRAMME IN TUMOURS WITH WT1 MUTATION

We were provided with a clue concerning the pathology of tumours involving WT1 mutation when the two nephroblastomas of a child with DDS were examined. As is often the case with inherited WT1 mutations this child had bilateral Wilms' tumours, one on the left kidney the other on the right kidney. Whereas one of the tumours had typical pathology, that is a mixture of epithelial structures, blastemal cells and stromal cells, the other tumour had very large regions that appeared to consist entirely of skeletal muscle. Immunohistochemical markers confirmed that skeletal muscle proteins such as myosin were being expressed in this tumour.

Skeletal muscle is known to develop through the action of the so-called myogenic genes, a group of transcription factors with the helix-loop-helix (HLH) domain, which include myoD, myogenin, Myf5 and Myf6. Recently we have examined whether these genes are expressed in Wilms' tumours and whether such expression is a common feature of tumours arising through WT1 mutation.

We have found that tumours arising through WT1 mutations have high levels of expression of these myogenic genes but that tumours not involving WT1 mutations do not express detectable levels. We have not been able to detect expression of these genes in normal developing kidney thus this appears to be true ectopic activity of myogenic genes.

This finding raises two interesting possibilities. First, that kidney stem cells are capable of differentiating into alternative mesodermal structures, including kidney, bone and cartilage but are normally repressed from doing this. Secondly, that when WT1 function is lost the strict direction of differentiation into epithelial cells is also lost and the stem cells are now capable of differentiating in various directions.

This also begs the question of whether WT1 can directly repress the differentiation of mesenchymal stem cells into muscle and other structures. To test this we have introduced constructs expressing the different spliced forms of WT1 into cultured C3H 10T1/2 cells, mesenchymal cells that can be induced to differentiate into muscle, cartilage and adipose

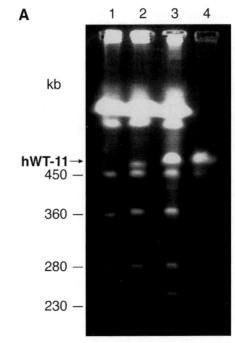

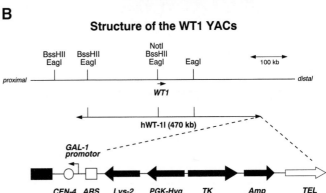

Fig. 2. Amplification and isolation of a large YAC containing the human WT1 gene. (A) Pulsed field gel electrophoresis of the YAC before and after purification; lane 1, chromosomes from *S. cerevisiae*; lane 2, chromosome preparation from *S. cerevisiae* containing the human WT1 YAC (hWT-1I) - see extra band at 470 kb; lane 3, human WT1 YAC after amplification stage (see Schedl et al., 1993); lane 4, the hWT-1I YAC cut out of the gel (as in lane 3) and rerun. (B) Map showing the position of the WT1 gene (70 kb) within the human insert together with features of the vector (see Schedl et al., 1993).

tissue. So far no effect of ectopic WT1 expression on the differentiation of these cells has been obtained; on the one hand there is no inhibition of differentiation into muscle, on the other hand we find no evidence of activation of epithelial markers that would have shown a direct effect of WT1 on mesenchyme to epithelial transition.

The only problems with these experiments were: (i) that we may not have been expressing sufficiently high levels of WT1 protein in these cells; and (ii) that the WT1 gene normally expresses four different forms of mRNA through alternative splicing. The ratio of these different forms is invariant in different mammals and in different tissues so that all the forms

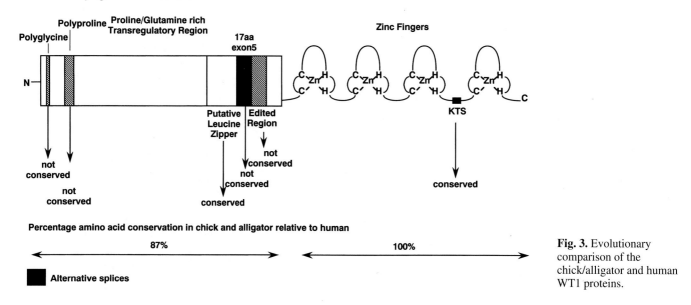

Percentage amino acid conservation in chick and alligator relative to human

87%

100%

■ Alternative splices

Fig. 3. Evolutionary comparison of the chick/alligator and human WT1 proteins.

may be necessary for WT1 to function, perhaps as a complex. If so, expression vectors encoding individual spliced forms may not be able to provide WT1 function. To circumvent this problem we are introducing the whole WT1 gene, which should express all the spliced forms on a YAC vector, both into cells in culture and into mice.

THE USE OF WT1 GENE-CONTAINING YACS FOR FUNCTIONAL STUDIES

As discussed above WT1 encodes four different splice forms of mRNA. All of these may be essential for function. Hence it is desirable to use the whole gene encoding all the different forms of the protein for expression studies. The problem here is that the complete gene is at least 70 kb in size and therefore too large to be included in conventional vectors. Hence we are using YAC vectors, which contain the human WT1 gene and up to 200 kb of flanking sequences upstream and downstream of the gene. If such YACs are introduced into mice or cells they should contain all the regulatory regions intact and should be able to carry out regulated splicing correctly (Schedl et al., 1993). Hence we have introduced one such YAC with a 500 kb insert into mice by direct pronuclear injection (Fig. 2). We have obtained a number of transgenic animals and are now waiting to see if these will transmit the YAC. If so the YAC will be transferred by conventional breeding to WT1 null mice to see if it can rescue the complete development of the mice. We will then create a whole range of modified WT1 YACs using the power of homologous recombination in yeast to generate mutations. Hence we are replacing the WT1 promoter with a constitutive promoter so that we can test whether ectopic expression of WT1 can both suppress muscle formation and direct the mesenchyme to epithelial transition in mice. Also we are making mutations that will disrupt individual splice forms to test the role of these forms during development. Finally, we are intending to create WT1 forms with missense mutations that are similar to those found in patients with DDS. Using these we would like to see whether we can create a mouse model for this condition.

THE EVOLUTION OF THE WT1 GENE AMONGST VERTEBRATES

We have been able to isolate full-length WT1 cDNAs from chicken and alligators and partial cDNAs including the zinc finger region from fish and amphibians (*Xenopus*). Sequencing of these cDNAs has shown that WT1 is highly conserved throughout its length but particularly in the zinc finger region, which maintains 99% identity throughout all the vertebrates (Fig. 3). This is particularly striking as the WT1 zinc fingers share 50-80% identity with the fingers of other known transcription factors. The zinc fingers of WT1 seem to be interchangeable with the related fingers of these other transcription factors. If this is the case why have the zinc fingers been constrained to diverge so much less during evolution? It suggests that there are additional functions for the zinc finger region, other than DNA binding, which we have not yet unravelled.

The +KTS/−KTS differential splice is conserved throughout all vertebrates proving that this must be functionally very important. However, the second alternative splice (±17 amino acids) could only be detected in mammals and not in birds or reptiles (Fig. 3) suggesting that this is a mammal-specific increase in complexity. Hence two WT1 isoforms can be encoded by chickens and alligators compared with four in all the mammals studied. Could the additional forms be involved in directing the production of mammal-specific structures in the genitourinary system? To test this we hope to introduce the WT1 gene from different vertebrates into WT1 null mice to see if they can rescue all the structures.

This work is supported by the Medical Research Council and a Howard Hughes International Scholarship Award to Drs Hastie and van Heyningen.

REFERENCES

Armstrong, J. F., Pritchard-Jones, K., Bickmore, W. A., Hastie, N. D. and Bard, J. B. L. (1992). The expression of the Wilms' tumour gene, WT1, in the developing mammalian embryo. *Mech. Dev.* **40**, 85-97.
Baird, P. N., Santos, A., Groves, J., Jadresic and Cowell, J. K. (1992).

Constitutional mutations in the WT1 gene in patients with Denys-Drash syndrome. *Hum. Mol. Genet.* **1**, 301-305.

Bickmore, W. A., Oghene, K., Little, M. H., Seawright, A., van Heyningen, V. and Hastie, N. D. (1992). Modulation of DNA binding specificity by alternative splicing of the Wilms' tumor WT1 gene transcript. *Science* **257**, 235-237.

Bruening, W., Bardeesy, N., Silverman, B. L., Cohn, R. A., Machin, G. A., Aronson, A. J., Housman, D. and Pelletier, J. (1992). Germline intronic and exonic mutations in the Wilms' tumour gene (WT1) affecting urogenital development. *Nature Genet.* **1**, 144-148.

Call, K. M., Glaser, T., Ito, C. Y., Buckler, A. J., Pelletier, J., Haber, D. A., Rose, E. A., Kral, A., Yeger, H., Lewis, W. H., Jones, C. and Housman, D. E. (1990). Isolation and characterization of a zinc finger polypeptide gene at the human chromosome 11 Wilms' tumor locus. *Cell* **60**, 509-520.

Drummond, I. A., Madden, S. L., Rohwer-Nutter, P., Bell, G. I., Sukhatme, V. P. and Rauscher, F. J. (1992). Repression of the insulin-like growth factor II gene by the Wilms' tumor suppressor WT1. *Science* **257**, 674-678.

Drummond, I. A., Rupprecht, H. D., Rohwer-Nutter, P., Lopez-Guisa, J., Madden, S. L., Rauscher, F. J. and Sukhatme, V. P. (1994). DNA recognition by splicing variants of the Wilms' tumor suppressor, WT1. *Mol. Cell. Biol.* **14**, 3800-3809.

Gessler, M., Poustka, A., Cavenee, W., Neve, R. L., Orkin, S. H. and Bruns, G A P. (1990). Homozygous deletion in Wilms' tumours of a zinc-finger gene identified by chromosome jumping. *Nature* **343**, 774-778.

Haber, D. A., Sohn, R. L., Buckler, A. J., Pelletier, J., Call, K. M. and Housman, D. E. (1991). Alternative splicing and genomic structure of the Wilms' tumor gene WT1. *Proc. Nat. Acad. Sci. USA* **88**, 9618-9622.

Haber, D. A. and Housman, D. E. (1992). Role of the WT1 gene in Wilms' tumour. *Cancer Surveys* **12**, 105-117.

Hastie, N. D. (1993). Wilms' tumour gene and function. *Curr. Opin. Genet. Dev.* **3**, 408-413.

Kreidberg, J. A., Sariola, H., Loring, J M., Maeda, M., Pelletier, J., Housman, D. and Jaenisch, R. (1993). WT1 is required for early kidney development. *Cell* **74**, 679-691.

Little, M. H., Williamson, K. A., Mannens, M., Kelsey, A., Gosden, C., Hastie, N. D. and van Heyningen, V. (1993). Evidence that WT1 mutations in Denys-Drash syndrome patients may act in a dominant-negative fashion. *Hum. Mol. Genet.* **2**, 259-264.

Madden, S. L., Cook, D. M., Morris, J. F., Gashler, A., Sukhatme, V. P. and Rauscher, F. J. (1991). Transcriptional repression mediated by WT1 Wilms' tumor gene product. *Science* **253**, 1550-1553.

Pelletier, J., Bruening, W., Kashtan, C. E., Mauer, S. M., Manivel, J. C., Striegel, J. E., Houghton, D. C., Junien, C., Habib, R., Fouser, L., Fine, R. N., Silverman, B. L., Haber, D. A. and Housman, D. (1991). Germline mutations in the Wilms' tumor suppressor gene are associated with abnormal urogenital development in Denys-Drash syndrome. *Cell* **67**, 437-447.

Pritchard-Jones, K., Fleming, S., Davidson, D., Bickmore, W., Porteous, D., Gosden, C., Bard, J., Buckler, A., Pelletier, J., Housman, D., van Heyningen, V. and Hastie, N. (1990). The candidate Wilms' tumour gene is involved in genitourinary development. *Nature* **346**, 194-197.

Rauscher, F. J., Morris, J. F., Tournay, O. E., Cook, D. M. and Curran, T. (1990). Binding of the Wilms' tumor locus zinc finger protein to the EGR-1 consensus sequence. *Science* **250**, 1259-1262.

Schedl, A., Montoliu, L., Kelsey, G. and Schutz, G. (1993). A yeast artificial chromosome covering the tyrosinase gene confers copy number-dependent expression in transgenic mice. *Nature* **362**, 258-261.

van Heyningen, V. and Hastie, N. D. (1992). Wilms' tumour: reconciling genetics and biology. *Trends Genet.* **8**, 16-21.

Werner, H. R. E., Gian, G., Drummond, I. A., Sukhatme, V. P., Rauscher, F. J., Sens, D. A., Garvin, A. J., LeRoith, D. and Roberts, C. T. (1993). Increased expression of the insulin-like growth factor I receptor gene, *IGF1R*, in Wilms tumor is correlated with modulation of *IGF1R* promoter activity by the WT1 Wilms tumor gene product. *Proc. Nat. Acad. Sci. USA* **90**, 5828-5832.

Journal of Cell Science, Supplement 18, 7-12 (1994)
Printed in Great Britain © The Company of Biologists Limited 1994

A developmental context for multiple genetic alterations in Wilms' tumor

Andrew P. Feinberg

Departments of Medicine, Molecular Biology & Genetics, and Oncology, Johns Hopkins University School of Medicine, 1064 Ross, 720 Rutland Avenue, Baltimore, MD 21205, USA

SUMMARY

Wilms' tumor has served as an example of Knudson's two-hit hypothesis of recessive tumor genes, but the genetics has proven to be surprisingly complex. WT1, a tumor suppressor gene on 11p13, is mutated in only a small fraction of Wilms' tumors, and a second chromosomal region, 11p15, harbors a second Wilms' tumor gene also involved in other cancers. In addition, loss of genomic imprinting, or parental origin-specific gene expression of at least two genes, appears to be an early step in Wilms' tumorigenesis and common cancers. Finally, genes on other chromosomes also play a role. I propose a model of Wilms' tumorigenesis in which multiple genetic alterations act within a specific developmental context, accounting for the epidemiological and pathological heterogeneity of Wilms' tumor, as well as the tissue specificity of the tumor types arising from alterations in these genes.

Key words: Wilms' tumor, WT1, 11p15 tumor suppressor gene, genomic imprinting, IGF2, H19

INTRODUCTION

Wilms' tumor (WT) has presented one of the most difficult genetic problems in molecular oncology, but ultimately it may prove to be one of the most informative. WT was one of the three tumors that led Knudson and Strong (1972) to their two-hit hypothesis of carcinogenesis. According to this model, patients with bilateral (i.e. multiple independent) tumors have a germline mutation and develop cancer at a younger age than children with unilateral tumors, who must develop two hits in a given somatic cell lineage. Comings (1973) also significantly contributed to these early ideas, in proposing that a recessive cancer gene could act as a dominantly inherited cancer predisposition syndrome, if a mutant allele were transmitted through the germline.

The hallmarks of a gene fitting Knudson's model are as follows:

(1) mutations in the causal gene should occur at high frequency in sporadically occurring tumors;

(2) loss of heterozygosity (LOH) in tumors should include the causal gene;

(3) re-introduction of the causal gene into tumor cells that are lacking a normal copy should, at least in part, abrogate the tumor phenotype, since the gene is by definition recessive;

(4) germline mutations in the gene should underlie familial cases of the tumor.

While another of the original three tumors, retinoblastoma, has met these criteria reasonably well, WT has been far more complicated, as will be discussed here. Neuroblastoma, which is beyond the scope of this article, is even less well understood. Some of the observations regarding the complexity of WT are summarized below, and they show that a simple two-hit model

of a single gene is incomplete. I believe that a large part of the answer in understanding them is to view these genetic alterations in the appropriate developmental context.

WILMS' TUMORS SHOW INFREQUENT MUTATIONS OF THE WT1 GENE ON 11P13

The discovery of a homozygous deletion in a Wilms' tumor using anonymous phage clones from the Los Alamos library was one of the first advances in positional cloning of cancer genes. It was accomplished after a heroic effort by the late Bill Lewis, working in a lonely surgery department laboratory at the Hospital for Sick Children in Toronto. Using these mapping reagents, and with considerable additional effort, David Housman's and Gail Bruns' laboratories cloned WT1. This gene was evidently a transcription factor, based upon its five zinc finger motifs resembling a DNA binding protein (Gessler et al., 1990; Call et al., 1990). The precise function of WT1 is still unclear, as its precise physiological targets are not completely understood. It shares a DNA binding motif with EGR-1 (Rauscher et al., 1990). However, it may also serve as a transcriptional inhibitor of IGF2 (Madden et al., 1991). Furthermore, additional DNA sequences to which it binds have been identified (Bickmore et al., 1994). WT1 has been reviewed elsewhere and will not be described in greater detail here (Hastie, 1993; Haber and Housman, 1992), except for three key aspects of the genetics of WT1:

(a) WT1 fulfills Knudson's two-hit hypothesis of carcinogenesis, that a germline mutation in a tumor suppressor gene predisposes individuals to multiple or bilateral tumors at an early age; and sporadic tumors arise from two hits in a somatic cell lineage. Thus, germline mutations in WT1 cause Drash syndrome, or genitourinary malformations plus WT (Pelletier et al., 1991), and WT1 is the tumor suppressor gene involved in the contiguous deletion syndrome WAGR (Wilms, aniridia, genitourinary malformation, mental retardation) (Huff et al., 1991). Also, sporadic tumors can show mutations in WT1, with loss of the normal allele (Huff et al., 1991; Brown et al., 1992; Baird et al., 1992), although mutations in a single allele have also been described (which could act as a dominant negative) (Haber et al., 1990; Kriedberg et al., 1994).

(b) Despite formal compliance with Knudson's model, the mutation frequency in sporadically occurring tumors is strikingly low, about 10% (Hastie, 1993; Little et al., 1992).

(c) About half of Wilms' tumors show loss of expression of WT1, as well as a pseudogene (WIT-1) transcribed in opposite orientation from the same promoter region (Huang et al., 1990). These tumors are characterized by a relatively early stage of differentiation (Huang et al., 1990), which has been referred to by Beckwith and colleagues as intralobar nephrogenic rest-like (or ILNR-like). ILNRs are residual fetal material often found in tumorous kidneys, or even in normal children (at least 1% of newborn infants), that resemble the immature interior of the developing unit of the kidney, the renal lobe (Beckwith et al., 1990). Tumors expressing WT1 (and WIT-1) tend to be perilobar nephrogenic rest-like (or PLNR-like) (Huang et al., 1990). PLNRs are residual fetal material resembling the more mature periphery of the renal lobe (Beckwith et al., 1990). An easy histological distinction between ILNRs and PLNRs is the presence in the former of heterologous tissue elements, such as muscle, suggesting a capacity for pleuripotent differentiation of early fetal kidney (Beckwith et al., 1990). These observations suggest genetic heterogeneity in the pathogenesis of WT.

WILMS' TUMORS INVOLVE INFREQUENT LOH OF WT1 BUT FREQUENT LOSS OF 11p15

Eric Fearon, Bert Vogelstein and I performed an experiment in 1982 that we thought might address Knudson's hypothesis. If two alleles are altered in sporadically occurring tumors, one of them might be altogether lost, which one could detect using polymorphic markers from the same chromosomal arm. The same approach was used by Cavenee and White, without our knowledge, to look at retinoblastoma. We did find loss of heterozygosity (LOH) in WT (Fearon et al., 1984). As our laboratory in Michigan eventually discovered, an important difference between WT and Rb is that, while chromosome 13 LOH includes the Rb gene (Friend et al., 1984), LOH on chromosome 11 does not generally involve 11p13 where the WAGR syndrome was mapped at the time, and where WT1 was later found. Thus, using a panel of markers from throughout 11p, we found that the common region of overlap of LOH was 11p15, not 11p13 (Reeve et al., 1989). LOH of 11p15 has also been reported in many common cancers, including bladder (30%) (Fearon et al., 1985), ovarian (50%) (Zheng et al., 1991), metastatic breast cancer (50%)(Ali et al., 1987), and lung (80%)(Weston et al., 1991). The specific involvement of 11p15 has been observed by several laboratories (Mannens et al., 1988; Wadey et al., 1990), although isolated loss of 11p13 does occur rarely (Wadey et al., 1990). In WT, the frequency

of 11p15 LOH is 30%, not very high compared to, for example, 17p loss in colorectal cancer, but 3-fold that of WT1 mutations. Even in the first report of WT1 mutation in sporadic WT, one copy of WT1 had been deleted and the other duplicated. However, the deletion-duplication event had arisen before the mutation, consistent with involvement of a second locus (Call et al., 1990).

WILMS' TUMORS INVOLVE A TUMOR SUPPRESSOR GENE ON 11p15

The implication of 11p15 LOH is that there is a second tumor suppressor gene on this chromosomal band, which is genetically unlinked to 11p13. In support of this idea, it was shown by Stanbridge's laboratory that, while chromosome 11 suppresses the growth of G401 cells (which are either a WT or rhabdoid tumor cell line), this activity does not require 11p13 but does require 11p15. They performed this experiment using radiation-treated chromosomes that had deleted either of the two regions (Dowdy et al., 1991).

We approached the same question directly, by transferring small parts of the chromosome to tumor cells, rather than using the whole chromosome with small parts missing. We term these reagents 'subchromosomal transferable fragments,' or STFs. They were generated by three steps: (1) introduction of a pSV2neo marker into a translocation chromosome 11/X (with 90% of 11 including all of 11p, and Xqter with the HPRT gene) monochromosome hybrid in mouse A9 cells; (2) microcell transfer and double selection with HAT and G418 (for chromosome 11 containing neo); and (3) irradiated microcell transfer into A9 cells, isolating a panel of hybrids with a portion of chromosome 11 (with neo) isolated from the rest of the chromosome. These STFs differ from conventional radiation hybrids in that they can be transferred into virtually any cell, such as a tumor cell, allowing one to score the recipient cell for a phenotype that is selected against, in this case growth inhibition or suppression of tumorigenicity (Koi et al., 1993).

Using STFs, we could show directly a growth inhibiting effect in vitro of a portion of 11p15, and we could map this activity to a 4 Mb region between the β-globin gene cluster and the insulin gene (Koi et al., 1993). Thus, there is a second tumor suppressor gene on chromosome 11, at band 11p15.

BECKWITH-WIEDEMANN SYNDROME (BWS), WHICH PREDISPOSES TO WT, MAPS TO 11p15

Another prediction of Knudson's model is that some families with WT should transmit germline mutations of the causal gene. Drash syndrome patients probably cannot do this because of their malformation. However, families with WT unlinked to chromosome 11 have also been described (Grundy et al., 1988; Huff et al., 1988).

We became interested in BWS when we identified two large kindreds with this disorder, which causes developmental overgrowth, organomegaly affecting the kidney, liver and tongue, and overproduction of IGF2 and hypoglycemia. Using polymorphic markers from 11p13 and 11p15, we mapped this disorder in both families to 11p15.5, close to the insulin gene.

BWS was genetically unlinked to 11p13 and WT1 (Ping et al., 1989).

Interestingly, WAGR-associated tumors are associated with ILNRs, representing an early stage of differentiation; and BWS-associated tumors are associated with PLNRs, representing a later stage of differentiation (Beckwith et al., 1990). Furthermore, Breslow and colleagues have observed that children with WT and hemihypertrophy (a characteristic of BWS), develop their tumors at a later age than children with WT and genitourinary malformations (a characteristic of WAGR). Thus, Breslow has suggested genetic heterogeneity in Wilms' tumorigenesis on strictly epidemiological grounds, the original gold standard of the genetics of this disorder (Breslow et al., 1988). The epidemiology is consistent with the idea of genetic heterogeneity suggested earlier.

BWS INVOLVES GENOMIC IMPRINTING

Finally, WT appears to involve genomic imprinting, a genetic alteration that is generating widespread excitement in cancer biology, and which further complicates the genetics of WT. In an effort to clone the BWS gene, we obtained cells lines from six patients with germline rearrangements involving 11p15. By deriving sequence tagged sites (STSs) from throughout this band, we obtained 22 YACs spanning over 6 Mb. With the collaboration of Jan Hoovers and Marcel Mannens, who performed fluorescent in situ hybridization with these YACs, we found that the germline rearrangements are distributed over a surprisingly large region of 5 Mb. Furthermore, all of these balanced rearrangements are derived from the maternally inherited chromosome. On the other hand, several patients with unbalanced duplications of 11p15 have also been reported, and all of these are paternally derived. Thus, the chromosomal translocations in BWS suggest that the maternal allele and paternal allele are different, or imprinted (Little et al., 1991).

Genomic imprinting is defined as parental origin-specific differential gene expression (Monk, 1988). BWS would appear to be an imprinted gene, with the paternal allele normally expressed and the maternal allele silent. Two working copies of the gene would cause disease. Thus, in the paternal duplications, there are now two working paternal copies. In the balanced rearrangements, the maternal allele has been moved to an autosome where it is transcriptionally activated, according to the model, and there are again two working copies of the gene and thus disease. Junien's laboratory found that 10% of BWS patients have paternal uniparental disomy, or a normal karyotype but with two paternal and no maternal 11p15 (Henry et al., 1991). These patients, too, would have two working copies of the gene.

WILMS' TUMOR SHOWS LOSS OF IMPRINTING OF IGF2 AND H19

In order to test the idea directly that genomic imprinting is involved in the pathogenesis of WT, we sought to determine whether two genes imprinted in mouse, and mapping to the BWS candidate region, are imprinted in man and abnormally imprinted in cancer. These are insulin-like growth factor-II (IGF2), an important autocrine and paracrine growth factor in a wide variety of childhood and adult tumors (El-Baldry et al., 1990; Bouffler et al., 1990); and H19, an untranslated RNA of obscure function (Brannan et al., 1990), which inhibits embryo growth in transgenic mice (Brunkow and Tilghman, 1991).

We used a known transcribed polymorphism in the H19 gene, and we identified a common polymorphism in an 800 nucleotide CA repeat in the IGF2 gene. This polymorphism is not apparent unless one labels either the 5′ or 3′ PCR primer and cleaves the product at a nonrepetitive *MvnI* site in the middle of the repeat. Using this approach, we found that H19 is transcribed from the maternal allele, and IGF2 from the paternal allele, as has been described in mouse (Rainier et al., 1993). This was the first direct evidence for an imprinted gene in man.

When we examined WT, we identified a novel type of mutation in man. In 70% of 17 tumors, including WT and a rhabdoid tumor, we found biallelic expression of IGF2. In 30% of tumors, there was biallelic expression of H19 (Rainier et al., 1993). This compares to a frequency of LOH of 30% and WT1 mutation of 10%. Reeve's laboratory also found biallelic expression of IGF2 in six WTs (Ogawa et al., 1993). Thus, this alteration is the most frequent yet described in WT. We have coined the term 'loss of imprinting,' or LOI, to describe this alteration. The term LOI has obvious appeal, but it also correctly does not imply mechanism, and is thus not biased toward gene activation or inactivation. It simply means loss of parental origin-specific differential gene expression.

LOI also perfectly fits the imprinting hypothesis of BWS, because in somatic tumors, there are two working copies of an imprinted gene, recapitulating in a Knudsonian way in somatic cells what is seen in the germline in some BWS patients. Also consistent with this model, we have observed LOI in normal tissue of some BWS patients, which has been reported by Weksberg et al. (1993). However, it remains unproven whether IGF2 is the BWS gene, as the frequency of LOI in normal tissue is relatively low. Nevertheless, there is no question that LOI can precede the development of malignancy.

GENE EXPRESSION IN TUMORS WITH LOI

If abnormal imprinting plays a causal role in tumorigenesis, then a prediction would be that those tumors with LOI should also show abnormal expression of the involved genes. To test this idea, we performed northern blot analysis of IGF2 and H19 on a large number of tumors, comparing them to tumors without LOI or LOH (as both alleles must be present to assess LOI). This is a more accurate control than unaffected kidney, which is embryologically dissimilar, or even fetal kidney, which varies greatly in developmental expression of IGF2 and H19. The prediction was that IGF2 levels should increase in tumors with LOI, and indeed we saw a two-fold increase in these tumors, compared to non-LOI non-LOH tumors. However, the difference was not statistically significant, as the level of expression of IGF2 varied greatly among tumors (Steenman et al., 1994).

Far more striking was the virtual absence of expression of H19 in those tumors that showed LOI of IGF2. Bear in mind that H19 and IGF2 are at least 100 kb apart on the genome, and thus these data provide strong evidence for their regulation by a common epigenetic mechanism. Tumors that showed

10   A. P. Feinberg

LOI of H19 nevertheless had down-regulated H19 (Steenman et al., 1994), indicating that LOI of IGF2 is the significant event. Consistent with that idea, all tumors with LOI of H19 also showed LOI of IGF2. Thus, biallelic expression of H19 (as detected by PCR) may be due to leakage to the paternal chromosome of a factor normally bound to the now unavailable maternal H19 allele, or 'cross-talk' as described in *Drosophila*. A more prosaic explanation is that tumor cells overexpressing H19 are selected against, leading to down regulation of H19 expression by other transcription factors.

DNA METHYLATION AND GENOMIC IMPRINTING IN WT

Many studies have shown an inverse relationship between DNA methylation and gene expression. However, it has been difficult to prove a causal link between the two in normal physiology, although altering DNA methylation can have dramatic effects on gene expression experimentally.

Nevertheless, there is strong circumstantial evidence linking genomic imprinting to DNA methylation. In the same issue of the journal in which our observations of LOI were reported, Surani's laboratory showed convincingly that a CpG island at the 5′ end of the H19 gene is methylated on the nonexpressed paternal allele and unmethylated on the expressed maternal allele. They accomplished this task by comparing embryos with maternal disomy for chromosome 7 (which harbors IGF2 and H19) to normal embryos. Maternally disomic embryos were hypomethylated in all tissues, and normal mice were hemimethylated, the exception being sperm DNA, which was hypomethylated (Ferguson-Smith et al., 1993). Thus, methylation marks the paternal allele, and it occurs after fertilization of the egg.

We used a similar but somewhat reciprocal approach to examine H19 methylation in man, by comparing DNA of normal individuals to that of BWS patients with paternal uniparental disomy for 11p15. Four such patients were found among 40 families studied. Like Surani's group, we found hemimethylation of a CpG island in all tissues but sperm, regardless of the state of gene expression. Thus, unlike traditional methylation studies, we are examining parental origin-specific tissue-independent DNA methylation, rather than tissue-specific methylation. In the UPD patients, both alleles were methylated, although not completely, consistent with the degree of somatic mosaicism for UPD itself (which is postzygotic in BWS) (Steenman et al., 1994).

These preliminary studies enabled us to determine whether LOI of IGF2 or H19 was associated with any alteration in imprint-specific DNA methylation. In every case with LOI of IGF2, which involves the maternal allele, the H19 CpG island was methylated, a paternal imprinting pattern. Thus, three changes occurred on the maternal chromosome, all switching it to a paternal epigenotype: activation of IGF2, loss of H19 expression, and methylation of the H19 CpG island (Steenman et al., 1994). Whether DNA methylation is the driving force in these alterations remains unclear, but the data are quite consistent with those from methyltransferase-deficient mice, in which the H19 CpG island is hypomethylated, and the paternal as well as maternal alleles of H19 are expressed (and IGF2 is

not). In both cases, IGF2 expression is inversely related to methylation of the H19 CpG island.

A MODEL OF WT: A DEVELOPMENTALLY SPECIFIC CASCADE OF GENETIC ALTERATIONS

I believe that WT, and childhood cancers in particular, should be viewed in a developmentally appropriate context (see Fig. 1). Thus, WT1 mutations appear to involve the earliest stages of nephrogenic development. WT1 knockout mice lack normal genitourinary development, and germline mutations are associated with genitourinary malformations (Kriedberg et al., 1994). According to the model, mutations in WT1 cause an arrest in early nephrogenic development, presenting a persistent target of nephrogenic precursor cells for subsequent tumorigenic events. Thus, WT1 mutations are quite similar to Rb mutations. Also, like Rb, WT1 is expressed in many mesodermal tissues, yet germline mutations are apparently only largely associated with a specific organ system.

The BWS gene, according to the model, is in large part responsible for expansion of a relatively well differentiated population of cells relatively late in nephrogenic development. It differs in its effects from WT1 in three critical ways. First, its role is later in nephrogenic development. Second, it affects the growth of a wider spectrum of embryonal tissues, including kidney, adrenal, liver, and muscle (Fig. 1).

Third, the abnormality of the BWS gene in cancer is in a new class of alterations, different from conventional transforming oncogenes and tumor suppressor genes. Here, the expression of the gene is tightly controlled, and overexpression of the gene (even two-fold from loss of imprinting), leads to overexpansion of cell populations. This overexpansion also presents an increased target for subsequent genetic changes, but it also leads to organomegaly, as seen in BWS, and its effects must occur within a critical developmental window. Thus, BWS patients are at risk for cancer only in early childhood, and they largely outgrow the developmental stigmata of the syndrome over time (Fig. 1). Furthermore, the BWS gene is involved in expansion of a larger group of tissues, accounting for a larger number of 'embryonal tumors' when overexpressed.

There is yet an additional genetic alteration on 11p in WT, involving a tumor suppressor gene on 11p15 distinct from the BWS gene. We know that these genes differ because a tumor-suppressing STF from 11p15 is centromeric to the imprinted region defined by the chromosomal translocation breakpoints in BWS patients, and to IGF2 and H19. However, the tumor suppressor gene is closely linked to the BWS gene and may even be involved in its regulation. Nevertheless, this suppressor gene, between the β-globin gene cluster and insulin, appears to be involved in a wide variety of common adult cancers, as well as childhood cancers. It is not necessarily imprinted itself, but loss of the gene would be expected to occur on the maternal chromosome, since paternal losses would by definition also usually delete the functioning copy of IGF2, which would be deleterious to tumor cell growth. The tumor suppressor gene is involved in growth arrest of an even larger number of tissues, with effects both in early development and adult life, accounting for 11p15 LOH in so many different types of tumors (Fig. 1).

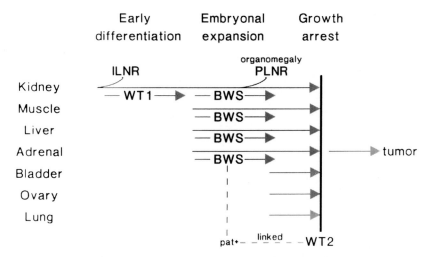

Fig. 1. A developmentally specific cascade of genetic alterations in Wilms' tumorigenesis. Mutation or loss of WT1, normally involved in differentiation, causes growth arrest of renal progenitor cells, leading to renal agenesis when present in the germline, and an expanded population of early developmental tumor precursor cells (ILNR, intralobar nephrogenic rests) when present in somatic cells. Loss of a regulatory gene or duplication of paternally expressed imprinted genes on 11p15, normally involved in embryonal expansion, leads to Beckwith-Wiedemann syndrome (BWS) when present in the embryo, and an expanded population of late developmental tumor precursor cells (PLNR, perilobar nephrogenic rests) when present in somatic cells. Mutation or loss of a distinct but genetically linked tumor suppressor gene on 11p15 (WT2) leads to impaired growth arrest as a late event in tumorigenesis. The spectrum of tumors arising from each of these genes depends on their role in normal development, as indicated.

There are surely other genetic alterations in Wilms' tumorigenesis. For example we and others have observed 16q loss in 20% of tumors, possibly involving the E-cadherin gene (Maw et al., 1992). One of the most interesting questions remaining to be answered is the mechanism of reduced expression of WT1 and WIT-1 in ILNR-like tumors. That both 11p13 genes show reduced expression in a concerted way suggests that a transcription factor binds to the region between these genes and is lacking in some Wilms' tumors. Perhaps this factor is related to familial WT unlinked to chromosome 11.

In conclusion, one of the most important lessons of molecular oncology is that multiple genes are involved in the pathogenesis of cancer, playing a role at steps of disease progression. The paradigm for this model has been colorectal cancer in adults (Fearon and Vogelstein, 1990). What distinguishes WT, and probably other childhood cancers, as well, is that these genetic alterations involve specific stages of differentiation and specific developmental lineages. These differences can in part explain the organ site specificity for cancer of these genes, as well as the developmental window for risk of malignancy in these patients, both key issues in our efforts to apply genetic knowledge to cancer prevention and treatment.

This work was supported by National Institutes of Health grants CA54358 and CA65145, and March of Dimes grant 0742.

REFERENCES

Ali, I. U., Lidereau, R., Theillet, C. and Callahan, R. (1987). Reduction to homozygosity of genes on chromosome 11 in human breast neoplasia. *Science* 238, 185-188.
Baird, P. N., Groves, N., Haber, D. A., Housman, D. E. and Cowell, J. K. (1992). Identification of mutations in the WT1 gene in tumours from patients with the WAGR syndrome. *Oncogene* 7, 2141-2149.
Beckwith, J. B., Kiviat, N. B. and Bonadio, J. F. (1990). Nephrogenic rests, nephroblastomatosis, and the pathogenesis of Wilms' tumor. *Pediatr. Pathol.* 1, 1-36.
Bickmore, W. A., Oghene, K., Little, M. H., Seawright, A., van Heyningen, V. and Hastie, N. D. (1994). Modulation of DNA binding specificity by alternative splicing of the Wilms' tumor wt1 gene transcript. *Science* 257, 235-237.
Bouffler, S. D., Jha, B. and Johnson, R. T. (1990). Multiple pathways of DNA double-strand break processing in a mutant Indian muntjac cell line. *Som. Cell. Mol. Genet.* 16, 451-460.
Brannan, C. I., Dees, E. c., Ingram, R. S. and Tilghman, S. M. (1990). The product of the H19 gene may function as an RNA. *Mol. Cell. Biol.* 10, 28-36.
Breslow, N., Beckwith, J. B., Ciol, M. and Sharples, K. (1988). Age distribution of Wilms' tumor: Report from the national Wilms' tumor study. *Cancer Res.* 48, 1653-1657.
Brown, K. W., Watson, J. E., Poirier, V., Mott, M. G., Berry, P. J. and Maitland, N. J. (1992). Inactivation of the remaining allele of the WT1 gene in a Wilms' tumour from a WAGR patient. *Oncogene* 7, 763-768.
Brunkow, M. E. and Tilghman, S. M. (1991). Ectopic expression of the H19 gene in mice causes prenatal lethality. *Genes Dev.* 5, 1092-1101.
Call, M., Glaser, T., Ito, C. Y., Buckler, A. J., Pelletier, J., Haber, D. A., Rose, E. A., Krai, A., Yeger, H., Lewis, W., Jones, C. and Housman, D. (1990). Isolation and characterization of a zinc finger polypeptide gene at the human chromosome 11 Wilms' tumor locus. *Cell* 60, 509-520.
Comings, E. (1973). A general theory of carcinogenesis. *Proc. Nat. Acad. Sci. USA* 70, 3324-3328.
Dowdy, S. F., Fasching, C. L., Araujo, D., Lai, K., Livanos, E., Weissman, B. E. and Stanbridge, E. J. (1991). Suppression of tumorigenicity in Wilms' tumor by the p15.5-p14 region of chromosome 11. *Science* 254, 293-295.
El-Badry, O. M., Minniti, C., Kohn, E. C., Houghton, P. J., Daughaday, W. H. and Helman, L. J. (1990). Insulin-like growth factor II acts as an autocrine growth and motility factor in human rhabdomyosarcoma tumors. *Cell Growth Differ.* 1, 325-331.
Fearon, E. R., Feinberg, A. P., Hamilton, S. H. and Vogelstein, B. (1985). Loss of genes on the short arm of chromosome 11 in bladder cancer. *Nature* 318, 377-380.
Fearon, E. P. and Vogelstein, B. (1990). A genetic model for colorectal tumorigenesis. *Cell* 61, 759-767.
Fearon, E. R., Vogelstein, B. and Feinberg, A. P. (1984). Somatic deletion and duplication of genes on chromosome 11 in Wilms' tumors. *Nature* 309, 176-178.
Ferguson-Smith, A. C., Sasaki, H., Cattanach, B. M. and Surani, M. A. (1993). Parental-origin-specific epigenetic modification of the mouse H19 gene, *Nature* 362, 751-755.
Friend, S. H., Bernards, R., Rogelj, S., Weinberg, R. A., Rapaport, J. M., Albert, D. M. and Dryja, T. P. (1986). A human DNA segment with properties of the gene that predisposes to retinoblastoma and osteosarcoma. *Nature* 323, 643-646.
Gessler, Poustka, A., Cavenee, W., Neve, R. L., Orkin, S. H. and Bruns, G. A. (1990). Homozygous deletion in Wilms' tumours of a zinc-finger gene identified by chromosome jumping. *Nature* 343, 774-778.
Grundy, P., Koufos, A., Morgan, K., Li, F. P., Meadows, A. T. and Cavenee, W. (1988). Familial predisposition to Wilms' tumour does not map to the short arm of chromosome 11. *Nature* 336, 374-376.
Haber, D. A., Buckler, A. J., Glaser, T., Call, K. M., Pelletier, J., Sohn, R. L., Douglass, E. C. and Housman, D. E. (1990). An internal deletion within

an 11p14 zinc finger gene contributes to the development of Wilms' tumor. *Cell* **61**, 1257-1269.

Haber, D. A. and Housman, D. E. (1992). Role of the WT1 gene in Wilms' tumour. *Cancer Surveys* **12**, 105-117.

Hastie, N. D. (1993). Wilms' tumour gene and function. *Curr. Opin. Genet. Dev.* **3**, 408-413.

Henry, I., Bonaitijk-Pellie, C., Chehensse, V., Beldjord, C., Schwartz, C., Utermann, G. and Junien, C. (1991). Uniparental paternal disomy in a genetic cancer-predisposing syndrome. *Nature* **351**, 665-667.

Huang, A., Campbell, C. E., Bonetta, L., McAndrews-Hill, M. S., Chilton-MacNeill, S., Coppes, M. J., Law, D. J., Feinberg, A. P., Yeger, H. and Williams, B. R. G. (1990). Tissue, developmental, and tumor-specific expression of divergent transcripts in Wilms' tumor. *Science* **250**, 991-994.

Huff, V., Compton, D., Chao, L., Strong, L., Geiser, C. and Saunders, G. (1988). Lack of linkage of familial Wilms' tumour to chromsomal band 11p13. *Nature* **336**, 377-378.

Huff, V., Miwa, H., Haber, D. A., Call, K. M., Housman, D., Strong, L. C. and Saunders, G. F. (1991). Evidence for WT1 as a Wilms' tumor (WT) gene: intragenic germinal deletion in bilateral WT. *Am. J. Hum. Genet.* **48**, 997-1003.

Knudson, A. G. and Strong, L. C. (1972). Mutation and cancer: A model for Wilms' tumor of the kidney. *J. Nat. Cancer Inst.* **48**, 313-324.

Koi, M., Johnson, L. A., Kalikin, L. M., Little, P. F. R., Nakamura, Y. and Feinberg, A. P. (1993). Tumor cell growth arrest caused by subchromosomal transferable DNA fragments from human chromosome 11. *Science* **260**, 361-364.

Kriedberg, J. A., Sariola, H., Loring, J. M., Maeda, M., Pelletier, J., Housman, D. and Jaenisch, R. (1994). WT-1 is required for early kidney development. *Cell* **74**, 679-691.

Little, M., van Heyningen, V. and Hastie, N. (1991). Dads and disomy and disease. *Nature* **351**, 609-610.

Little, M. H., Prosser, J., Condie, A., Smith, P. J., van Heyningen, V. and Hastie, N. D. (1992). Zinc finger point mutations within the WT1 gene in Wilms' tumor patients. *Proc. Nat. Acad. Sci. USA* **89**, 4791-4795.

Madden, S. L., Cook, D. M., Morris, J. F., Gashler, A., Sukhatme, V. P. and Rauscher, F. J. III (1991). Transcriptional repression mediated by the WT1 Wilms' tumor gene product. *Science* **253**, 1550-1553.

Mannens, M., Slater, R. M., Heyting, C., Bliek, J., de Kraker, J., Coad, N., de Pagter-Holthuizen, P. and Pearson, P. L. (1988). Molecular nature of genetic changes resulting in loss of heterozygosity of chromosome 11 in Wilms' tumours. *Hum. Genet.* **81**, 41-48.

Maw, M. A., Grundy, P. E., Millow, L. J., Eccles, M. R., Dunn, R. S., Smith, P. J., Feinberg, A. P., Law, D. J., Paterson, M. C., Telzerow, P. E., Callen, D. F., Thompson, A. D., Richards, R. I. and Reeve, A. E. (1992). A third Wilms' tumor locus on chromosome 16q. *Cancer Res.* **52**, 3094-3098.

Monk, M. (1988). Genomic imprinting. *Genes Dev.* **2**, 921-925.

Ogawa, O., Eccles, M. R., Szeto, J., McNoe, L. A., Yun, K., Maw, M. A., Smith, P. J. and Reeve, A. E. (1993). Relaxation of insulin-like growth factor II gene imprinting implicated in Wilms' tumour. *Nature* **362**, 749-751.

Pelletier, J., Bruening, W., Kashtan, C. E., Mauer, S. M., Manivel, J. C., Striegel, J. E., Houghton, D. C., Junien, C., Habib, R., Fouser, L. and Housman, D. (1991). Germline mutations in the Wilms' tumor suppressor gene are associated with abnormal urogenital development in Denys-Drash syndrome. *Cell* **67**, 437-447.

Ping, A. J., Reeve, A. E., Law, D. J., Young, M. R., Boehnke, M. and Feinberg, A. P. (1989). Genetic linkage of Beckwith-Wiedemann syndrome to 11p15. *Am. J. Hum. Genet.* **44**, 720-723.

Rainier, S., Johnson, L. A., Dobry, C. J., Ping, A. J., Grundy, P. E. and Feinberg, A. P. (1993). Relaxation of imprinted genes in human cancer. *Nature* **362**, 747-749.

Rauscher, F. J., Morris, J. F., Tournay, O. E., Cook, D. M. and Curran, T. (1990). Binding of the Wilms' tumor locus zinc finger protein to the EGR-1 consensus sequence. *Science* **250**, 1259-1262.

Reeve, A. E., Sih, S. A., Raizis, A. M. and Feinberg, A. P. (1989). Loss of allelic heterozygosity at a second locus on chromosome 11 in sporadic Wilms' tumor cells. *Mol. Cell. Biol.* **9**, 1799-1803.

Steenman, M. J. C., Rainier, S., Dobry, C. J., Grundy, P., Horon, I. and Feinberg, A. P. (1994). Loss of imprinting of IGF2 is linked to reduced expression and abnormal methylation of H19 in Wilms' tumor. *Nature Genet.* (in press).

Wadey, R. B., Pal, N., Buckle, B., Yeomans, E., Pritchard, J. and Cowell, J. K. (1990). Loss of heterozygosity in Wilms' tumour involves two distinct regions of chromosome 11. *Oncogene* **5**, 901-907.

Weksberg, R., Shen, D. R., Fei, Y. L., Song, Q. L. and Squire, J. (1993). Disruption of insulin-like growth factor 2 imprinting in Beckwith-Weidemann syndrome. *Nature Genet.* **5**, 143-150.

Weston, A., Willey, J. C., Modali, R., Sugimura, H., McDowell, E. M., Resau, J., Light, B., Haugen, A., Mann, D. L., Trump, B. F. and Harris, C. C. (1991). Differential DNA sequence deletions from chromosomes 3, 11, 13, and 17 in squamous-cell carcinoma, large-cell carcinoma, and adenocarcinoma of the human lung. *Proc. Nat. Acad. Sci. USA* **86**, 5099-5103.

Zheng, J., Robinson, W. R., Ehlen, T., Yu, M. C. and Dubeau, L. (1991). Distinction of low grade from high grade human ovarian carcinomas on the basis of losses of heterozygosity on chromosomes 3, 6, and 11 and HER-2/neu gene amplification. *Cancer Res.* **51**, 4045-4051.

Journal of Cell Science, Supplement 18, 13-17 (1994)
Printed in Great Britain © The Company of Biologists Limited 1994

The role of the *p53* and *Rb-1* genes in cancer, development and apoptosis

Martin L. Hooper

Cancer Research Campaign Laboratories, Department of Pathology, University of Edinburgh, Teviot Place, Edinburgh EH8 9AG, UK

SUMMARY

Gene targeting using embryonal stem cells has been used to generate strains of mice with inactivating mutations at the *Rb-1* and *p53* tumour suppressor loci. Mice heterozygous for a null allele of *Rb-1* do not show retinoblastomas but instead develop pituitary tumours. Homozygotes die at between 10 and 14 days' gestation and show increased levels of both cell division and cell death by apoptosis in the haematopoietic and nervous systems. This is consistent with the view that the *Rb-1* gene product plays a general role in the maturation of precursor cells. In contrast, mice heterozygous for a null allele of *p53* are predisposed to a spectrum of tumours, while the corresponding homozygotes are viable but show a very high tumour incidence. Thymocytes from *p53* homozygotes, unlike wild-type thymocytes, do not show increased levels of apoptosis following treatment with DNA-damaging agents, while response to its induction by other agents is unaltered. Similarly, epithelial cells from the crypts of both small and large intestine of *p53*-deficient mice are resistant to the induction of apoptosis by γ-irradiation. In contrast, two other early responses of wild-type crypts to γ-irradiation, namely the G_2 block and the reduction in bromodeoxyuridine incorporation, are both largely intact in *p53*-deficient mice. These observations are consistent with the view that *p53* is responsible for monitoring DNA damage so that damaged cells can be either repaired or eliminated prior to division.

Key words: oncosuppressor gene, cancer, development, apoptosis

INTRODUCTION

An oncosuppressor gene is one whose normal function prevents the development of one or more types of cancer; such genes are also known as tumour suppressor genes or antioncogenes (reviewed by Knudson, 1993). A powerful way of investigating how such genes function is to examine the consequences of inactivating them in an experimental animal. This can be done using gene targeting in embryonal stem (ES) cells (reviewed by Hooper, 1992). These cells, established in culture from the pluripotent inner cell mass cells of the peri-implantation embryo, retain the capacity to colonise the somatic tissues and germ line of chimaeras produced by injecting them into blastocyst-stage embryos. Designed mutations can be introduced into chosen genes by introducing into the cultured cells a gene targeting DNA vector and isolating cells in which the vector has undergone homologous recombination with the endogenous gene. These mutations can then be introduced via chimaeras into the mouse germ line. I will describe the application of this approach to the *Rb-1* and *p53* oncosuppressor genes.

THE *RB-1* GENE

The paradigm for oncosuppressor genes is the retinoblastoma susceptibility gene *RB-1*. Retinoblastoma is a tumour of the retina occurring predominantly in early childhood which, although relatively uncommon, is of interest in that about 40% of all cases are familial. Knudson (1971) proposed that these tumours arise as a result of two mutational events, of which one is present in the germline in familial cases. Recent molecular analysis has shown this to be correct, and demonstrated that both events involve modification or loss of the same gene, *RB-1*. More than 90% of individuals constitutively heterozygous for an *RB-1* mutation develop retinoblastoma as a result of a somatic event occurring in one or more cells of the retina, or of its precursor tissues, that eliminates the function of the wild-type allele, usually by allele loss (reviewed by Knudson, 1993). The exact cell type of origin of retinoblastoma is the subject of some dispute, with advocates of primitive neurotubular cell, glial cell and photoreceptor cell origin, the last possibility being most easily reconcilable with biochemical, immunocytochemical and morphological properties (Rootman et al., 1987). Photoreceptor-like ultrastructural features are particularly marked in benign tumours, termed retinomas or retinocytomas, which develop in a small proportion of *RB-1* heterozygotes and are thought to result from loss of the residual wild-type allele in a more mature stage of the retinoblastoma precursor cell type (Gallie et al., 1982). These tumours have been described as cone-like (Margo et al., 1983), although this should not be over-interpreted since the organisational features that distinguish rods from cones would probably be obscured in a tumour. In addition to retinal tumours, about 15% of *RB-1* heterozygotes develop osteosarcomas. *RB-1* allele loss is also seen in sporadic lung, breast, prostate and bladder carcinomas, although no increase in incidence of these tumours is seen in germline heterozygotes (see Knudson, 1993).

The *RB-1* gene codes for a 105 kDa protein that is present in most cell types and undergoes cell cycle-dependent changes in phosphorylation as a result of the action of cyclin-dependent kinase and phosphoprotein phosphatase activity (see Hollingsworth et al., 1993). The hypophosphorylated protein associates with the cell nucleus and binds to transcription factors such as E2F, with effects that depend upon the transcription factor and in some cases also on the cell type. Transcription of genes containing an E2F recognition site is inhibited by the binding of the *RB-1* gene product; such genes include several whose products are required during S phase. It appears to depend upon the phase of the cell cycle whether E2F is predominantly associated with the *RB-1* gene product or with one of two other related proteins, p107 or p130 (Cao et al., 1992; Shirodkar et al., 1992; Li et al., 1993; Hannon et al., 1993; Cobrinik et al., 1993) and it is likely that this provides a further level at which the expression of E2F-dependent genes can be regulated. A different control element is implicated in the stimulation of *c-fos* expression by the *RB-1* gene product (Robbins et al., 1990). Further levels of complexity may be present in the form of feedback control loops, one involving *RB-1* and TGF-β1 possibly involved in the regulation of *c-myc* expression (see Hollingsworth et al., 1993) and another involving *RB-1* and a cyclin-dependent kinase inhibitor, p16^{INK4} (Serrano et al., 1993). Numerous proteins other than transcription factors also associate with the *RB-1* gene product, implicating it in mechanisms unrelated to the control of gene expression. The importance of *RB-1* in cell cycle regulation is emphasised by the fact that several tumour viruses have independently evolved proteins that bind to the hypophosphorylated gene product and thus inactivate it, examples being SV40 T antigen, adenovirus E1A protein and human papillomavirus E7 protein (see Hollingsworth et al., 1993).

Rb-1 MUTANT MICE

The corresponding murine gene, designated *Rb-1,* has 91% sequence homology to the human gene and is widely expressed in mouse tissues (Bernards et al., 1989; Szekely et al., 1992). In collaboration with the laboratory of Dr Anton Berns at the Netherlands Cancer Institute, we have used gene targeting to introduce mutations into the mouse *Rb-1* gene (Clarke et al., 1992). Two other groups have also done so (Lee et al., 1992; Jacks et al., 1992). All three groups have reported similar results, and in what follows I will discuss principally our own data, with reference to those of the other groups where appropriate. We used two targeting vectors to generate the mutant *Rb-1* alleles, designed to insert, respectively, the selectable marker genes *neo* and *hyg,* in each case under the control of the *pgk-1* promoter, into exon 19 of the *Rb-1* gene (Clarke et al., 1992). Both insertions carry translation termination codons in all three reading frames and polyadenylation signals, so that in the targeted allele the *Rb-1* reading frame is truncated upstream of the coding sequences for SV40 T antigen-binding domain number 2, which is essential for the function of the gene product (Hu et al., 1990). We therefore consider both targeted alleles as null alleles.

In contrast to the situation in humans, no retinoblastomas have to date been detected in mice heterozygous for a null allele of *Rb-1*. We have considered a number of possible explanations for this. First, because of their smaller size and shorter lifespan, mice may simply have a lower probability of a somatic mutation occurring in the retina during the period when it is susceptible to tumour development, so that only a very small proportion of heterozygotes develop retinoblastomas. However, as the aggregate number of heterozygous animals examined by the three groups increases, this hypothesis becomes progressively less tenable. Second, mice may differ from humans in the level of exposure of their retinas to some required environmental agent. As laboratory mice are maintained under conditions of artificial light and are active principally in the hours of darkness, one candidate for such an environmental agent is sunlight. Intriguingly, published incidences of human retinoblastoma are significantly correlated with geographical latitude (Fig. 1) and more recent data also show this trend (M. L. Hooper and D. M. Parkin, unpublished), indicating that this hypothesis is worthy of further investiga-

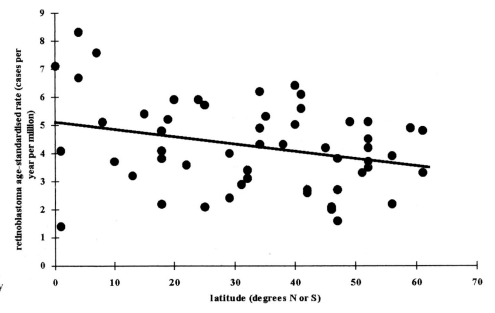

Fig. 1. Effect of geographical latitude on retinoblastoma incidence. Age-standardised rates for the first 14 years of life are taken from Parkin et al. (1988). A linear regression has been fitted to the data using the GLIM statistical package (Numerical Algorithms Group, Oxford). The slope, −0.02606 ± s.e. 0.01158, is significantly different from zero (*t*=2.250, *P*<0.05).

tion. Third, there may be a need in the mouse for an additional genetic event or events. Two observations suggest that this idea should be taken seriously: (i) retinoblastomas are uncommon if not non-existent in veterinary practice (Hogan and Albert, 1991), suggesting that humans may be unusually susceptible; (ii) it is possible to induce retinoblastoma in the mouse by expressing SV40 T antigen in the retina, thereby inactivating both the *Rb-1* and *p53* gene products (Windle et al., 1990). However, crossing into our *Rb-1* mutant stock the null allele of *p53* described below has not led to the development of any retinoblastomas (A. R. Clarke et al., unpublished observations). Fourth, in view of the relationship to photoreceptor cells discussed above, it may be significant that the photoreceptors of the predominantly nocturnal mouse are almost exclusively rods, while humans also possess cones of three different spectral sensitivities (see Bowmaker, 1991). Notwithstanding the absence of retinoblastomas in *Rb-1* heterozygous mice, pituitary adenocarcinomas develop in most if not all of these animals (Jacks et al., 1992; Hu et al., 1994; D. J. Harrison et al., unpublished observations). Hu et al. (1994) report that these tumours develop in the intermediate lobe of the pituitary, which is present only in vestigial form in adult humans. They produce α-melanocyte stimulating hormone, suggesting that they originate from corticotrope cells and, interestingly, also show patchy expression of the photoreceptor S-antigen (Hu et al., 1994).

No instance of constitutional homozygosity for a null *RB-1* allele has been reported in humans, and so the production of *Rb-1* mutant mice allowed the consequences of germline homozygosity at this locus to be studied for the first time. When heterozygous mice were intercrossed, no homozygotes survived to term, and examination of midgestation embryos revealed that homozygotes showed abnormalities in the haematopoietic and nervous systems, in both cases involving increased levels of cell death by apoptosis and overabundant or ectopic mitosis (Clarke et al., 1992; Lee et al., 1992; Jacks et al., 1992). The tissues affected correlate well with sites of high-level *Rb-1* expression (Szekely et al., 1992) and are those in which maturation of a dividing precursor cell population to a postmitotic differentiated cell occurs earliest in embryonic development, suggesting that *Rb-1* has a generalised role in the maturation of precursor cells. The presence of abnormalities in both cell division and cell death is consistent with the hypothesis that *Rb-1* functions to maintain cells in a quiescent state in which they show reduced levels of both mitosis and apoptosis (Dive and Wyllie, 1993). Interestingly, at least part of the *Rb-1*-deficient phenotype appears not to be cell-autonomous, since *Rb-1*-deficient embryonal stem cells can give rise to phenotypically normal mature B and T lymphocytes in chimaeras produced by injecting them into blastocysts homozygous for a mutation in the *Rag-2* gene (Chen et al., 1993).

THE *p53* GENE

The *p53* gene, originally discovered by virtue of its ability to form a complex with SV40 T antigen (Lane and Crawford, 1979), was at first thought to be an oncogene, but it was subsequently realised that the allele initially cloned and studied was, in fact, a mutant allele, and the wild-type gene functions

as an oncosuppressor (see Knudson, 1993). Its loss is the most common allele loss in human malignancy, and germline heterozygosity for a mutant allele causes Li-Fraumeni syndrome, a predisposition to a spectrum of tumours of which breast and brain tumours are the most common (reviewed by Knudson, 1993). The gene encodes a sequence-specific DNA-binding protein that activates the expression of a reporter gene adjacent to the binding site (reviewed by Vogelstein and Kinzler, 1992). The protein is phosphorylated in a cell cycle-dependent manner, and following DNA damage its levels rise as a result of post-translational stabilisation, leading to G_1 growth arrest. It has been shown recently that the G_1 arrest is mediated by a 21 kDa cyclin-dependent kinase inhibitor, variously designated WAF-1, Cip-1 or sdi-1, whose expression is induced by p53 protein (reviewed by Nasmyth and Hunt, 1993). Loss of wild-type *p53* is associated with genomic instability, which has led to the proposal that the p53 protein functions to prevent cells entering S phase before DNA damage has been repaired (Lane, 1992). Studies on cultured cell lines have also implicated *p53* in the regulation of apoptosis (Yonish-Rouach et al., 1991; Shaw et al., 1992). Some mutant alleles of *p53* exert a dominant negative effect and are able, in the presence of wild-type *p53*, to immortalise normal early-passage cells in culture and cooperate with *ras* to induce transformation of embryo fibroblasts. This effect depends on the ability of the mutant protein to sequester wild-type protein into inactive oligomers. Such alleles lack the ability of the wild-type allele to suppress the transformation of embryo fibroblasts by other oncogenes, which is itself not dependent on ability to oligomerise (see Slingerland et al., 1993).

p53 MUTANT MICE

Mice with a targeted mutation in the *p53* gene were first reported by Donehower et al. (1992), who found that heterozygous animals developed tumours at low frequency, while homozygotes developed normally to birth but all developed tumours, of various types, in the first few months of life. Although the targeted allele carried by these mice was designed as a null allele, the possibility could not be rigorously excluded that an active polypeptide fragment could be produced from the 3′ end of the modified gene. However, we have used gene targeting to produce mice with a *p53* allele in which exons 2 to 6 are replaced by an insert that, as described above for *Rb-1*, truncates the reading frame, producing an unambiguously null allele (Clarke et al., 1993), and these mice behave similarly. Homozygous mice develop tumours, predominantly T cell lymphomas, during the first six months of life; in heterozygotes, which develop tumours later, soft tissue sarcomas are relatively more important (Purdie et al., 1994). Some mice developed pathological signs without obvious tumour development, and most of these showed reactive lymphoid hyperplasia, suggesting a perturbation of the immune system. A similar tumour spectrum has been reported in a third *p53* mutant strain (Jacks et al., 1994). Small differences in tumour spectrum between strains are probably a consequence of differences in genetic background (Harvey et al., 1993a). Most tumours in our *p53* heterozygotes had suffered loss of the wild-type *p53* allele, indicating that the gene behaves as a classical oncosuppressor. In contrast to the pituitary tumours

16   M. L. Hooper

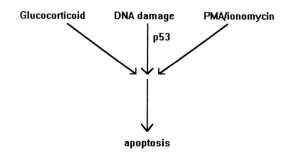

Fig. 2. Pathways to apoptosis in thymocytes. PMA (phorbol myristoyl 13-acetate) and ionomycin provide a stimulus that mimics the effect of crosslinking the T-cell antigen receptor, thereby modelling the physiological process of negative selection in the thymus (see Clarke et al., 1993).

occurring in the *Rb-1* heterozygotes, most of the tumours in *p53* heterozygous and homozygous mice contained an aneuploid or polyploid cell population as assessed by flow cytometry, consistent with the concept that, in the absence of functional *p53,* cells enter division without having repaired DNA damage, and this leads to abnormalities in chromosome segregation (Lane, 1992).

An important clue to the mechanism underlying the tumour suppressor activity of *p53* was provided by studies of thymocyte apoptosis. Wild-type thymocytes placed in culture in serum-free medium spontaneously undergo apoptosis over a 1- to 2-day period, and the rate of this apoptosis can be stimulated by a variety of stimuli including physiological agents such as glucocorticoids and DNA-damaging agents such as γ-radiation. Thymocytes from *p53* homozygous mice showed normal response to agents of the former class, but were resistant to induction of apoptosis by agents of the second class (Clarke et al., 1993; Lowe et al., 1993b). Heterozygous cells showed an intermediate response. This suggested that stimuli can feed into the apoptosis pathway via different routes, and that *p53* is required in a branch route linking DNA damage to the main apoptosis pathway (Fig. 2).

In order to investigate whether this behaviour is peculiar to thymocytes, we have also examined the response of epithelial cells of intestinal crypts to γ-irradiation in vivo. Four hours after irradiation, crypt cells from both small intestine and colon of wild-type mice showed abundant apoptosis, but corresponding cells from *p53* homozygotes were completely resistant to induction of apoptosis. Again, cells from heterozygotes showed an intermediate response. In contrast, two other early responses of wild-type crypts to γ-irradiation, namely reduction in the proportion of cells in S phase, as assessed by the bromodeoxyuridine labelling index, and growth arrest in the G2 phase of the cell cycle (reviewed by Potten, 1990) were both largely intact in *p53*-deficient animals (Clarke et al., 1994). Merritt et al. (1994) also observed resistance of intestinal epithelial cells from *p53* homozygous mutant mice to induction of apoptosis by γ-irradiation, although they did not observe a reduction in the response of cells from heterozygotes, perhaps because they used a higher irradiation dose. In both studies the low background level of apoptosis in the intestine appeared to be *p53*-independent, indicating that, as with thymocytes, *p53* is required to link

apoptosis to DNA damage rather than being required for apoptosis per se. This is consistent with the observation that the development of homozygous *p53*-deficient mice to birth is normal, implying no anomalies in developmental programmed cell death (Donehower et al., 1992), and with the finding that *p53* is not required for the apoptosis that occurs in prostatic glandular cells following androgen ablation (Berges et al., 1993).

An important question that remains is that of how cells make a decision between different *p53*-mediated responses to DNA damage, i.e. a decision between entry into growth arrest, thereby possibly allowing DNA repair, and entry into apoptosis. Relevant to this question is recent work of Lowe et al. (1993a) who showed, using fibroblasts of different *p53* genotypes, that the apoptotic response in these cells is seen only when G1 growth arrest is bypassed by expressing the adenovirus E1A protein in the cells, suggesting that in general the choice of response depends upon what other genes the cell is expressing. Fibroblasts from *p53* mutant mice have also been used to confirm that p53-deficiency promotes genetic instability and to show that it facilitates immortalisation (Harvey et al., 1993b). Enhanced proliferative potential has been noted in a variety of cell types from *p53*-deficient mice (Tsukuda et al., 1993).

It seems reasonable to conclude that the reason that *p53*-deficient mice develop tumours is that damaged, potentially tumourigenic cells fail to be eliminated by the normal apoptotic pathway and instead grow into tumours. This emphasises the fact that the regulation of cell death can be as important as the regulation of cell division in determining whether tumours develop. It also has implications for cancer therapy in that some anti-cancer drugs appear to exert their cytotoxic effect by induction of the endogenous apoptotic pathway (reviewed by Dive and Wyllie, 1993) and therefore loss of *p53*, the most common allele loss in human cancer, may be an important mechanism of resistance to such drugs. The advent of novel drugs specifically designed to activate the natural suicide pathway of the cell is likely to provide valuable therapeutic agents for the treatment of cancer in future years.

I am grateful to Alan Clarke, David Harrison, Jill Bubb, Charles Patek, John Mullins and Max Parkin for helpful suggestions. Work in my laboratory is supported by the Cancer Research Campaign.

REFERENCES

Berges, R. R., Furuya, Y., Remington, L., English, H. F., Jacks, T. and Isaacs, J. T. (1993). Cell proliferation, DNA repair, and p53 function are not required for programmed death of prostatic glandular cells induced by androgen ablation. *Proc. Nat. Acad. Sci. USA* **90**, 8910-8914.
Bernards, R., Schackleford, G. M., Gerber, M. R., Horowitz, J. M., Friend, S. H., Schartl, M., Bogenmann, E., Rapaport, J. M., McGee, T., Dryja, T. P. and Weinberg, R. A. (1989). Structure and expression of the murine retinoblastoma gene and characterization of its encoded protein. *Proc. Nat. Acad. Sci. USA* **86**, 6474-6478.
Bowmaker, J. K. (1991). The evolution of vertebrate visual pigments and photoreceptors. In *Vision and Visual Dysfunction*, vol. 2 (ed. J. R. Cronly-Dillon and R. L. Gregory) pp. 63-81. London: Macmillan Press.
Cao, L., Faha, B., Dembski, M., Tsai, L.-H., Harlow, E. and Dyson, N. (1992). Independent binding of the retinoblastoma protein and p107 to the transcription factor E2F. *Nature* **355**, 176-179.
Chen, J., Gorman, J. R., Stewart, V., Williams, B., Jacks, T. and Alt, F. W. (1993). Generation of normal lymphocyte populations by Rb-deficient embryonic stem cells. *Curr. Biol.* **3**, 405-413.

Clarke, A. R., Robanus Maandag, E., van Roon, M., van der Lugt, N. M. T., van der Valk, M., Hooper, M. L., Berns, A. and te Riele, H. (1992). Requirement for a functional *Rb-1* gene in murine development. *Nature* **359**, 328-330.

Clarke, A. R., Purdie, C. A., Harrison, D. J., Morris, R. G., Bird, C. C., Hooper, M. L. and Wyllie, A. H. (1993). Thymocyte apoptosis induced by p53-dependent and independent pathways. *Nature* **362**, 849-852.

Clarke, A. R., Gledhill, S., Hooper, M. L., Bird, C. C. and Wyllie, A. H. (1994). p53-dependence of early apoptotic and proliferative responses within the mouse intestinal epithelium following γ-irradiation. *Oncogene* **9**, 1767-1773.

Cobrinik, D., Whyte, P., Peeper, D. S., Jacks, T. and Weinberg, R. A. (1993). Cell cycle-specific association of E2F with the p130 E1A-binding protein. *Genes Dev.* **7**, 2392-2404.

Dive, C. and Wyllie, A. H. (1993). Apoptosis and cancer chemotherapy. In *Frontiers in Pharmacology: Cancer Chemotherapy* (ed. J. A. Hickman and T. T. Tritton), pp 21-56. Oxford: Blackwell Scientific.

Donehower, L. A., Harvey, M., Slagle, B. M., McArthur, M. J., Montgomery, C. A. Jr, Butel, J. S. and Bradley, A. (1992). Mice deficient for p53 are developmentally normal but susceptible to spontaneous tumours. *Nature* **356**, 215-221.

Gallie, B. L., Ellsworth, R. M., Abramson, D. H. and Phillips, R. A. (1982). Retinoma: spontaneous regression of retinoblastoma or benign manifestation of the mutation? *Brit. J. Cancer* **45**, 513-521.

Hannon, G. J., Demetrick, D. and Beach, D. (1993). Isolation of the Rb-related p130 through its interaction with CDK2 and cyclins. *Genes Dev.* **7**, 2378-2391.

Harvey, M., McArthur, M. J., Montgomery, C. A. Jr, Bradley, A. and Donehower, L. A. (1993a). Genetic background alters the spectrum of tumors that develop in p53-deficient mice. *FASEB J.* **7**, 938-943.

Harvey, M., Sands, A. T., Weiss, R. S., Hegi, M. E., Wiseman, R. W., Pantazis, P., Giovanella, B. C., Tainsky, M. A., Bradley, A. and Donehower, L. A. (1993b). *In vitro* growth characteristics of embryo fibroblasts isolated from p53-deficient mice. *Oncogene* **8**, 2457-2467.

Hogan, R. N. and Albert, D. M. (1991). Does retinoblastoma occur in animals? *Prog. Vet. Comp. Ophthalmol.* **1**, 73-82.

Hollingsworth, R. E. Jr, Hensey, C. E. and Lee, W.-H. (1993). Retinoblastoma protein and the cell cycle. *Curr. Opin. Genet. Dev.* **3**, 55-62.

Hooper, M. L. (1992). *Embryonal Stem Cells: Introducing Planned Changes into the Animal Germline.* Harwood Academic Publishers gmbh, Chur, Switzerland.

Hu, N., Gutsmann, A., Herbert, D. C., Bradley, A., Lee, W.-H. and Lee, E. Y.-H. P. (1994). Heterozygous *Rb-1*$^{\Delta20}$/+ mice are predisposed to tumours of the pituitary gland with a nearly complete penetrance. *Oncogene* **9**, 1021-1027.

Hu, Q., Dyson, N. and Harlow, E. (1990). The regions of the retinoblastoma protein needed for binding to adenovirus E1A or SV40 large T antigen are common sites for mutations. *EMBO J.* **9**, 1147-1155.

Jacks, T., Fazeli, A., Schmitt, E. M., Bronson, R. T., Goodell, M. A. and Weinberg, R. A. (1992). Effects of an Rb mutation in the mouse. *Nature* **359**, 295-300.

Jacks, T., Remington, L., Williams, B. O., Schmitt, E. M., Halachmi, S., Bronson, R. T. and Weinberg, R. A. (1994). Tumour spectrum analysis in p53 mutant mice. *Curr. Biol.* **4**, 1-7.

Knudson, A. G. (1971). Mutation and cancer: statistical study of retinoblastoma. *Proc. Nat. Acad. Sci. USA* **68**, 820-823.

Knudson, A. G. (1993). Antioncogenes and human cancer. *Proc. Nat. Acad. Sci. USA* **90**, 10914-10921.

Lane, D. P. and Crawford, L. V. (1979). T antigen is bound to a host protein in SV40-transformed cells. *Nature* **278**, 261-263.

Lane, D. P. (1992). Cancer: p53, guardian of the genome. *Nature* **358**, 15-16.

Lee, E. Y.-H. P., Chang, C.-Y., Hu, N., Wang, Y.-C. J., Lai, C.-C., Herrup, K., Lee, W.-H. and Bradley, A. (1992). Mice deficient for Rb are nonviable and show defects in neurogenesis and haematopoiesis. *Nature* **359**, 288-294.

Li, Y., Graham, C., Lacy, S., Duncan, A. M. V. and Whyte, P. (1993). The adenovirus E1A-associated 130-kD protein is encoded by a member of the retinoblastoma gene family and physically interacts with cyclins A and E. *Genes Dev.* **7**, 2366-2377.

Lowe, S. W., Ruley, H. E., Jacks, T. and Housman, D. E. (1993a). p53-dependent apoptosis modulates the cytotoxicity of anticancer agents. *Cell* **74**, 957-967.

Lowe, S. W., Schmitt, E. M., Smith, S. W., Osborne, B. A. and Jacks, T. (1993b). p53 is required for radiation-induced apoptosis in mouse thymocytes. *Nature* **362**, 847-849.

Margo, C., Hidayat, A., Kopelman, J. and Zimmerman, L. E. (1983). Retinocytoma: a benign variant of retinoblastoma. *Arch. Ophthalmol.* **101**, 1519-1531.

Merritt, A. J., Potten, C. S., Kemp, C. J., Hickman, J. A., Balmain, A., Lane, D. P. and Hall, P. A. (1994). The role of p53 in spontaneous and radiation-induced apoptosis in the gastrointestinal tract of normal and p53-deficient mice. *Cancer Res.* **54**, 614-617.

Nasmyth, K. and Hunt, T. (1993). Cell cycle: Dams and sluices. *Nature* **366**, 634-635.

Parkin, D. M., Stiller, C. A., Bieber, A., Draper, G. J., Terracini, B. and Young, J. L. (1988). International incidence of childhood cancer. *Int. Agency Res. Cancer Sci. Publ.* **87**.

Potten, C. S. (1990). A comprehensive study of the radiobiological response of the murine (BDF1) small intestine. *Int. J. Radiat. Biol.* **58**, 925-973.

Purdie, C. A., Harrison, D. J., Peter, A., Dobbie, L., White, S., Howie, S. E. M., Salter, D. M., Bird, C. C., Wyllie, A. H., Hooper, M. L. and Clarke, A. R. (1994). Tumour incidence, spectrum and ploidy in mice with a large deletion in the p53 gene. *Oncogene* **9**, 603-609.

Robbins, P. D., Horowitz, J. M. and Mulligan, R. C. (1990). Negative regulation of human *c-fos* expression by the retinoblastoma gene product. *Nature* **346**, 668-671.

Rootman, J., Carruthers, J. D. A. and Miller, R. R. (1987). Retinoblastoma. *Perspect. Pediatr. Pathol.* **10**, 208-258.

Serrano, M., Hannon, G. J. and Beach, D. (1993). A new regulatory motif in cell-cycle control causing specific inhibition of cyclin D/CDK4. *Nature* **366**, 704-707.

Shaw, P., Bovey, R., Tardy, S., Sahli, R., Sordat, B. and Costa, J. (1992). Induction of apoptosis by wild-type p53 in a human colon tumour-derived cell line. *Proc. Nat. Acad. Sci. USA* **89**, 4495-4499.

Shirodkar, S., Ewen, M., DeCaprio, J. A., Morgan, J., Livingston, D. M. and Chittenden, T. (1992). The transcription factor E2F interacts with the retinoblastoma product and a p107-cyclin A complex in a cell cycle-regulated manner. *Cell* **68**, 157-166.

Slingerland, J. M., Jenkins, J. R. and Benchimol, S. (1993). The transforming and suppressor functions of p53 alleles: effects of mutations that disrupt phosphorylation, oligomerization and nuclear translocation. *EMBO J.* **12**, 1029-1037.

Szekely, L., Jiang, W.-Q., Bulic-Jakus, F., Rosen, A., Ringertz, N., Klein, G. and Wiman, K.G. (1992). Cell type and differentiation dependent heterogeneity in retinoblastoma protein expression in SCID mouse fetuses. *Cell Growth Differ.* **3**, 149-156.

Tsukuda, T., Tomooka, Y., Takai, S., Ueda, Y., Nishikawa, S., Yagi, T., Tokunaga, T., Takeda, N., Suda, Y., Abe, S., Matsuo, I., Ikawa, Y. and Aizawa, S. (1993). Enhanced proliferative potential in culture of cells from p53-deficient mice. *Oncogene* **8**, 3313-3322.

Vogelstein, B. and Kinzler, K. W. (1992). p53 Function and dysfunction. *Cell* **70**, 523-526.

Windle, J. J., Albert, D. M., O'Brien, J. M., Marcus, D. M., Disteche, C. M., Bernards, R. and Mellon, P. L. (1990). Retinoblastoma in transgenic mice. *Nature* **343**, 665-669.

Yonish-Rouach, E., Resnitzky, D., Lotem, J., Sachs, L., Kimchi, A. and Oren, M. (1991). Wild-type p53 induces apoptosis of myeloid leukaemic cells that is inhibited by interleukin-6. *Nature* **352**, 345-347.

Journal of Cell Science, Supplement 18, 19-33 (1994)
Printed in Great Britain © The Company of Biologists Limited 1994

Drosophila in cancer research: the first fifty tumor suppressor genes

Kellie L. Watson*, Robin W. Justice and Peter J. Bryant

Developmental Biology Center, University of California, Irvine, CA 92717, USA

*Present address: Department of Molecular and Cellular Biology, Harvard University, Cambridge, MA 02138, USA

SUMMARY

In *Drosophila*, over 50 genes have been identified in which loss-of-function mutations lead to excess cell proliferation in the embryo, in the central nervous system, imaginal discs or hematopoietic organs of the larva, or in the adult gonads. Twenty-two of these genes have been cloned and characterized at the molecular level, and nine of them show clear homology to mammalian genes. Most of these mammalian genes had not been previously implicated in cell proliferation control. Overgrowth in some of the mutants involves conversion to a cell type that, in normal development, shows more cell proliferation than the original cell type. Thus the neurogenic mutants, including *Notch*, show conversion of epidermal cells to neuroblasts, leading to the 'neurogenic' phenotype of excess nervous tissue. The ovarian tumor mutants show conversion of the female germ line to a cell type resembling the male germ line, which undergoes more proliferation than the female germ line. Mutations of the *fat* locus cause hyperplastic overgrowth of imaginal discs, in which the epithelial structure is largely intact. The predicted fat protein product is a giant relative of cadherins, supporting indications from human cancer that cadherins play an important

role in tumor suppression. Mutations in the *lethal(2)giant larvae* and *lethal(1)discs large* genes cause neoplastic overgrowth of imaginal discs as well as the larval brain. The *dlg* gene encodes a membrane-associated guanylate kinase homolog that is localized at septate junctions between epithelial cells. This protein is a member of a family of homologs that also includes two proteins found at mammalian tight junctions (ZO-1 and ZO-2) and a protein found at mammalian synaptic junctions (PSD-95/SAP90). Genes in which mutations cause blood cell overproduction include *aberrant immune response-8*, which encodes the RpS6 ribosomal protein and *hopscotch*, which encodes a putative non-receptor protein tyrosine kinase. The gene products identified by ovarian tumor mutants do not show clear amino acid sequence homology to known proteins. *Drosophila* provides an opportunity to rapidly identify and characterize tumor suppressor genes, many of which have mammalian homologs that might also be involved in cell proliferation control and tumor suppression.

Key words: *Drosophila*, tumor suppressor gene, loss-of-function mutation

INTRODUCTION

It is becoming increasingly clear that the deregulated cell growth seen in neoplasia is associated with genetic alterations, which can be multiple and progressive. Proto-oncogenes are activated in a dominant fashion by mutation, chromosome translocation or gene amplification (Bishop, 1991), whereas tumor suppressor genes (TSGs) are inactivated or lost by mutation, chromosome loss, mitotic recombination or gene conversion (Lasko et al., 1991; Fig. 1a,b). The identification of genes in both categories is, of course, important to a full understanding of cancer.

Human TSGs usually have been identified by genetic mapping of tumor susceptibility loci followed by positional cloning, and/or by analyzing the changes in somatic cell DNA that occur during tumor development (Stanbridge, 1990). The protein products of TSGs include cell adhesion proteins, putative signal transduction molecules, transcription factors and molecules involved in cell cycle control. They apparently mediate many different steps in the production and transduction of growth-control signals.

Model experimental systems have not contributed greatly to the discovery of human TSGs, but they have the potential to do so. In this article we show how the genetic procedures available in *Drosophila* are now making it possible to quickly identify and characterize new tumor suppressor genes in this organism, and we discuss the possible functions of their mammalian homologs.

TSG IDENTIFICATION IN *DROSOPHILA*

In *Drosophila*, mutations in over 50 genes cause either hyperplastic or neoplastic overgrowth of various proliferating cell populations in the embryonic, larval and adult stages (Tables 1-5). The mutants vary in the degree to which the overgrowing tissue shows neoplastic characteristics such as loss of differentiated structure and invasiveness. However, for simplicity, since in all cases loss of function leads to overgrowth, we classify these genes as tumor suppressor genes (TSGs). Mutations in most of them are recessive lethals that cause death in pre-adult stages; TSGs that function only in the gonads are

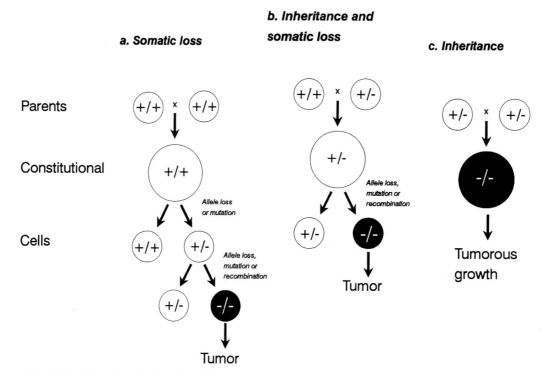

Fig. 1. Three ways in which cells can lose both copies of the normal allele of a TSG. (a) The first allele is lost by mutation, and the second is lost by a second mutation or by mitotic recombination between the two homologous chromosomes. (b) One mutant allele is inherited from a parent, and the second is lost by a second mutation or by mitotic recombination between the two homologous chromosomes. (c) A mutant allele (or a deficiency of the gene) is inherited from each of the two heterozygous parents, giving a zygote that lacks TSG function. Growth abnormalities are expected to arise at the time in development when the normal TSG functions.

exceptional in that they allow survival to adulthood but then cause sterility.

One of the technical advantages of using *Drosophila* as a model system is the availability of balancer chromosomes that make it possible to maintain recessive lethal mutations as stable heterozygous stocks. From such stocks it is simple to produce and study homozygous animals that have lost TSG function in every cell of the body (Fig. 1c). Another technical advantage is that radiation-induced or FLP recombinase-induced mitotic recombination (Golic and Lindquist, 1989) can be used to generate homozygous mutant clones in an otherwise heterozygous animal (Bryant et al., 1993), mimicking the allele loss observed in human tumors (Fig. 1b). Lastly, the ability to alter, reintroduce and manipulate transposable elements in the *Drosophila* genome (Sentry and Kaiser, 1992; Brand and Perrimon, 1993) is providing a series of powerful new tools for the identification and analysis of TSGs and other genes. Several large-scale mutagenesis screens involving mobilization of P elements (Watson et al., 1991; Török et al., 1993) have contributed greatly to our knowledge of *Drosophila* TSGs.

Twenty-two *Drosophila* TSGs have been characterized at the molecular level (Tables 1-5). Nine of them (*Notch, shibire, fat, twins, expanded, lethal(1)discs large, lethal(2)giant larvae, hopscotch* and *aberrant immune response-8*) show obvious homology to human genes, most of which had not been previously recognized as TSGs. This work is therefore contributing to our understanding of oncogenesis by identifying new candidate TSGs in man. Clearly, the further analysis

of this system could lead to the rapid identification of the molecular nature of many more TSG products, and it is likely that these will have functional equivalents in human cells. Many of the known elements controlling cell growth and differentiation (for example, the EGF, FGF and insulin receptors, TGFβ, cyclins, cdc genes, many oncogenes, tyrosine kinases, G proteins, homeobox genes) are highly conserved between human and *Drosophila* (Merriam et al., 1991), making it likely that many tumor-suppressing functions are also conserved.

TSGs FUNCTIONING IN THE EMBRYO

'Neurogenic' genes

A group of *Drosophila* genes with possible roles in tumor suppression is represented by the zygotic 'neurogenic' genes, the prototype being *Notch* (*N*; Artavanis-Tsakonas et al., 1991) (Table 1). The best-known phenotype caused by mutations of the *N* locus is hyperplasia of the embryonic nervous system in which excessive numbers of ectodermal cells adopt the neuroblast fate and delaminate from the ectodermal layer, rather than adopting the alternative epidermal fate (Poulson, 1937). Detailed study of these embryos shows that not only neuroblasts, but also other cell types that delaminate from the ectoderm (sensory neurons, peripheral glial cells and oenocytes) are overproduced (Hartenstein et al., 1992). Although excess neuronal and other cells are produced in these mutant embryos, the phenotype results from the initial determination of excess precursors rather than continuous cell pro-

Table 1. Genes in which mutations cause overgrowth of the nervous system in *Drosophila* embryos (the 'neurogenic' phenotype)

Gene	Symbol	Locus*	Site*	(Predicted) gene product	Reference
Notch	*N*	1-3.0	3B4	Transmembrane protein with EGF repeats	Gateff and Schneiderman, 1974; Wharton et al., 1985a; Artavanis-Tsakonas et al., 1991
lethal(1)discs large	*dlg*	1-34.8	10B8-9	Septate junction-associated guanylate kinase homolog	Woods and Bryant, 1989, 1991
shibire	*shi*	1-52.1	13F-14A1	Dynamin homolog	Poodry, 1990; Chen et al., 1991; Van der Bliek and Meyerowitz, 1991
big brain	*bib*	2-34.7	27D-31E	Transmembrane channel	Rao et al., 1990; Artavanis-Tsakonas et al., 1991
mastermind	*mam*	2-70.3	50C20-23	Nuclear protein rich in homopolymers	Smoller et al., 1990; Artavanis-Tsakonas et al., 1991
neuralized	*neu*	3-50	86C1-D8	Zinc finger protein	Artavanis-Tsakonas et al., 1991; Price et al., 1993
Delta	*Dl*	3-66.2	92A2	Transmembrane protein with EGF repeats	Alton et al., 1989; Artavanis-Tsakonas et al., 1991
Enhancer of split complex	*E(spl)-C*	3-89	96F11-14	G protein (β subunit) plus seven basic helix-loop-helix proteins	Hartley et al., 1988; Delidakis and Artavanis-Tsakonas, 1992; Knust et al., 1992

*Locus and site from Lindsley and Zimm, 1992 or from listed references.

Table 2. Genes in which mutations cause larval brain overgrowth in *Drosophila*

Gene	Symbol	Locus*	Site*	(Predicted) gene product	Reference
lethal(1)discs large	*dlg*	1-34.8	10B8-9	Septate junction-associated guanylate kinase homolog	Woods and Bryant, 1989, 1991
lethal(2)giant larvae	*l(2)gl*	2-0.0	21A	Cell membrane-associated, 78 and 127 kDa	Gateff and Schneiderman, 1974; Mechler et al., 1985; Klämbt and Schmidt, 1986; Jacob et al., 1987
lethal(2)79/18	*l(2)79/18*	2-	22C		Török et al., 1993
lethal(2)giant discs	*lgd*	2-42.7	32A-E		Bryant and Levinson, 1985
lethal(2)37Cf	*brat*	2-53.9	37C5-7	Novel, 99 kDa, pI = 9.25	Wright, 1987; Hankins, 1991
lethal(2)82/25	*l(2)82/25*	2-	35D-E		Török et al., 1993
lethal(2)43/1	*l(2)43/1*	2-	38CD		Török et al., 1993; M. Buratovich and P. J. Bryant, unpublished
lethal(2)90/37	*l(2)90/37*	2-	48		Török et al., 1993
lethal(2)115/12	*l(2)115/12*	2-	50		Török et al., 1993
lethal(3) malignant brain tumor	*l(3)mbt*	3-93	97E8-F11		Loffler et al., 1990; Gateff et al., 1993
lethal(3)1A1	*1A1*	3-	92B		T. Uemura, personal communication; P. J. Bryant, unpublished
prune;Killer of prune	*pn;awd^{K-pn}*	1-0.8; 3-102.9	2E2-3; 100C-D	GAP protein?; nucleoside diphosphate kinase	Teng et al., 1991b; Hackstein, 1992

*Locus and site from Lindsley and Zimm, 1992 or from listed references.

liferation, so the mutant phenotype does not constitute a tumor in the usual sense. However, transplantation studies do show that tissue from embryos lacking *N* function can develop into teratoma-like growths that can be serially cultured (Gateff and Schneiderman, 1974). Unfortunately it is not clear whether this effect is due to loss of *N* function per se or to the loss of a closely linked gene in the deficiency used in these experiments. The *N* gene encodes a 2703 amino acid transmembrane protein with 36 cysteine-rich domains homologous to epidermal growth factor (EGF) and three copies of the cysteine-rich *lin-12/N* repeat in the extracellular portion (Wharton et al., 1985a; Kidd et al., 1986; Fig. 2). In the cytoplasmic domain the protein contains a PEST motif (Rogers et al., 1986) and an OPA repeat (Wharton et al., 1985b), both thought to be associated with high protein turnover rate (Rogers et al., 1986). It also includes six ankyrin repeats, each composed of a 33 amino acid sequence homologous to a repeated sequence in the cell-cycle control genes *cdc10* of *Schizosaccharomyces pombe* and *SW16* of *Saccharomyces cerevisiae* (Breeden and Nasmyth, 1987). Immunolocalization experiments show that the Notch protein is localized at the cell membrane in embryos (Johansen et al., 1989) and in adherens junctions of the imaginal disc epithelium (Artavanis-Tsakonas et al., 1991; Fehon et al., 1991).

The human homolog of Notch, TAN-1, shows the same

Table 3. Genes in which mutations cause imaginal disc overgrowth in *Drosophila*

Gene	Symbol	Locus*	Site*	(Predicted) gene product	Reference
lethal(1)discs large	*dlg*	1-34.8	10B8-9	Septate junction-associated guanylate kinase homolog	Woods and Bryant, 1989, 1991
lethal(2)giant larvae	*l(2)gl*	2-0.0	21A	Cell membrane-associated 78 and 127 kDa	Gateff and Schneiderman, 1974; Mechler et al., 1985; Klämbt and Schmidt, 1986; Jacob et al., 1987
expanded	*ex*	2-0.1	21C1-2	Protein 4.1 family	Boedigheimer and Laughon, 1993; Boedigheimer et al., 1993
lethal(2)79/18	*l(2)79/18*	2-	22C		Török et al., 1993
lethal(2)fat	*fat*	2-12	24D8	Giant cadherin-like molecule	Bryant et al., 1988; Mahoney et al., 1991
lethal(2)giant discs	*lgd*	2-42.7	32A-E		Bryant and Schubiger, 1971; Bryant and Levinson, 1985
lethal(2)161/28	*l(2)161/28*	2-	43B		Török et al., 1993
lethal(2)90/37	*l(2)90/37*	2-	48E		Török et al., 1993
lethal(2)131/7	*l(2)131/7*	2-	48E		Török et al., 1993
lethal(2)115/12	*l(2)115/12*	2-	50E		Török et al., 1993
lethal(2)106/22†	*l(2)106/22*	2-	57		Török et al., 1993
lethal(2) tumorous imaginal discs	*tid*	2-104	59F4-6		Loffler et al., 1990; Kurzik-Dumke et al., 1992
lethal(3)c43	*hyd*	3-49.0	85E	Novel	Martin et al., 1977; Mansfield et al., 1994
twins	*tws*	3-	85F	Protein phosphatase 2A	Uemura et al., 1993
lethal(3)9C3	*l(3)9C3*	3-	90D		T. Uemura, personal communication
lethal(3)1A1	*1A1*	3-	93E1-9		T. Uemura, personal communication; P. J. Bryant, unpublished
lethal(3)malignant brain tumor	*l(3)mbt*	3-93	97E8-F11		Loffler et al., 1990; Gateff et al., 1993
warts‡	*wts*	3-	100A7-B1		Justice and Bryant, 1992
lethal(3)discs overgrown	*dco*	3-	100A7-B7		Jursnich et al., 1990

*Locus and site from Lindsley and Zimm, 1992 or from listed references.
†Only labial and antenna discs affected.
‡Phenotype known only from mitotic recombination clones.

domain structure as Notch, with amino acid identities in the range of 50-70% (Fig. 2). It was discovered as a gene spanning the 9q34 breakpoint in a series of translocations found in T lymphoblastic neoplasms (Ellisen et al., 1991). In addition to bearing the translocation chromosome, the tumor cells show frequent loss of the remaining normal chromosome 9. A likely interpretation is that the translocation inactivates one copy of *TAN-1* and that neoplasia is promoted when the second allele is lost from cells already carrying the translocation. Such an association between loss of both functional copies of a gene and the onset of malignancy would be similar to the behavior of other tumor suppressor genes. Thus for both *Drosophila* and human homologs there is preliminary evidence that these genes may function as TSGs.

It has been suggested that Notch function at the cell membrane may be translated into effects on gene expression through a pathway involving transcription factors encoded by other genes in which mutations cause overproduction of neuroblasts in the embryo (the 'neurogenic' class, Table 1; Artavanis-Tsakonas et al., 1991). If so, this effect could be mediated by the ankyrin repeats of Notch. Ankyrin repeats like those in Notch are found in members of the IκB family, proteins that interact with and inhibit the function of members of the rel/NF-κB group of sequence-specific transcription activators by blocking their translocation into the nucleus (Geisler et al., 1992; Kidd, 1992). N and TAN-1 may represent transmembrane relatives of IκB that interact directly with transcription factors, possibly at times when the latter are localized transiently in the cytoplasm.

Another possibly important aspect of Notch action is its interaction with the *Serrate* gene product, another transmembrane protein with EGF-like repeats in its extracellular domain (Fleming et al., 1990). Cells expressing Notch show adhesion to Serrate-expressing cells (Rebay et al., 1991), suggesting a direct interaction between the proteins, and a role for Serrate in cell proliferation control is indicated by the reduced proliferation seen in imaginal discs of *Serrate* mutant larvae, as well as the additional proliferation seen in imaginal discs containing regions that over-express Serrate (Speicher et al., 1994).

Mutations at the *shibire* (*shi*) locus also produce a neuralized phenotype as described for *Notch*, and tissues transplanted from mutant embryos give rise to transplantable tumorous growths (Hummon and Costello, 1988; Poodry, 1990). The predicted amino acid sequence of the *Drosophila shi* gene product shows 68-69% identity of amino acid sequence to that of both rat and human dynamin (Chen et al., 1991; Van der Bliek and Meyerowitz, 1991), a protein that acts as a GTP-binding motor functioning in vesicle trafficking and meiotic spindle separation (Obar et al., 1991). Vesicle trafficking may be required in the intercellular transfer of signals controlling cell fates, as with the products of *wingless* (Van den Heuvel et al., 1989; González et al., 1991) and *boss* (Cagan et al., 1992), which appear to be transported within and between cells in vesicles. Such a requirement has not been demonstrated for signals controlling cell proliferation, but one possibility is suggested by the finding that the Ash/Grb-2 adaptor protein, which is essential for Ras activation and therefore possibly involved in cell proliferation control, co-precipitates with

Table 4. Genes in which mutations cause overgrowth of larval hematopoietic tissues in *Drosophila*

Gene	Symbol	Locus*	Site*	(Predicted) protein product	Reference
lethal(1)air1	*air1*	1-0.5-2.1	1C3-E1;	2B15-18	Watson et al., 1991
lethal(1)air2	*air2*	1-2.8-4.3	1E3-4		Watson et al., 1991
lethal(1)air6	*air6*	1-15.0	5A1-E8		Watson et al., 1991
lethal(1)air7	*air7*	1-15.9	7A6-8		Watson et al., 1991
lethal(1)air8	*air8*	1-22.3	7C4-9	RpS6 ribosomal protein	Watson et al., 1991, 1992; Stewart and Denell, 1993
lethal(1)air9	*air9*	1-20.0	7C9-D10		Watson et al., 1991
lethal(1)air11	*air11*	1-29.0	8A5-9A2; 11A7-13F10		Watson et al., 1991
multi sex combs^malignant blood neoplasm	*mxc^mbn*		8D3-9		Santamaria and Randsholt, 1994
hopscotch^Tumorous-lethal	*hop^Tum-l*	1-34.5	10B6-8	Non-receptor protein tyrosine kinase (Jak family)	Hanratty and Ryerse, 1981; Hanratty and Dearolf, 1993; Zinyk et al., 1993; Binari and Perrimon, 1994
lethal(1)air13	*air13*	1-35.4	8A5-9A2; 11A7-13F10		Watson et al., 1991
lethal(1)air15	*air15*	1-55.6	11A7-13F10		Watson et al., 1991
lethal(2)168/14	*l(2)168/14*	2-	23B		Török et al., 1993
lethal(2)144/1	*l(2)144/1*	2-	31A		Török et al., 1993
lethal(2)86/34	*l(2)86/34*	2-	37D		Török et al., 1993
lethal(2)43/1	*l(2)43/1*	2-	38CD		Török et al., 1993; M. Buratovich and P. J. Bryant, unpublished
lethal(2)65/24	*l(2)65/24*	2-	48A		Török et al., 1993
lethal(2)90/37	*l(2)90/37*	2-	48E		Török et al., 1993
lethal(2)131/7†	*l(2)131/7*	2-	48E		Török et al., 1993
lethal(2)154/1†	*l(2)154/1*	2-	48E		Török et al., 1993
lethal(2)211/5	*l(2)211/5*	2-	51		Török et al., 1993
lethal(2)30/7	*l(2)30/7*	2-	55DE		Török et al., 1993
lethal(2)88/10	*l(2)88/10*	2-	56A		Török et al., 1993; M. Buratovich and P. J. Bryant, unpublished
lethal(2) malignant blood neoplasm	*l(2)mbn*	2-			Gateff et al., 1984
lethal(3) malignant blood neoplasm-1	*l(3)mbn-1*	3-13.3	64F4-5	Cytokeratin homolog	Shrestha and Gateff, 1986; Konrad et al., 1994
lethal(3)malign ant blood neoplasm-2	*l(3)mbn-2*	3-	87		Mechler, 1990
prune;Killer of prune	*pn;awdK-pn*	1-0.8; 3-102.9	2E2-3; 100C-D	GAP protein?; nucleoside diphosphate kinase	Teng et al., 1991b; Hackstein, 1992

*Locus and site from Lindsley and Zimm, 1992 or from listed references.
†*l(2)131/7* and *l(2)154/1* are allelic to *l(2)90/37* but are phenotypically distinct (Török et al., 1993).

Table 5. Genes in which mutations cause ovarian or gonial cell tumors in *Drosophila*

Gene	Symbol	Locus*	Site*	(Predicted) gene product	Reference
ovo	*ovo*	1-10.2	4E2	Zinc finger protein	Mével-Ninio et al., 1991; Mohler, 1977
female sterile(1)1621, sans-fille, liz	*fs(1)1621, snf*	1-11.7	4F1-5A1		Gollin and King, 1981; Salz, 1992
Sex-lethal	*Sxl*	1-19.2	6F4-7B3	RNA-binding protein	Bell et al., 1988; McKearin and Spradling, 1990
ovarian tumors	*otu*	1-23.2	7F1	Novel, proline-rich	Steinhauer et al., 1989; Geyer et al., 1993; Sass et al., 1993
fused	*fu*	1-59.5	17C3-D2	Ser/thr protein kinase	Therond et al., 1993; King et al., 1957
female sterile(1)231	*fs(1)231*	1-			King et al., 1957
female sterile(2)of Bridges	*fs(2)B*	2-5			King et al., 1957
narrow	*nw*	2-83?	54A-55A		King et al., 1957
benign(2)gonial cell neoplasm	*b(2)gcn*	2-106.7	60A3-7		Loffler et al., 1990
bag-of-marbles	*bam*	3-85	96C	Novel	McKearin and Spradling, 1990

*Locus and site from Lindsley and Zimm, 1992 or from listed references.

dynamin from PC12 cells (Miki et al., 1994). Interaction between these proteins would provide a link between signal transduction pathways important in cell proliferation control, and endocytic processes.

Mutations in several genes other than *Notch* and *shi* give rise to the neuralized phenotype (Artavanis-Tsakonas et al., 1991; Hartenstein et al., 1992; Table 1); these include *neuralized* (*neu*), *mastermind* (*mam*), *Delta* (*Dl*), *big brain* (*bib*) and the

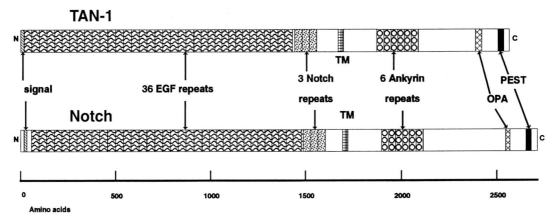

Fig. 2. Domain comparison between *Drosophila* Notch and human TAN-1 (after Ellisen et al., 1991). Both proteins contain a signal sequence, 36 tandemly repeated epidermal growth factor (EGF) domains, three tandemly-repeated Notch domains, a transmembrane domain (TM), six ankyrin domains, an OPA domain and a PEST domain. C, carboxy terminus; N, amino terminus.

Enhancer of split complex (*E(spl)-C*). Unfortunately, the appropriate transplantation tests to identify neoplastic growth like that seen with *N* and *shi* have not been reported for these genes. Therefore, whether or not they should be considered true TSGs must await further analysis.

TSGs FUNCTIONING IN BRAIN DEVELOPMENT

Several genes have been found to be necessary to control proliferation in the developing central nervous system of the larva. In wild-type larvae, the central nervous system is composed of two brain hemispheres and a ventral ganglion. The brain hemispheres are surrounded by a single layer of glial cells (the perineurium) together with an extracellular matrix, the neurilemma. The outer cortical region of the brain hemispheres contains several cell types (Gateff et al., 1984): neuroblasts, functioning as stem cells; ganglion mother cells, which are derived from the neuroblasts; and differentiated cells including neurons, neurosecretory cells and glial cells. The mass of axons making up the neuropile is in the center of the hemispheres. The lateral part of each hemisphere is occupied by the inner and outer proliferation centers - layers of neuroblasts that give rise to the optic lobes during metamorphosis. Between the two proliferation centers are several layers of ganglion mother cells and neurons.

Mutations in brain TSGs cause dramatic enlargement (to 2-5× the normal volume) of the two brain hemispheres, usually with no noticeable effect on the ventral ganglion. In the three cases that have been investigated in detail (*lethal(2)giant larvae (lgl)*, Gateff and Schneiderman, 1974; *brain tumor (brat)*, Hankins, 1991; and *lethal(3)malignant brain tumor (l(3)mbt)*, Gateff et al., 1993) the mutant brain hemispheres contain large numbers of undifferentiated cells, interpreted as small undifferentiated neuroblasts (*brat*), or as neuroblasts and ganglion mother cells (*lgl* and *l(3)mbt*). The predominance of neuroblasts leads to the suggestion that these growths are neuroblastomas (Gateff and Schneiderman, 1974; Hankins, 1991; Gateff et al., 1993). The *lgl* brain hemispheres contain all of the cell types found in wild-type animals, but they are intermingled rather than separated into well-defined layers and proliferation centers. In *l(3)mbt* mutants, the brain is disorganized

and the excess growth seems to obliterate at least part of the neuropile and to cause fragmentation of the remaining neuropile. In all three mutants, pieces of the mutant larval brain continue to grow by cell proliferation when transplanted into the abdomens of wild-type adults, and the body cavity becomes filled with cells interpreted as neuroblasts (*brat*) or neuroblasts and ganglion mother cells (*lgl* and *l(3)mbt*). Tumor cell types include neurons in the case of *brat*, and 'preganglion cells' and polyploid giant cells in the case of *lgl*. In all three mutants tumor cells invade host tissues such as ovaries, fat body, gut, and thoracic muscles, and in *lgl* the invasiveness has been confirmed by the use of genetic markers to distinguish the transplanted cells from the host (Timmons et al., 1993). For *lgl* and *l(3)mbt* the tumors are lethal to the host, supporting the idea that they should be considered malignant neuroblastomas (Gateff and Schneiderman, 1974).

lethal(2)giant larvae (lgl)

Although the *lgl* gene was the first TSG in any organism to be identified, cloned and sequenced (Klämbt et al., 1989), an understanding of how its product functions has been elusive. cDNA sequencing predicts the existence of two protein products, one of which is predicted to be 78 kDa and the other 127 kDa due to the addition of a C-terminal tail (Jacob et al., 1987). Neither sequence contains a transmembrane domain or other recognizable functional domain. The 78 kDa product is sufficient for tumor suppression, as judged by transformation rescue experiments (Jacob et al., 1987). Immunocytochemical studies show that the lgl protein is localized mainly in the cytoplasm, but about 20% is membrane-associated during early embryonic stages. At late embryonic stages the protein becomes restricted to the lateral surfaces of midgut and salivary gland epithelial cells, and to the neuropile of the central nervous system (Klämbt and Schmidt, 1986; Klämbt et al., 1989; Mechler and Strand, 1990; Strand et al., 1991). This pattern of embryonic expression is somewhat puzzling since the midgut and salivary gland are not abnormal in mutant animals, and since homozygous mutant *lgl* embryos can successfully develop and reach late third instar before they show the characteristic brain and imaginal disc tumors. These findings could be explained if the mutant embryos are rescued by maternally derived gene products (Schmidt, 1989). The lgl

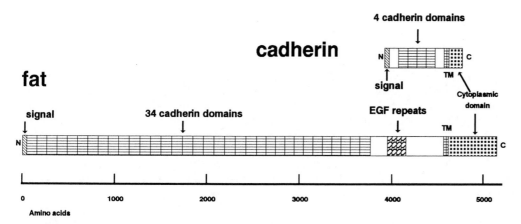

Fig. 3. Domain comparisons between the *Drosophila* fat protein and a typical vertebrate cadherin (Mahoney et al., 1991). The predicted fat product contains 34 extracellular domains with sequence similarity to the four extracellular domains of typical cadherins, and contains four epidermal growth factor (EGF) repeats that are not found in cadherins. In the predicted fat protein the first cadherin domain occurs immediately after the signal sequence, whereas in typical cadherins the signal sequence is followed by approximately 100 amino acids that are cleaved off to produce the mature protein. There is no significant homology between fat and cadherin in the cytoplasmic domain. C, carboxy terminus; N, amino terminus; TM, transmembrane domain.

protein is also expressed in the late third instar, in imaginal discs and in the neuroblasts of the larval brain (Klämbt and Schmidt, 1986), which are the tissues that show overgrowth in the mutant. In general, the protein seems to be present in tissues that are near or at the end of their proliferative growth phase, consistent with the conclusion from phenotypic studies that lgl plays a role in arresting cell proliferation. A mouse homolog of lgl has been identified as a gene under the control of the Hox-C8 homeobox gene, by immunopurification of DNA sequences that bind to Hox-C8 in native chromatin (Tomotsune et al., 1993). The predicted amino acid sequence shows about 41% identity to that of *Drosophila* lgl, and the gene is expressed at high levels in the nervous system.

brat has also been cloned and cDNAs sequenced (Hankins, 1991), but the sequence shows no clear homology to any other sequence and reveals no clues about the protein's function.

prune-killer-of-prune (pn;awd^{K-pn}) and neurofibromatosis

An unusual genetic interaction occurs in *Drosophila* between recessive mutations at the *prune* (*pn*) locus and the dominant *Killer-of-prune* allele of the *abnormal wing disc* gene (*awd^{K-pn}*; Teng et al., 1991a), and this genetic combination gives rise to an unusual tumorous phenotype. Animals carrying both of these mutations exhibit hypertrophy of the brain perineurium, the neuroglia and the lymph glands (Hackstein, 1992), and they die as late larvae. This is the only reported example of a TSG functioning in glial cells in *Drosophila*. The *awd* gene encodes a nucleoside diphosphate (NDP) kinase that is 78% identical to the mammalian Nm23 protein, which was identified by its low expression in cell lines with high metastatic potential (Rosengard et al., 1989). It has been proposed that NDP kinases regulate developmental processes and metastasis by increasing the availability of GTP, which activates GTP-binding proteins (Liotta et al., 1991). It has also been proposed that the *pn* gene product may be a GTPase activating protein (GAP), based on its slight similarity to bovine GAP (Teng et al., 1991b; but see Barnes and Burglin, 1992; Venkatesh and Teng, 1992, for a discussion of this putative similarity). These ideas and some phenotypic similarities have led to the formulation of a detailed model relating the *Drosophila* double mutant *pn;awd^{K-pn}* to human neurofibromatosis (Hackstein, 1992).

TSGs FUNCTIONING IN IMAGINAL DISCS

Mutations in some genes cause hyperplastic overgrowth of imaginal discs, in which the disc tissue retains most of its epithelial structure and is able to secrete cuticle during metamorphosis after transplantation to a larval host. In contrast in another group of mutants, the mutant imaginal discs lose their epithelial structure to varying extents, and lose their ability to differentiate after transplantation into a larval host. The latter are called neoplastic overgrowth mutants.

Hyperplastic overgrowth mutants

fat: a TSG encoding a putative cell adhesion molecule

Lethal mutations at the *fat* locus cause overgrowth of all of the imaginal discs, and the overgrowth is classified as hyperplasia because the tissues retain their single-layered epithelial structure and their ability to differentiate (Bryant et al., 1988; Mahoney et al., 1991). The gene is transcribed in the embryonic ectoderm and larval imaginal discs (Mahoney et al., 1991). Sequencing of overlapping partial cDNAs indicates that the gene product is a transmembrane protein with strong sequence homology in its extracellular domain to calcium-dependent cell adhesion molecules (cadherins; Fig. 3). However, the predicted product is much larger than typical cadherins, with 34 extracellular domains corresponding to the four domains of typical cadherins, as well as four EGF-like repeats and other cysteine-rich regions in the extracellular domain. The cytoplasmic domain shows no significant homology to that of typical cadherins. Some of the excess tissue from the overgrown imaginal discs in *fat* mutants is shed as vesicles during the pupal stage, supporting the idea that the gene product is required for epithelial cell adhesion as well as proliferation control.

In human patients, loss or reduction of E-cadherin expression has been reported in breast, head-and-neck, gastric, colorectal, bladder, prostate and liver cancer (Schipper et al., 1991; Shimoyama and Hirohashi, 1991; Field, 1992; Bringuier et al., 1993; Mayer et al., 1993; Morton et al., 1993; Nigam et al., 1993; Oka et al., 1993; Oda et al., 1994), and E-cadherin loss is correlated with invasiveness of carcinoma and epithelial cell lines (Behrens et al., 1989; Frixen et al., 1991; Doki et al., 1993). Treatment with anti-E-cadherin antibodies can cause non-invasive carcinoma and epithelial cell lines to become invasive (Behrens et al., 1989; Frixen et al., 1991), and invasiveness of carcinoma cell lines can be prevented by transfection with E-cadherin cDNA (Frixen et al., 1991). These correlative findings are highly suggestive of an important role of E-cadherin in preventing the transition to tumorous and/or invasive growth. Even more intriguing is the possibility that the human E-cadherin gene located at 16q22.1 (Natt et al., 1989) may correspond to a TSG identified by loss of heterozygosity in this genetic region in hepatocellular, breast, and prostate carcinomas (Carter et al., 1990; Sato et al., 1990; Tsuda et al., 1990; Zhang et al., 1990). If E-cadherin plays an important role in tumor suppression, the *fat* locus may provide a useful model system for investigating the mechanism of this effect. Both E-cadherin and the fat protein may play important direct roles in proliferation control, perhaps by initiating a signal transduction process at the cell membrane. Alternatively, their roles may be simply to support cell adhesion as a crucial prerequisite for the cell signalling events that control proliferation and for the mechanical attachments that prevent metastasis.

Other hyperplastic overgrowth mutants

Three more genes in which mutations cause hyperplastic imaginal disc overgrowth have been cloned. The *hyperplastic discs (hyd)* gene (=*l(3)c43*; Martin et al., 1977) encodes a novel protein with a region homologous to a part of poly(A)-binding proteins (Mansfield et al., 1994). Alterations at the *twins* locus cause an overgrowth phenotype in which the posterior part of the wing disc is duplicated with mirror-image symmetry (Uemura et al., 1993). cDNAs representing the *twins* gene encode a product with 75-78% amino acid identity to the regulatory B subunits of human protein phosphatase 2A (Uemura et al., 1993). The *expanded* locus, in which mutations result in overgrowth of the posterior part of the wing disc and parts of the leg and antenna discs (Boedigheimer and Laughon, 1993), encodes a member of the protein 4.1 family of membrane-cytoskeletal linker molecules that includes the NF2 (neurofibromatosis type 2) tumor suppressor (Boedigheimer et al., 1993).

Neoplastic overgrowth mutants

discs-large: a TSG encoding a junctional protein

Mutations in the *lethal(1)discs large (dlg)* gene cause neoplastic imaginal disc overgrowth; the mutant tissues, which are normally single-layered, become disorganized masses and lose the ability to develop into adult parts after transplantation into normal hosts. This is similar to the effect on imaginal discs produced by mutations in the *lgl* gene (Gateff and Schneiderman, 1974). The *dlg* gene encodes several products including a 960 amino acid protein DlgA (Fig. 4) that is expressed in most epithelial tissues as well as other tissues throughout development (Woods and Bryant, 1989, 1991). The carboxy-terminal 179 amino acids of DlgA show strong homology (35.5% identity) to yeast guanylate kinase (GUK; Berger et al., 1989), an enzyme that transfers a phosphate group from ATP to GMP, converting it to GDP. Although the GMP-binding features of yeast GUK are highly conserved in DlgA, the putative ATP-binding site has a 3 amino acid deficiency (Koonin et al., 1992) suggesting that the protein may simply bind GMP or catalyze a reaction other than phosphorylation of GMP. DlgA also contains the 59 amino acid SH3 domain (Musacchio et al., 1992), which is found in many membrane-

associated signal transduction proteins and mediates binding to other proteins, including GTPase-activating proteins (Ren et al., 1993). It also has an OPA domain and a PEST domain, as mentioned above for the Notch protein. The N-terminal half of the molecule contains three copies of a newly identified 91 amino acid motif called DHR (previously GLGF; Cho et al., 1992), of unknown function (Fig. 4).

In epithelial cells the Dlg protein is localized in an apical belt of the lateral cell membrane at the position of a specialized structure, called the septate junction, which connects cell neighbors (Woods and Bryant, 1991). The role of these junctions is unknown, although they have often been considered the invertebrate equivalent of vertebrate tight junctions (Noirot-Timothee and Noirot, 1980). The Dlg protein is required for septate junction structure as shown by the absence or reduction of septate junctions in *dlg* mutant larvae (D. F. Woods and P. J. Bryant, unpublished). The analysis of this gene suggests that cell interactions important for growth control occur at septate junctions, and that the interactions may regulate the production of guanine nucleotides that act as messenger molecules within the cell.

Four human homologs of *dlg* have been identified, and none was previously suspected to be involved in tumor suppression (Fig. 4; Woods and Bryant, 1993). We refer to this growing family of gene products as MAGUKs (membrane-associated guanylate kinase homologs). Three of the mammalian MAGUKs are associated with cell junctions: ZO-1 and ZO-2 are two well-known components of epithelial tight junctions, while PSD95/SAP-90 is a component of synaptic junctions in the brain.

ZO-1 is a major protein component of epithelial and endothelial tight junctions (Anderson et al., 1988; Itoh et al., 1993; Willott et al., 1993). It shows clear homology to DlgA in the DHR, SH3, and GUK domains, but it differs from it in the presence of a large proline-rich C-terminal extension (Fig. 4). The ZO-1 GUK domain shows 29% identity of amino-acid sequence with the DlgA GUK domain and 24% with pig GUK, and it has a well conserved Mg^{2+}-binding site (the B motif) including the Asp residue implicated in direct interaction with the Mg^{2+} cofactor (Yan and Tsai, 1991). However, ZO-1 has a 32 amino acid deficiency within the GUK domain as compared to DlgA and pig GUK, and this deficiency removes four of the ten residues expected to interact with GMP. The A-motif of ZO-1 has the same three amino acid deficiency as in DlgA, and is also missing an otherwise highly conserved lysine residue. These features would appear to make it unlikely that ZO-1 functions as a guanylate kinase and suggest that it might not even interact with GMP. The ZO-1 amino acid sequence shows 14.6-44.8% identity with DlgA in the other domains (Fig. 4).

The second mammalian MAGUK is ZO-2 (Fig. 4; Jesaitis and Goodenough, 1994), another protein component of epithelial tight junctions that has been shown to bind to ZO-1 (Gumbiner et al., 1991). The available predicted amino acid sequence shows the presence of DHR3, SH3 and GUK domains, together with a proline-rich C-terminal domain that is considerably shorter than that of ZO-1. The sequence is incomplete at the N-terminal end, so it is still possible that DHR1 and DHR2 domains are present. The sequence is more similar to that of ZO-1 than to the other known members of the MAGUK family.

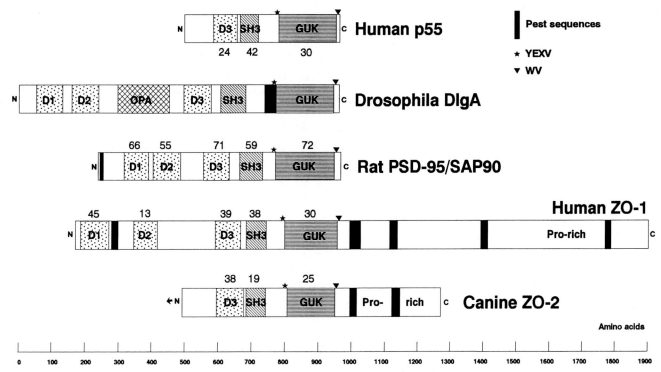

Fig. 4. Comparison of the modular structures of human p55 (Ruff et al., 1991), *Drosophila* DlgA (Woods and Bryant, 1991), rat PSD-95/SAP90 (Cho et al., 1992; Kistner et al., 1993), human ZO-1 (Willott et al., 1993) and canine ZO-2 (Jesaitis and Goodenough, 1994). D1, D2, D3, discs-large homologous regions (DHRs), previously designated GLGF (Cho et al., 1992); SH3, src-homology region 3 (Musacchio et al., 1992); GUK, guanylate kinase-homologous region; OPA, repetitive sequence (Wharton et al., 1985b). Domain boundaries and sequence identities were determined using the BLAST algorithm (Altschul et al., 1990) on line at the National Center for Biotechnology Information, and the multiple alignment program MACAW (Schuler et al., 1991). Numbers outside the boxes indicate percentage amino acid identity compared with the corresponding domain of DlgA. Regions shown in black are PEST sequences, scoring >6.0 on the PESTFIND program (Rogers et al., 1986). Arrow indicates incomplete sequence.

The third mammalian DlgA homolog is a protein localized in synaptic junctions and named either PSD-95 (Cho et al., 1992) or SAP90 (Kistner et al., 1993) (Fig. 4). The deduced amino acid sequence of this protein shows strong homology (about 67% identity) to DlgA throughout its length, and includes three DHRs, an SH3 and a modified GUK. The PSD-95/SAP90 sequence shows strong conservation of the GMP-binding site and has the same deficiency as DlgA in the putative ATP-binding site, suggesting that its function is similar to that of the *Drosophila* protein (Koonin et al., 1992).

The fourth mammalian MAGUK is the heavily palmitoylated phosphoprotein p55, which was purified from red blood cell membrane ghosts and copurifies with the cytoskeletal actin-bundling protein dematin, protein 4.1, and actin (Ruff et al., 1991). p55 shows striking similarity to the DlgA protein in the DHR3, SH3, and GUK domains (Fig. 4; Ruff et al., 1991; Bryant and Woods, 1992). The ATP-binding site of p55 does not show a deficiency like those seen in the junction-associated MAGUKs, but it does show a K to R substitution that might affect enzyme activity. The p55 gene is located near the tip of the long arm of the X chromosome, between the genes encoding the blood-clotting protein, factor VIII, and the enzyme glucose-6-phosphate dehydrogenase (Metzenberg and Gitschier, 1992).

p55 binds with high affinity to protein 4.1, which is thought to link the cytoskeleton to the cell membrane, and to the trans-membrane protein glycophorin C (Alloisio et al., 1993; Marfatia et al., 1994). Protein 4.1 and glycophorin C also bind to each other, suggesting the existence of a ternary complex at the erythrocyte plasma membrane. Genetic loss of either protein 4.1 or glycophorin C leads to loss of p55 and to abnormal erythrocyte shape in the hereditary elliptocytoses, indicating that the complex plays a critical role in stabilizing the erythrocyte plasma membrane. Isoforms of p55, protein 4.1 and glycophorin C are present in many cell types in addition to blood cells (Metzenberg and Gitschier, 1992; Marfatia et al., 1994), so similar membrane-associated complexes may exist in these other cell types. Also, the strong similarity between p55 and other MAGUKs raises the possibility that the MAGUKs are components of similar membrane-associated molecular complexes that might be important structural components of cell junctions.

TSGs FUNCTIONING IN BLOOD CELL DEVELOPMENT

In *Drosophila*, mutations at more than 25 loci lead to a characteristic larval phenotype including hyperplastic hematopoietic organs, excess blood cells in circulation, and melanizing aggregates formed by the mutant blood cells (Table 4). The hematopoietic organs are the lymph glands, which line the dorsal vessel at its anterior end and give rise to two distinct populations of hemocytes (blood cells): the plasmatocytes and the crystal cells (Rizki, 1978; Gateff et al., 1984). Three of these genes (*aberrant immune response-8, lethal(3)malignant blood neoplasm-1* and *hopscotch*) have been cloned and characterized at the molecular level.

aberrant immune response-8: a TSG encoding a ribosomal protein

The *aberrant immune response-8* (*air8*) locus was the first TSG affecting the functioning of the *Drosophila* hematopoietic system that was characterized at the molecular level. Animals mutant for the *air8* locus show a generalized slowing of larval growth, but they also exhibit gross hypertrophy, hyperplasia and melanization of the larval lymph glands (Watson et al., 1991). Blood cells are overproduced and their differentiation is altered such that lamellocytes, not normally produced until the late larval or pupal stage, are found both in the lymph glands and in circulation. The normal role of lamellocytes is to aggregate and form melanized capsules around foreign objects during an immune response, but in *air8* animals the lamellocytes aggregate and form large melanotic tumors in the absence of a foreign challenge. The mutant animals die during the late larval stage. Transplantation of *air8* lymph glands into permissive hosts results in the formation of melanotic tumors and an increased rate of host death when compared to wild-type lymph gland transplants (Watson, 1993).

The product of the *air8* gene, predicted from cDNA sequencing, shows 75% identity and 95% similarity to the human ribosomal protein S6 (Watson et al., 1992; Fig. 5). On northern blots, the 1 kb RpS6 transcript is barely detectable in hemizygous *air8* larvae but is very abundant in *air8* revertant animals and in wild-type animals throughout development. Thus a loss or major reduction in RpS6 expression appears to result in tumor formation in the *Drosophila* hematopoietic system. Two other RpS6 gene mutations (*RpS6^WG1288* and *RpS6^hen*) have been identified (Watson et al., 1992; Stewart and Denell, 1993) and shown to result in reduced RpS6 transcription although the hematopoietic tissues in these mutants have not been analyzed for neoplastic properties. Expression of a single wild-type RpS6 gene in germ-line transformants is sufficient to rescue the lethality associated with the *RpS6^WG1288* and *RpS6^hen* mutations, and to partially rescue the phenotype of the *RpS6^air8* mutation (K. Watson, unpublished).

In mammals, RpS6 is the major phosphoprotein of the 40 S ribosomal subunit, occupying the mRNA-binding site (Ballou et al., 1988). Its phosphorylation, on a cluster of serine residues at the C terminus (Fig. 5), represents the end-point of a mitogen-stimulated serine/threonine phosphorylation cascade triggered by growth factor binding at the cell surface (Pelech and Sanghera, 1992; Posada and Cooper, 1992). RpS6 phosphorylation is developmentally regulated, and can be stimulated in quiescent cells by treatments that increase protein synthesis and cell proliferation such as serum growth factors, insulin, tumor promoting agents, transforming viruses, mitogens and chemical carcinogens (see Traugh and Pendergast, 1986, for review). The mitogenic stimulation of RpS6 phosphorylation is reversible, and rapid dephosphorylation occurs when cells are deprived of serum or exposed to other treatments that arrest growth (Glover, 1982; Traugh and Pendergast, 1986). Similarly, cultured blood cells derived from

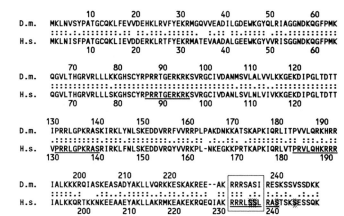

Fig. 5. Sequence comparison between *Drosophila* (D.m.; Watson et al., 1992) and human (H.s.; Pata et al., 1992) RpS6 ribosomal proteins (from Watson et al., 1992). The *Drosophila* RpS6 protein is encoded by the *air8* gene. Both sequences include four copies of a nuclear localization signal (underlined), and a cluster of serine residues at the C terminus. Some of these serines in the human protein (shaded) are sites of phosphorylation by a variety of kinases and an S6-kinase (Ferrari et al., 1991). The kinase recognition sequence is boxed. Alignments were made using the FASTA program (Pearson and Lipman, 1990).

air8 mutant animals become quiescent when deprived of insulin and can be stimulated to proliferate when insulin is added back to the medium (K. L. Watson, unpublished). RpS6 and other ribosomal phosphoprotein mRNAs are overexpressed in human colon carcinomas and liver metastases (Barnard et al., 1992).

In view of the correlations between RpS6 phosphorylation and growth, the loss of RpS6 expression accompanied by tumor formation in the *air8* mutant appears paradoxical. But one way that RpS6 may play a role in controlling cell growth is through the selective translation of particular mRNAs due to different rates of mRNA initiation or translation (Ballou et al., 1988; Erikson, 1991). If the regulated genes included some that are directly involved in tissue-specific cell proliferation control, the loss of RpS6 expression could slow growth in some tissues while accelerating it in others.

The human RpS6 shares many features with *Drosophila* RpS6 including a polypyrimidine tract at the transcription start site, short untranslated regions, the first intron beginning after the second codon and the absence of consensus TATA or CAAT sequence motifs in the 5′ regulatory region (Antoine and Fried, 1992). The chromosome location of the human RpS6 gene is 9p21, a chromosome region at which genetic alterations are associated with acute lymphoblastic leukemia (ALL), acute myeloid leukemia (AML) and pleomorphic adenoma of the salivary gland (Antoine and Fried, 1992). This raises the possibility of RpS6 mutations being involved in human tumorigenesis.

lethal(3)malignant blood neoplasm-1 (l(3)mbn-1)

Mutations in the *l(3)mbn-1* gene cause hyperplasia of the lymph glands, abnormal differentiation of plasmatocytes and lamellocytes, invasion of the larval tissues by blood cells and lethality in the late larval stage (Konrad et al., 1994). The gene produces a 2.6 kb transcript during embryonic and larval stages of development and two transcripts of 1.4 and 1.8 kb in pupae and adults. The predicted gene product contains 796 residues bearing some similarity in the C-terminal domain to the G-S repeats found in human cytokeratins K1 and K10 (Konrad et al., 1994). It is unclear what role this protein performs in blood cells or how loss of the function leads to overproliferation of blood cells.

hopscotch^{Tumorous lethal} (*hop*^{Tum-l}): a TSG encoding a tyrosine kinase

Loss-of-function mutations in the *hopscotch (hop)* gene result in small imaginal organs, and mutant animals die at the larval/pupal stage (Binari and Perrimon, 1994). Wild-type *hop* activity is required maternally for the proper segmentation of embryos (Binari and Perrimon, 1994). Conceptual translation of *hop* cDNAs yields a 1,177 amino acid protein proposed to be a member of the Janus family of non-receptor protein tyrosine kinases (JAKs) (Binari and Perrimon, 1994). Although most lesions in the *hop* gene lead to undersized imaginal tissues, one unusual allele (*hop*^{Tum-l}) results in the dominant overproduction of lamellocytes (Hanratty and Dearolf, 1993; Zinyk et al., 1993). The *hop*^{Tum-l} mutation is complex in that the dominant transformation of hemocytes is temperature-insensitive whereas the recessive lethality and dominant enhancement of melanotic tumors is temperature-sensitive (Hanratty and Ryerse, 1981; Silvers and Hanratty, 1984; Nappi and Carton, 1986). The alteration in the *hop* gene that causes this complex phenotype, and its effect on kinase activity, is not known.

The double mutant *pn;awd*^{K-pn} (see above) suppresses the hematopoietic defect in *hop*^{Tum-l} mutant animals (Zinyk et al., 1993). This interaction has led to the suggestion that the wild-type products of the *awd, pn,* and *hop* genes may function in a common hematopoietic regulatory pathway (Zinyk et al., 1993).

TSGs FUNCTIONING IN GONAD DEVELOPMENT

Ovarian tumor mutants

These mutants are characterized by the production of large numbers of poorly differentiated germ cells in the adult ovary, causing female sterility. In the normal ovary each egg chamber contains one oocyte and fifteen nurse cells, which together represent the progeny from four successive divisions of a single cystoblast. In the ovarian tumor mutants (Table 5) the germ cells overproliferate to produce a mass of much smaller cells that show some cytological features characteristic of spermatocytes (Pauli et al., 1993). In *Sxl, snf* and *otu* these cells also show expression of male-specific enhancer traps (Wei et al., 1994). Since in the normal male the spermatocytes show much more proliferation than oogonial cells, it has been suggested that the ovarian tumor phenotype is a result of sex transformation in the germ line (Pauli and Mahowald, 1990; Steinmann-Zwicky, 1992). Indeed, mutations in some genes known to function in somatic cell sex determination (*Sex-lethal* and *sans-fille*) also give rise to ovarian tumors. The expression of some male-specific enhancer traps is restricted to the testis apex in normal males, but is much more widespread in the ovarian tumors. Furthermore, some cells in the tumors show cytological features of nurse cells (female germ-line cells)

while expressing male-specific genes (Wei et al., 1994). These results suggest that the ovarian tumor phenotype is not due simply to sex transformation but that it also involves the over-proliferation of cells that are in an early stage of germ-cell development and/or show incomplete sex transformation.

ovarian tumor (otu)

Mutations in this gene yield a variety of phenotypes including excess cell proliferation and differentiation defects during oogenesis (Geyer et al., 1993; Sass et al., 1993). The most severe mutants lack germ cell proliferation; less severe mutants develop tumorous ovarian chambers, and the least severe ones exhibit some oocyte/nurse cell differentiation but fail to complete oogenesis (Geyer et al., 1993; Sass et al., 1993). In *otu* null mutants, ovaries contain tumorous egg chambers indicating that *otu* function is required for the control of normal germ cell proliferation (Geyer et al., 1993). This gene produces two 3.2 kb alternatively spliced, ovary-specific transcripts that differ in their temporal expression (Geyer et al., 1993; Sass et al., 1993). P-element insertions in the *otu* promoter and noncoding regions affect the levels of *otu* expression and this variable expression is correlated with the severity of the mutant phenotype even though transcript initiation occurs at the major start site (Sass et al., 1993). The predicted product is proline-rich and hydrophilic (Steinhauer et al., 1989), but the amino acid sequence is otherwise unrevealing.

Gonial cell tumors

Mutations in two genes give rise to tumorous adult gonads in both sexes. Null mutations in the *bag of marbles* (*bam*) gene result in the formation of abnormal germ cell clusters with increased cell numbers in both ovaries and testes (McKearin and Spradling, 1990). The *bam* gene gives rise to a 2.2 kb transcript, expressed in both male and female gonads, that encodes a protein with some similarity to the central portion of the otu protein (see above; McKearin and Spradling, 1990). Unfortunately, the protein sequence does not immediately reveal a putative functional role for this protein other than the presence of a PEST sequence, which is usually correlated with protein instability or rapid turnover (Rogers et al., 1986). The sequence and phenotypic similarity between *otu* and *bam* suggests that they may have related functions. Mutations in *benign(2)gonial cell neoplasm* also cause tumorous growth of the germ line in both males and females. The ring canals that join nurse cells to the oocyte in the wild type are missing in the ovaries of this mutant, suggesting that the differentiation of the female germ line does not progress beyond the gonial stage; the male germ line also fails to progress beyond the gonial stage (Gateff and Mechler, 1989).

FUTURE DIRECTIONS

In this article, we have shown the utility of *Drosophila* as a model system for identifying and analyzing TSG functions. At least nine cloned *Drosophila* TSGs (*Notch, shibire, fat, twins, expanded, lethal(1)discs large, lethal(2)giant larvae, hopscotch* and *aberrant immune response-8*) have human homologs that may have important roles in growth control and differentiation. Many more TSGs have been identified in *Drosophila* but not yet cloned, and these may direct attention to additional mammalian homologs. Furthermore, not all chromosomes have been exhaustively screened for such mutations and it is therefore very likely that many more TSGs remain to be discovered. Little effort has been devoted to finding mutations that cause overgrowth in embryonic stages or in mesodermal tissues, so that even more genes could probably be found by searching for mutations with such phenotypes. In addition to its utility for rapidly discovering new TSGs, *Drosophila* provides a variety of genetic methods that will be useful in analyzing the interactions and functions of these genes at the molecular, cellular and developmental levels.

The authors' research is supported by grants from the National Institutes of Health and the National Science Foundation.

REFERENCES

Alloisio, N., Venezia, N. D., Rana, A., Andrabi, K., Texier, P., Gilsanz, F., Cartron, J.-P., Delaunay, J. and Chishti, A. H. (1993). Evidence that red blood cell protein p55 may participate in the skeleton-membrane linkage that involves protein 4.1 and glycophorin C. *Blood* **82**, 1323-1327.

Alton, A. K., Fechtel, K., Kopczynski, C. C., Shepard, S. B., Kooh, P. J. and Muskavitch, M. A. (1989). Molecular genetics of *Delta*, a locus required for ectodermal differentiation in *Drosophila*. *Dev. Genet.* **10**, 261-272.

Altschul, S. F., Gish, W., Miller, W., Myers, E. W. and Lipman, D. J. (1990). Basic local alignment search tool. *J. Mol. Biol.* **215**, 403-410.

Anderson, J. M., Stevenson, B. R., Jesaitis, L. A., Goodenough, D. A. and Mooseker, M. S. (1988). Characterization of ZO-1, a protein component of the tight junction from mouse liver and Madin-Darby canine kidney cells. *J. Cell Biol.* **106**, 1141-1149.

Antoine, M. and Fried, M. (1992). The organization of the intron-containing human S6 ribosomal protein (rpS6) gene and determination of its location at chromosome 9p21. *Hum. Mol. Genet.* **1**, 565-570.

Artavanis-Tsakonas, S., Delidakis, C. and Fehon, R. G. (1991). The *Notch* locus and the cell biology of neuroblast segregation. *Annu. Rev. Cell Biol.* **7**, 427-452.

Ballou, L. M., Jeno, P. and Thomas, G. (1988). Control of S6 phosphorylation during the mitogenic response. *Advan. Exp. Med. Biol* **231**, 445-452.

Barnard, G. F., Staniunas, R. J., Bao, S., Mafune, K.-i., Steele, G. D., Gollan, J. L. and Chen, L. B. (1992). Increased expression of human ribosomal phosphoprotein P0 messenger RNA in hepatocellular carcinoma and colon carcinoma. *Cancer Res.* **52**, 3067-3072.

Barnes, T. M. and Burglin, T. R. (1992). Prune function? *Nature* **355**, 504-505.

Behrens, J., Mareel, M. M., Van Roy, F. M. and Birchmeier, W. (1989). Dissecting tumor cell invasion: epithelial cells acquire invasive properties after the loss of uvomorulin-mediated cell-cell adhesion. *J. Cell Biol.* **108**, 2435-2447.

Bell, L. R., Maine, E. M., Schedl, P. and Cline, T. W. (1988). Sex-lethal, a Drosophila sex determination switch gene, exhibits sex-specific RNA splicing and sequence similarity to RNA binding proteins. *Cell* **55**, 1037-1046.

Berger, A., Schiltz, E. and Schulz, G. E. (1989). Guanylate kinase from *Saccharomyces cerevisiae*. Isolation and characterization, crystallization and preliminary X-ray analysis, amino acid sequence and comparison with adenylate kinases. *Eur. J. Biochem.* **184**, 433-443.

Binari, R. and Perrimon, N. (1994). Stripe-specific regulation of pair-rule genes by *hopscotch*, a putative Jak family tyrosine kinase in *Drosophila*. *Genes Dev.* **8**, 300-312.

Bishop, J. M. (1991). Molecular themes in oncogenesis. *Cell* **64**, 235-248.

Boedigheimer, M., Bryant, P. and Laughon, A. (1993). Expanded, a negative regulator of cell proliferation in *Drosophila*, shows homology to the NF2 tumor suppressor. *Mech. Dev.* **44**, 83-84.

Boedigheimer, M. and Laughon, A. (1993). *expanded*: a gene involved in the control of cell proliferation in *Drosophila* imaginal discs. *Development* **118**, 1291-1301.

Brand, A. H. and Perrimon, N. (1993). Targeted gene expression as a means of altering cell fates and generating dominant phenotypes. *Development* **118**, 401-415.

Breeden, L. and Nasmyth, K. (1987). Similarity between cell-cycle genes of budding yeast and fission yeast and the *Notch* gene of *Drosophila*. *Nature* **329**, 651-654.

Bringuier, P. P., Umbas, R., Schaafsma, H. E., Karthaus, H. F. M., Debruyne, F. M. J. and Schalken, J. A. (1993). Decreased E-cadherin immunoreactivity correlates with poor survival in patients with bladder tumors. *Cancer Res.* **53**, 3241-3245.

Bryant, P. J. and Schubiger, G. (1971). Giant and duplicated imaginal discs in a new lethal mutant of *Drosophila melanogaster*. *Dev. Biol.* **24**, 233-263.

Bryant, P. J. and Levinson, P. Y. (1985). Intrinsic growth control in the imaginal primordia of *Drosophila* and the autonomous action of a lethal mutation causing overgrowth. *Dev. Biol.* **107**, 355-363.

Bryant, P. J., Huettner, B., Held, L. I. Jr, Ryerse, J. and Szidonya, J. (1988). Mutations at the *fat* locus interfere with cell proliferation control and epithelial morphogenesis in *Drosophila*. *Dev. Biol.* **129**, 541-554.

Bryant, P. J. and Woods, D. F. (1992). A major palmitoylated membrane protein of human erythrocytes shows homology to yeast guanylate kinase and to the product of a *Drosophila* tumor suppressor gene. *Cell* **68**, 621-622.

Bryant, P. J., Watson, K. L., Justice, R. W. and Woods, D. F. (1993). Tumor suppressor genes encoding proteins required for cell interactions and signal transduction in *Drosophila*. *Development* **119** (suppl.) 239-249.

Cagan, R. L., Krämer, H., Hart, A. C. and Zipursky, S. L. (1992). The *bride of sevenless* and *sevenless* interaction: internalization of a transmembrane ligand. *Cell* **69**, 393-399.

Carter, B. S., Ewing, C. M., Ward, W. S., Treiger, B. F., Aalders, T. W., Schalken, J. A., Epstein, J. I. and Isaacs, W. B. (1990). Allelic loss of chromosomes 16q and 10q in human prostate cancer. *Proc. Nat. Acad. Sci. USA* **87**, 8751-8755.

Chen, M. S., Obar, R. A., Schroeder, C. C., Austin, T. W., Poodry, C. A., Wadsworth, S. C. and Vallee, R. B. (1991). Multiple forms of dynamin are encoded by *shibire*, a *Drosophila* gene involved in endocytosis. *Nature* **351**, 583-586.

Cho, K.-O., Hunt, C. A. and Kennedy, M. B. (1992). The rat brain postsynaptic density fraction contains a homolog of the *Drosophila discs-large* tumor suppressor protein. *Neuron* **9**, 929-942.

Delidakis, C. and Artavanis-Tsakonas, S. (1992). The Enhancer of split [E(spl)] locus of Drosophila encodes seven independent helix-loop-helix proteins. *Proc. Nat. Acad. Sci. USA* **89**, 8731-8735.

Doki, Y., Shiozaki, H., Tahara, H., Inoue, M., Oka, H., Iihara, K., Kadowaki, T., Takeichi, M. and Mori, T. (1993). Correlation between E-cadherin expression and invasiveness *in vitro* in a human esophageal cancer cell line. *Cancer Res.* **53**, 3421-3426.

Ellisen, L. W., Bird, J., West, D. C., Soreng, A. L., Reynolds, T. C., Smith, S. D. and Sklar, J. (1991). *TAN-1*, the human homolog of the *Drosophila Notch* gene, is broken by chromosomal translocations in T lymphoblastic neoplasms. *Cell* **66**, 649-661.

Erikson, R. L. (1991). Structure, expression, and regulation of protein kinases involved in the phosphorylation of ribosomal protein S6. *J. Biol. Chem.* **266**, 6007-6010.

Fehon, R. G., Johansen, K., Rebay, I. and Artavanis-Tsakonas, S. (1991). Complex cellular and subcellular regulation of *Notch* expression during embryonic and imaginal development of *Drosophila*: Implications for *Notch* function. *J. Cell Biol.* **113**, 657-669.

Ferrari, S., Bandi, H. R., Hofsteenge, J., Bussian, B. M. and Thomas, G. (1991). Mitogen-activated 70K S6 kinase. Identification of *in vitro* 40 S ribosomal S6 phosphorylation sites. *J. Biol. Chem.* **266**, 22770-22775.

Field, J. K. (1992). Oncogenes and tumour-suppressor genes in squamous cell carcinoma of the head and neck. *Eur. J. Cancer [B]* **28B**, 67-76.

Fleming, R. J., Scottgale, T. N., Diederich, R. J. and Artavanis-Tsakonas, S. (1990). The gene *Serrate* encodes a putative EGF-like transmembrane protein essential for proper ectodermal development in *Drosophila melanogaster*. *Genes Dev.* **4**, 2188-2201.

Frixen, U. H., Behrens, J., Sachs, M., Eberle, G., Voss, B., Warda, A., Lochner, D. and Birchmeier, W. (1991). E-cadherin-mediated cell-cell adhesion prevents invasiveness of human carcinoma cells. *J. Cell Biol.* **113**, 173-185.

Gateff, E. A. and Schneiderman, H. A. (1974). Developmental capacities of benign and malignant neoplasms of *Drosophila*. *Roux's Arch. Dev. Biol.* **176**, 23-65.

Gateff, E., Shrestha, R. and Akai, H. (1984). Comparative ultrastructure of wild-type and tumorous cells of *Drosophila*. *Insect Ultrastruct.* **2**, 559-578.

Gateff, E. A. and Mechler, B. M. (1989). Tumor-suppressor genes of *Drosophila melanogaster*. *CRC Crit. Rev. Oncogen.* **1**, 221-245.

Gateff, E., Löffler, T. and Wismar, J. (1993). A temperature-sensitive brain tumor suppressor mutation of *Drosophila melanogaster*: Developmental studies and molecular localization of the gene. *Mech. Dev.* **41**, 15-31.

Geisler, R., Bergmann, A., Hiromi, Y. and Nüsslein-Volhard, C. (1992).

cactus, a gene involved in dorsoventral pattern formation of *Drosophila*, is related to the IkappaB gene family of vertebrates. *Cell* **71**, 613-621.

Geyer, P. K., Patton, J. S., Rodesch, C. and Nagoshi, R. N. (1993). Genetic and molecular characterization of *P* element-induced mutations reveals that the *Drosophila ovarian tumor* gene has maternal activity and a variable null phenotype. *Genetics* **133**, 265-278.

Glover, C. V. C. (1982). Heat shock induces rapid dephosphorylation of a ribosomal protein in *Drosophila*. *Proc. Nat. Acad. Sci. USA* **79**, 1781-1785.

Golic, K. G. and Lindquist, S. (1989). The FLP recombinase of yeast catalyzes site-specific recombination in the *Drosophila* genome. *Cell* **59**, 499-509.

Gollin, S. M. and King, R. C. (1981). Studies of *fs(1)1621*, a mutation producing ovarian tumors in *Drosophila melanogaster*. *Dev. Genet.* **2**, 203

González, F., Swales, L., Bejsovec, A., Skaer, H. and Martínez-Arias, A. (1991). Secretion and movement of *wingless* protein in the epidermis of the *Drosophila* embryo. *Mech. Dev.* **35**, 43-54.

Gumbiner, B., Lowenkopf, T. and Apatira, D. (1991). Identification of a 160-kDa polypeptide that binds to the tight junction protein ZO-1. *Proc. Nat. Acad. Sci. USA* **88**, 3460-3464.

Hackstein, J. H. P. (1992). The *lethal prune/Killer-of-prune* interaction of *Drosophila* causes a syndrome resembling human neurofibromatosis (NF1). *Eur. J. Cell Biol.* **58**, 429-444.

Hankins, G. R. (1991). *Analysis of a* Drosophila *Neuroblastoma Gene*. Ph.D. thesis, University of Virginia, Charlottesville, Virginia, USA.

Hanratty, W. P. and Ryerse, J. S. (1981). A genetic melanotic neoplasm of *Drosophila melanogaster*. *Dev. Biol.* **83**, 238-249.

Hanratty, W. P. and Dearolf, C. R. (1993). The *Drosophila Tumorous-lethal* hematopoietic oncogene is a dominant mutation in the *hopscotch* locus. *Mol. Gen. Genet.* **238**, 33-37.

Hartenstein, A. Y., Rugendorff, A., Tepass, U. and Hartenstein, V. (1992). The function of the neurogenic genes during epithelial development in the *Drosophila* embryo. *Development* **116**, 1203-1220.

Hartley, D. A., Preiss, A. and Artavanis-Tsakonas, S. (1988). A deduced gene product from the *Drosophila* neurogenic locus, *enhancer of split*, shows homology to mammalian G-protein beta subunit. *Cell* **55**, 785-795.

Hummon, M. and Costello, W. (1988). Induced neuroma formation and target muscle perturbation in the giant fiber pathway of the *Drosophila* temperature-sensitive mutant *shibire*. *Roux's Arch. Dev. Biol.* **197**, 383-393.

Itoh, M., Nagafuchi, A., Yonemura, S., Kitani-Yasuda, T. and Tsukita, S. (1993). The 220-kD protein colocalizing with cadherins in non-epithelial cells is identical to ZO-1, a tight junction-associated protein in epithelial cells: cDNA cloning and immunoelectron microscopy. *J. Cell Biol.* **121**, 491-502.

Jacob, L., Opper, M., Metzroth, B., Phannavong, B. and Mechler, B. M. (1987). Structure of the *l(2)gl* gene of *Drosophila* and delimitation of its tumor suppressor domain. *Cell* **50**, 215-225.

Jesaitis, L. A. and Goodenough, D. A. (1994). Molecular characterization and tissue distribution of ZO-2, a tight junction protein homologous to ZO-1 and the *Drosophila* discs-large tumor suppressor protein. *J. Cell Biol.* **124**, 949-961.

Johansen, K. M., Fehon, R. G. and Artavanis-Tsakonas, S. (1989). The *Notch* gene product is a glycoprotein expressed on the cell surface of both epidermal and neuronal precursor cells during *Drosophila* development. *J. Cell Biol.* **109**, 2427-2440.

Jursnich, V. A., Fraser, S. E., Held, L. I. J., Ryerse, J. and Bryant, P. J. (1990). Defective gap-junctional communication associated with imaginal disc overgrowth and degeneration caused by mutations of the *dco* gene in *Drosophila*. *Dev. Biol.* **140**, 413-429.

Justice, R. W. and Bryant, P. J. (1992). *warts*, a new tumor suppressor gene in *Drosophila melanogaster*. *Mol. Biol. Cell* **3**, 174a (abstract).

Kidd, S., Kelley, M. R. and Young, M. W. (1986). Sequence of the *Notch* locus of *Drosophila melanogaster*: relationship of the encoded protein to mammalian clotting and growth factors. *Mol. Cell. Biol.* **6**, 3094-3108.

Kidd, S. (1992). Characterization of the *Drosophila cactus* locus and analysis of interactions between *cactus* and *dorsal* proteins. *Cell* **71**, 623-636.

King, R. C., Burnett, R. G. and Staley, N. A. (1957). Oogenesis in adult *Drosophila melanogaster*. IV. Hereditary ovarian tumors. *Growth* **21**, 239-261.

Kistner, U., Wenzel, B. M., Veh, R. W., Cases-Langhoff, C., Garner, A. M., Appeltauer, U., Voss, B., Gundelfinger, E. D. and Garner, C. C. (1993). SAP90, a rat presynaptic protein related to the product of the *Drosophila* tumor suppressor gene *dlg-A*. *J. Biol. Chem.* **268**, 4580-4583.

Klämbt, C. and Schmidt, O. (1986). Developmental expression and tissue

distribution of the *lethal(2)giant larvae* protein of *Drosophila melanogaster*. *EMBO J.* **5**, 2955-2961.

Klämbt, C., Müller, S., Lützelschwab, R., Rossa, R., Totzke, F. and Schmidt, O. (1989). The *Drosophila melanogaster l(2)gl* gene encodes a protein homologous to the cadherin cell-adhesion molecule family. *Dev. Biol.* **133**, 425-436.

Knust, E., Schrons, H., Grawe, F. and Campos-Ortega, J. A. (1992). Seven genes of the *Enhancer of split* complex of *Drosophila melanogaster* encode helix-loop-helix proteins. *Genetics* **132**, 505-518.

Konrad, L., Becker, G., Schmidt, A., Klöckner, T., Kaufer-Stillger, G., Dreschers, S., Edström, J.-E. and Gateff, E. (1994). Cloning, structure, cellular localization, and possible function of the tumor suppressor gene *lethal(3)malignant blood neoplasm-1* of *Drosophila melanogaster*. *Dev. Biol.* **163**, 98-111.

Koonin, E. V., Woods, D. F. and Bryant, P. J. (1992). dlg-R proteins: modified guanylate kinases. *Nature Genet.* **2**, 256-257.

Kurzik-Dumke, U., Phannavong, B., Gundacker, D. and Gateff, E. (1992). Genetic, cytogenetic and developmental analysis of the *Drosophila melanogaster* tumor suppressor gene *lethal(2)tumorous imaginal discs (1(2) tid)*. *Differentiation* **51**, 91-104.

Lasko, D., Cavenee, W. and Nordenskjold, M. (1991). Loss of constitutional heterozygosity in human cancer. *Annu. Rev. Genet.* **25**, 281-314.

Lindsley, D. L. and Zimm, G. G. (1992). *The Genome of* Drosophila melanogaster. New York: Academic Press.

Liotta, L. A., Steeg, P. S. and Stetler-Stevenson, W. G. (1991). Cancer metastasis and angiogenesis: an imbalance of positive and negative regulation. *Cell* **64**, 327-336.

Loffler, T., Wismar, J., Sass, H., Miyamoto, T., Becker, G., Konrad, L., Blondeau, M., Protin, U., Kaiser, S., Graf, P., Haas, M., Schuler, G., Schmidt, J., Phannavong, B., Gundacker, D. and Gateff, E. (1990). Genetic and molecular analysis of six tumor suppressor genes in *Drosophila melanogaster*. *Environ. Health Perspect.* **88**, 157-161.

Mahoney, P. A., Weber, U., Onofrechuk, P., Biessmann, H., Bryant, P. J. and Goodman, C. S. (1991). The *fat* tumor suppressor gene in *Drosophila* encodes a novel member of the cadherin gene superfamily. *Cell* **67**, 853-868.

Mansfield, E., Hersperger, E., Biggs, J. and Shearn, A. (1994). Genetic and molecular analysis of *hyperplastic discs*, a gene whose product is required for regulation of cell proliferation in *Drosophila melanogaster* imaginal discs and germ cells *Dev. Biol.* **165**, 507-526.

Marfatia, S. M., Lue, R. A., Branton, D. and Chishti, A. H. (1994). *In vitro* binding studies suggest a membrane-associated complex between erythroid p55, protein 4. 1, and glycophorin C. *J. Biol. Chem.* **269**, 8631-8634.

Martin, P., Martin, A. and Shearn, A. (1977). Studies of *l(3)c43*[hs1] a polyphasic, temperature-sensitive mutant of *Drosophila melanogaster* with a variety of imaginal disc defects. *Dev. Biol.* **55**, 213-232.

Mayer, B., Johnson, J. P., Leitl, F., Jauch, K. W., Heiss, M. M., Schildberg, F. W., Birchmeier, W. and Funke, I. (1993). E-cadherin expression in primary and metastatic gastric cancer: Down-regulation correlates with cellular dedifferentiation and glandular disintegration. *Cancer Res.* **53**, 1690-1695.

McKearin, D. M. and Spradling, A. C. (1990). *bag-of-marbles*: A *Drosophila* gene required to initiate both male and female gametogenesis. *Genes Dev.* **4**, 2242-2251.

Mechler, B. M., McGinnis, W. and Gehring, W. J. (1985). Molecular cloning of *lethal(2)giant larvae*, a recessive oncogene of *Drosophila melanogaster*. *EMBO J.* **4**, 1551-1557.

Mechler, B. (1990). The fruit fly *Drosophila* and the fish *Xiphophorus* as model systems for cancer studies. *Cancer Surv.* **9**, 505-527.

Mechler, B. M. and Strand, D. (1990). Tumor suppression in *Drosophila*. *Immunol. Ser.* **51**, 123-144.

Merriam, J., Ashburner, M., Hartl, D. L. and Kafatos, F. C. (1991). Toward cloning and mapping the genome of *Drosophila*. *Science* **254**, 221-225.

Metzenberg, A. and Gitschier, J. (1992). The gene encoding the palmitoylated erythrocyte membrane protein, p55, originates at the CpG island 3' to the factor VIII gene. *Hum. Mol. Genet.* **1**, 97-101.

Mével-Ninio, M., Terracol, R. and Kafatos, F. C. (1991). The *ovo* gene of *Drosophila* encodes a zinc finger protein required for female germ line development. *EMBO J.* **10**, 2259-2266.

Miki, H., Miura, K., Matuoka, K., Nakata, T., Hirokawa, N., Orita, S., Kaibuchi, K., Takai, Y. and Takenawa, T. (1994). Association of Ash/Grb-2 with dynamin through the Src homology 3 domain. *J. Biol. Chem.* **269**, 5489-5492.

Mohler, J. D. (1977). Developmental genetics of the *Drosophila* egg. I.

Identification of 50 sex-linked cistrons with maternal effects on embryonic development. *Genetics* **85**, 259-272.

Morton, R. A., Ewing, C. M., Nagafuchi, A., Tsukita, S. and Isaacs, W. B. (1993). Reduction of E-cadherin levels and deletion of the α-catenin gene in human prostate cancer cells. *Cancer Res.* **53**, 3585-3590.

Musacchio, A., Gibson, T., Lehto, V.-P. and Saraste, M. (1992). SH3 - An abundant protein domain in search of a function. *FEBS Lett.* **307**, 55-61.

Nappi, A. J. and Carton, Y. (1986). Cellular immune responses and their genetic aspects in *Drosophila*. In *Immunity in Invertebrates* (ed. M. Brehelin), pp. 171-187. Berlin: Springer-Verlag.

Natt, E., Magenis, R. E., Zimmer, J., Mansouri, A. and Scherer, G. (1989). Regional assignment of the human loci for uvomorulin (UVO) and chymotrypsinogen B (CTRB) with the help of two overlapping deletions on the long arm of chromosome 16. *Cytogenet. Cell Genet.* **50**, 145-148.

Nigam, A. K., Savage, F. J., Boulos, P. B., Stamp, G. W. H., Liu, D. and Pignatelli, M. (1993). Loss of cell-cell and cell-matrix adhesion molecules in colorectal cancer. *Br. J. Cancer* **68**, 507-514.

Noirot-Timothee, C. and Noirot, C. (1980). Septate and scalariform junctions in arthropods. *Int Rev. Cytol.* **63**, 97-140.

Obar, R. A., Shpetner, H. S. and Vallee, R. B. (1991). Dynamin: a microtubule-associated GTP-binding protein. *J. Cell Sci. Suppl.* **14**, 143-145.

Oda, T., Kanai, Y., Oyama, T., Yoshiura, K., Shimoyama, Y., Birchmeier, W., Sugimura, T. and Hirohashi, S. (1994). E-cadherin gene mutations in human gastric carcinoma cell lines. *Proc. Nat. Acad. Sci. USA* **91**, 1858-1862.

Oka, H., Shiozaki, H., Kobayashi, K., Inoue, M., Tahara, H., Kobayashi, T., Takatsuka, Y., Matsuyoshi, N., Hirano, S., Takeichi, M. and Mori, T. (1993). Expression of E-cadherin cell adhesion molecules in human breast cancer tissues and its relationship to metastasis. *Cancer Res.* **53**, 1696-1701.

Pata, I., Hoth, S., Kruppa, J. and Metspalu, A. (1992). The human ribosomal protein S6 gene: Isolation, primary structure and location in chromosome 9. *Gene* **121**, 387-392.

Pauli, D. and Mahowald, A. P. (1990). Germ-line sex determination in *Drosophila melanogaster*. *Trends Genet.* **6**, 259-264.

Pauli, D., Oliver, B. and Mahowald, A. P. (1993). The role of the *ovarian tumor* locus in *Drosophila melanogaster* germ line sex determination. *Development* **119**, 123-134.

Pearson, W. R. and Lipman, D. J. (1990). Improved tools for biological sequence comparison. *Proc. Nat. Acad. Sci. USA* **85**, 2444-2448.

Pelech, S. L. and Sanghera, J. S. (1992). Mitogen-activated protein kinases: versatile transducers for cell signaling. *Trends. Biochem. Sci.* **17**, 233-238.

Poodry, C. A. (1990). *shibire*, a neurogenic mutant of *Drosophila*. *Dev. Biol.* **138**, 464-472.

Posada, J. and Cooper, J. A. (1992). Molecular signal integration. Interplay between serine, threonine, and tyrosine phosphorylation. *Mol. Biol Cell* **3**, 583-592.

Poulson, D. F. (1937). Chromosomal deficiencies and the embryonic development of *Drosophila melanogaster*. *Proc. Nat. Acad. Sci. USA* **23**, 133-137.

Price, B. D., Chang, Z., Smith, R., Bockheim, S. and Laughon, A. (1993). The *Drosophila neuralized* gene encodes a C_3HC_4 zinc finger. *EMBO J.* **12**, 2411-2418.

Rao, Y., Jan, L. Y. and Jan, Y. N. (1990). Similarity of the product of the *Drosophila* neurogenic gene *big brain* to transmembrane channel proteins. *Nature* **345**, 163-167.

Rebay, I., Fleming, R. J., Fehon, R. G., Cherbas, L., Cherbas, P. and Artavanis-Tsakonas, S. (1991). Specific EGF repeats of Notch mediate interactions with Delta and Serrate: implications for Notch as a multifunctional receptor. *Cell* **67**, 687-699.

Ren, R., Mayer, B. J., Cicchetti, P. and Baltimore, D. (1993). Identification of a ten-amino acid proline-rich SH3 binding site. *Science* **259**, 1157-1161.

Rizki, T. M. (1978). The circulatory system and associated cells and tissues. In *The Genetics and Biology of Drosophila*, vol. 2b, (ed. M. Ashburner and T. R. F. Wright), pp. 397-452. New York, Academic Press.

Rogers, S., Wells, R. and Rechsteiner, M. (1986). Amino acid sequences common to rapidly degraded proteins: the PEST hypothesis. *Science* **234**, 364-368.

Rosengard, A. M., Krutzsch, H. C., Shearn, A., Biggs, J. R., Barker, E., Margulies, I. M., King, C. R., Liotta, L. A. and Steeg, P. S. (1989). Reduced Nm23/Awd protein in tumour metastasis and aberrant *Drosophila* development. *Nature* **342**, 177-180.

Ruff, P., Speicher, D. W. and Husain-Chishti, A. (1991). Molecular identification of a major palmitoylated erythrocyte membrane protein containing the *src* homology 3 motif. *Proc. Nat. Acad. Sci. USA* **88**, 6595-6599.

Salz, H. K. (1992). The genetic analysis of *snf*: A *Drosophila* sex determination gene required for activation of *Sex-lethal* in both the germline and the soma. *Genetics* **130**, 547-554.

Santamaria, P. and Randsholt, N. B. (1994). Characterization of a region of the X chromosome of *Drosophila* including *multi sex combs* (*mxc*) a *Polycomb group* gene which also functions as a Tumour suppressor. *Mol. Gen. Gnet.* (in press).

Sass, G. L., Mohler, J. D., Walsh, R. C., Kalfayan, L. J. and Searles, L. L. (1993). Structure and expression of hybrid dysgenesis-induced alleles of the *ovarian tumor* (*otu*) gene in *Drosophila melanogaster*. *Genetics* **133**, 253-263.

Sato, T., Tanigami, A., Yamakawa, K., Akiyama, F., Kasumi, F., Sakamoto, G. and Nakamura, Y. (1990). Allelotype of breast cancer: cumulative allele losses promote tumor progression in primary breast cancer. *Cancer Res.* **50**, 7184-7189.

Schipper, J. H., Frixen, U. H., Behrens, J., Unger, A., Jahnke, K. and Birchmeier, W. (1991). E-cadherin expression in squamous cell carcinomas of head and neck: Inverse correlation with tumor dedifferentiation and lymph node metastasis. *Cancer Res.* **51**, 6328-6337.

Schmidt, O. (1989). A recessive tumor gene function in Drosophila is involved in adhesion. *J. Neurogenet.* **5**, 95-98.

Schuler, G. D., Altschul, S. F. and Lipman, D. J. (1991). A workbench for multiple alignment construction and analysis. *Proteins* **9**, 180-190.

Sentry, J. W. and Kaiser, K. (1992). P element transposition and targeted manipulation of the *Drosophila* genome. *Trends Genet.* **8**, 329-331.

Shimoyama, Y. and Hirohashi, S. (1991). Cadherin intercellular adhesion molecule in hepatocellular carcinomas: Loss of E-cadherin expression in an undifferentiated carcinoma. *Cancer Lett.* **57**, 131-135.

Shrestha, R. and Gateff, E. (1986). Ultrastructure and cytochemistry of the tumorous blood cells in the mutant *lethal(3)malignant blood neoplasm* of *Drosophila melanogaster*. *J. Invert. Pathol.* **48**, 1-12.

Silvers, M. and Hanratty, W. P. (1984). Alterations in the production of hemocytes due to a neoplastic mutation of *Drosophila melanogaster*. *J. Invert. Pathol.* **44**, 324-328.

Smoller, D., Friedel, C., Schmid, A., Bettler, D., Lam, L. and Yedvobnick, B. (1990). The *Drosophila* neurogenic locus *mastermind* encodes a nuclear protein unusually rich in amino acid homopolymers. *Genes Dev.* **4**, 1688-1700.

Speicher, S. A., Thomas, U., Hinz, U. and Knust, E. (1994). The *Serrate* locus of *Drosophila* and its role in morphogenesis of the wing imaginal discs: Control of cell proliferation. *Development* **120**, 535-544.

Stanbridge, E. J. (1990). Human tumor suppressor genes. *Annu. Rev. Genet.* **24**, 615-657.

Steinhauer, W. R., Walsh, R. C. and Kalfayan, L. J. (1989). Sequence and structure of the *Drosophila melanogaster ovarian tumor* gene and generation of an antibody specific for the *ovarian tumor* protein. *Mol. Cell. Biol.* **9**, 5726-5732.

Steinmann-Zwicky, M. (1992). How do germ cells choose their sex? *Drosophila* as a paradigm. *BioEssays* **14**, 513-518.

Stewart, M. J. and Denell, R. (1993). Mutations in the *Drosophila* gene encoding ribosomal protein S6 cause tissue overgrowth. *Mol. Cell. Biol.* **13**, 2524-2535.

Strand, D., Torok, I., Kalmes, A., Schmidt, M., Merz, R. and Mechler, B. M. (1991). Transcriptional and translational regulation of the expression of the *l(2)gl* tumor suppressor gene of *Drosophila melanogaster*. *Advan. Enzyme Regul.* **31**, 339-350.

Teng, D. H. F., Bender, L. B., Engele, C. M., Tsubota, S. and Venkatesh, T. (1991a). Isolation and characterization of the *prune* locus of *Drosophila melanogaster*. *Genetics* **128**, 373-380.

Teng, D. H. F., Engele, C. M. and Venkatesh, T. R. (1991b). A product of the *prune* locus of *Drosophila* is similar to mammalian GTPase-activating protein. *Nature* **353**, 437-440.

Therond, P., Busson, D., Guillemet, E., Limbourg-Bouchon, B., Preat, T., Terracol, R., Tricoire, H. and Lamour-Isnard, C. (1993). Molecular organisation and expression pattern of the segment polarity gene *fused* of *Drosophila melanogaster*. *Mech. Dev.* **44**, 65-80.

Timmons, L., Hersperger, E., Woodhouse, E., Xu, J., Liu, L.-Z. and Shearn, A. (1993). The expression of the *Drosophila awd* gene during normal development and in neoplastic brain tumors caused by *lgl* mutations. *Dev. Biol.* **158**, 364-379.

Tomotsune, D., Shoji, H., Wakamatsu, Y., Kondoh, H. and Takahashi, N. (1993). A mouse homologue of the *Drosophila* tumour-suppressor gene *l(2)gl* controlled by Hox-C8 *in vivo*. *Nature* **365**, 69-72.

Török, T., Tick, G., Alvarado, M. and Kiss, I. (1993). *P-lacW* insertional mutagenesis on the second chromosome of *Drosophila melanogaster*: isolation of lethals with different overgrowth phenotypes. *Genetics* **135**, 71-80.

Traugh, J. A. and Pendergast, A. M. (1986). Regulation of protein synthesis by phosphorylation of ribosomal protein S6 and aminoacyl-tRNA synthetases. *Prog. Nucl. Acid. Res. Mol. Biol.* **33**, 195-230.

Tsuda, H., Zhang, W. D., Shimosato, Y., Yokota, J., Terada, M., Sugimura, T., Miyamura, T. and Hirohashi, S. (1990). Allele loss on chromosome 16 associated with progression of human hepatocellular carcinoma. *Proc. Nat. Acad. Sci. USA* **87**, 6791-6794.

Uemura, T., Shiomi, K., Togashi, S. and Takeichi, M. (1993). Mutation of *twins* encoding a regulator of protein phosphatase 2A leads to pattern duplication in *Drosophila* imaginal discs. *Genes Dev.* **7**, 429-440.

Van den Heuvel, M., Nusse, R., Johnston, P. and Lawrence, P. A. (1989). Distribution of the *wingless* gene product in *Drosophila* embryos: a protein involved in cell-cell communication. *Cell* **59**, 739-749.

Van der Bliek, A. M. and Meyerowitz, E. M. (1991). Dynamin-like protein encoded by the *Drosophila shibire* gene associated with vesicular traffic. *Nature* **351**, 411-414.

Venkatesh, T. R. and Teng, D. H. F. (1992). Reply. *Nature* **355**, 505.

Watson, K. L., Johnson, T. K. and Denell, R. E. (1991). *Lethal(1)aberrant immune response* mutations leading to melanotic tumor formation in *Drosophila melanogaster*. *Dev. Genet.* **12**, 173-187.

Watson, K. L., Konrad, K. D., Woods, D. F. and Bryant, P. J. (1992). *Drosophila* homolog of the human S6 ribosomal protein is required for tumor suppression in the hematopoietic system. *Proc. Nat. Acad. Sci. USA* **89**, 11302-11306.

Watson, K. L. (1993). *Mutations in a Ribosomal Protein Gene Lead to Blood Cell Neoplasia in Drosophila*. Ph.D. thesis, University of California, USA.

Wei, G., Oliver, B., Pauli, D. and Mahowald, A. P. (1994). Evidence for sex transformation of germline cells in ovarian tumor mutants of *Drosophila*. *Dev. Biol.* **161**, 318-320.

Wharton, K. A., Johansen, K. M., Xu, T. and Artavanis-Tsakonas, S. (1985a). Nucleotide sequence from the neurogenic locus *Notch* implies a gene product that shares homology with proteins containing EGF-like repeats. *Cell* **437**, 567-581.

Wharton, K. A., Yedvobnick, B., Finnerty, V. and Artavanis-Tsakonas, S. (1985b). *opa*: A novel family of transcribed repeats shared by the *Notch* locus and other developmentally regulated loci in *D. melanogaster*. *Cell* **40**, 55-62.

Willott, E., Balda, M. S., Fanning, A. S., Jameson, B., Van Itallie, C. and Anderson, J. M. (1993). The tight junction protein ZO-1 is homologous to the *Drosophila* discs-large tumor suppressor protein of septate junctions. *Proc. Nat. Acad. Sci. USA* **90**, 7834-7838.

Woods, D. F. and Bryant, P. J. (1989). Molecular cloning of the *lethal(1)discs large-1* oncogene of *Drosophila*. *Dev. Biol.* **134**, 222-235.

Woods, D. F. and Bryant, P. J. (1991). The *discs-large* tumor suppressor gene of *Drosophila* encodes a guanylate kinase homolog localized at septate junctions. *Cell* **66**, 451-464.

Woods, D. F. and Bryant, P. J. (1993). ZO-1, DlgA and PSD-95/SAP90: homologous proteins in tight, septate and synaptic cell junctions. *Mech. Dev.* **44**, 85-89.

Wright, T. R. F. (1987). The genetics of biogenic amine metabolism, sclerotization, and melanization in *Drosophila melanogaster*. *Advan. Genet.* **24**, 127-222.

Yan, H. G. and Tsai, M. D. (1991). Mechanism of adenylate kinase. Demonstration of a functional relationship between aspartate 93 and Mg^{2+} by site-directed mutagenesis and proton, phosphorus-31, and magnesium-25 NMR. *Biochemistry* **30**, 5539-5546.

Zhang, W. D., Hirohashi, S., Tsuda, H., Shimosato, Y., Yokota, J., Terada, M. and Sugimura, T. (1990). Frequent loss of heterozygosity on chromosomes 16 and 4 in human hepatocellular carcinoma. *Jpn J. Cancer Res.* **81**, 108-111.

Zinyk, D. L., McGonnigal, B. G. and Dearolf, C. R. (1993). Drosophila awdK-pn, a homologue of the metastasis suppressor gene nm23, suppresses the Tum-1 haematopoietic oncogene. *Nature Genet.* **4**, 195-201.

Journal of Cell Science, Supplement 18, 35-42 (1994)
Printed in Great Britain © The Company of Biologists Limited 1994

Pax genes in development

Ahmed Mansouri, Anastassia Stoykova and Peter Gruss

Max-Plank-Institut für biophysikalische Chemie, Abteilung Molekulare Zellbiologie, Am Fassberg, D-37077 Göttingen, Germany

SUMMARY

The *Pax* gene family consists of nine members encoding nuclear transcription factors. Their temporally and spatially restricted expression pattern during embryogenesis suggests that they may play a key role during embryogenesis.

Direct evidence for the important role of the *Pax* genes during embryonic development has been demonstrated by the correlation of mouse developmental mutants and human syndromes with mutations in some *Pax* genes. To date three *Pax* genes have been shown to be mutated in undulated, *Splotch* and *small eye*, respectively. In man, *Pax-3* is mutated in the Waardenburg syndrome, while in aniridia *Pax-6* is mutated.

Key words: *Pax* gene, mutant, human disease

INTRODUCTION

The mechanisms that control embryonic development are highly conserved among different organisms such as *Drosophila*, mouse and nematodes and has led to the isolation of many developmental control genes, which are shared between different species including mammals.

Based on sequence homology to the *Drosophila* segmentation genes (Bopp et al., 1986; Frigerio et al., 1986; Coté et al., 1987; Baumgartner et al., 1987), a family of paired box-containing genes has been isolated in the mouse (Deutsch et al., 1988; Dressler et al., 1988; Plachov et al., 1990; Jostes et al., 1991; Asano and Gruss, 1992; Wallin et al., 1993; Stapleton et al., 1993; for review see Deutsch and Gruss, 1991; Fritsch and Gruss, 1993; Chalepakis et al., 1993; Gruss and Walther, 1992; Noll, 1993). The paired box has been highly conserved during evolution and paired box encoding genes have been found in different organisms such as zebrafish (Krauss et al., 1991), chicken (Goulding et al., 1993a) and man (Burri et al., 1989).

The *Pax* gene family now consists of nine members, referred to as *Pax-1* to *Pax-9*. Unlike the *Hox* genes they are not clustered and are localised on different loci (Walther et al., 1991; Wallin et al., 1993; Stapleton et al., 1993).

Like several other developmental control genes, *Pax* proteins act as transcription factors, since they display sequence-specific DNA-binding activity (Chalepakis et al., 1991; Treisman et al., 1991; Dressler and Douglas, 1992; Zannini et al., 1992; Fickenscher et al., 1993; Czerny et al., 1993; Epstein et al., 1994) and can activate transcription. This is also in agreement with the nuclear localisation of *Pax-1*, *Pax-2*, *Pax-5* and *Pax-6* (Dressler and Douglas, 1992; Adams et al., 1992; R. Fritsch and P. Gruss, unpublished data).

Three conserved motifs exist in the *Pax* proteins (Fig. 1). A DNA-binding domain of 128 amino acids, the paired domain, which is located close to the amino terminus of the *Pax* proteins. A second DNA-binding domain of 61 amino acids, the paired-type homeodomain, is localised at the 3′ end of the paired box of *Pax-3*, *Pax-4*, *Pax-6* and *Pax-7*. In contrast, *Pax-2*, *Pax-5* and *Pax-8* only contain the first helix of this domain, thus missing the whole helix-loop-helix part of the second DNA-binding motif, while *Pax-1* and *Pax-9* are missing the whole homeobox sequences. In addition (except for *Pax-4* and *Pax-6*), all the *Pax* proteins share a conserved octapeptide, which is localised between the paired- and the homeodomains and whose function remains unknown. According to the genomic organisation and the paired domain sequence similarities, *Pax* genes can be subdivided into 5 subgroups. The paralogous genes within a subgroup share common intron-exon boundaries, similar protein structure and related expression pattern during development (*Pax-1* and *Pax-9*; *Pax-2*, *Pax-5* and *Pax-8*; *Pax-3* and *Pax-7*).

In this article we will summarise the expression patterns of *Pax* genes during mouse development and correlate the expression domains with the phenotypes observed in some mouse mutants and in human diseases, where specific *Pax* genes are mutated. Finally we will discuss what we can learn from the developmental defects in the *Pax* mutants about the function of the *Pax* genes during development.

EXPRESSION PATTERN DURING MOUSE DEVELOPMENT

Pax genes in neural development

The potential importance of the *Pax* genes is reflected by their expression pattern during development. A common feature of all *Pax* genes, except for *Pax-1* and *Pax-9*, is that they exhibit spatially and temporally restricted expression patterns in the developing nervous system. This strongly suggests that they may play a crucial role in the regionalisation of the neural tube and brain. (Fig. 2).

The first group of the *early genes*, which contain both the paired- and the homeodomain (*Pax-3*, *Pax-6* and *Pax-7*) start to be expressed around day 8.5 pc., before the onset of cellular differentiation. Up to day 10.5 pc. their expression domains are confined to the ventricular zone of the entire developing CNS (epichordal and prechordal part). Thereafter, the expression of *Pax-3* and *Pax-7* is retracted from the telencephalon, while in all stages *Pax-6* is not expressed in the mesencephalic roof and maintains a caudal limit of expression at the level of the posterior commissure (Walther and Gruss, 1991; Stoykova and Gruss, 1994; Goulding et al., 1991; Jostes et al., 1991).

The group of the *late genes*, which harber no paired-type homeodomain (*Pax-2*, *Pax-5* and *Pax-8*) are first detected around day 9.5-10.5 pc. Their expression domains are confined only to postmitotic cells in the epichordal part of the neural tube with a rostral limit of expression at the midbrain-hindbrain boundary. It should be noted, however, that *Pax-5* transcripts are detected in the posterior mesencephalic tegmentum (Asano and Gruss, 1992; Adams et al., 1992) and is strongly expressed on both sides of the fovea isthmi. The fact that the expression of all *Pax* genes in the epichordal part of the neural tube extends up to the midbrain hindbrain boundary, thus surpassing the most rostral expression limit of the *Hox* genes (Keynes et al., 1990), suggests a role for *Pax* genes in the regionalisation of the most rostral part of the hindbrain.

Recent evidence support the idea that *Pax* genes are involved in the specification of the midbrain-hindbrain boundary: injection of an antibody against *Pax(zf-b)* protein (probable homolog of *Pax-2* in the mouse) results in a failure of the normal isthmus development (Krauss et al., 1992). Disruption of *Pax-2*, *Pax-5* and *Pax-8* by homologous recombination in embryonic stem cells will help to elucidate their role in the regionalisation of the midbrain-hindbrain area. Furthermore their interaction with other genes already known to play such a role (En-1, En-2 and Wnt-1) (Davis et al., 1988; Davidson et al., 1988; Wilkenson et al., 1987) can also be studied.

Pax genes also show restricted expression domains along the dorso-ventral (D-V) axis of the developing neural tube. The specific location of the cells along the D-V axis appears to be a prerequisite for the commitment of the precursor cells to a distinct phenotype: motor neurons (in basal plate), commissural neurons and neurons involved in sensory pathway (in alar plate), interneurons and preganglionic sympathetic and parasympathetic neurons (intermediate plate). Inductive signals from the underlying notochord and floor plate determine the dorsoventral regionalisation of the spinal cord (van Straaten et al., 1988; Placzek et al., 1990). During development, the paralogous genes *Pax-3* and *Pax-7* are expressed in the ventricular zone of the alar subdivision of the neural tube. Only the *Pax-3* expression domain includes the roof plate, the neural crest and its derivatives (Goulding et al., 1991; Jostes et al., 1991).

In contrast, *Pax-6* transcripts are detected in the ventricular zone of the intermediate and basal plate, partially overlapping with *Pax-3* and *Pax-7* at the upper region (Walther and Gruss, 1991). As shown in notochord transplantation experiments in chick the restriction of the *Pax-6* and *Pax-3* expression domain along the D-V axis is under the influence of the notochord (Goulding et al., 1993a). This support the notion that the expression of these genes is related to the D-V patterning of the developing spinal cord.

In the developing neural tube the paralogous genes *Pax-2*, *Pax-5* and *Pax-8* are expressed in two longitudinal columns of

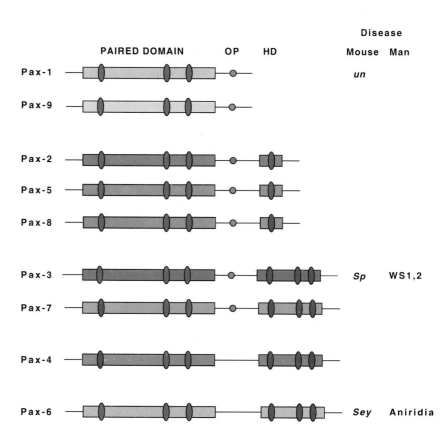

Fig. 1. Protein structure of the *Pax* genes. Paired and homeodomain (HD) are presented in boxes and α-helices from paired- and homeodomain are shown by violet ovals. A blue circle indicates the octapeptide, OP. The paralogous genes are grouped together. Corresponding mouse mutants and human diseases are indicated. *un*, *undulated*; *Sp*, *Splotch*; WS1,2, Waardenburg syndrome type 1 and type 2.

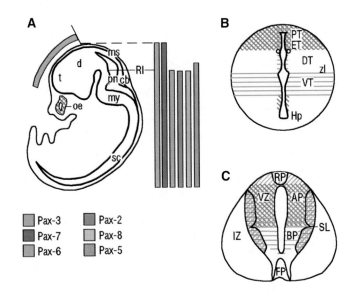

Fig. 2. Schematic representation of *Pax* gene expression in midgestation embryo brain. The major expression domains of the *Pax* genes are indicated in different colours. (A) Limits of expression of *Pax* genes along the A-P axis of developing CNS. (B) 'Segment-like' expression domain of *Pax-3*, *Pax-6* and *Pax-7* in developing diencephalon. (C) Restricted expression patterns of *Pax* genes along D-V axis of developing spinal cord. AP, alar plate; BP, basal plate; cb, cerebellum; d, diencephalon; DT, dorsal thalamus; ET, epithalamus; FP, floor plate; Hp, hypothalamus; IZ, intermediate zone; ms, mesencephalon; my, myelencephalon; oe, olfactory epithelium; pn, pons; PT, pretectum; RI, rhombencephalic isthmus; RP, roof plate; sc, spinal cord; SL, sulcus limitans; t, telencephalon.

the intermediate gray on both sides of sulcus limitans (Nornes et al., 1990; Plachov et al., 1990; Asano and Gruss, 1992; Adams et al., 1992). Expression of the *Pax-2* homologue in zebrafish is consistent with a role in the fate determination of the progenitor cells to the specific phenotype of the interneuron (Püschel et al., 1992; Mikkola et al., 1992).

Recent neuroanatomical and molecular analyses have shown that the segmental organisation of the hindbrain is determined by the differential expression of combinations of *Hox* genes (Lumsden, 1990; McGinnis and Krumlauf, 1992). In contrast, the molecular mechanisms that control the regionalisation and differentiation of the embryonic forebrain are still largely unknown. A large number of genes have been identified that are expressed in spatially restricted domains that outline longitudinal and transverse domains in the developing forebrain. Consistent with the restricted expression pattern of numerous genes in the CNS, recently, new models for the neuromeric organisation of the forebrain have been proposed (Puelles and Rubenstein, 1993; Figdor and Stern, 1993).

The expression domains of several *Pax* genes during development were found to respect anatomical boundaries that relate to former neuromeric territories. Around day 10.5 pc, thus before morphological appeerance of segmentation in the developing diencephalon, the main expression domain of *Pax-6* is confined to the ventral thalamus (the former parencephalon posterior), while *Pax-3* and *Pax-7* transcripts are detected in the epithalamus and entire pretectum (former synencephalon). Further, in a comparative in situ analysis in midgestation and

adult brain, a similar transcript distribution along the anterior-posterior axis for *Pax* genes has been observed (Stoykova and Gruss, 1994). Similar to the situation in the embryonic brain (see Fig. 2), in the adult brain transcripts of six *Pax* genes are detected in distinct isthmic nuclei; in the midbrain three *Pax* genes (*Pax-5*, *Pax-6* and *Pax-7*) are expressed, while in the telencephalon and anterior diencephalon only *Pax-6* is detected. In many cases, a correlation exist between the expression of different *Pax* genes in defined brain structures and the respective domains of their origin in the embryonic brain. Therefore, the products of *Pax* genes may not only be important for the regionalisation of the developing nervous system, but also involved in the differentiation and/or maintenance of specific structures in the mature brain. The identification of *Pax* genes involved in specific mouse mutants and their corresponding human syndromes support this idea.

Some *Pax* genes show expression consistent with a role in the *inductive process* underlying the formation of sensory organs. The lens and cornea of the eye are formed by the interaction of different cell layers. When the optic vesicle contacts a specific region of the head ectoderm, the ectoderm thickens into the lens placodes. All structures of developing eye (optic placode, optic vesicle, sulcus, retina, lens and cornea) express *Pax-6*; thus inductive and responsive tissues express *Pax-6*. (Walther and Gruss, 1991). *Pax-6* is also expressed in the developing olfactory epithelium (Walther and Gruss, 1991).

The otic vesicle is derived from the otic placode, which invaginates towards the neural tube. *Pax-2* has been detected in the otic vesicle of the mouse (Nornes et al., 1990) and zebrafish (Krauss et al., 1991; Püschel et al., 1992). *Pax(zf-b)* has been shown to exhibit the highest level of expression close to the neural tube surface. Therefore this gene and, in homology, *Pax-2* have been suggested to be involved in the formation of the inner ear, in response to some secreted signal, from the neural tube (Püschel et al., 1992).

Expression in the mesoderm

Some *Pax* genes are also expressed in the segmented mesoderm (*Pax-1*, *Pax-9*, *Pax-3* and *Pax-7*; Deutsch et al., 1988; Dietrich et al., 1993; Wallin et al., 1994; Goulding et al., 1991; Williams and Ordahl, 1994; Jostes et al., 1991) and in the developing excretory system (*Pax-2* and *Pax-8*; Dressler et al., 1990; Plachov et al., 1990).

Pax-1 expression is seen at day 8.5 pc. in the ventral half of the newly formed somite and mRNA is later detected in the sclerotome cells migrating to surround the notochord. This domain of expression later gives rise to a segmented structure called the intervertebral disc anlagen (Deutsch et al., 1988; Dietrich et al., 1993; Wallin et al., 1994).

During gastrulation *Pax-3* is expressed in the primitive streak (Goulding et al., 1993a). At day 8.0 pc *Pax-3* is detected in the undifferentiated somite before it looses its epithelial morphology. The expression of *Pax-3* is later confined to the dorsal half of the somite. At day 9 pc *Pax-3* and *Pax-7* are expressed in the dermomyotome (Jostes et al., 1991). Here *Pax-3* is expressed at higher levels in the dorsolateral than the dorsomedial half. At the early limb bud stage, *Pax-3* expression is extended from the lateral edge of the dermomyotome into the limb. Transplantation experiments in the chick-quail marking system (Williams and Ordahl, 1994) demonstrate that *Pax-3* labels the migratory muscle precursor cells

Legend for Fig. 2:
- Pax-3
- Pax-7
- Pax-6
- Pax-2
- Pax-8
- Pax-5

entering the limb to form skeletal muscle in this part of the body, suggesting that *Pax-3* is probably necessary for the migratory process of these cells. (Williams and Ordahl, 1994; Bober et al., 1994). At later stages only *Pax-7* is detected in the intercostal muscle, while *Pax-3* is downregulated.

The paralogous genes *Pax-2* and *Pax-8* are expressed also in the developing kidney (Dressler et al., 1990; Plachov et al., 1990), while *Pax-5* is detected in B lymphocytes and testis (Adams et al., 1992).

The *Pax-2* mRNA is detected during kidney development namely in the pro- and mesonephros tubuli (Dressler et al., 1990). After induction of the metanephros *Pax-2* protein is present in the mesenchymal condensations and its early epithelial derivatives. With the further differentiation of the epithelium, *Pax-2* is downregulated. Therefore it has been suggested (Dressler et al., 1990) that *Pax-2* may play a role in the conversion of the mesenchyme to epithelium during kidney organogenesis. This is also supported by experiments showing *Pax-2* expression in Wilms tumors (Dressler and Douglas, 1992).

Mutations in *Pax* genes

Direct evidence for the crucial role of the *Pax* genes during development has been demonstrated by the correlation of mouse developmental mutants with mutations in certain *Pax* genes. Three *Pax* genes have been correlated with mouse mutants (for review see Hastie, 1991; Chalepakis et al., 1993; Tremblay and Gruss, 1994; Stuart et al., 1994) and two with corresponding human syndromes (for review see Hill and Van Heyningen, 1992; Strachan and Reed, 1994).

Pax-1 has been found to be mutated in *undulated* (*un*) mice (Balling et al., 1988), a recessive mutation that exhibits skeletal abnormalities in the vertebral column and sternum (Grüneberg, 1950, 1954). Their phenotype is clearly correlated with the expression pattern of *Pax-1* in sclerotome (Deutsch et al., 1988; Koseki et al., 1993; Wallin et al., 1994; Dietrich et al., 1993). A point mutation (change from Gly to Ser) in the paired domain of *Pax-1* results in a reduction of DNA-binding affinity (Chalepakis et al., 1991), interfering with the transcriptional activity of the *Pax-1* protein. Two other *undulated* alleles are known: *undulated* extensive (*un^ex*) and *undulated* shorttail (*un^s*), where *Pax-1* is also involved (Balling et al., 1992). In *un^ex* it has been shown that the RNA level of *Pax-1* is highly reduced (Balling et al., 1992) and that a deletion of at least 28.2 kb is located within the 3′ end of the gene, which eliminates the terminal exon and the Poly A signal (Dietrich and Gruss, 1994, unpublished). In *un^s* a large chromosomal deletion has been detected (Balling et al., 1992) of at least 48.3 kb, which includes the *Pax-1* gene thus removing the *Pax-1* locus and 38 kb flanking sequences (Dietrich and Gruss, 1994, unpublished; Wallin et al., 1994). *un^s* exhibits the most severe phenotype and is semidominant, while *un* and *un^ex* are recessive.

Pax-3 has been shown to be mutated in the mouse mutant *Splotch* (*Sp*, spontaneous mutation; splice site defect; exon 4 skipped and truncation within paired domain; Russell, 1947; Epstein et al., 1991a,b, 1993; Goulding et al., 1993b). In humans, *Pax-3* mutations have been correlated with Waardenburg syndrome (Tassabehji et al., 1992, 1993; Baldwin et al., 1992; Morell et al., 1992). The *Pax-3* mutation in *Splotch* mice is semidominant. The heterozygous mice have white spotting of the abdomen, tail and feet, probably due to the absence of

melanocyte migration to these regions (Auerbach, 1954). The homozygous mice die at midgestation stage with severe defects in closure of the neural tube (exencephaly, meningocele and spina bifida) and multiple defects in structures of neural crest origin (schwann cells, spinal ganglia and melanocytes; Auerbach, 1954; Franz, 1989, 1990; Moase and Trasler, 1989). It is of interest to notice that neural tube defect and deficiency in neural crest-derived structures are independent from each other. In addition, the development of the muscle in the limb (fore- and hindlimb) and in the associated shoulder is impaired (Franz et al., 1993; Bober et al., 1994; Goulding et al., 1994). However the muscles of the neck, of the head and of the body wall are not affected (Franz et al., 1993) possibly due to the specific expression of the paralogous gene *Pax-7* in this region (Jostes et al., 1991). Detailed analysis revealed that the dermomyotome is disorganised and the limbs are devoid of *Pax-3* expressing cells (Franz, et al., 1993; Bober et al., 1994; Goulding et al., 1994). The reduction of axial muscles, which is more prominent in caudal segments, also follows the rostrocaudal gradient observed in the neural crest defects.

The described defects in *Splotch* mice correlate very well with the expression domains of *Pax-3* in neural crest cells, in the dermomyotome and in the neural tube. However, it is not clear whether the neural tube defect is due specifically to the absence of the *Pax-3* protein or not, since other mouse mutants like *curly tail* also show this phenotype (Copp et al., 1988). Five other *Splotch* alleles have been described: *Sp^{2H}* (X-irradiation-induced mutant of 32 bp deletion within exon 5; truncation within homeodomain; Epstein et al., 1991a), *Sp^r* (*Splotch retarded*; X-irradiation-induced mutation with a deletion of *Pax-3* and several other genes; Epstein et al., 1991b), *Sp^d* (*Splotch delayed*; point mutation within the paired box: Gly to Arg; Vogan et al., 1993) and *Sp^{4H}* (*Splotch 4H*, X-irradiation-induced mutant with a deletion of *Pax-3*; Goulding et al., 1993b) and *Splotch1H* (*Sp1H*, undefined X-irradiation-induced mutant). The phenotype is almost identical in most *splotch* alleles known so far. The most severe phenotype is expressed by *Sp^r*, which die before implantation. (Evans et al., 1988), while *Sp^d* exhibit only spina bifida and die after birth (Dickie, 1964).

Waardenburg syndrome is an autosomal dominant disorder with incomplete penetrance (McKusick, 1992). It is clinically and genetically heterogenous. The Waardenburg syndrome consists of numerous defects of neural crest derivatives: deafness, pigmentation deficiency (heterochromia irides; white forelock and white skin patches) and lateral displacement of the inner corner of the eye. Based on the presence or absence of the lateral displacement of the inner corner of the eye the Waardenburg syndrome is classified into two categories: type 1 (WS1) and type 2 (WS2). In both WS1 and WS2 *Pax-3* has been found to be mutated (Tassebehji et al., 1992, 1993). The cause of the deafness in Waardenburg syndrome patients is not clear. However, it has been often observed that frequently pigmentation defects are associated with deafness in mice and man (Steel and Smith, 1992).

In the mouse *small eye* (*sey*) mutant and its corresponding human syndrome aniridia (Shaw et al., 1960), *Pax-6* has been found to be mutated. The small eye homozygous mutant is recognised by complete loss of the eyes and the nasal cavities do not develop (Pritchard and Clayton, 1974). Like *Splotch*, *small eye* display a semidominant trait and heterozygous mice are characterized by smaller eyes. A number of different *Sey* alleles have been described (*Sey*, spontaneous mutation; *Sey^H*, X-irradiation mutant; *Sey^Neu*, ethylnitrosourea induced; *Sey^Dey*, spontaneous mutation). The most severe phenotype is exhibited by *Sey^H* where the homozygous animals die shortly after implantation and have a large chromosomal deletion including *Pax-6* and possibly other genes (Hill et al., 1991). In the spontaneouly occurring *Sey* there is an in-frame stop codon before the homeobox of *Pax-6* (Hill et al., 1991), while in *Sey^Dey* a deletion of the *Pax-6* gene (Glaser et al., 1990) has been found. In *Sey^Neu* a splice defect in the *Pax-6* gene results in a truncated protein lacking the last 115 amino acids but containing both the paired- and the homeobox (Hill et al., 1991). Most of the described mutations result in the same phenotype, suggesting a loss of function mutation.

Also in the rat there is a small eye mutation, where the *Pax-6* gene is involved (Matsuo et al., 1993; Fujiwara et al., 1994) and the phenotype is similar to that described in the mouse.

Pax-6 mutations in aniridia range from single base pair mutations to large deletions (Ton et al., 1991; Hill et al., 1991; Jordan et al., 1992; Glaser et al., 1992). The patients suffer from complete or partial absence of the iris. Cornea, lens, retina and optic nerve are also affected. Recently, mutations at the *Pax-6* locus in man have been described for Peter's anomaly (heterogeneous anterior segment malformations; Hanson et al., 1994).

All the phenotypes described for the small eye in mouse and rat and aniridia in human correlate very well with the expression of the *Pax-6* gene in the affected structures.

Finally, in human tumours *PAX-3* has been found to be mutated (Barr et al., 1993). In alveolar rhabdomyosarcoma cell lines the *PAX-3* gene is rearranged and translocated to a region of chromosome 13, where its 5′ end is fused to a gene of the forkhead family termed FKHR (Galili et al., 1993) or ALV (Shapiro et al., 1993). Recently also *PAX-7* has been found to be rearranged in a variant of alveolar rhabdomyosarcoma. *PAX-7* is involved in a translocation of t(1; 13)(p36; q14) and the 5′ end of the gene is fused to the 3′ end of the FKHR region (Davis et al., 1994). This indicates that deregulation of *Pax* gene expression may be involved in tumorgenesis, which supports the previous observation that overexpression of *Pax* genes transforms fibroblasts and the resulting foci develop into tumours in nude mice (Maulbecker and Gruss, 1993).

Phenotypes and function

The availability of *Pax* developmental mutants is a valuable tool to analyse the function of the *Pax* genes. The phenotypes characterized in *Splotch*, *undulated*, *small eye* and in the human syndromes Waardenburg and aniridia correlate very well with their expression pattern and highlights the fact that *Pax* genes are involved in the control of embryonic development in different cell types.

The described mutations *Splotch* and *small eye* seem to be loss of function mutations, since different mutations exhibit the same phenotype in most cases.

From all the mutants, except *undulated*, the *Pax* protein threshold seems to play an important role in *Pax* gene function. This is documented by the semidominance of *small eye* and *Splotch* phenotypes in the mouse and dominance of Wardenburg and aniridia diseases in man. Another example is given by the different undulated alleles. The phenotypes ranges from

mild skeletal abnormalities to complete lack of vertebral bodies in the lumbar region and enhances the idea of phenotypic dependence on the *Pax* protein concentration (Hill and Hanson, 1992). DNA binding studies using *undulated* (Chalepakis et al., 1991), splotch or Wardenburg mutations (Chalepakis et al., 1994) could clearly show that these mutations affect DNA binding of the *Pax* proteins. In Waardenburg Brazil, where the invariant Pro residue is substituted by a Leu residue in the paired box, the DNA binding is even completely abolished (Chalepakis et al., 1994), suggesting that this invariant position in the paired domain is essential for DNA binding of the paired domain. The further biochemical analysis of such mutations will help to map the transcription activation domains essential for *Pax* function.

At the cellular level, *Pax* genes seem to be expressed in specific cell types: *Pax-3*, *Pax-7* and *Pax-6* are detected in mitotically active cells in the ventricular zone of developing neural tube and could play a role in cell growth. *Pax-2* is specifically related to the differentiating spinal cord interneurons (Mikkola et al., 1992). In addition *Pax-3* is possibly involved in the emigration of neural crest cells, which is delayed in *Splotch* mice (Moase and Trasler, 1990). It has been suggested that N-CAM is involved in this latter process (Moase and Trasler, 1991), however, it is not known if N-CAM is regulated by *Pax-3*. Using muscle-specific markers and morphological analysis, it has been shown that in splotch mice the development of the shoulder and limb muscle is disturbed, while body wall and axial muscle develop normally (Franz et al., 1993; Bober et al., 1994; Goulding et al., 1994). The mechanism described for the neural crest emigration defect could be identical in the migration process of muscle cell precursors to the limb. However *Pax-3* can also be involved in the differentiation and/or proliferation of these cells.

In vitro experiments using antisense oligonucleotides to inhibit *Pax-5* protein synthesis demonstrate, that this gene could be involved in the proliferation of B lymphocytes (Wakatsuki et al., 1994).

In rat and mouse *small eye* the *Pax-6* mutation seems also to interfere with the migration of the neural crest (Matsuo et al., 1993; Schmahl et al., 1993) cells. By using vital dye labelling, it was shown that anterior midbrain neural crest migration in the rat *sey* mutant is disturbed. Neural crest cells accumulate in areas adjacent to the anterior cardinal vein and around the optic vesicle and further migration to the frontonasal area is inhibited. Since *Pax-6* is not expressed in neural crest cells (Walther et al., 1991), the impaired migration in the rat *small eye* mutant could be linked to the perturbation of the normal expression of a downstream target gene of *Pax-6*, involved in this process. This mechanism is similar to that described for the *Splotch* mice, where N-CAM is abnormally expressed (Moase and Trasler, 1991) and possibly also a downstream gene of *Pax-3*.

Pax genes may also be involved in the determination of certain tissue structures. Thus *Pax-6* could play a role in the induction of the lens during eye development. In vitro ablation experiments in the chick, however, suggest that *Pax-6* may be necessary for the early determination of the lens-competent regions (Li et al., 1994).

Also *Pax-2* has been shown to be involved in specifying certain tissues. Using antisense oligonucleotides to *Pax-2* (Rothenpieler and Dressler, 1993) in kidney organ culture, it has been shown that *Pax-2* is possibly required for the conversion of the mesenchyme to epithelium in kidney development.

Finally it should be kept in mind that *Pax* genes are paralogous genes, sharing many expression domains, which may implicate some redundancy. In *Splotch* mice axial muscle develops normally, which could be a compensation from *Pax-7*, the paralogous gene to *Pax-3*.

There is a need for more mutants to try to elucidate the function of the *Pax* genes. The homologous recombination approach is a powerful tool to mutate the whole *Pax* family in mice and to achieve double and triple mutants that will allow us to identify the redundant parts possibly present in each paralogous group.

Furthermore, since the *Pax* protein concentration seems to play a crucial role for their appropriate function it is of interest to deregulate the *Pax* protein thresholds by generating gain of function mouse mutants by overexpressing *Pax* proteins ectopically and specifically in certain tissues. Also promoter swap experiments in transgenic mice by using homologous recombination approach in ES cells (for example expressing *Pax-7* under the promoter of *Pax-3*) will be useful in order to distinguish the specific function of the paralogous *Pax-3* and *Pax-7* genes during development.

We thank Paolo Bonaldo and Edward Stuart for critically reading the manuscript and Ralf Altschäffel for the photographs. This work was supported by the Max-Planck Society.

REFERENCES

Adams, B., Dörfler, P., Aguzzi, A., Kozmik, Z., Urbanek, P., Maurer-Fogy, I. and Busslinger, M. (1992). Pax-5 encodes the transcription factor BSAP and is expressed in B lymphocytes, the developing CNS and adult testis. *Genes Dev.* **6**, 1589-1607.

Asano, M. and Gruss, P. (1992). Pax-5 is expressed at the midbrain-hindbrain boundary during mouse development. *Mech. Dev.* **39**, 29-39.

Auerbach, R. (1954). Analysis of the developmental effects of a lethal mutation in the house mouse. *J. Exp. Zool.* **127**, 305-329.

Baldwin, C. T., Hoth, C. F., Amos, J. A., Da-Silva, E. O. and Milunsky, A. (1992). An exonic mutation in the HuP2 paired domain gene causes Waardenburg's syndrome. *Nature* **355**, 637-638.

Balling, R., Deutsch, U. and Gruss, P. (1988). *Undulated*, a mutation affecting the development of the mouse skeleton, has a point mutation in the paired box of *Pax-1*. *Cell* **55**, 531-535.

Balling, R., Lau, C. F., Dietrich, S., Wallin, J. and Gruss, P. (1992). Development of the skeletal system. In *Postimplantation Development in the Mouse*, vol. 165, pp. 132-143. Wiley: Chichester.

Barr, F. G., Galili, N., Holick, J., Biegel, J. A., Rovera, G. and Emanuel, B. S. (1993). Rearrangement of the PAX3 paired box gene in the paediatric solid tumour alveolar rhabdomyosarcoma. *Nature Genet.* **3**, 113-117.

Baumgartner, S., Bopp, D., Burri, M. and Noll, M. (1987). Structure of two genes at the *gooseberry* locus related to the *paired* gene and their spatial expression during embryogenesis. *Genes Dev.* **1**, 1247-1267.

Bober, E., Franz, T., Arnold, H. H., Gruss, P. and Tremblay, P. (1994). Pax-3 is required for the development of limb muscles: a possible role for the migration of dermomyotomal muscle progenitor cells. *Development* **120**, 603-612.

Bopp, D., Burri, M., Baumgartner, S., Frigerio, G. and Noll, M. (1986). Conservation of a large protein domain in the segmentation gene *paired* and in functionally related genes of *Drosophila*. *Cell* **47**, 1033-1040.

Burri, M., Tromvoukis, Y., Bopp, D., Frigerio, G. and Noll, M. (1989). Conservation of the paired domain in metazoans and its structure in three isolated human genes. *EMBO J.* **8**, 1183-1190.

Chalepakis, G., Fritsch, R., Fickenscher, H., Deutsch, U., Goulding, M. D. and Gruss, P. (1991). The molecular basis of the undulated/ Pax-1 mutation. *Cell* **66**, 873-884.

Chalepakis, G., Stoykova, A., Wijnholds, J., Tremblay, P. and Gruss, P. (1993). Pax: Gene regulators in the developing nervous system. *J. Neurobiol.* **24**, 1367-1384.

Chalepakis, G., Goulding, M., Read, A., Strachan, T. and Gruss, P. (1994). Molecular basis of splotch and Waardenburg Pax-3 mutations. *Proc. Nat. Acad. Sci. USA* **91**, 3685-3689.

Copp, A. J., Brook, F. A. and Roberts, H. J. (1988). A cell-type-specific abnormality of cell proliferation in mutant (curly tail) mouse embryos developing spinal neural tube defects. *Development* **104**, 285-295.

Coté, S., Preiss, A., Haller, J., Schuh, R., Kienlin, A., Seifert, E. and Jäckle, H. (1987). The *gooseberry-zipper* region of *Drosophila*: five genes encode different spatially restricted transcripts in the embryo. *EMBO J.* **6**, 2793-2801.

Czerny, T. Schaffner, G. and Busslinger, M. (1993). DNA sequence recognition by Pax proteins: bipartite structure of the paired domain and its binding site. *Genes Dev.* **7**, 2048-2061.

Davidson, D., Graham, E., Sime, C. and Hill, R. (1988). A gene with sequence similarity to *Drosophila engrailed* is expressed during the development of the neural tube and vertebrate in the mouse. *Development* **104**, 315-316.

Davis, C. A., Noble-Topham, S. E., Rossant, J. and Joyner, A. L. (1988). Expression of the homeobox-containing gene *En-2* delineates a specific region of the developing mouse brain. *Genes Dev.* **2**, 1736-1744.

Davis, R. J., D'Cruz, C. M., Lovell, M. A., Biegel, J. A. and Barr, F. G. (1994). Fusion of *PAX-7* to FKHR by the variant t(1; 13)(p36; q14) Translocation in alveolar rhabdomyosarcoma. *Cancer Res.* **54**, 2869-2872.

Deutsch, U., Dressler, G. and Gruss, P. (1988). Pax1, a member of a paired box homologous murine gene family, is expressed in segmented structures during development. *Cell* **53**, 617-625.

Deutsch, U. and Gruss, P. (1991). Murine paired domain proteins as regulatory factors of embryonic development. *Semin Dev. Biol.* **2**, 413-424.

Dickie, M. M. (1964). New Splotch alleles in the mouse. *J. Hered.* **55**, 97-101.

Dietrich, S., Schubert, F. and Gruss, P. (1993). Altered Pax gene expression in murine notochord mutants: the notochord is required to initiate and maintain ventral identity in the somite. *Mech. Dev.* **44**, 189-207.

Dressler, G. R., Deutsch, U., Balling, R., Simon, D., Guenet, J.-L. and Gruss, P. (1988). Murine genes with homology to *Drosophila* segmentation genes. *Development* **104** (suppl.), 181-186.

Dressler, G. R., Deutsch, U., Chowdhury, K., Nornes, H. O. and Gruss, P. (1990). Pax2, a new murine paired-box-containing gene and its expression in the developing excretory system. *Development* **109**, 787-795.

Dressler, G. R. and Douglas, E. C. (1992). Pax-2 is a DNA binding protein expressed in embryonic kidney and Wilms tumors. *Proc. Nat. Acad. Sci. USA* **89**, 1179-1183.

Epstein, D. J., Vekemans, M. and Gros, P. (1991a). Splotch (Sp^{2H}), a mutation affecting development of the mouse neural tube, shows a deletion within the paired homeodomain of Pax-3. *Cell* **67**, 767-774.

Epstein, D. J., Malo, D., Vekemans, M. and Gros, P. (1991b). Molecular characterisation of a deletion encompassing the splotch (*Sp*) mutation on chromosome 1. *Genomics* **10**, 89-93.

Epstein, D. J., Vogan, K. J., Trasler, D. G. and Gros, P. (1993). A mutation within intron 3 of the Pax-3 gene produces aberrantly spliced mRNA transcripts in the splotch (sp) mouse mutant. *Proc. Nat. Acad. Sci.* **90**, 532-536.

Epstein, J., Jiexing, C., Glaser, T., Jepeal, L. and Maas, R. (1994). Identification of a Pax paired domain recognition sequence and evidence for DNA-dependent conformational changes. *J. Biol. Chem.* **269**, 8355-8361.

Evans, E. P., Burtenshaw, M. D., Beechey, C. V. and Searle, A. G. (1988). A Splotch locus deletion visible by Giemsa banding. *Mouse News Letter* **81**, 66.

Fickenscher, H., Chalepakis, G. and Gruss, P. (1993). Murine Pax-2 protein is a sequence specific transactivator with expression in the genital system. *DNA* **12**, 381-391.

Figdor, M. C. and Stern C. D. (1993). Segmental organisation of embryonic diencephalon. *Nature* **363**, 630-634.

Franz, T. (1989). Persistant truncus arteriosus in the splotch mutant mouse. *Anat. Embryol.* **180**, 457-464.

Franz, T. (1990). Defective ensheathment of motoric nerves in the splotch mutant mouse. *Acta Anat.* **138**, 246-253.

Franz, T., Kothary, R., Surani, M. A. H., Halata, Z. and Grim, M. (1993). The splotch mutation interferes with muscle development in the limbs. *Anat. Embryol.* **187**, 153-160.

Frigerio, G., Burri, M., Bopp, D., Baumgartner, S. and Noll, M. (1986). Structure of the segmentation gene *paired* and the Drosophila PRD gene sets a part of the gene network. *Cell* **47**, 735-746.

Fritsch, R. and Gruss, P. (1993). Murine paired box containing genes. In *Cell-Cell Signalling in Vertebrate Development* (ed. E. Robertson, F. R. Maxfield and H. J. Vogel), pp. 229-245. Academic Press: New York.

Fujiwarw, M., Uchida, T., Osumi-Yamashita, N. and Eto, K. (1994). Uchida rat (*rSey*): a new mutant rat with craniofacial abnormalities resembling those of the mouse *Sey* mutant. *Differentiation* **57**, 31-38.

Galili, N., Davis, R. J., Fredericks, W. J., Mukhopadhyay, S., Rauscher, F. R., Emanuel, B. S., Rovera, G. and Barr, F. G. (1993). Fusion of a fork head domain gene to *PAX3* in the solid tumour alveolar rhabdomyosarcoma. *Nature Genet.* **5**, 230-235.

Glaser, T., Lane, J. and Housman, D. (1990). A mouse model of the aniridia-Wilms tumor deletion syndrome. *Science* **250**, 823-827.

Glaser, T., Walton, D. S. and Maas, R. L. (1992). Genomic structure, evolutionary conservation and aniridia mutations in the human *PAX6* gene. *Nature Genet.* **2**, 232-239.

Goulding, M. D., Chalepakis, G., Deutsch, U., Erselius, J. R. and Gruss, P. (1991). Pax3, a novel murine DNA binding protein expressed during early neurogenesis. *EMBO J.* **10**, 1135-1147.

Goulding, M. D., Lumsden, A. and Gruss, P. (1993a). Signals from the notochord and floor plate regulate the region specific expression of two Pax genes in the developing spinal cord. *Development* **117**, 1001-1016.

Goulding, M. D., Sterrer, S., Fleming, J., Balling, R., Nadeau, J. Moore, K., Brown, S. D. M., Steel, K. P. and Gruss, P. (1993b). Analysis of the Pax-3 gene in the mouse mutant splotch. *Genomics* **17**, 355-363.

Goulding, M., Lumsden, A. and Paquette, A. J. (1994). Regulation of Pax-3 expression in the dermomyotome and its role in muscle development. *Development* **120**, 957-971.

Grüneberg, H. (1950). Genetical studies on the skeleton of the mouse. II. Undulated and its modifiers. *J. Genetics* **50**, 142-173.

Grüneberg, H. (1954). Genetical studies on the skeleton of the mouse. XII. The development of undulated. *J. Genetics* **52**, 441-455.

Gruss, P. and Walther, C. (1992). Pax in development. *Cell* **69**, 719-722.

Hanson, I. M., Fletcher, J. M., Jordan, T., Brown, A., Taylor, D., Adams, R. J., Punnet, H. H. and van Heyningen, V. (1994). Mutations at the *PAX6* locus are found in heterogeneous anterior segment malformations including Peters' anomaly. *Nature Genet.* **6**, 168-173.

Hastie, N. D. (1991). Pax in our time. *Curr. Biol.* **1**, 342-344.

Hill, R. E., Favor, J., Hogan, B. L. M., Ton, C. C. T., Saunders, G. F., Hanson, I. M., Prosser, J., Jordan, T., Hastie, N. D. and van Heyningen, V. (1991). Mouse *Small eye* results from mutations in a paired-like homeobox-containing gene. *Nature* **354**, 522-525.

Hill, R. E. and Hanson, I. M. (1992). Molecular genetics of the Pax family. *Curr. Opin. Cell Biol.* **4**, 967-972.

Hill, R. E. and Van Heyningen, V. (1992). Mouse mutations and human disorders. *Trends Genet.* **8**, 119-120.

Jordan, T., Hanson, I., Zaletayev, D., Hodgson, S., Prosser, J., Seawright, A., Hastie, N. and van Heyningen, V. (1992). The human *PAX6* gene is mutated in two patients with aniridia. *Nature Genet.* **1**, 328-332.

Jostes, B., Walther, C. and Gruss, P. (1991). The murine paired box gene, *Pax7*, is expressed specifically during the development of the nervous and muscular system. *Mech. Dev.* **33**, 27-38.

Keynes, R., Cook, G., Davies, J., Lumsden, A., Norris, W. and Stern, C. (1990). Segmentation and the development of the vertebrate nervous system. *J. Physiol. (Paris)* **84**, 27-32.

Koseki, H., Wallin, J., Wilting, J., Mizutani, Y., Kispert, A., Ebensperger, C., Herrmann, B. G., Christ, B. and Balling, R. (1993). A role for *Pax-1* as a mediator of notochord signals during the dorsoventral specification of vertebrae. *Development* **119**, 649-660.

Krauss. S., Johansen, T., Korzh, V. and Fjose, A. (1991). Expression of the zebrafish paired box gene pax[zfb] during early neurogenesis. *Devlopment* **113**, 1193-1206.

Krauss, S., Johansen, T., Korzh, V. and Fjose, A. (1992). Expresion of zebrafish Pax genes suggests a role in early brain regionalisation. *Nature* **353**, 267-270.

Li, H.-S., Yang, J.-M., Jacobson, R. D., Pasko, D. and Sundin, O. (1994). Pax-6 is first expressed in a region of ectoderm anterior to early neural plate: Implications for stepwise determination of the lens. *Dev. Biol.* **162**, 181-194.

Lumsden, A. (1990). The cellular basis of segmentation in the developing hinbrain. *Trends Neurosci.* **13**, 329-335.

Matsuo, T., Osumi-Yamashita, N., Noji, S., Ohuchi, H., Koyama, E., Myokai, F., Matsuo, N., Taniguchi, S., Doi, H., Iseki, S., Ninomiya, Y., Fujiwara, M., Watanabe, T. and Eto, K. (1993). A mutation in the Pax-6 gene in rat small eye is associated with impaired migration of midbrain cells *Nature Genet.* **3**, 299-304.

Maulbecker, K. and Gruss, P. (1993). The oncogenic potential of Pax genes. *EMBO J.* **12**, 2361-2367.

McGinnis and Krumalauf (1992).

McKusick, V. A. (1992). *Mendelian Inheritance in man.* Johns Hopkins University Press, Baltimore.

Mikkola, J., Fjose, A., Kuwada, J. Y., Wilson, S., Guddal, P. H. and Krauss, S. (1992). The paired domain-containing factor *pax[b]* is expressed in specific commissural interneurons in zebrafish embryos. *J. Neurobiol.* **23**, 933-945.

Moase, C. E. and Trasler, D. G. (1989). Spinal ganglia reduction in the Splotch-delayed mouse neural tube defect mutant. *Teratology* **40**, 67-75.

Moase, C. and Trasler, D. G. (1990). Delayed neural crest emigration from Sp and Spd mouse neural tube explants. *Teratology* **42**, 171-182.

Moase, C. and Trasler, D. G. (1991). N-CAM alterations in splotch neural tube defect mouse embryos. *Development* **113**, 1049-1058.

Morell, R., Friedman, T. B., Moeljopawiro, S., Hartono, Soewito and Asher, J. H. Jr (1992). A frameshift mutation in the Hup2 paired domain of the probable human homolog of murine Pax-3 is responsible for Waardenburg syndrome type 1 in an indonesian family. *Hum. Mol. Genet.* **1**, 243-247.

Noll, M. (1993). Evolution and role of Pax genes. *Curr. Opin. Genet. Dev.* **3**, 595-605.

Nornes, H. O., Dressler, G. R., Knapik, E. W., Deutsch, U. and Gruss, P. (1990). Spatially and temporally restricted expression of Pax2 during murine neurogenesis. *Development* **109**, 797-809.

Plachov, D., Chowdhury, K., Walther, C., Simon, D., Guenet, J.-L. and Gruss, P. (1990). Pax8, a murine paired box gene expressed in the developing excretory system and thyroid gland. *Development* **110**, 643-651.

Placzek, M., Tessier-Lavigne, M., Yamada, T., Jessel, T. and Dodd, D. (1990). Mesodermal control of neural cell identity: Floor plate induction by the notochord. *Science* **250**, 985-988.

Pritchard, D. J. and Clayton, R. M. (1974). Abnormal lens capsule carbohydrate associated with the dominant gene small eye in the mouse. *Exp. Eye Res.* **19**, 335-340.

Puelles, L. and Rubenstein, J. L. R. (1993). Expression patterns of homeobox and other putative regulatory genes in the embryonic mouse forebrain suggest a neuromeric organization. *Trends Neurosci.* **16**, 472-479.

Püschel, A. W., Westerfield, M. and Dressler, G. R. (1992). Comparative analysis of Pax-2 protein distributions during neurulation in mice and zebrafish. *Mech. Dev.* **38**, 197-208.

Rothenpieler, U. W. and Dressler, G. R. (1993). *Pax-2* is required for mesenchyme-to-epithelium conversion during kidney development. *Development* **119**, 711-720.

Russell, W. L. (1947). Splotch, a new mutation in the house mouse Mus musculus. *Genetics* **32**, 107.

Schmahl, W., Knoediseder, M., Favor, J. and Davidson, D. (1993). Defects of neuronal migration and the pathogenesis of cortical malformations are associated with small eye (sey) in the mouse, a point mutation at the Pax-6 locus. *Acta Neuropathol.* **86**, 126-135.

Shapiro, D. N., Sublett, J. E., Li, B., Downing, J. R. and Naeve, C. W. (1993). Fusion of *PAX3* to a member of the forkhead family of transcription factors in human alveolar rhabdomyosarcoma. *Cancer Res.* **53**, 5108-5112.

Shaw, M. W., Falls, H. F. and Neel, J. V. (1960). Congenital aniridia. *Am. J. Hum. Genet.* **12**, 389-415.

Stapleton, P., Weith, A., Urbanek, P., Kozmik, Z. and Busslinger, M. (1993). Chromosomal localization of seven Pax genes and cloning of a noval family member, Pax-9. *Nature Genet.* **3**, 292-298.

Steel, K. P. and Smith, R. J. H. (1992). Normal hearing in Splotch (Sp/+), the mouse homologue of Waardenburg syndrome type 1. *Nature Genet.* **2**, 75-79.

Stoykova, A. and Gruss, P. (1994). Roles of Pax-genes in developing and adult brain as suggested by expression patterns. *J. Neurosci.* **14**, 1395-1412.

Strachan, T. and Reed, A. P. (1994). Pax genes. *Curr. Biol.* **4**, 427-438.

Stuart, E. T., Kioussi, C. and Gruss, P. (1994). Mammalian Pax genes. *Annu. Rev. Genetics* (in press).

Tassabehji, M., Read, A. P., Newton, V. E., Harris, R., Balling, R., Gruss, P. and Strachan, T. (1992). Waardenburg's syndrome patients have mutation in the human homologue of the Pax-3 paired box gene. *Nature* **355**, 635-636.

Tassabehji, M., Read, A. P., Newton, V. E., Patton, M., Gruss, P., Harris, R. and Strachan, T. (1993). Mutations in the PAX-3 paired box gene causing Waardenburg syndrome Type 1 and Type 2. *Nature Genet.* **3**, 26-30.

Ton, C. C. T, Hirvonen, H., Miwa, H., Weil, M. W., Monaghan, P., Jordan, T., Van Heyningen, V., Hastie, N. D., Meijers-Heijboer H., Drechsler, M.,

Royer-Pokora, B., Collins, F., Swaroop, A., Strong, L. C. and Saunders, G. F. (1991). Positional cloning and characterizationof a paired box- and homeobox-containing gene from Aniridia Region. *Cell* **67**, 1059-1074.

Tremblay, P. and Gruss, P. (1994). Pax: Genes for mice and men. *Phamac. Ther.* (in press).

Treisman, J., Harris, E. and Desplan, C. (1991). The paired box encodes a second DNA-binding domain in the paired homeodomain protein. *Genes Dev.* **5**, 594-604.

van Straaten, H. W., Hekking, J. W., Wiertz-Hoessels, E. J., Thors, F. and Drukker, J. (1988). Effect of the notochord on the differentiation of a floor plate area in the neural tube of the chick embryo. *Anat. Embryol.* **177**, 317-324.

Vogan K. J., Epstein, D. J., Trasler, D. G. and Gros, P. (1993). The Splotch delayed (Spd) mouse mutant carries a point mutation within the paired box of the Pax-3 gene. *Genomics* **17**, 364-369.

Wakatsuki, Y., Neurath M. F., Max, E. M. and Strober, W. (1994). *J. Exp. Med.* **179**, 1099-1108.

Walther, C. and Gruss, P. (1991). Pax-6, a murine paired box gene, is expressed in the developing CNS. *Development* **113**, 1435 1449.

Walther, C., Guenet, J.-L., Simon, D., Deutsch, U., Jostes, B., Goulding, M. D., Plachov, D., Balling, R. and Gruss, P. (1991). Pax: a murine multigene family of paired box containing genes. *Genomics* **11**, 424-434.

Wallin, J., Mizutani, Y., Imai, K., Miyashita, N., Moriwaki, K., Taniguchi, M., Koseki, H. and Balling, R. (1993). A new Pax gene, Pax-9, maps to mouse chromosome 12. *Mammalian Genome* **4**, 354-358.

Wallin, J., Witting, J., Haruhiko, K., Fritsch, R., Christ, B. and Balling, R. (1994). The role of Pax-1 in axial skeleton development. *Development* **120**, 1109-1121.

Wilkinson, D. G., Bailes, J. A. and McMahon, A. P. (1987). Expression of the proto-oncogene *int-1* is restricted to specific neural cells in the developing mouse embryo. *Cell* **50**, 79-88.

Williams, B. A. and Ordahl, C. P. (1994). Pax-3 expression in segmental mesoderm marks early stages in myogenic cell specification. *Development* **120**, 785-796.

Zannini, M., Francis-Lang, H., Plachov, D. and Di Lauro, R. (1992). Pax-8, a paired domain-containing protein, binds to a sequence overlapping the recognition site of a homeodomain and activates transcription from two thyroid-specific promoters. *Mol. Cell Biol.* **12**, 4230-4241.

Journal of Cell Science, Supplement 18, 43-49 (1994)
Printed in Great Britain © The Company of Biologists Limited 1994

Mutations of the *RET* proto-oncogene in the multiple endocrine neoplasia type 2 syndromes and Hirschsprung disease

Darrin P. Smith[1], Charis Eng[1,2] and Bruce A. J. Ponder[1,*]

[1]CRC Human Cancer Genetics Research Group, Department of Pathology, University of Cambridge, Cambridge, UK
[2]Division of Medical Oncology, Division of Cancer Epidemiology and Control, Dana-Farber Cancer Institute, Department of Medicine, Harvard Medical School, Boston, USA

SUMMARY

Distinct point mutations in the *RET* proto-oncogene are the cause of the inherited multiple endocrine neoplasia type 2 syndromes (MEN 2), and the congenital gut disorder Hirschsprung disease. The site and type of these mutations suggests that they have differing effects on the activity of the receptor tyrosine kinase encoded by *RET*. The normal function of the *RET* receptor tyrosine kinase has yet to be determined. However, this has been investigated by the inactivation of the *RET* gene in transgenic mice. The developmental abnormalities apparent in these mice, together with the observation that the major tissues affected in MEN 2 and Hirschsprung disease have a common origin in the embryonal neural crest, suggest that *RET* encodes a receptor for a developmental regulator involved in the genesis of a variety of neural crest derivatives, and in the organogenesis of the kidney.

Key words: *RET* proto-oncogene, receptor tyrosine kinase, inherited cancer syndrome, MEN 2, Hirschsprung disease

INTRODUCTION AND CLINICAL CONSIDERATIONS

The multiple endocrine neoplasia (MEN) type 2 syndromes and Hirschsprung disease (HSCR) are neurocristopathies or disorders involving neural crest and its derivatives. MEN 2 is an autosomal dominantly inherited cancer syndrome in which developmental abnormalities may be associated with tumour development. HSCR is not a cancer syndrome. It is the congenital absence of autonomic ganglia of the gut.

There are 3 types of MEN 2, which differ in the spectrum of tissues involved (Table 1). Families with MEN 2A have: medullary thyroid carcinoma (MTC), a tumour of the thyroid C-cells; phaeochromocytoma, a tumour of the adrenal medulla, in approximately 50% of individuals; and either hyperplasia or adenoma of the parathyroids in approximately 25% of individuals (Schimke, 1984). While thyroid C-cells and the adrenal medulla are neural crest derivatives, the parathyroids develop from the third and fourth branchial arches and are therefore derived from endoderm (Moore, 1982). Families with familial medullary thyroid carcinoma (FMTC) have MTC only (Farndon et al., 1986). The majority of patients with MEN 2A and FMTC present in their second to fourth decades of life. However, clinical evidence for C-cell hyperplasia is present in as many as 10% of gene carriers by the age of 10 (Ponder et al., 1988), suggesting that C-cell hyperplasia may begin in utero or in childhood. By the time they are 30, clinical screening evidence of C-cell hyperplasia is present in almost 100% of patients. MEN 2B is similar to MEN 2A but is characterised by earlier age of tumour onset and such developmental abnormalities as intestinal ganglioneuromatosis, marfanoid habitus and atypical facies (Schimke et al., 1968; Chong et al., 1975). The ganglioneuromatosis results from hyperplasia and dysplasia of the autonomic ganglia of the gut, which is also derived from the neural crest.

Hirschsprung disease is a congenital disorder characterised by functional intestinal obstruction resulting in megacolon. Abdominal distention and the inability to defecate manifest early in infancy. The functional intestinal obstruction is caused by the absence of the ganglion cells within Meissner's and Auerbach's plexuses (Okamoto and Ueda, 1967). This is in contrast to the ganglioneuromatosis observed in MEN 2B. This observation, together with the fact that tissues of neural crest origin are involved in MEN 2, suggests that MEN 2 and HSCR share a common aetiology.

GENETICS

MEN 2 is inherited as an autosomal dominant trait, with age-related penetrance (Ponder et al., 1988). Approximately 50% of MEN 2A gene carriers will manifest with symptoms by the age of 55, and 70% by the age of 70 (Ponder, 1985; Ponder et

Table 1. Summary of tissues involved in the MEN 2 syndromes and in Hirschsprung disease*

Syndrome	Thyroid C-cells (tumour)	Adrenal medulla (tumour)	Parathyroid (hyperplasia/ adenoma)	Enteric ganglia (increased/ absent)
MEN 2A	+	+ (50%)	+ (~25%)	↓↓ (rare families only)
FMTC	+	-	-	-
MEN 2B	+	+ (50%)	-	↑↑
Hirschsprung	-	-	-	↓↓

*Eng et al. 1994.

al., 1988). HSCR often occurs sporadically. Sometimes, HSCR is familial and is inherited as an autosomal dominant trait with low penetrance, estimated at 30%. Rarely, a few families with MEN 2A or FMTC have been reported in which some members affected with MEN 2A or FMTC also have histopathologically proven aganglionosis, consistent with the diagnosis of HSCR (Frilling et al., 1992; Verdy et al., 1982).

LOCALISATION OF THE SUSCEPTIBILITY GENES FOR MEN 2 AND HSCR

Linkage analysis, i.e. the examination of the segregation of alleles at a disease locus with respect to alleles at a known marker locus, revealed that the susceptibility gene(s) for all 3 syndromes of MEN 2 was localised to a small interval on chromosome sub-band 10q11.2 (Carson et al., 1990; Gardner et al., 1993; Lairmore et al., 1991; Mathew et al., 1987; Simpson et al., 1987). Only one previously identified gene, the *RET* proto-oncogene, which codes for a receptor tyrosine kinase expressed in neural crest-derived tissues (see below), was known to lie within the 480 kb MEN 2A region (Mole et al., 1993).

Similarly, linkage analysis applied to large kindreds with HSCR demonstrated that the susceptibility locus for HSCR was on chromosome sub-band 10q11.2 (Angrist et al., 1993; Lyonnet et al., 1993). Further, 5 patients were described with HSCR and partial deletion of chromosome sub-band 10q11.2 (Fewtrell et al., 1994; Luo et al., 1993; Martucciello et al., 1992). Each of these deletions encompasses the *RET* proto-oncogene.

Further study of the *RET* proto-oncogene led to the identification of different mutations that predispose to the MEN 2 syndromes and HSCR.

RET ENCODES A RECEPTOR TYROSINE KINASE

By the criterion of structural similarity the *RET* proto-oncogene encodes a receptor tyrosine kinase (RTK) (Takahashi et al., 1988, 1989). RTKs are transmembrane proteins mediating cell-cell signalling. The intracellular tyrosine kinase domain is activated by ligand interaction with the extracellular domain (reviewed by Pawson and Schlessinger, 1993; Resh, 1993; Pazin and Williams, 1992). The prevailing concept of mechanism of receptor activation (demonstrated for EGF, PDGF and CSF-1 receptors) is that ligand binding induces receptor dimerisation. This, in turn, activates intracellular signal transduction pathways by inducing autophosphorylation of the receptor's intracellular domain. This is accompanied by interaction of the phosphotyrosines generated with cellular proteins, and the phosphorylation of a range of cytoplasmic substrates. The ligand(s) of *RET* has yet to be identified, and perhaps the only clue to the identity of a *RET* ligand is the observation that the extracellular domain of RET shares homology with the extracellular domain of the cadherin superfamily (Schneider, 1992). Cadherins are transmembrane proteins that mediate cell-cell adhesion principally (although probably not exclusively) by homophilic interactions (Takeichi, 1991, Inuzuka et al., 1991). This raises the possibility that RET signalling may be activated by a homophilic cell-cell interaction, or by a heterophilic interaction with another cadherin superfamily member. The D*trk* RTK of

Drosophila shares homology with neural cell adhesion molecules of the immunoglobulin superfamily, and is activated by such a homophilic adhesive interaction (Pulido et al., 1992). Many of the events in the downstream signalling pathway of *RET* can be predicted by analogy to the better studied RTKs. Some of these events have begun to be investigated by the use of an EGF receptor-*RET* chimaera, in which the extracellular domain of *RET* has been replaced by the extracellular domain of the EGF receptor (Santoro et al., 1994). EGF activation of the chimaera results in cell growth, transformation and phosphorylation of downstream target proteins.

Activated forms of the *RET* proto-oncogene were originally identified by transfection of tumour DNA into fibroblasts. *RET* was found to be activated by juxtaposition of 3′ *RET* sequences with 5′ sequences from other genes. *RET* activation occurred during the transfection assay, and activated *RET* was not found in the original tumour DNAs (from T cell lymphoma, colon carcinoma and gastric carcinoma) (Takahashi et al., 1985; Takahashi and Cooper, 1987; Ishizaka et al., 1988, 1989; Koda, 1988). Activated *RET* has subsequently been found in vivo only in papillary thyroid carcinoma (PTC) (Grieco et al., 1990; Lanzi et al., 1992; Bongarzone et al., 1993). In 25% of PTC, the 3′ tyrosine kinase domain of *RET* is fused to the 5′ terminal region of other genes that induce dimerisation and constitutive tyrosine kinase activity.

THE ROLE OF *RET* DURING EMBRYOGENESIS

The normal function of *RET* has yet to be determined. However, the discovery that *RET* mutations predispose to neurocristopathies suggests a central role for *RET* in the migration, proliferation or differentiation of neural crest derivatives. Further clues to the function of *RET* have been obtained from an examination of the expression pattern of *RET* mRNA, and the phenotype of mice in which the *RET* gene has been inactivated.

The expression pattern of *RET* mRNA

In the post-implantation mouse embryo, *RET* mRNA is expressed in a temporally and spatially dynamic pattern in subsets of cells in the central nervous system (motor neuron lineages of the hind brain and spinal cord, neuroretina), the peripheral nervous system (autonomic nervous system, enteric nervous system, sensory ganglia), and the secretory system (nephrotome, Wolffian duct) (Pachnis et al., 1993). This suggests that *RET* plays an important role in control of normal mammalian embryogenesis.

RET expression in subsets of the migratory neural crest cells originating from the hind brain and their derivatives is of particular interest in relationship to the disease phenotypes associated with *RET* mutations. It suggests that, as with HSCR mutations, MEN 2 mutations may act during the development of the affected tissue. The thyroid C-cells, adrenal chromaffin cells, mucosal ganglia, cranial mesenchyme and enteric ganglia, which are affected in MEN 2 and HSCR, are derivatives of the hind brain neural crest. Their precursors express *RET* during embryogenesis, both in the hind brain neural crest and in their transient location in the posterior branchial arches. The parathyroid gland, also affected in MEN 2A, is not a neural crest derivative, but is derived from the endoderm of the posterior branchial arches, which strongly expresses *RET* during embryogenesis. This reveals a common developmental link between the tissues affected in diseases linked to *RET* mutations.

In the adult mouse, strong *RET* expression is found in the brain and salivary gland, with weaker expression in the heart and spleen (Pachnis et al., 1993). Low but detectable levels of expression are also found in the thyroid C cells, but no expression is detectable in the adrenal chromaffin cells. In contrast, MTCs and phaeochromocytomas strongly express *RET*, as do neuroblastomas, which are also tumours of neuroectodermal origin (e.g. Santoro et al., 1990; Takahashi et al., 1991).

The phenotype of *RET* 'knock-out' mice

The *RET* gene has been disrupted in mice by homologous recombination in embryonic stem cells (Schuchardt et al., 1994). *RET*+/- mice develop apparently normally; however, *RET*-/- mice die soon after birth and show a lack of enteric neurons throughout the entire length of the gut, and severe renal abnormalities.

The lack of enteric neurons in *RET*-/- is similar to HSCR in man, and emphasises the role of *RET* in the development of the enteric nervous system.

The renal agenesis or severe dysgenesis in *RET*-/- mice reveals a role for *RET* in kidney development which was implied by *RET* expression during embryogenesis in the Wolffian duct. The ureteric bud, an outgrowth of the Wolffian duct, induces adjacent metanephric mesenchyme to form the epithelium of the glomerulus and tubules. Reciprocally, the ureteric mesenchyme induces the ureteric bud to grow and branch to form the collecting system. Given *RET* expression in the tip of the ureteric bud, and the lack of kidney tissue in *RET* deficient mice it is tempting to speculate that *RET* transduces a signal (a *RET* ligand) from the kidney mesenchyme, which induces growth and budding of the ureteric bud.

It will be interesting to see if viable wild-type and *RET*-/- chimaeric mice can be made in order to analyse the effects of the loss of *RET* in later life.

GERMLINE MUTATIONS OF THE *RET* PROTO-ONCOGENE IN MEN 2 AND HSCR

Missense mutations of the *RET* proto-oncogene have been found in the constitutional DNA of the majority of patients with MEN 2A, FMTC and MEN 2B (Carlson et al., 1994; Donis-Keller et al., 1993; Eng et al., 1994; Hofstra et al., 1994; Mulligan et al., 1993b, 1994a,b). In MEN 2A and FMTC, the mutations alter 1 of 5 cysteine residues in exons 10 and 11 within the cysteine-rich domain of *RET* (Fig. 1; Table 2). There is a correlation between the particular cysteine residue that has been mutated and the spectrum of tissue involvement. Thus, mutation at cysteine 634, which accounts for over 75% of mutations, is more frequent in families with MEN 2A (Mulligan et al., 1994a), whereas mutation at the other cysteine codons is more frequent in families with FMTC (Mulligan et al., 1994a). Moreover, within the group of families with mutation at codon 634, the particular mutation that changes cysteine (TGC) to arginine (CGC), is significantly associated with parathyroid involvement (but not with phaeochromocytoma) (Mulligan et al., 1994a). Evidence against a founder effect to explain this

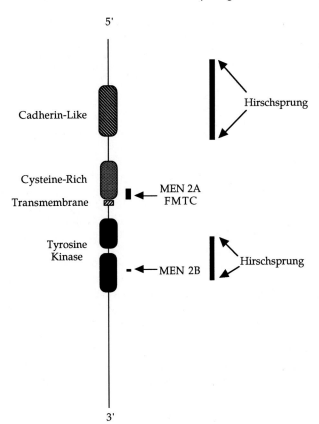

Fig. 1. Schematic representation of the *RET* proto-oncogene and summary of point mutations found in the MEN 2 syndromes and Hirschsprung disease (adapted from Eng et al., 1994, with permission).

Table 2. Summary of published germline mutations in exons 10 and 11 of *RET* in MEN 2A and FMTC*

Cys codon no.	Mutation to	Number of cases	
		MEN 2A	FMTC
634	Arg	38	0
634	Gly	4	0
634	Phe	3	2
634	Ser	4	0
634	Trp	2	0
634	Tyr	10	1
620	Arg	4	2
620	Phe	1	0
620	Tyr	1	1
618	Arg	2	1
618	Gly	1	0
618	Phe	1	0
618	Ser	4	4
618	Tyr	0	1
611	Trp	0	1
611	Tyr	2	2
609	Tyr	1	0

*Donis-Keller et al., 1993; Mulligan et al., 1994; Xue et al., 1994.

association has been obtained by examining the haplotypes on which codon 634 cysteine → arginine mutations have occurred (E. Gardner et al., 1994).

Table 3. Summary of germline mutations of *RET* codon 918 in MEN 2B

	Total patients	Mutation	No mutation
Carlson et al., 1994	34	34	0
Eng et al., 1994*	29	27	2
Hofstra et al., 1994	9	9	0

*Including unpublished data.

In contrast to MEN 2A and FMTC, a single missense mutation affecting codon 918, altering a methionine (ATG) to a threonine (ACG), has been found in all but 2 patients with MEN 2B (Fig. 1; Table 3) (Carlson et al., 1994; Eng et al., 1994; Hofstra et al., 1994). The 2 patients without the codon 918 mutation did not differ clinically from the rest of the patients with mutations (Eng et al., 1994).

Excluding the cases of HSCR with partial deletion of chromosome sub-band 10q11.2, 23 sporadic and 25 familial cases of HSCR have been examined for mutations in *RET*. Of these 48, 2 sporadic and 8 familial cases were found to have point mutations scattered along the extracellular and tyrosine kinase domains of *RET* (Fig. 1) (Edery et al., 1994; Romeo et al., 1994). Seven had missense mutations in the extracellular domain of *RET*, 2 had nonsense mutations in exon 3 and 1 had a frameshift mutation predicted to result in truncated protein (Table 4).

SOMATIC MUTATIONS OF THE *RET* PROTO-ONCOGENE IN SPORADIC TUMOURS

Although MTC and phaeochromocytoma are component tumours of the MEN 2 syndromes, they also occur as truly sporadic, i.e. noninherited, tumours. By analogy with other inherited cancer syndromes, one might expect that somatic *RET* mutations corresponding to the germline mutations observed in MEN 2A and MEN 2B would be involved in the tumourigenesis of these sporadic tumours. Of 31 sporadic MTC, 10 (32%) had somatic MEN 2B-type mutations (codon 918, changing ATG to ACG) (Table 5) (Eng et al., 1994; Hofstra et al., 1994). Donis-Keller et al. (1993) reported only one of an unknown number of sporadic MTC to have a mutation in exon 10 or 11: this was a 6 bp deletion, which removed cysteine 630 (Donis-Keller et al., 1993). In contrast to sporadic MTC, 1 of 12 (8%) apparently sporadic phaeochromocytoma had a somatic mutation of codon 918 and 2 (16%) had somatic missense mutations affecting cysteine 620 (Eng et al., 1994). Unfortunately, corresponding germline DNA was not available for the 2 phaeochromocytomas that had cysteine 620 mutations. No MTC and phaeochromocytoma from patients with MEN 2A or FMTC had a codon 918 mutation. Since only 3 of 20 *RET* exons have been analysed for somatic mutations in these tumours, it is possible that mutations elsewhere in *RET* (other exons or promoter) may also play a role in tumourigenesis.

TUMOURIGENESIS IN MEN 2 TUMOURS

Hyperplasia of the thyroid C-cells and adrenal chromaffin cells

Table 4. Summary of germline *RET* mutations in Hirschsprung disease*

Reference	*RET* exon	Codon no.	Amino acid	Mutated to
Edery et al., 1994	2	32	ser	leu
	2	64	pro	leu
	3	136	glu	stop
	3	180	arg	stop
	5	330	arg	gln
	6	393	phe	leu
Romeo et al., 1994	6	373	ala	frameshift
	13	765	ser	pro
	15	897	arg	gln
	17	972	arg	gly

*Exclusive of 5 microscopic and submicroscopic deletions encompassing *RET* on chromosome sub-band 10q11.2.

Table 5. Summary of somatic *RET* mutations in sporadic tumours

Sporadic tumour	Total analysed	Codon 918	MEN 2A region
MTC*,†	31	10	0*,‡
Phaeo*	12	1	2

*Eng et al., 1994.
†Hofstra et al., 1994.
‡Excluding somatic mutations in the MEN 2A region reported by Donis-Keller et al., 1993 (total MTC analysed not reported).

has been observed in patients with MEN 2. It is not known if this hyperplasia is monoclonal or polyclonal. Germline mutation of a single allele of *RET* is believed to be the initiating event in familial MEN 2 tumours. This first event may be sufficient to promote multiple foci of hyperplasia in neuroendocrine organs. If the hyperplasia were monoclonal, it would argue for the germline mutation being the initiating event but subsequent molecular events would likely be necessary for progression. However, if the hyperplasia were polyclonal, then germline mutation of *RET* would be the only event necessary for hyperplasia. Because of the possible mechanism of action of RET (see below) and because loss of heterozygosity of markers on chromosome sub-band 10q11.2 is the exception rather than the rule in MEN 2 and MEN 2-related tumours (Mulligan et al., 1993a), loss of activity of the second *RET* allele probably does not occur. Indeed, it has been shown, by RT-PCR, that both alleles of *RET* are transcribed in MEN 2 and MEN 2-related tumours (Mulligan et al., 1993b). However, it is possible that a second point mutation on the other *RET* allele occurs in the process of tumourigenesis. Subsequent somatic mutations, involving 1p, 3p, 11p, 17p and 22q (Mulligan et al., 1993a), within the already hyperplastic tissues may lead to formation of MTC and phaeochromocytoma. There is little or no data available with regards to involvement of known oncogenes in this multistep process of oncogenesis in these tumours. Since loss of heterozygosity of markers on these chromosome regions, where there are known tumour suppressor genes, has been demonstrated (Mulligan et al., 1993), subsequent loss of activity of one or more tumour suppressors probably plays a role in tumour formation. Known tumour suppressor genes in the regions of loss include the *VHL* gene on 3p, *WT1* on 11p13, *p53* on 17p and *NF2* on 22q.

POSSIBLE EFFECTS OF THE MUTATIONS ON RET PROTEIN FUNCTION

The effects of the different *RET* mutations on receptor function remain to be determined. However, certain predictions can be made.

HSCR mutations

The nonsense mutations in HSCR are predicted to result in a highly truncated RET protein that will almost certainly be inactive. Hence, HSCR *RET* mutations in general probably create an inactive or partially active *RET* allele. This is consistent with the deletion of one *RET* allele in some patients with HSCR (Martucciello et al., 1992; Fewtrell et al., 1994; Luo et al., 1993). It is possible that the missense mutations in HSCR create an inactive RET protein that can also act as a dominant negative by inhibiting the activity of the RET protein derived from the normal allele by the formation of inactive heterodimers. The precursors of the enteric ganglia, and perhaps the ureteric bud, are more sensitive to the reduced dosage of *RET* than the other tissues that express *RET* during embryogenesis, since these tissues (notably the C-cell and chromaffin cell precursors) are apparently normal in HSCR.

Whereas in man, apparently heterozygous inactivation of *RET* is sufficient to result in the phenotype (although with markedly incomplete penetrance), in the mice studied so far, heterozygous disruption of a *RET* allele is not sufficient to give rise to an HSCR phenotype (Schuchardt et al., 1994). However, the homozygous *RET* 'knock-out' mice do display the absence of enteric ganglion cells of the myenteric and submucosal plexus, which characterises HSCR. This difference, and the incomplete penetrance of HSCR mutations in man, suggests that dosage effects and perhaps genetic background may be important. *RET* 'knock-out' mice also show severe renal abnormalities. In man kidney defects have not been previously recorded in association with HSCR, but now a few rare families with HSCR and renal dysplasias are being observed (our unpublished observations).

MEN 2 mutations

Although there is as yet no formal proof, it seems likely that the *RET* mutations in MEN 2 are dominant at the level of the cell. If so, this is in contrast to the other inherited cancer syndromes where the predisposing mutations have consistently been associated with loss of function. The evidence that MEN 2 mutations are dominant and activating is three-fold: (1) the absence of *RET* allele loss and concomitant expression of the wild-type *RET* allele in MEN 2B- and MEN 2A-related tumours argues for an activating rather than an inactivating mutation; (2) the contrasting effects of MEN 2B and HSCR mutations on enteric ganglion cells (overgrowth rather than absence) suggests these mutations have opposite effects, that is, the MEN 2B mutation results in an active *RET* allele; (3) heterozygous disruption of a *RET* allele in mice does not result in an MEN 2 phenotype (Schuchardt et al., 1994).

Variable penetrance of expression of MEN 2A and MEN 2B within a single family (Easton et al., 1989), and variable spectrum of tissue involvement suggest that, as with HSCR, the germline mutation is not the only determinant of phenotype and that the possible effects of genetic background should also be considered. Substantial phenotypic variability is also seen between family members in other inherited cancer syndromes.

For example, colon cancer syndromes caused by mutation in the APC gene (Leppert et al., 1990; Spirio et al., 1992). In a mouse model of familial colon cancer it has been possible to map the chromosomal location of a major modifier gene affecting the phenotypic expression of the APC mutation (Dietrich et al., 1993). The same *RET* mutation can result in FMTC or MEN 2A (Table 2; Mulligan et al., 1994a). This observation points to a more specific effect of genetic background. Since FMTC and MEN 2A families 'breed true' the genetic modifier must be closely linked to *RET*, and is perhaps the *RET* allele in which the disease mutation occurs.

The possible ways in which MEN 2A and MEN 2B mutations may activate the RET protein such that it is dominant at the cellular level are discussed below.

MEN 2A and FMTC mutations

If, indeed, the MEN 2A and FMTC mutations are activating, it is likely that they serve to enhance receptor dimerisation. There are now several examples of enhanced dimerisation associated with the oncogenic activation of RTKs. *RET* itself, *met*, and *trk* are activated by genomic rearrangements that generate hybrids containing the 3′ tyrosine kinase domain linked to upstream sequences, which act as a constitutive dimerisation interface (Bongarzone et al., 1993; Rodrigues and Park, 1993; Greco et al., 1992). Ligand-independent aggregation and oncogenic activation of the *neu* RTK is associated with a more subtle mutation, an amino acid substitution in the transmembrane domain (Weiner et al., 1989). The c-*fms* RTK provides a precedent for oncogenic activation by a missense mutation in the extracellular domain (Roussel et al., 1988). This mutation leads to a constitutive increase in autophosphorylation. Studies with the *neu* RTK indicate a possible mechanism (Cao et al., 1992) by which the MEN 2A and FMTC mutations may enhance receptor dimerisation. Introduction of an extra cysteine residue proximal to the transmembrane domain induces receptor dimerisation, probably by the formation of inter-receptor disulphide bonds. Loss of a cysteine residue in MEN 2A and FMTC *RET* may free another cysteine residue normally involved in an intra-receptor disulphide bond allowing such a mechanism to operate.

MEN 2A and FMTC mutations occur in conserved cysteine residues in the cysteine-rich region close to the transmembrane domain. The analogous region in the EGF receptor has been implicated in the formation of a ligand-binding pocket (Lax et al., 1988, 1989). It is possible that MEN 2A and FMTC mutations do not induce receptor dimerisation per se; instead, these mutations may activate RET by increasing the affinity of the extracellular domain for a ligand or ligands.

The correlation of different MEN 2A mutations with different patterns of involvement of C cells, adrenal medulla and parathyroid may imply that the mutations differ in their effects on tissue-specific interactions between RET and another protein (possibly a ligand), or that these tissues differ in their sensitivity to a partially activated RET protein. Alternatively, the mutations may vary in their effects on differentially expressed *RET* splice variants. Multiple splice variants are common in RTKs, and 3′ alternate splicing of *RET* has already been identified (Tahira et al., 1990).

The MEN 2B mutation

Methionine-918 is strongly conserved within the substrate

recognition pocket of the tyrosine kinase catalytic core of receptor tyrosine kinases (Hanks et al., 1988). Hence, mutation of this residue to a threonine in MEN 2B is predicted to strongly affect catalytic activity. This effect, however, is unlikely to be inactivating because a threonine at the equivalent position is strongly conserved in *src*-related and *abl*-related cytoplasmic tyrosine kinases (Hanks et al., 1988). Instead, two effects singly or in combination are among the possible consequences of this mutation. The mutation may cause increased or ligand-independent activation of RET. The mutation causes RET to more closely resemble the cytoplasmic tyrosine kinases, which have no ligand. Src, for example, is activated by the dephosphorylation of a regulatory C-terminal phosphotyrosine (Cooper and Howell, 1993). Second, a ligand-dependent or -independent change in substrate specificity of the tyrosine kinase enzymatic activity may be the result of the mutation.

A striking observation from the analysis of whether MEN 2 mutations occur somatically in sporadic tumours is that the MEN 2B mutation is common in sporadic MTC, whereas MEN 2A mutations have not been found (Table 5; Eng et al., 1994). This may be explained by a greater susceptibility of the *RET* gene to the MEN 2B mutation. However, this could also indicate that a shorter time-window (perhaps during development of the thyroid gland) exists during which the MEN 2A mutations are active and somatically occurring mutations can lead to MTC.

Whatever the actual effects of MEN 2 mutations may be, it is clear, given the differences between MEN 2A and MEN 2B, that simple constitutive activation of the normal *RET* signalling pathway cannot be the consequence of both mutations. Determination of the precise biological consequences of these mutations presents an exciting challenge.

We thank our colleagues, especially Dr Lois M. Mulligan and Dr Stanislas Lyonnet, who contributed to this work. The work in our laboratory is supported by programme grants from the Cancer Research Campaign and a CRC Dana-Farber Cancer Institute Fellowship (C.E.). B.A.J.P. is a Gibb Fellow of the CRC.

REFERENCES

Angrist, M., Kauffman, E., Slaugenhaupt, S. A., Matise, T. C., Puffenberger, E. G., Washington, S. S., Lipson, A., Cass, D. T., Reyna, T., Weeks, D. E., Sieber, W. and Chakravarti, A. (1993). A gene for Hirschsprung disease (megacolon) in the pericentromeric region of human chromosome 10. *Nature Genet.* **4**, 351-356.

Bongarzone, I., Monzini, N., Borrello, M. G., Carcano, C., Ferraresi, G., Arighi, E., Mondellini, P., Dell Porta, G. and Pierotti, M. A. (1993). Molecular characterisation of a thyroid tumor-specific transforming sequence formed by the fusion of *ret* tyrosine kinase and the regulatory subunit RI of cyclic AMP-dependent protein kinase A. *Mol. Cell. Biol.* **13**, 358-366.

Cao, H., Bangalore, L., Dompe, C., Bormann, B.-J. and Stern, D. F. (1992). An extra cysteine proximal to the transmembrane domain induces differential cross-linking of p185^{neu} and p185^{neu*}. *J. Biol. Chem.* **267**, 20489-20492.

Carlson, K. M., Dou, S., Chi, D., Scavarda, N., Toshima, K., Jackson, C. E., Wells, S. A., Goodfellow, P. J. and Donis-Keller, H. (1994). Single missense mutation in the tyrosine kinase catalytic domain of the *RET* protooncogene is associated with multiple endocrine neoplasia type 2B. *Proc. Nat. Acad. Sci. USA* **91**, 1579-1583.

Chong, G. C., Beahrs, O. H., Sizemore, G. W. and Woolner, L. H. (1975). Medullary carcinoma of the thyroid gland. *Cancer* **33**, 695-704.

Carson, N. L., Wu, J., Jackson, C. E., Kidd, K. K. and Simpson, N. E. (1990). The mutation for medullary thyroid carcinoma with parathyroid tumours (MTC with PTs) is closely linked to the centromeric region of chromosome 10. *Am. J. Hum. Genet.* **47**, 946-951.

Cooper, J. A. and Howell, B. (1993). The when and how of src regulation. *Cell* **73**, 1051-1054.

Dietrich, W. F., Lander, E. S., Smith, J. S., Moser, A. R., Gould, K. A., Luongo, C., Borenstein, N. and Dove, W. (1993). Genetic identification of *Mom-1* a major modifier locus affecting *Min*-induced intestinal neoplasia in the mouse. *Cell* **75**, 631-639.

Donis-Keller, H., Dou, S., Chi, D., Carolson, K. M., Toshima, K., Lairmore, T. C., Howe, J. R., Moley, J. F., Goodfellow, P. and Wells, S. A. (1993). Mutations in the *RET* proto-oncogene are associated with MEN 2A and FTMC. *Hum. Mol. Genet.* **2**, 851-856.

Easton, D. F., Ponder, M. A., Cummings, T., Gagel, R. F., Hansen, H. H., Reichlin, S., Tashjian, A. H., Telenius-Berg, M., Ponder, B. A. J. and the CRC Medullary Thyroid Group. (1989). The clinical and age-at-onset distribution for the MEN-2 syndrome. *Am. J. Hum. Genet.* **44**, 208-215.

Edery, P., Lyonnet, S., Mulligan, L. M., Pelet, A., Dow, E., Abel, L., Holder, S., Nihoul-Fekete, C., Ponder, B. A. J. and Munnich, A. (1994). Mutations of the *RET* proto-oncogene in Hirschsprung's disease. *Nature* **367**, 378-380.

Eng, C., Smith, D. P., Mulligan, L. M., Nagai, M. A., Healey, C. S., Ponder, M. A., Gardner, E., Scheumann, G. F. W., Jackson, C. E., Tunnacliffe, A. and Ponder, B. A. J. (1994). Point mutation within the tyrosine kinase domain of the *RET* proto-oncogene in multiple endocrine neoplasia type 2B and related sporadic tumours. *Hum. Mol. Genet.* **3**, 237-241.

Farndon, J. R., Leight, G. S., Dilley, W. G., Baylin, S. B., Smallridge, R. C., Harrison, T. S. and Wells, S. A. Jr (1986). Familial medullary thyroid carcinoma without associated endocrinopathies: a distinct clinical entity. *Br. J. Surg.* **73**, 278-281.

Fewtrell, M. S., Tam, P. K. H., Thomson, A. H., Fitchett, M., Currie, J., Huson, S. M. and Mulligan, L. M. (1994). Hirschsprung's disease associated with a deletion of chromsome 10 (q11. 2q21. 2): a further link with the neurocristopathies? *J. Med. Genet.* (in press).

Frilling, A., Becker, H. and Roehr, H.-D. (1992). Unusual features of multiple endocrine neoplasia. *Henry Ford Hosp. Med. J.* **40**, 233-235.

Gardner, E., Mulligan, L. M., Eng, C., Healey, C. S., Kwok, J. B. J., Ponder, M. A. and Ponder, B. A. J. (1994). Haplotype analysis of MEN 2 mutations. *Hum. Mol. Genet.* (in press).

Gardner, E., Papi, L., Easton, D. F., Cummings, T., Jackson, C. E., Kaplan, M., Love, D. R., Mole, S. E., Moore, J. K., Mulligan, L. M., Norum, R. A., Ponder, M. A., Reichlin, S., Stall, G., Telenius, H., Telenius-Berg, M., Tunnacliffe, A. and Ponder, B. A. J. (1993). Genetic linkage studies map the multiple endocrine neoplasia type 2 loci to a small interval on chromosome 10q11. 2. *Hum. Mol. Genet.* **2**, 241-246.

Greco, M., Pierotti, M. A., Bongarzone, I., Pagliardini, S., Lanzi, C. and Dell Porta, G. (1992). Trk-t1 is a novel oncogene formed by the fusion of tpr and trk genes in human papillary thyroid carcinomas. *Oncogene* **7**, 237-242.

Grieco, M., Santoro, M., Berlingieri, M. T., Melillo, R. M., Donghi, R., Bongarzone, I., Pierotti, M. A., Della Porta, G., Fusco, A. and Vecchio, G. (1990). PTC is a novel rearranged form of the *ret* proto-oncogene and is frequently expressed *in vivo* in human papillary thyroid carcinomas. *Cell* **60**, 557-563.

Hanks, S. K., Quinn, A. M. and Hunter, T. (1988). The protein kinase family: conserved features and deduced phylogeny of the catalytic domain. *Science* **241**, 42-52.

Hofstra, R. M. W., Landsvater, R. M., Ceccherini, I., Stulp, R. P., Steelwagen, T., Luo, Y., Pasini, B., Hoppener, J. W. M., van Amstel, H. K. P., Romeo, G., Lips, C. J. M. and Buys, C. H. C. M. (1994). A mutation in the *RET* proto-oncogene asociated with multiple endocrine neoplasia type 2B and sporadic medullary thyroid carcinoma. *Nature* **367**, 375-376.

Inuzuka, H., Miyatani, S. and Takeichi, M. (1992). R-cadherin: a novel Ca^{2+}-dependent cell-cell adhesion molecule expressed in the retina. *Neuron* **7**, 69-79.

Ishizaka, Y., Tahira, T., Ochiai, M., Ikeda, I., Sugimura, T. and Nagao, M. (1988). Molecular cloning and characterisation of the human retII oncogene. *Oncogene Res.* **3**, 193-197.

Ishizaka, Y., Ochiai, M., Tahira, T., Ikeda, I., Sugimura, T. and Nagao, M. (1989). Activation of the retII oncogene without sequences encoding a transmembrane domain and transforming activity of two retII oncogene products differing in carboxy termini due to alternative splicing. *Oncogene* **4**, 789-794.

Koda, T. (1988). Ret gene from a human stomach cancer. *Hokaido J. Med. Sci.* **63**, 913-924.

Lairmore, T. C., Howe, J. R., Korte, J. A., Dilley, W. G., Aine, I., Aine, E., Wells, S. A. and Donis-Keller, H. (1991). Familial medullary thyroid carcinoma and multiple endocrine neoplasia type 2B map to the same region of chromosome 10 as multiple endocrine neoplasia type 2A. *Genomics* **9**, 181-192.

Lanzi, C., Borrello, M. G., Bongarzone, I., Migliazza, A., Fusco, A., Grieco, M., Santoro, M., Gambetta, R. A., Zunio, F., Della Porta, G. and Pierotti, M. (1992). Identification of the product of two oncogenic rearranged forms of the ret proto-oncogene in papillary thyroid carcinomas. *Oncogene* **7**, 2189-2194.

Lax I., Burgess, H. W., Bellot, F., Ullrich, A., Schlessinger, J. and Givol, D. (1988). Location of a major receptor-binding domain for epidermal growth factor by affinity labelling. *Mol. Cell. Biol.* **8**, 1831-1834.

Lax, I., Bellot, F., Howk, R., Ullrich, A., Givol, D. and Schlessinger, J. (1989). Functional analysis of the ligand binding site of EGF-receptor utilizing chimeric chicken/human receptor molecules. *EMBO J.* **8**, 421-427.

Leppert, M., Burt, R., Hughes, J. P., Samowitz, W., Nakamura, Y., Woodward, S., Gardner, E., Lalouel, J.-M. and White, R. (1990). Genetic analysis of an inherited predisposition to colon cancer in a family with variable number of adenomatous polyps. *New Eng. J. Med.* **322**, 904-908.

Luo, Y., Ceccherini, I., Pasini, B., Matera, I., Bicocchi, M. P., Barone, V., Bocciardi, R., Kaariaiainen, H., Weber, D., Devoto, M. and Romeo, G. (1993). Close linkage with the *RET* proto-oncogene and boundaries of deletion mutations in autosomal dominant Hirschsprung disease. *Hum. Mol. Genet.* **2**, 1803-1808.

Lyonnet, S., Bolino, A., Pelet, A., Abel, L., Nihoul-Fekete, C., Briard, M. L., Mok-Siu, V., Kaariainen, H., Martucciello, G., Lerone, M., Puliti, A., Luo, Y., Weissenbach, J., Devoto, M., Munnich, A. and Romeo, G. (1993). A gene for Hirschsprung disease maps to the proximal long arm of chromosome 10. *Nature Genet.* **4**, 346-350.

Martucciello, G., Bicocchi, M. P., Dodero, P., Lerone, M., Cirillo, M. S., Puliti, A., Gimelli, G., Romeo, G., Jasonni, V. (1992). Total colonic aganglionosis with interstitial deletion of the long arm of chromosome 10. *Pediatr. Surg. Intern.* **7**, 308-310.

Mathew, C. G. P., Chin, K. S., Easton, D. F., Thorpe, K., Carter, C., Liou, G. I., Fong, S.-L., Bridges, C. D. B., Haak, H., Nieuwenhuijzen Krusman, A. C., Schifter, S., Hansen, H. H., Telenius, H., Telenius-Berg, M. and Ponder, B. A. J. (1987). A linked genetic marker for multiple endocrine neoplasia type 2A on chromosome 10. *Nature* **328**, 527-528.

Mole, S. E., Mulligan, L. M., Healey, C. S., Ponder, B. A. J. and Tunnacliffe, A. (1993). Localisation of the gene for multiple endocrine neoplasia type 2A to a 480 kb region in chromosome band 10q11. 2. *Hum. Mol. Genet.* **2**, 247-252.

Moore, K. L. (1982). The branchial apparatus and the head and neck. In *The Developing Human*, 3rd edn, pp. 179-215. Philadelphia: W. B. Saunders Co.

Mulligan, L. M., Gardner, E., Smith, B. A., Mathew, C. G. P. and Ponder, B. A. J. (1993a). Genetic events in tumor initiation and progression in multiple endocrine neoplasia. *Genes Chrom. Cancer* **6**, 166-177.

Mulligan, L. M., Kwok, J. B. J., Healey, C. S., Elsdon, M. J., Eng, C., Gardner, E., Love, D. R., Mole, S. E., Moore, J. K., Papi, L., Ponder, M. A., Telenius, H., Tunnacliffe, A. and Ponder, B. A. J. (1993b). Germ-line mutations of the *RET* proto-oncogene in multiple endocrine neoplasia type 2A. *Nature* **363**, 458-460.

Mulligan, L. M., Eng, C., Healey, C. S., Clayton, D., Kwok, J. B. J., Gardner, E., Ponder, M. A., Frilling, A., Jackson, C. E., Lehnert, H., Neumann, H. P. H., Thibodeau, S. N. and Ponder, B. A. J. (1994a). Specific mutations of the RET proto-oncogene are related to disease phenotype in MEN 2A and FMTC. *Nature Genet* **6**, 70-74.

Mulligan, L. M., Eng, C., Healey, C. S., Ponder, M. A., Feldman, G. L., Li, P., Jackson, C. E. and Ponder, B. A. J. (1994b). A *de novo* mutation of the *RET* proto-oncogene in a patient with MEN 2A. *Hum. Mol. Genet.* **3**, 1007-1008.

Okamoto, E. and Ueda, T. (1967). Embryogenesis of intramural ganglia of the gut and its relation to Hirschsprung disease. *J. Pediatr. Surg.* **10**, 437-443.

Pachnis, V. E., Mankoo, B. and Costantini, F. (1993). Expression of the *c-ret* proto-oncogene during mouse embryogenesis. *Development* **119**, 1005-1017.

Pawson, T. and Schlessinger, J. (1993). SH2 and SH3 domains. *Curr. Biol.* **3**, 434-442.

Pazin, M. J. and Williams, L. T. (1992). Triggering signaling cascades by receptor tyrosine kinases. *Trends Biochem. Sci.* **17**, 374-378.

Ponder, B. A. J. (1985). Medullary thyroid carcinoma: screening the family of the apparently sporadic case. In *Familial Cancer* (ed. H. J. Muller and W. Weber), pp. 112-114. Basel: Karger.

Ponder, B. A. J., Ponder, M. A., Coffey, R., Pembrey, M., Gagel, R. F., Telenius-Berg, M., Semple, P. and Easton, D. F. (1988). Risk estimation

and screening in families of patients with medullary thyroid carcinoma. *Lancet* i, 397-400.

Pulido, D., Sonsoles, C., Koda, T., Modolell, J. and Barbacid, M. (1992). D*trk*, a *Drosophila* gene related to the *trk* family of neurotrophin receptors, encodes a novel class of neural cell adhesion molecule. *EMBO J.* **11**, 391-404.

Resh, M. D. (1993). Interaction of tyrosine kinase oncoproteins with cellular membranes. *Biochim. Biophys. Acta* **1155**, 307-322.

Rodrigues, G. A. and Park, M. (1993). Dimerization mediated through a leucine zipper activates the oncogenic potential of the *met* receptor tyrosine kinase. *Mol. Cell. Biol.* **13**, 6711-6722.

Romeo, G., Ronchetto, P., Luo, Y., Barone, V., Seri, M., Ceccherini, I., Pasini, B., Bocciardi, R., Lerone, M., Kaarlainen, H. and Martucceillo, G. (1994). Point mutations affecting the tyrosine kinase domain of the *RET* proto-oncogene in Hirschsprung's disease. *Nature* **367**, 377-378.

Roussel, M. F., Downing, J. R., Rettenmeir, C. W. and Sherr, C. J. (1988). A point mutation in the extracellular domain of the human CSF-1 receptor (*c-fms* proto-oncogene product) activates its transforming potential. *Cell* **55**, 979-988.

Santoro, M., Rosato, R., Grieco, M., Berlingieri, M. T., Luca-Colucci D'Amato, G., de Franciscis, V. and Fusco, A. (1990). The *ret* proto-oncogene is consistently expressed in human pheochromocytomas and thyroid medullary carcinomas. *Oncogene* **5**, 1595-1598.

Santoro, M., Wong, W. T., Aroca, P., Santos, E., Matoskova, B., Grieco, M., Fusco, A. and Di Fiore, P. P. (1994). An epidermal growth factor receptor/ret chimera generates mitogenic and trasforming signals: evidence for a *ret*-specific signaling pathway. *Mol. Cell. Biol.* **14**, 663-675.

Schimke, R. N., Hartmann, W. H., Prout, T. E. and Rimoin, D. L. (1968). Syndrome of bilateral pheochromocytoma, medullary thyroid carcinoma and multiple neuromas. *New Engl. J. Med.* **279**, 1-7.

Schimke, R. N. (1984). Genetic aspects of multiple endocrine neoplasia. *Annu. Rev. Med.* **35**, 25-31.

Schneider, R. (1992). The human protooncogene *ret*: a communicative cadherin? *Trends Biochem. Sci.* **17**, 468-469.

Schuchardt, A., D' Agati, V., Larsson-Blomberg, L., Costantini, F. and Pachnis, V. (1994). The *c-ret* receptor tyrosine kinase gene is required for the development of the kidney and the enteric nervous system. *Nature* **367**, 380-383.

Simpson, N. E., Kidd, K. K., Goodfellow, P. J., McDermid, H., Myers, S., Kidd, J. R., Jackson, C. E., Duncan, A. M. V., Farrer, L. A., Brasch, K., Castiglione, C., Genel, M., Gertner, J., Greenberg, C. R., Gusella, J. F., Holden, J. J. A. and White, B. N. (1987). Assignment of multiple endocrine neoplasia type 2A to chromosome 10 by linkage. *Nature* **328**, 528-530.

Spirio, L., Otterud, B., Stauffer, D., Lynch, H., Lynch, P., Watson, P., Lanspa, S., Smyrk, T., Cavalieri, J., Howard, L., Burt, R., White, R. and Leppert, M. (1992). Linkage of a variant or attenuated form of adenomatous polyposis coli to the adenomatous polyposis coli (APC) locus. *Am. J. Hum. Genet.* **51**, 92-100.

Tahira, T., Ishizaka, Y., Itoh, F., Sugimura, T. and Nagao, M. (1990). Characterization of ret proto-oncogene mRNA encoding two isoforms of the protein product in a human neuroblastoma cell line. *Oncogene* **5**, 97-102.

Takahashi, M., Ritz, J. and Cooper, G. M. (1985). Activation of a novel human transforming gene, ret, by DNA rearrangement. *Cell* **42**, 581-588.

Takahashi, M. and Cooper, G. M. (1987). *RET* fusion protein encodes a fusion protein homologous to tyrosine kinases. *Mol. Cell. Biol.* **7**, 1378-1385.

Takahashi, M., Buma, Y., Iwamoto, T., Inaguma, Y., Ikeda, H. and Hiai, H. (1988). Cloning and expression of the *ret* proto-oncogene encoding a receptor tyrosine kinase with two potential transmembrane domains. *Oncogene* **3**, 571-578.

Takahashi, M., Buma, Y. and Hiai, H. (1989). Isolation of ret proto-oncogene cDNA with an amino-terminal signal. *Oncogene* **4**, 805-806.

Takahashi, M., Buma, Y. and Taniguchi, M. (1991). Identification of ret proto-oncogene products in neuroblastoma and leukemia cells. *Oncogene* **6**, 297-301.

Takeichi, M. (1991). Cadherin cell adhesion receptors as a morphogenetic regulator. *Science* **251**, 1451-1455.

Verdy, M., Weber, A. M., Roy, C. C., Morin, C. L., Cadotte, M. and Brochu, P. (1982). Hirschsprung's disease in a family with multiple endocrine neoplasia type 2. *J. Pediatr. Gastroenterol. Nutr.* **1**, 603-607.

Weiner, D. B., Liu, J., Cohen, J. A., Williams, W. V. and Greene, M. I. (1989). A point mutation in the *neu* oncogene mimics ligand induction of receptor aggregation. *Nature* **339**, 230-231.

Xue, F., Yu, H., Maurer, L. H., Memoli, V. A., Nutile-McMenemy, N., Schuster, M. K., Bowden, D. W., Mao, J.-i. and Noll, W. W. (1994). Germline RET mutations in MEN 2A and FMTC and their detection by simple DNA diagnostic test. *Hum. Mol. Genet.* **3**, 635-638.

Journal of Cell Science, Supplement 18, 51-55 (1994)
Printed in Great Britain © The Company of Biologists Limited 1994

bcl-2 in cancer, development and apoptosis

David M. Hockenbery

Fred Hutchinson Cancer Research Center, Seattle, WA, USA

SUMMARY

The bcl-2 gene provides a window on the basic cellular machinery of apoptosis or programmed cell death, a process involved in virtually all biologic events in multicellular organisms, but particularly relevant to neoplasia and development. bcl-2 gene function supports cell survival and appears to lie at a nodal point in pathways leading to activation or execution of apoptosis. Carcinogenesis may involve several steps at which cell death programs are normally activated and are bypassed in cancer cells, including apoptotic pathways activated by several oncogenes. Functional redundancy and the complexity of the regulation of cell survival are demonstrated by the less than expected phenotype of bcl-2 knockout mice and the cloning of several bcl-2 related genes, some of which promote cell death. The molecular function for bcl-2 is unknown, but several lines of evidence support a role in protection from oxidative stress. These studies suggest that many environmental perturbations and genetic pathways converge to disrupt a metabolic balance between oxidant generation and anti-oxidant defenses.

Key words: oncogene, cell death, oxidative stress

INTRODUCTION

As has been the case for genes involved in cellular proliferation and activation, an important cellular gene controlling programmed cell death was discovered by a search for novel oncogenes. *bcl-2* was identified as an oncogene involved in the t(14;18) translocation that is characteristic of follicular lymphoma, a human B cell malignancy (Tsujimoto et al., 1984; Bakhshi et al., 1985; Cleary and Sklar, 1985). *bcl-2* on chromosome 18q and the immunoglobulin heavy chain gene locus on chromosome 14q are broken and rejoined in a balanced translocation, creating a chromosomal context in which transcriptional deregulation of *bcl-2* occurs.

Initial assays for cell transforming properties were disappointing and a potential role for *bcl-2* in oncogenesis was lacking until the experiments of Vaux et al. (1988) were reported. Introduction of *bcl-2* into an interleukin-3-(IL-3)-dependent cell line led, not to factor-independent growth, but to factor-independent survival. Subsequent experiments confirmed the ability of *bcl-2* to inhibit the expression of an apoptotic cell death program following factor withdrawal independent of cell cycle effects (Nunez et al., 1990; Hockenbery et al., 1990). The overexpression of a normal bcl-2 protein is the important oncogenic event in human follicular lymphoma and can be partially recreated in transgenic models. The generation of *bcl-2*-transgenic mice using the *bcl-2*-promoter and cDNA and immunoglobulin heavy chain enhancer demonstrated the consequences in the B cell lineage of deregulated cell survival (McDonnell et al., 1989). Dramatic polyclonal expansion of mature B lymphocytes precedes development of diffuse immunoblastic B cell lymphomas in the second year of life. A high proportion of these tumors have rearrangements of *c-myc* as a second genetic alteration (McDonnell and Korsmeyer, 1991).

Although several groups have reported similar results in the B cell lineage (Strasser et al., 1991b; Katsumata et al., 1992), oncogenic effects of bcl-2 in other cell types have not been as evident. Targeted overexpression of bcl-2 in thymic lymphocytes, mammary and intestinal epithelium, and myeloid populations has not produced tumors, although occasional T cell neoplasms have been reported in mice bearing immunoglobulin enhancer-*bcl-2* transgenes (Sentman et al., 1991; Lagasse and Weissman, 1993; D. M. Hockenbery, unpublished observations).

bcl-2 FUNCTION IN CANCER

One model for bcl-2 action in oncogenesis relies on the dual effects of proliferation and cell death in homeostatic regulation of cell populations, suggesting that abnormalities in both pathways may lead to clonal selection and neoplasia (Korsmeyer, 1992). Documentation of an extended lifespan of tumor cells is lacking in most cases, however, and is presumably not the case in tumors with a demonstrably high cell turnover, such as Burkitt's lymphoma. The requirement for a deregulated cell survival mechanism may be temporally restricted to the period of early acquisition of several genetic lesions, when the constraints of physiologic cell turnover may be a limiting factor on clonal evolution. B lymphocytes, which survive only several days in the peripheral circulation without antigenic stimulation, may be one lineage and differentiation stage with this requirement.

Another model would propose a more targeted role for bcl-2 in neoplasia in which bcl-2 is highly synergistic with specific cellular oncogenes. This concept follows the recognition that several oncogenes that function in cell activation and proliferation pathways have a paradoxical effect of promoting cell death by apoptosis. This tendency is unmasked by adverse growth conditions or blockade of cell proliferation. This connection between cell proliferation and apoptosis was originally demonstrated for c-myc, and has been shown to be relieved by overexpression of bcl-2 (Evan et al., 1992; Bissonnette et al., 1992; Fanidi et al., 1992). Tumorigenesis in cell lines and transgenic models is dramatically accelerated by co-expression of c-myc and bcl-2 (Strasser et al., 1990). Progression of human lymphoid tumors with deregulated c-myc and bcl-2 suggests that these observations hold true in naturally occurring tumors (Lee et al., 1989). Additional cellular oncogenes have been found that can predispose cells to undergo apoptosis, including c-rel and c-fos (Smeyne et al., 1993; Abbadie et al., 1993).

Deregulation of bcl-2 may also function as a survival mechanism in cancer cells predisposed to cell death by environmental factors. bcl-2 acts as a broad anti-apoptotic factor and opposes cell deaths following ionizing radiation, cancer drugs and hormonal manipulations (Sentman et al., 1991; Strasser et al., 1991a; Miyashita and Reed, 1993). Apoptosis may also be triggered by withdrawal of extracellular matrix interactions, suggesting that tumor growth pattern and metastasis may impose an apoptosis-inducing stress (see article by C. Streuli, this issue). Several non-lymphoid neoplasms, including prostate, lung, colon and breast express high levels of bcl-2, although a genetic alteration in *bcl-2* has not been demonstrated (McDonnell et al., 1992; Pezzella et al., 1993; Bronner et al., 1994; D. M. Hockenbery, unpublished observations).

bcl-2 FUNCTION IN DEVELOPMENT

The identification of an anti-apoptotic function of bcl-2 in cancer and in in vitro assays has produced much interest in the potential normal in vivo functions of this gene. Apoptotic cell deaths are abundant in developmental processes of many organisms (Sulston and Horvitz, 1977; Abrams et al., 1993). These appear to be essential events in higher organisms, leading to important morphogenetic changes such as loss of interdigital webs, and functional matching of cell populations in the nervous system, resulting in the death of up to 85% of neurons that are born (Cowan et al., 1984). bcl-2 is expressed in a limited number of tissues in the adult, including T and B lymphocytes, hemopoietic cells, epithelia, and neurons (Hockenbery et al., 1991). Predictions of a determinative role for bcl-2 in life or death decisions in vivo are best supported by study of germinal centres in lymphoid follicles. Germinal centres are sites with high rates of apoptotic cell death of B cells during humoral immune responses to T cell-dependent antigens (MacLennan and Gray, 1986). Cell death operates as a selective mechanism for expansion of B cell clones bearing high-affinity immunoglobulin antigen receptors. Diversity in immunoglobulin receptors is created by hypermutation of the rearranged immunoglobulin genes of one or two B cells that are recruited to the germinal centre, where expansion and hypermutation take place in the centroblastic zone. A need for survival cues becomes evident as these cells cease proliferating and accumulate in the centrocytic zone. Limiting amounts of cognate antigen are localized within the germinal centre on dendritic cells, provoking a competition for antigen-antigen receptor interactions won by B cells bearing mutated, high-affinity receptors. The evidence suggests that these cells are the survivors of germinal centre reactions, emigrating as memory B cells or plasma cells characteristic of the mature immune response. The remainder of B cells generated in the germinal centre succumb to apoptosis. The primary role of bcl-2 in this selection scheme is suggested by the vigorous regulation of bcl-2 expression that is observed. B lymphocytes that are recruited to the germinal centre and undergo expansion as centroblasts have down-regulated the abundant bcl-2 expression characteristic of circulating B cells to undetectable levels (Hockenbery et al., 1991; Pezzella et al., 1990). This remains true for the majority of centrocytes in the area of the germinal centre with high rates of apoptotic death, with the exception of rare single cells that stain positively for bcl-2.

In vitro study of centrocytes reveals the probable course of events. Germinal centre lymphocytes undergo an accelerated apoptotic death in vitro unless specific signals are present. These include immunoglobulin receptor stimulation and the co-stimulatory ligands anti-CD40 antibody or rCD23 protein plus interleukin-1 (Liu et al., 1991). These factors likely represent antigen-antibody binding in the context of cell-cell and cytokine-receptor interactions present in the germinal centre environment. bcl-2 protein, significantly, is induced by both sets of stimuli. Thus, in the germinal centre reaction, down-regulation of bcl-2 appears to set up an apoptotic reaction and is the target of positively-selecting stimuli to rescue cells from an apoptotic end. The apparent complexity of bcl-2 regulation in germinal centres is further increased by in situ RNA hybridization studies, which revealed abundant bcl-2 RNA throughout the germinal centre, suggesting a predominant post-transcriptional mechanism (Chleq-Deschamps et al., 1993).

bcl-2 is expressed more widely in the developing fetus, notably in many neuronal populations, the retina, and limb buds. The expression pattern of bcl-2 is, in some instances, inversely related to topographically-restricted sites of apoptotic death, such as interdigital webs (Veis et al., 1993).

FUNCTIONAL REDUNDANCY AND bcl-2-RELATED GENES

Transgenic mice with deletions of single genes by homologous recombination provide a stringent test for the essential function of genes during development. Two gene 'knockout' models of bcl-2 have been reported (Veis et al., 1993; Nakayama et al., 1993). Surprisingly, except for a slight growth retardation, development proceeds normally in these mice and normal births are reported with no excess mortality for mice with homozygously deleted bcl-2. Three tissue-specific phenotypes are evident post-natally. Lymphoid organs undergo massive involution by apoptosis within the first 2 months of life, although thymic and B cell maturation initially proceed normally. These mice undergo early deaths, probably more related to a polycystic kidney lesion apparent soon after birth. Finally, a pattern of progressive graying during the second hair follicle cycle develops, although hair pigmentation at birth is normal (Veis et al., 1993).

The results in mice with deleted bcl-2 suggests a level of functional redundancy for bcl-2, particularly during developmental stages. Recently, several genes homologous to bcl-2 have been cloned, which may explain models based on redundant gene function. Two genes, *bax* and *bcl-x*, encode proteins that lack one or more regions evolutionarily conserved in bcl-2 (Oltvai et al., 1993; Boise et al., 1993). Both of these, when co-expressed with bcl-2, produce inhibition of bcl-2 function in survival assays. bax was isolated by co-immuno-precipitation with bcl-2 and has been demonstrated to form het-erodimeric complexes with bcl-2 (Oltvai et al., 1993). The ratio of bcl-2 to bax protein within a cell appears to act as a 'rheostat' predicting cell survival following apoptotic triggers.

bcl-x, cloned by low-stringency hybridization of a cDNA library, produces alternatively-spliced mRNAs, one of which encodes an inhibitor of bcl-2 function, bcl-x$_S$, lacking 2 domains conserved in bcl-2. A larger protein, bcl-x$_L$, is encoded by a second mRNA and retains all conserved domains identified in bcl-2. This bcl-x product inhibits apoptotic death and appears to be functionally equivalent to bcl-2. bcl-x$_L$ and bcl-x$_S$ appear to be regulated independently and are expressed in different cell types. Additional bcl-2 family members, mcl-1 and A1, have recently been cloned from hematopoietic cells, but have not been functionally characterized (Kozopas et al., 1993; Lin et al., 1993). bcl-2 is part of a still larger family of homologous proteins, including cell death inhibitors found in the DNA viruses adenovirus, Epstein-Barr virus, African swine fever virus and herpesvirus saimiri (White, 1993; Cleary et al., 1986; Neilan et al., 1993; Albrecht et al., 1992). Sequence

homology is strongest in two short regions, BH1 and BH2 (Fig. 1). Homologous genes have also been found in mouse, chicken, rat and *Caenorhabditis elegans* (Negrini et al., 1987; Eguchi et al., 1992; Reed, 1994; Hengartner and Horvitz, 1994).

Knowledge of redundancy in bcl-2 function may help to explain one conundrum in the literature. Down-regulation of bcl-2 expression precedes cell death in many models and, if prevented in gene transfection experiments, cell death is impeded. These results suggest that some stimuli that induce apoptosis have bcl-2 down-regulation as their target. However, attempts to induce cell death by decreasing bcl-2 function, using anti-sense oligonucleotides or overexpression of an inhibitor such as bax, still require an apoptotic trigger (Oltvai et al., 1993; Reed et al., 1990). The intracellular changes produced by an apoptotic stimulus, such as serum deprivation, are therefore poorly understood. If more than a single bcl-2-like protein is expressed and involved in maintaining cellular viability, attempts to reproduce the events of serum deprivation by down-regulating one member of this family may be insufficient. It may only increase the apoptotic response to serum deprivation, if the effect of serum deprivation is to down-regulate all bcl-2-like proteins below some threshold level. This is, in fact, the sensitization response that is observed after bcl-2 down-regulation, including assays of cells from bcl-2 'knockout' mice.

Why are there multiple bcl-2 family members? One potential

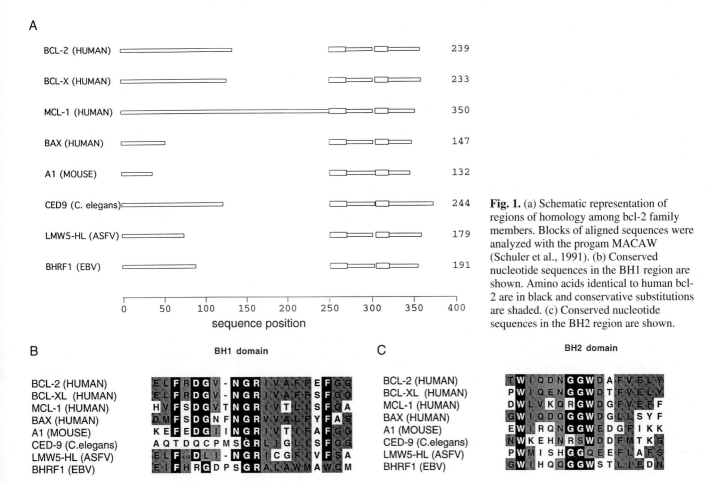

Fig. 1. (a) Schematic representation of regions of homology among bcl-2 family members. Blocks of aligned sequences were analyzed with the progam MACAW (Schuler et al., 1991). (b) Conserved nucleotide sequences in the BH1 region are shown. Amino acids identical to human bcl-2 are in black and conservative substitutions are shaded. (c) Conserved nucleotide sequences in the BH2 region are shown.

explanation is suggested by the pattern of bcl-2 expression within a cell lineage. Hemopoietic precursors of myeloid, erythroid and megakaryotic lineage express bcl-2, but more mature, post-mitotic progeny lack bcl-2. We have recently demonstrated that quiescent, pluripotent hemopoietic cells with 'stem cell' features also lack bcl-2. This pattern of bcl-2 expression within a limited number of differentiation or developmental stages of a lineage is seen in other cell types, such as complex epithelia. If some bcl-2-like proteins have non-overlapping distributions, perhaps each stage in a lineage of a cell will have a member(s) of this family of proteins actively maintaining cell viability. This would mean that cellular transitions would result in down-regulation of one bcl-2 family member and up-regulation of another. This might provide an efficient check on any cells that fail to execute normal developmental or differentiation programmes. These cells, which may fail to exit the cell cycle in G_0 or fail to express the correct receptor for a trophic factor, would automatically undergo apoptosis by losing expression of one family member and failing to induce another. A family of genes would increase the complexity of regulatory strategies that could be used in different lineages or stages of differentiation. This model would also suggest that in vitro models of apoptotic cell death after various exogenous treatments may be variations on a theme used in vivo, in which cell cycle arrest, DNA damage or factor-withdrawal could converge to down-regulate intracellular survival factors.

APOPTOTIC MECHANISMS AND bcl-2 FUNCTION

Mechanisms of apoptotic cell death must be closely linked to the function of bcl-2, since bcl-2 has been shown in experimental models to block almost all examples of apoptotic death. There is also room for those cell deaths not responsive to bcl-2 overexpression to remain part of the larger category of bcl-2-responsive deaths, if high levels of inhibitory proteins like bax are present.

The subcellular localization of bcl-2 may provide a clue to its function. bcl-2 has been found associated with mitochondria, nuclear membrane, and smooth endoplasmic reticulum (Hockenbery et al., 1990: Jacobson et al., 1993; Monaghan et al., 1992). These sites have in common an oxidation-reduction function that can result in oxygen-free radical generation. Several stimuli that can produce apoptosis are linked to oxidative stress, including ionizing radiation, tumor necrosis factor and phorbol esters.

To investigate the possibility that reactive oxygen species (ROS) play a wider role in apoptosis, we examined the model of interleukin-3 (IL-3)-withdrawal-induced cell death (Hockenbery et al., 1993). Pretreatment of IL-3-dependent FL5.12 cells with either N-acetylcysteine, a direct free radical scavenger that increases intracellular glutathione levels, or vitamin E, a chain-terminating antioxidant, gave partial protection from factor withdrawal-induced apoptosis. To achieve enhanced antioxidant effects, stable transfectants of FL5.12 cells were made with glutathione peroxidase or manganese superoxide dismutase (MnSOD) cDNAs and evaluated for response to factor withdrawal. While overexpression of MnSOD had no effect in this model, glutathoine peroxidase provided substantial protection. These results suggested that ROS participated in factor withdrawal-induced cell death. In view of the recognized effects of oxidative stress in gene induction and modification of protein function, a role in cell signaling or a more direct role in cell damage could be envisaged. The specificity for peroxides activity suggests that peroxidase are the relevant ROS involved in apoptosis.

A useful assay of ROS-mediated cellular damage is the analysis of lipid peroxidation. A fluorescent lipid analog, cis-parinaric acid (CPA) has been used as an indirect measure of lipid peroxidation in flow cytometric assays. CPA is distributed to all cellular membranes and remains stably fluorescent unless it is peroxidized, which involves a molecular rearrangement with loss of fluorescent properties. We examined the model of dexamethasone-induced apoptosis of a T cell hybridoma, 2B4 cells, for the advantage of a more synchronized apoptotic response. 2B4 cells that are bcl-2-transfected remained viable after dexamethasone treatment and showed no loss of CPA fluorescence. To the contrary, control 2B4 cells died by apoptosis and showed an early diminution of CPA fluorescence by 4 hours after dexamethasone that progressively increased during the incubation. An early marker of apoptotic cell death in this model, DNA fragmentation, occurred at 10-11 hours. This result suggests that early ROS-mediated cell damage occurs and increases during the time period when other cellular events in apoptosis take place. Finally, we asked if the effect of bcl-2 in preventing lipid peroxidation was at the level of ROS generation or at a downstream point. Menadione is a toxic vitamin K derivative that causes intracellular formation of superoxide radical by redox cycling. Cells treated with menadione undergo apoptosis, which is blocked by bcl-2 at lower menadione doses. Generation of superoxide radical can be measured by oxygen consumption in the presence of cyanide, an inhibitor of oxidative phosphorylation. bcl-2 protected cells demonstrated no change in the rate of superoxide production as measured in this assay, implying a downstream, antioxidant function for bcl-2. Further studies using a flow cytometric indicator of peroxide generation, dichlorofluorescein, confirmed that bcl-2 did not inhibit the generation of ROS. Interestingly, the effect of dexamethasone as a trigger of apoptotic death does not appear to be mediated by an increase in ROS generation. As pro-oxidant effects can be achieved by decreases in antioxidant levels, this mechanism may be operative in dexamethasone-induced apoptosis. If bcl-2 directly or indirectly acts as an antioxidant, the models of apoptosis in which bcl-2 down-regulation occurs might also fit this model.

Why would cells use oxidative damage as a general effector mechanism in programmed cell deaths? ROS have been shown to stimulate gene transcription, regulate transcription factors, and activate components of signal transduction pathways. As described for the role of nitric oxide as a second messenger, ROS may be tightly regulated within a cell to achieve desired physiologic effects and avoid pathologic effects. Global cellular programs, such as cell proliferation and differentiation, respond to changes in redox environment. If variations in ROS levels regulate some of these programs, a novel view of cellular oxidant/antioxidant balance as a labile, dynamic control element may be required. Exaggerated responses or prolonged down-regulation of balancing antioxidants could readily result in apoptotic cell death.

The author is a Lucille P. Markey Scholar and this work was supported by a grant from the Lucille P. Markey Charitable Trust.

REFERENCES

Abbadie, C., Kabrun, N., Bouali, F. et al. (1993). High levels of c-rel expression are associated with programmed cell death in the developing avian embryo and in bone marrow cells in vitro. *Cell* **75**, 899-912.

Abrams, J. M., White, K., Fessler, L. I. and Steller, H. (1993). Programmed cell death during *Drosophila* embryogenesis. *Development* **117**, 29-43.

Albrecht, J. C., Nicholas, J., Cameron, K. R., Newman, C., Fleckenstein, B. and Honess, R. W. (1992). Herpesvirus saimiri has a gene specifying a homologue of the cellular membrane glycoprotein CD59. *Virology* **190**, 527-530.

Bakhshi, A., Jensen, J. P., Goldman, P. et al. (1985). Cloning the chromosomal breakpoint of t(14;18) human lymphomas: clustering around J$_H$ on chromosome 14 and near a transcriptional unit on chromosome 18. *Cell* **41**, 899-906.

Bissonnette, R. P., Echeveri, F., Mahboubi, A. and Green, D. (1992). Apoptotic cell death induced by c-myc is inhibited by bcl-2. *Nature* **359**, 552-554.

Boise, L. H., Gonzalez-Garcia, M., Postema, C. E. et al. (1993). bcl-x, a bcl-2-related gene that functions as a dominant regulator of apoptotic cell death. *Cell* **74**, 597-608.

Bronner, M. P., Culin, C., Reed, J. and Furth, E. (1994). Bcl-2 protooncogene and the gastrointestinal mucosal epithelial tumor progression model. *Am. J. Pathol.* (in press).

Chleq-Deschamps, C. M., LeBrun, D. P., Huie, P. et al. (1993). Topographical dissociation of BCL-2 messenger RNA and protein expression in human lymphoid tissues. *Blood* **81**, 293-298.

Cleary, M. L. and Sklar, J. (1985). Nucleotide sequence of a t(14;18) chromosomal breakpoint in follicular lymphoma and demonstration of a breakpoint-cluster region near a transcriptionally active locus on chromosome 18. *Proc. Nat. Acad. Sci. USA* **82**, 7439-7443.

Cleary, M. L., Smith, S. D. and Sklar, J. (1986). Cloning and structural analysis of cDNAs for bcl-2 and a hybrid bcl-2/immunoglobulin transcript resulting from the t(14;18) translocation. *Cell* **47**, 19-28.

Cowan, W. M., Fawcett, J. W., O'Leary, D. D. M. and Stanfield, B. B. (1984). Regressive events in neurogenesis. *Science* **225**, 1258-1265.

Eguchi, Y., Ewart, D. L. and Tsujimoto, Y. (1992). Isolation and characterization of the chicken bcl-2 gene: expression in a variety of tissues including lymphoid and neuronal organs in adult and embryo. *Nucl. Acids Res.* **20**, 4187-4192.

Evan, G. I., Wyllie, A. H., Gilbert, C. S. et al. (1992). Induction of apoptosis in fibroblasts by c-myc protein. *Cell* **69**, 119-128.

Fanidi, A., Harrington, E. A. and Evan, G. (1992). Cooperative interaction between c-myc and bcl-2 proto-oncogenes. *Nature* **359**, 554-556.

Hengartner, M. O. and Horvitz, H. R. (1994). C. elegans cell survival gene ced-9 encodes a functional homolog of the mammalian proto-oncogene bcl-2. *Cell* **76**, 665-676.

Hockenbery, D., Nunez, G., Milliman, C., Schreiber, R. D. and Korsmeyer, S. J. (1990). Bcl-2 is an inner mitochondrial membrane protein that blocks programmed cell death. *Nature* **348**, 334-336.

Hockenbery, D. M., Zutter, M., Hickey, W., Nahm, M. and Korsmeyer, S. J. (1991). BCL2 protein is topographically restricted in tissues characterized by apoptotic death. *Proc. Nat. Acad. Sci. USA* **88**, 6961-6965.

Hockenbery, D. M., Oltvai, Z. N., Yin, X.-M. et al. (1993). Bcl-2 functions in an antioxidant pathway to prevent apoptosis. *Cell* **75**, 241-251.

Jacobsen, M. D., Burne, J. F., King, M. P. et al. (1993). Bcl-2 blocks apoptosis in cells lacking mitochondrial DNA. *Nature* **361**, 365-369.

Katsumata, M., Siegel, R. M., Louie, D. C. et al. (1992). Differential effects of Bcl-2 on T and B cells in transgenic mice. *Proc. Nat. Acad. Sci. USA* **89**, 11376-11380.

Korsmeyer, S. J. (1992). Bcl-2 initiates a new category of oncogenes: regulators of cell death. *Blood* **80**, 879-886.

Kozopas, K. M., Yang, T., Buchan, H. L., Zhou, P. and Craig, R. W. (1993). MCL1, a gene expressed in programmed myeloid differentiation, has sequence similarity to BCL2. *Proc. Nat. Acad. Sci. USA* **90**, 3516-3520.

Lagasse, E. and Weissman, I. L. (1993). bcl-2 inhibits apoptosis of neutrophils but not their engulfment by macrophages. *J. Exp. Med.* **179**, 1047-1052.

Lee, J. T., Innes, D. J. and Williams, M. E. (1989). Sequential bcl-2 and c-myc oncogene rearrangements associated with the clinical transformation of non-Hodgkin's lymphoma. *J. Clin. Invest.* **84**, 1454-1459.

Lin, E., Orlofsky, A., Berger, M. and Prystowsky, M. (1993). Characterization of A1, a novel hemopoietic-specific early-response gene with sequence similarity to bcl-2. *J. Immunol.* **151**, 1979-1988.

Liu, Y.-J., Mason, D. Y., Johnson, G. D. et al. (1991). Germinal center cells express bcl-2 protein after activation by signals which prevent their entry into apoptosis. *Eur. J. Immunol.* **21**, 1905-1910.

MacLennan, I. C. M. and Gray, D. (1986). Antigen-driven selection of virgin and memory B cells. *Immunol. Rev.* **91**, 61-65.

McDonnell, T. J., Deane, N., Platt, F. M. et al. (1989). bcl-2-immunoglobulin transgenic mice demonstrate extended B cell survival and follicular lymphoproliferation. *Cell* **57**, 79-88.

McDonnell, T. J. and Korsmeyer, S. J. (1991). Progression from lymphoid hyperplasia to high-grade malignant lymphoma in mice transgenic for the t(14;18). *Nature* **349**, 254-256.

McDonnell, T. J., Troncoso, P., Brisbay, S. M. et al. (1992). Expression of the protooncogene bcl-2 in the prostate and its association with emergence of androgen-independent prostate cancer. *Cancer Res.* **523**, 6940-6944.

Miyashita, T. and Reed, J. C. (1993). Bcl-2 oncoprotein blocks chemotherapy-induced apoptosis in a human leukemia cell line. *Blood* **81**, 151-157.

Monaghan, P., Robertson, D., Amos, T. A. S. et al. (1992). Ultrastructural localization of Bcl-2 protein. *J. Histochem. Cytochem.* **40**, 1819-1825.

Nakayama, K., Nakayama, K., Nagashi, I. et al. (1993). Disappearance of the lymphoid system in bcl-2 homozygous mutant chimeric mice. *Science* **261**, 1584-1588.

Negrini, M., Silini, E., Kozak, C., Tsujimoto, Y. and Croce, C. M. (1987). Molecular analysis of mbcl-2: structure and expression of the murine gene homologous to the human gene involved in follicular lymphomas. *Cell* **49**, 455-463.

Neilan, J., Lu, Z., Afonso, C., Kutish, G., Sussman, M. and Rock, D. (1993). An African swine fever virus gene with similarity to the proto-oncogene bcl-2 and the Epstein-Barr virus gene BHRF1. *J. Virol.* **67**, 4391-4394.

Nunez, G., London, L., Hockenbery, D., Alexander, M., McKearn, J. P. and Korsmeyer, S. J. (1990). Deregulated Bcl-2 gene expression selectively prolongs survival of growth-factor-deprived hemopoietic cell lines. *J. Immunol.* **144**, 3602-3610.

Oltvai, Z. N., Milliman, C. L. and Korsmeyer, S. J. (1993). Bcl-2 heterodimerizes in vivo with a conserved homolog, Bax, that accelerates programmed cell death. *Cell* **74**, 609-619.

Pezzella, F., Tse, A. G. D., Cordell, J. L., Pulford, K. A. F., Guter, K. C. and Mason, D. Y. (1990). Expression of the Bcl-2 oncogene protein is not specific for the 14;18 translocation. *Am. J. Pathol.* **137**, 225-232.

Pezzella, F., Turley, H., Kuzu, I. et al. (1993). bcl-2 protein in non-small-cell lung carcinoma. *New Eng. J. Med.* **329**, 690-694.

Reed, J. C., Cuddy, M., Haldar, S. et al. (1990). BCL2-mediated tumorigenicity of a human T-lymphoid cell line: synergy with MYC and inhibition by BCL2 antisense. *Proc. Nat. Acad. Sci. USA* **87**, 3600-3664.

Reed, J. C. (1994). Bcl-2 and the regulation of programmed cell death. *J. Cell Biol.* **124**, 1-6.

Schuler, G. C., Altschul, S. F. and Lipman, D. J. (1991). A workbench for multiple alignment construction and analysis. *Prot. Struct. Funct. Genet.* **9**, 180-190.

Sentman, C. L., Shutter, J. R., Hockenbery, D., Kanegawa, O. and Korsmeyer, S. J. (1991). bcl-2 inhibits multiple forms of apoptosis but not negative selection in thymocytes. *Cell* **67**, 879-888.

Smeyne, R. J., Vendrell, M., Hayward, M. et al. (1993). Continuous c-fos expression precedes programmed cell death *in vivo*. *Nature* **363**, 166-169.

Strasser, A., Harris, A. W., Bath, M. L. and Cory, S. (1990). Novel primitive lymphoid tumors induced in transgenic mice by cooperation between myc and bcl-2. *Nature* **348**, 331-333.

Strasser, A., Harris, A. W. and Cory, S. (1991a). bcl-2 transgene inhibits T cell death and perturbs thymic self-censorship. *Cell* **67**, 889-899.

Strasser, A., Whittingham, S., Vaux, D. L. et al. (1991b). Enforced BCL2 expression in B-lymphoid cells prolongs antibody responses and elicits autoimmune disease. *Proc. Nat. Acad. Sci. USA* **88**, 8661-8665.

Sulston, J. E. and Horvitz, H. R. (1977). Post-embryonic cell lineages of the nematode *Caenorhabditis elegans*. *Dev. Biol.* **56**, 110-156.

Tsujimoto, Y., Finger, L. R., Yunis, J., Nowell, P. C. and Croce, C. M. (1984). Cloning of the chromosome breakpoint of neoplastic B cells with the t(14;18) chromosome translocation. *Science* **226**, 1097-1099.

Vaux, D. L., Cory, S. and Adams, J. M. (1988). Bcl-2 gene promotes haemopoietic cell survival and cooperates with c-myc to immortalize pre-B cells. *Nature* **335**, 440-442.

Veis, D. J., Sorenson, C. M., Shutter, J. R. and Korsmeyer S. J. (1993). Bcl-2 deficient mice demonstrate fulminant lymphoid apoptosis, polycystic kidneys, and hypopigmented hair. *Cell* **75**. 241-251.

White, E. (1993). Death-defying acts: a meeting review on apoptosis. *Genes Dev.* **7**, 2277-2284.

Journal of Cell Science, Supplement 18, 57-61 (1994)
Printed in Great Britain © The Company of Biologists Limited 1994

Coupling of DNA replication and mitosis by fission yeast rad4/cut5

Yasushi Saka[1], Peter Fantes[2] and Mitsuhiro Yanagida[1]

[1]Department of Biophysics, Faculty of Science, Kyoto University, Sakyo-ku, Kyoto 606, Japan
[2]Institute of Cell and Molecular Biology, Darwin's Building, King's Buildings, University of Edinburgh, Edinburgh EH9 3JR, UK

SUMMARY

The fission yeast cut5+ (identical to rad4+) gene is essential for S phase. Its temperature-sensitive (ts) mutation causes mitosis while S phase is inhibited: dependence of mitosis upon the completion of S phase is abolished. If DNA is damaged in mutant cells, however, cell division is arrested. Thus the checkpoint control system for DNA damage is functional, while that for DNA synthesis inhibition is not in the cut5 mutants. Transcription of the cut5+ gene is not under the direct control of cdc10+, which encodes a transcription factor for the START of cell cycle. The transcript level does not change during the cell cycle. The protein product has four distinct domains and is enriched in the nucleus. Its level does not alter during the cell cycle. The N-domain is important for cut5 protein function: it is essential for complementation of ts cut5 mutations and its overexpression blocks cell division. Furthermore, it resembles the N-terminal repeat domain of proto-oncoprotein Ect2, which, in the C-domain, contains a regulator-like sequence for small G proteins. We discuss a hypothesis that the cut5 protein is an essential component of the checkpoint control system for the completion of DNA synthesis. The restraint of mitosis until the completion of S phase is mediated by the cut5 protein, which can sense the state of chromosome duplication and negatively interacts with M phase regulators such as cdc25 and cdc2.

Key words: checkpoint control, DNA damage repair, DNA replication, mitosis, oncogene

INTRODUCTION

In the normal vegetative cycle cells increases in size before division. In early embryos, however, cells divide without this size increase step, and a large number of cells of reduced sizes are produced. In another situation, cell size greatly increases without cell division, and a giant cell is formed with numerous nuclei. In any of these three types of cell division, DNA replication and mitosis (nuclear division) have to be coordinated, otherwise cells lacking a nucleus or having a polyploid nucleus would be produced. Events leading from DNA replication to mitosis and from mitosis to DNA replication thus must be precisely regulated. Replication of chromosome DNA in S phase is followed by the G_2 phase. Then, cells enter M phase with chromosome condensation, spindle apparatus formation and sister chromatid separation. All of these mitotic events precede cell division.

We have employed the fission yeast *Schizosaccharomyces pombe* as a model organism to study the cell division cycle. Under a vegetative condition, this yeast has a long G_2 phase, which occupies two-thirds of the entire cell cycle period, whereas the G_1 phase is very short. Cell size increases twice during G_2. Under limited nitrogen source, haploid heterothalic cells cease to divide and remain in a state with a 1C DNA content. If they can conjugate with other cells of the opposite mating type, zygotic cells are formed and then enter meiosis.

Fission yeast mutations called *cut* (*c*ell *u*ntimely *t*orn; Hirano et al., 1986; Samejima et al., 1993) disrupt coordination between M phase and cytokinesis; cell division takes place

in the absence of normal nuclear division. There are approximately twenty *cut+* genes known; in this article, we discuss the role of the *cut5+* gene in the cell division cycle. The reason for our interest in this particular gene is that the *cut5* mutation abolishes the dependence between the S and M phases (Saka and Yanagida, 1993). DNA synthesis is defective while nuclear and cell division take place in the *cut5* mutant (Fig. 1). DNA synthesis is not inhibited in most other *cut* mutants, which makes the phenotype of the *cut5* mutation unique. Furthermore, *cut5* mutations are radiation (UV and X-ray)-sensitive at the permissive temperature. Results of gene cloning indicated that the *cut5+* gene is identical to *rad4+*, which was previously cloned and sequenced by Fenech et al. (1991). The role of the *cut5+* gene thus seemed intriguing, as it is implicated in DNA replication/repair and in the restraint of mitosis/cytokinesis.

UNCOUPLING OF THE S AND M PHASES IN *cut5* MUTANTS

How can M phase be uncoupled from S phase in the *cut5* mutant ? A system similar to the checkpoint control (Weinert and Hartwell, 1988) originally described for DNA damage recovery may not be functional in this mutant. The checkpoint control system would operate to monitor the progression from S phase to M phase. If S phase is blocked, subsequent M phase does not take place. This negative feedback control (Murray, 1992) becomes evident in DNA replication mutants or wild-

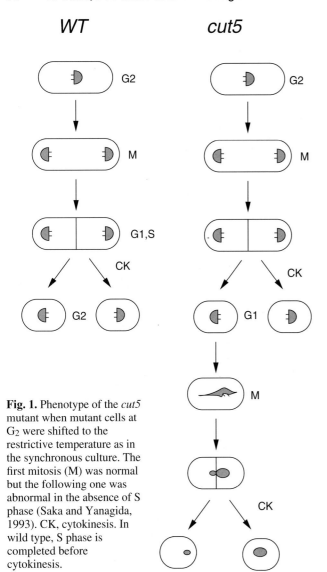

Fig. 1. Phenotype of the *cut5* mutant when mutant cells at G$_2$ were shifted to the restrictive temperature as in the synchronous culture. The first mitosis (M) was normal but the following one was abnormal in the absence of S phase (Saka and Yanagida, 1993). CK, cytokinesis. In wild type, S phase is completed before cytokinesis.

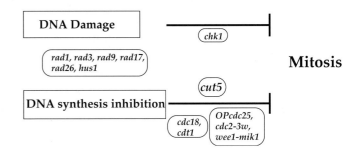

Fig. 2. Checkpoint control systems for DNA damage and DNA synthesis inhibition. Some mutations like *rad1*, *rad3*, *rad9*, *rad17*, *rad26*, *hus1* cause defects in both types of checkpoints (see Sheldrick and Carr, 1993). Mutation in *chk1* (*rad27*) affects only the damage checkpoint, while *cdc2-3w*, overexpression of *cdc25$^+$* (OP cdc25) and *wee1-mik1* mutations disrupt the replication checkpoint. The *cdc18$^+$* and *cdt1$^+$* genes are potential components for the replication checkpoint. The *cut5$^+$* is shown to be required for the progression of DNA replication and the essential component for the replication checkpoint (Saka et al., 1994).

type cells inhibited by hydroxyurea (HU), an inhibitor of DNA synthesis. In *cut5* mutants this monitoring system for the completion of S phase might be disrupted (Fig. 2). Not only mitosis but also cell division takes place at 36°C in the mutants in the absence of S phase (Saka and Yanagida, 1993). The *cut5$^+$* gene product could thus be considered to act as one component of such a checkpoint control system. Alternatively, the *cut5$^+$* gene is required only for the progression of S phase, and its loss may not be detected by the checkpoint system, which allows uncoupled mitotic events to take place.

GENES IMPLICATED IN NEGATIVE REGULATION OF MITOTIC ENTRY BEFORE THE COMPLETION OF S PHASE

Phenotypes strongly similar to those of ts *cut5* mutants were recently reported for null mutants of the fission yeast *cdc18$^+$* and *cdt1$^+$* genes, both of which are essential for cell viability (Kelly et al., 1993; Hofmann and Beach, 1994). The null mutants in these genes are defective in DNA replication and

cause mitotic events. Temperature-sensitive *cdc18* mutant cells are arrested with 2C DNA contents, but the null mutant cells fail to synthesize DNA (Kelly et al., 1993). The *cdt1$^+$* gene was isolated by an immunoprecipitation-PCR (polymerase chain reaction) cycle used to isolate physically the genomic DNA sequences that are bound to the *cdc10$^+$* gene product, a transcription factor for START (Hofmann and Beach, 1994).

Characteristically, expression of the *cdc18$^+$* and *cdt1$^+$* genes is cell cycle-regulated in a manner dependent on the *cdc10$^+$* gene (Fig. 3). Transcripts of these genes peak during S phase. The 5′ upstream region of the genes contained the *Mlu*I motifs known to be the binding site for the transcription complex in which the cdc10 protein is a component (Lowndes et al., 1992). Furthermore, ectopic expression of the *cdc18$^+$* or *cdt1$^+$* gene can complement a ts mutation of *cdc10* at restrictive or semi-permissive temperature. The products of the *cdc18$^+$* and *cdt1$^+$* genes were thought to be the major downstream targets of the *cdc10$^+$* gene. The product of *cdc18$^+$* is similar to that of the budding yeast *CDC6* gene (Bueno and Russell, 1992). The *CDC6* gene was postulated to play a dual role by positively regulating DNA synthesis and negatively regulating M phase, consistent with the results obtained from study on the fission yeast *cdc18$^+$* gene (Kelly et al., 1993). The amino acid sequences of the *cdt1$^+$* genes do not resemble any known protein. The roles of these gene products in DNA replication are largely unknown. They are putative components of the checkpoint control that prevents mitosis from occurring until S phase is completed.

Other fission yeast mutations such as rad1 are known, which abolish normal dependency between the S and M phases when DNA is damaged or cell cycle progression is blocked before the completion of DNA synthesis (Fig. 2; Enoch et al., 1992; Sheldrick and Carr, 1993). However, the above identified genes have not been shown to be essential for DNA replication, unlike the *cut5$^+$*, *cdc18$^+$* and *cdt1$^+$* genes. Studies by

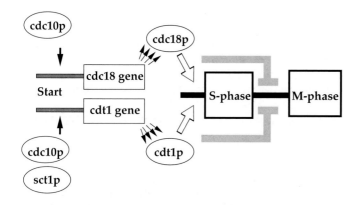

Fig. 3. Two genes *cdc18+* and *cdt1+* are essential for viability. Their mutations cause mitosis while replication is blocked. Expression of these two genes is under the direct transcriptional control of the START gene *cdc10+* (indicated by small arrows). These gene products (cdc18p and cdt1p) are required for S phase (indicated by large arrows) and restrain mitosis until the completion of S phase (Kelly et al., 1993; Hofmann and Beach, 1994).

fusion experiments and microinjection have led to the proposal that in mammalian cells, dose-dependent inhibitors of mitosis are present in G₁ and S phase cells.

One of our main questions about the nature of the *cut5+* gene product has been whether it may operate in the same or a similar pathway as that of *cdc18+* and *cdt1+*. If so, one question to be addressed is how these gene products interact.

DNA SYNTHESIS DEFECT AND MITOTIC PHENOTYPES OF *cut5* MUTANTS

Temperature-sensitive (ts) *cut5* mutants display at the restrictive temperature (36°C) the chromosomes pulled with the extended mitotic spindle in the absence of DNA replication (Fig. 1; Saka and Yanagida, 1993). By FACS (fluorescence activated cell scanning) analysis, the amount of DNA was shown to be approximately 1C after 3 hours at 36°C. Cells did not die in the absence of DNA replication, but subsequent mitotic events were lethal. As a large fraction of *cut5* mutant cells exponentially grown at 26°C were in the G₂ phase, the transfer of those cells to 36°C caused two or three rounds of cell division, the first (with 2C DNA) was normal and the second (with 1C DNA) mostly lethal. Cells containing less than 1C DNA were produced by successive aberrant cell divisions. When cells containing 1C DNA in the nitrogen-deprived medium were released at 36°C in the complete medium, DNA synthesis was blocked in the first cell cycle and mitosis and cell division followed. The synchronous culture analysis of *cut5* cells at 36°C showed that mitotic events occurred prematurely in the absence of S phase; the interval required for cell division was only 80 minutes, much shorter than the normal generation time (120 minutes at 36°C). These results clearly demonstrated that the restraint for mitosis and cell division was lost in *cut5* mutants if DNA synthesis did not occur.

The effect of HU on *cut5* mutants supported the above conclusion. Cell division accompanying the *cut* phenotype took place when *cut5* mutant cells were incubated in the presence of HU at 36°C (Saka et al., 1994). When mutant cells were first arrested in S phase by the addition of HU at 26°C and then shifted to 36°C, cell division still occurred. As the checkpoint control system was activated at 26°C by the addition of HU, the cell division phenotype suggested that the cut5 protein was a part of the replication checkpoint system.

Chromosomal DNAs in *cut5* mutant cells at 36°C were not like those of wild-type cells (Saka et al., 1994). Pulsed field gel (PFG) electrophoresis showed that the usual wild-type PFG chromosomal DNA bands were not present in DNA from *cut5* mutants that had been incubated at 36°C for 3 hours, indicating that none of the three chromosomal DNAs entered the gel. The three bands were obtained, however, from a *cdc10-cut5* mutant. Chromosomal DNA bands in *cdc18* mutant cells also showed the reduced efficiency of larger chromosomes I and II to enter the gel (Kelly et al., 1993). The PFG bands of cells treated with HU are unable to enter the agarose gel (Hennessy et al., 1991). Although the precise nature of the chromosomal DNAs accumulated in *cut5* mutant cells is unknown, replication was initiated to some degree. The *cut5* phenotypic expression was altered by the presence or the absence of *cdc10+*.

CELL DIVISION BLOCK PRODUCED BY UV IRRADIATION

Gene cloning of the *cut5+* gene indicated that it was identical to the *rad4+* gene previously reported by Fenech et al. (1991). The *rad4+* gene is one of many *rad+* genes identified in fission yeast and is known to be required for the repair of X-ray- and UV-damaged DNA. The *rad4* mutant is exceptional among *rad* mutants isolated, as it displays the ts lethal phenotype (Duck et al., 1976); it is sensitive to X-ray and UV at the permissive temperature. Consistent with this, *cut5* mutants are sensitive to UV and X-rays at the permissive temperature (Saka and Yanagida, 1993). The *rad4+* gene, however, has not been classified as one of the checkpoint genes for DNA damage recovery (Al-Khodairy et al., 1992; Rowley et al., 1992). Cell cycle is delayed if *rad4* cells are irradiated at 26°C.

We examined whether cell division of the *cut5* mutant at 36°C was blocked if mutant cells were irradiated with UV (Saka et al., 1994), and clearly found that it was severely inhibited by moderate doses of UV radiation. Using 4-nitroquinoline oxide (4NQO), which also causes DNA damage, we found that a concentration as low as 1 µg/ml also blocked cell division of the *cut5* mutant. These results strongly suggest that the checkpoint system for DNA damage is functional in *cut5* mutant cells at 36°C.

Fission yeast DNA repair mutants such as *rad1* lose checkpoint control for both DNA synthesis and damage (Al-Khodairy et al., 1992). However, the *chk1* mutant is defective only in the DNA damage checkpoint (Walworth et al., 1993) while *cdc2-3w*, overproduced *cdc25+* and *wee1-mik1* mutants are impaired only in the monitoring of the completion of DNA synthesis (Fig. 1; Enoch and Nurse, 1990, 1991; Lundgren et al., 1991). Thus the loss of checkpoint control in *cut5* mutants parallels the case of these mutations. The *cut5+* gene may form a link for DNA replication with these cell cycle regulators.

LEVELS OF cut5 TRANSCRIPT AND PROTEIN DURING THE CELL CYCLE

To examine the functional similarity between $cut5^+$, $cdc18^+$ and $cdt1^+$ proteins, it was essential to learn whether the expression of $cut5^+$ is cell cycle-regulated in a $cdc10$-dependent manner. Wild-type synchronous culture was performed, and RNAs were prepared for northern blot probed with the $cut5^+$ gene (Saka et al., 1994). There was no significant change in the level of transcript during the cell cycle, in contrast to the transcript of the $cdc22^+$ gene, which peaked during S phase (Gordon and Fantes, 1986). Then RNAs were prepared from extracts of cells including $cdc10$ mutants cultured at 36°C for 0-6 hours. No change in the level of transcript was found in $cdc10$ mutant RNAs (Saka et al., 1994); instead, an increase in the transcript level was found in mitotically arrested cells ($nda3$-311 and $nuc2$-663). These results established that transcription of the $cut5^+$ gene is neither cell cycle regulated nor directly controlled by the $cdc10^+$ gene. The function of the $cut5^+$ gene may not be in the same pathway as $cdc18^+$ and $cdt1^+$.

THE PRODUCT OF THE cut5⁺ GENE IS SIMILAR TO AN ONCOPROTEIN

The $cut5^+$ gene encodes a putative 74 kDa (designated p74) polypeptide (Fenech et al., 1991; Saka and Yanagida, 1993; Lehmann, 1993). Close sequence alignment indicates that the protein product consists of four distinct domains: two repetitive domains and two hydrophilic domains (Fig. 4). Its N-terminal to the central domain resembles human XRCC1, which is implicated in DNA damage repair (Thompson et al., 1990). We found that the NH_2-domain of a proto-oncogene product Ect2 (Miki et al., 1993) is similar to that of the cut5 protein (Saka et al., 1994). Ect2 contains a sequence similar to the regulator for small G proteins in the COOH domain. The NH_2-domain seems to act negatively, and the gene truncating the NH_2-region causes a striking increase in transformation efficiency. Consistently, the NH_2-domain of the cut5 protein also blocks cell division (Saka et al., 1994). Cells are arrested in G_2 without cell elongation.

The cut5 protein was identified by immunoblot using antibodies against the fusion protein. Although p74 was identified in cell extracts, several cleaved protein products were detected (Saka et al., 1994). The cleavage seemed to take place in the boundaries of different domains.

Immunofluorescence microscopy established that the protein product is enriched in the nucleus. The cut5 protein may be bound to chromatin or directly bound to DNA. The localization pattern is similar to that of type I phosphatase dis2 and DNA topoisomerase II (Ohkura et al., 1989; Shiozaki and Yanagida, 1992). No change in localization was recognized during the cell division cycle. Consistently, the level of protein in the synchronous culture quantified by immunoblot was kept constant during the cell cycle (Saka et al., 1994).

REGULATION OF THE cut5 PROTEIN DURING THE CELL CYCLE

cut5 protein function is quite intriguing: it appears to play a positive role in replication/repair and a negative one in mitosis and cytokinesis. We previously proposed that the cut5 protein might have altered its function in different stages of the cell cycle and mark single and twin chromatids differently (Saka and Yanagida, 1993). The single chromatid marked with cut5 is accessible for DNA synthesis and delays mitosis. The duplicated twin chromatids marked differently by cut5 have lost the ability to restrain the onset of M phase and are amenable to mitosis and cytokinesis. The cut5 protein may sense the state of chromosomes (either single or duplicated chromatids) and can send the signal to the mitotic regulators. To investigate the possible regulation of the cut5 protein during the cell cycle, it is critical to identify and determine the function of a protein(s) with which it interacts.

No significant cell cycle change has been found in the levels of transcript and protein product. If the cut5 protein is regulated during the cell cycle, it might be at the level of post-translation such as protein phosphorylation. It remains to be examined whether the cut5 protein is phosphorylated. The protein product is cleaved but no cell cycle change has been found in the cleavage patterns.

As an initial attempt to identify genes that may interact with $cut5^+$, crosses were made with known mutants defective in the cell division cycle, and the double mutant phenotypes were examined (Saka et al., 1994). Temperature-sensitive double mutants $cdc25$-$cut5$, $cdc2$-$cut5$ and $cdc13$-$cut5$ showed the cdc phenotype (cell elongation and single nucleus) but most other double mutants were $cut5$-like (the cut phenotype) at restrictive temperature. This indicated that cdc25, cdc13 (cyclin B) and cdc2 proteins are required for the mitotic phenotype when the cut5 protein is inactivated. One of these cell cycle regulator proteins may be negatively regulated by the cut5 protein before the completion of S phase. A likely candidate is cdc25 or cdc2, as their mutations ($OPcdc25$ and $cdc2$-$3w$; Enoch and Nurse, 1990 and 1991) abolished the dependence of mitosis on DNA replication. Alternatively, wee1 and mik1 kinases, which inhibit entry into mitosis might be positively regulated by the cut5 protein. These mitotic regulators may be the receivers of

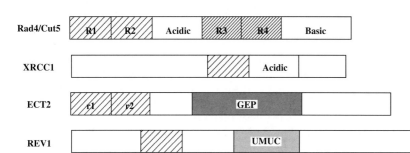

Fig. 4. cut5 consists of four domains: two repetitive (dashed lines) and two hydrophilic (acidic and basic) domains. The N-terminal domain partly resembles the human DNA repair protein XRCC1, proto-oncogene product Ect2 and the budding yeast DNA repair protein Rev1. Similar regions are indicated by the boxes with slashed lines. See text for details.

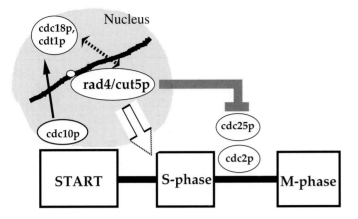

Fig. 5. Hypothetical pathway of the cut5-dependent replication checkpoint. See text for details.

the signal sent from the cut5 protein, which can distinguish the single and twin chromatids.

We found another exceptional double mutant, which did not show the *cut* phenotype at restrictive temperature: *cut5* and *ppe1* deleted cells were viable at 36°C, producing colonies (our unpublished result). The *ppe1⁺* gene encodes a serine/threonine protein phosphatase (Shimanuki et al., 1993) alternatively called esp1 (Matsumoto and Beach, 1993). The single *ppe1* deletion mutant is cold-sensitive (cs), sterile and pear-shaped (Shimanuki et al., 1993; Matsumoto et al., 1993). Interestingly, the deletion of *ppe1⁺* not only rescues the ts phenotype of *cut5* but also that of the *pim1* mutant (Matsumoto and Beach, 1993). The *pim1⁺* gene product is similar to the human RCC1 protein, which is also related to the coupling of M phase and S phase (Matsumoto and Beach, 1991).

One possible hypothesis is that cut5 is an essential component, forming the checkpoint for coupling of the S and M phases. It is not known how ppe1 phosphatase is implicated in this checkpoint. The cut5 protein function may be regulated directly or indirectly by ppe1 phosphatase. The cut5 protein is a nuclear protein, possibly a chromatin protein, and its activity, directly or indirectly regulated by the states of the chromosome, is essential for the progression of DNA synthesis. When replication is completed, the M phase regulator is activated possibly as a result of the inactivation of the cut5 protein.

This work was supported by a grant (Specially Promoted Research) from the Ministry of Education, Science and Culture of Japan. P.F. was supported by a visiting professorship from the British Council and the Ministry of Education, Science and Culture of Japan.

REFERENCES

Al-Khodairy, F. and Carr, A. M. (1992.). DNA repair mutants defining G₂ checkpoint pathways in *Schizosaccharomyces pombe*. *EMBO J.* **11**, 1343-1350.

Bueno, A. and Russell, P. (1992). Dual functions of CDC6: a yeast protein required for DNA replication also inhibits nuclear division. *EMBO J.* **6**, 2167-2176.

Duck, P., Nasim, A. and James, A. P. (1976). Temperature-sensitive mutant of *Schizosaccharomyces pombe* exhibiting enhanced radiation sensitivity. *J. Bacteriol.* **128**, 536-539.

Enoch, T. and Nurse, P. (1990). Mutation of fission yeast cell cycle control genes abolishes dependence of mitosis on DNA replication. *Cell* **60**, 665-673.

Enoch, T. and Nurse, P. (1991). Coupling M phase and S phase: Control maintaining the dependence of mitosis on chromosome replication. *Cell* **65**, 921-923.

Enoch, T., Carr, T. and Nurse, P. (1992). Fission yeast genes involved in coupling mitosis to completion of DNA replication. *Genes Dev.* **6**, 2035-2046.

Fenech, M., Carr, A. M., Murray, J., Watts, F. Z. and Lehmann, A. R. (1991). Cloning and characterization of the *rad4* gene of *Schizosaccharomyces pombe*; a gene showing short regions of sequence similarity to the human *XRCC1* gene. *Nucl. Acids Res.* **19**, 6737-6741.

Gordon, C. B. and Fantes, P. (1986). The *cdc22* gene of *Schizosaccharomyces pombe* encodes a cell cycle regulated transcript. *EMBO J.* **5**, 2981-2985.

Hennessy, K. M., Lee, A., Chen, E. and Botstein, D. (1991). A group of interacting yeast DNA replication genes. *Genes Dev.* **5**, 958-969.

Hirano, T., Funahashi, S., Uemura, T. and Yanagida, M. (1986). Isolation and characterization of *Schizosaccharomyces pombe* cut mutants that block nuclear division but not cytokinesis. *EMBO J.* **5**, 2973-2979.

Hofmann, J. F. X. and Beach, D. (1994). cdt1 is an essential target of the Cdc10/Sct1 transcription factor: requirement for DNA replication and inhibition of mitosis. *EMBO J.* **13**, 425-434.

Kelly, T. J., Martin, S., Forsburg, S. L., Stephen, R. J., Ausso, A. and Nurse, P. (1993). The fission yeast *cdc18⁺* gene product couples S phase to start and mitosis. *Cell* **74**, 371-382.

Lehmann, A. R. (1993). Duplicated region of sequence similarity to the human *XRCC1* DNA repair gene in the *Schizosaccharomyces pombe* rad4/cut5 gene. *Nucl. Acids Res.* **21**, 5274.

Lowndes, N. F., McInerny, C. J., Johnson, A. L., Fantes, P. A. and Johnston, L. H. (1992). Control of DNA synthesis genes in fission yeast by the cell-cycle gene *cdc10⁺*. *Nature* **355**, 449-453.

Lundgren, K., Walworth, N., Booher, R., Dembski, M., Kirschner, M. and Beach, D. (1991). mik1 and wee1 cooperate in the inhibitory tyrosine phosphorylation of cdc2. *Cell* **64**, 1111-1122.

Matsumoto, T. and Beach, D. (1991). Premature initiation of mitosis in yeast lacking RCC1 or an interacting GTPase. *Cell* **66**, 347-360.

Matsumoto, T. and Beach, D. (1993). Interaction of the pim1/spi1 mitotic checkpoint with a protein phosphatase. *Mol. Biol. Cell* **4**, 337-345.

Miki, T., Smith, C. L., Long, J. E., Eva, A. and Fleming, T. P. (1993). Oncogene ect2 is related to regulators of small GTP-binding protein. *Nature* **362**, 462-465.

Murray, A. W. (1992). Creative blocks: cell cycle checkpoints and feedback controls. *Nature* **359**, 599-604.

Nurse, P. (1990). Universal control mechanism regulating onset of M phase. *Nature* **344**, 503-508.

Ohkura, H., Kinoshita, N., Miyatani, S., Toda, T. and Yanagida, M. (1989). The fission yeast *dis2⁺* gene required for chromosome disjoining encodes one of two putative type 1 protein phosphatases. *Cell* **57**, 997-1007.

Rowley, R., Subramini, S. and Young, P. G. (1992). Checkpoint controls in *Schizosaccharomyces pombe: rad1*. *EMBO J.* **11**, 1335-1342.

Saka, Y. and Yanagida, M. (1993). Fission yeast *cut5⁺* gene required for the onset of S phase and the restraint of M phase is identical to the radiation-damage repair gene *rad4⁺*. *Cell* **74**, 383-393.

Saka, Y., Fantes, P., Sutani, T., McInerny, C., Creanor, J. and Yanagida, M. (1994). Fission yeast cut5 links nuclear chromatin and M-phase regulator in the replication checkpoint control. *EMBO J.* (in press).

Samejima, I., Matsumoto, T., Nakaseko, Y., Beach, D. and Yanagida, M. (1993). Identification of seven new cut genes involved in *Schizosaccharomyces pombe* mitosis. *J. Cell Sci.* **105**, 135-143.

Sheldrick, K. S. and Carr, A. M. (1993). Feedback controls and G₂ checkpoints: Fission yeast as a model system. *BioEssays* **15**, 775-782.

Shimanuki, M., Kinoshita, N., Ohkura, H., Yoshida, T., Toda, T. and Yanagida, M. (1993). Isolation and characterization of the fission yeast protein phosphatase gene *ppe1⁺* involved in cell shape control and mitosis. *Mol. Biol. Cell* **4**, 303-313.

Shiozaki, K. and Yanagida, M. (1992). Functional dissection of the phosphorylated termini of fission yeast DNA topoisomerase II. *J. Cell Biol.* **119**, 1023-1036.

Thompson, L. H., Brookman, K. W., Jones, J. J., Allen, S. A. and Carrano, A. V. (1990). Molecular cloning of the human XRCC1 gene, which corrects defective DNA strands repair and sister chromatid exchange. *Mol. Cell. Biol.* **10**, 6160-6171.

Walworth, N., Davey, S. and Beach, D. (1993). Fission yeast chk1 protein kinase links rad checkpoint pathway to cdc2. *Nature* **363**, 368-371.

Weinert, T. A. and Hartwell, L. H. (1988). The RAD9 gene controls the cell cycle response to DNA damage in *Saccharomyces cerevisiae*. *Science* **241**, 317-322.

Journal of Cell Science, Supplement 18, 63-68 (1994)
Printed in Great Britain © The Company of Biologists Limited 1994

Regulation of the cell cycle timing of Start in fission yeast by the *rum1⁺* gene

Sergio Moreno[1,*], Karim Labib[1], Jaime Correa[2] and Paul Nurse[2]

[1]Instituto de Microbiología Bioquímica, CSIC/Universidad de Salamanca, Edificio Departamental, Campus Miguel de Unamuno, 37007 Salamanca, Spain
[2]ICRF Cell Cycle Group, Lincoln's Inn Fields, London WC2A 3PX, UK

*Author for correspondence

SUMMARY

We have identified the *rum1⁺* gene as a new regulator of the G_1-phase of the fission yeast cell cycle. *rum1⁺* determines the cell cycle timing of Start, by maintaining cells in a pre-Start state until they have attained a minimal critical mass. Cells lacking *rum1⁺* are unable to arrest in pre-Start G_1 in response to nitrogen starvation and are subsequently sterile. In addition, *rum1⁺* prevents entry into mitosis from pre-Start G_1, as shown by the fact that *cdc10* mutants in the absence of *rum1⁺* undergo lethal mitosis without entering S-phase.

Key words: *rum1⁺*, Start, cell cycle, *Schizosaccharomyces pombe*

INTRODUCTION

Progression from the G_1-phase of the cell cycle to the onset of chromosomal DNA replication requires a process of cell cycle commitment in a wide variety of eukaryotes from yeast to humans. In the yeasts *Saccharomyces cerevisiae* and *Schizosaccharomyces pombe* this process of commitment, termed Start, defines a period in late G_1 beyond which cells can no longer undergo other developmental fates, such as sexual differentiation (Hartwell, 1974; Nurse, 1975; Nurse and Bisset, 1981). At Start, yeast cells monitor the extracellular microenviroment (presence or absence of nutrients, sexual pheromones, etc.) and either make a commitment to progression through the mitotic cell cycle, appropiate for cells growing in rich medium, or undergo cell cycle arrest in G_1 as a prelude to conjugation and meiosis, appropiate for nutritionally starved cells (Hartwell, 1974; Nurse, 1975; Nurse and Bisset, 1981). Before cells can pass Start, they must grow sufficiently to attain a critical cell mass, and small cells in G_1 cannot undergo S-phase until they reach this mass (Hartwell, 1974; Nurse, 1975; Nurse and Thuriaux, 1977; Nasmyth et al., 1979). In fission yeast the p34^cdc2 protein kinase is known to be required for progression past Start (Nurse and Bisset. 1981), together with the transcription factors encoded by the genes *cdc10⁺* (Nurse, 1981) and *res1⁺/sct1⁺* (Tanaka et al., 1992; Caligiuri and Beach, 1993). Candidate G_1 cyclins are encoded by *puc1⁺* (Forsburg and Nurse, 1991) and *cig2⁺* (Bueno and Russell, 1993; Connolly and Beach, 1994; Obara-Ishihara and Okayama, 1994) but a clear role for these cyclins in the mitotic cell cycle remains to be established.

Here we describe the identification and characterization of the gene *rum1⁺*, encoding a 25 kDa protein important for determining the duration of the G_1-phase. Overexpression of *rum1⁺* initially causes cell cycle delay in G_1, since the critical mass required for Start is increased relative to wild-type cells. These

cells undergo multiple rounds of S-phase in the absence of mitosis, leading to very long cells with increased ploidy. When *rum1⁺* is deleted, the critical cell mass required at Start is reduced and the pre-Start G_1 interval is eliminated, indicating that *rum1⁺* is a major element determining the timing of Start. *rum1⁺* is also important in restraining mitosis until G_1 is finished: when *rum1⁺* is deleted in a mutant that normally blocks at Start, cells proceed to undergo mitosis and cell division. Therefore *rum1⁺* is important for defining the G_1 status of a fission yeast cell.

MATERIALS AND METHODS

Strains and media

S. pombe strains used in this study were *972 h⁻, leu1-32 h⁻, ade6-M210/ade6-M216 ura4-D18/ura4-D18 leu1-32/leu1-32 h⁺/h⁻, ade6-704 leu1-32 h⁺, cdc10-129 h⁻, cdc2-L7 h⁻, cdc2-M26 h⁻* and *wee1-50 h⁻*. *Escherichia coli* strain DH5α was used for routine cloning. *S. pombe* and *E. coli* were manipulated following standard procedures (Moreno et al., 1991; Sambrook et al., 1989).

rum1⁺ overexpression experiments, DAPI staining, DNA and protein content determination

To induce *rum1⁺* expression from the regulatable *nmt1⁺* promoter, a *S. pombe leu1-32 h⁻* strain transformed with pREP3X-*rum1⁺* or an integrant constructed by transforming the strain *ade6-704 leu1-32 h⁺* with the plasmid pREP3X(sup3-5)-*rum1⁺* were grown to mid-exponential phase in minimal medium containing 5 μg/ml thiamine at 32°C. Cells were fixed in cold 70% ethanol, stained with DAPI and photographed using a Zeiss Axioscop photomicroscope (Moreno et al., 1991). DNA content was determined by a FACScan (fluorescence activated cell analyser; Becton-Dickinson; Sazer and Sherwood, 1990) and by the diphenylamine method of Bostock (1970) with the modification of Gendimenico et al. (1988). Protein content was determined using the BCA kit assay (Pierce). Cell number was measured using a Coulter counter.

Constructing a *rum1⁺* deletion

A 2.1 kb *Cla*I fragment in *rum1⁺* was replaced with the *ura4⁺* gene in a 6.1 kb *rum1⁺* genomic clone. This construction was used to delete the *rum1⁺* gene using a diploid strain *ade6-M210/ade6-M216 ura4-D18/ura4-D18 leu1-32/leu1-32 h⁺/h⁻*. Stable ura⁺ diploids were obtained and tetrads were dissected after sporulation. Although there was a general reduction in the viability of the spores from these tetrads in comparison with a wild-type control, uracil prototrophic haploid colonies with the *rum1⁺* gene deleted grew well in YE5S indicating that the *rum1⁺* gene was not essential in a wild-type background.

Nitrogen starvation

Cells were grown in minimal medium to mid-exponential phase, washed 6 times with nitrogen-free minimal medium and resuspended in this medium at a concentration of 2×10^6 cells/ml.

RESULTS

rum1⁺ overexpression inhibits the cell cycle both in G₁ and G₂

The *rum1⁺* gene was isolated screening for genes that when overproduced induce extra rounds of DNA replication in the absence of mitosis (Moreno and Nurse, 1994). A 1.5 kb cDNA derived from a gene we called *rum1⁺* (for *r*eplication *u*ncoupled from *m*itosis) induced over-replication when over-expressed, generating very long cells with a giant nucleus (Fig. 1A). Flow cytometry analysis during a time course revealed an increase in DNA content, showing discrete peaks of 1C, 2C, 4C, 8C, 16C, etc., indicating that the increase in DNA content was a consequence of complete rounds of DNA replication (Fig. 1B). This is also supported by the fact that a short pulse of *rum1⁺* overexpression converts more than 50% of cells into viable diploids and tetraploids. Overproduction of the rum1 protein therefore produces a cell cycle consisting exclusively of complete rounds of DNA replication, without intervening mitosis.

Examination of very early time points shows that the first effect of *rum1⁺* overexpression is the accumulation of cells with a 1C DNA content (10-20% of the total), indicating a delay in G₁. We measured the DNA and protein content during *rum1⁺* induction and found that whilst both DNA and protein content per cell increased in parallel, the protein/DNA ratio was elevated in the over-replicating cells by 10% in relation to wild type and by 65% in relation to a *wee1* mutant (see Table 1), indicating that the cell mass at which S-phase takes place is increased. This means that elevated *rum1⁺* expression results in a delay of S-phase until cells attain a larger mass, suggesting that the *rum1⁺* gene product acts as a transient inhibitor of progression through G₁ into S-phase. This provides an explanation for the appearance of the 1C population early on in the induction.

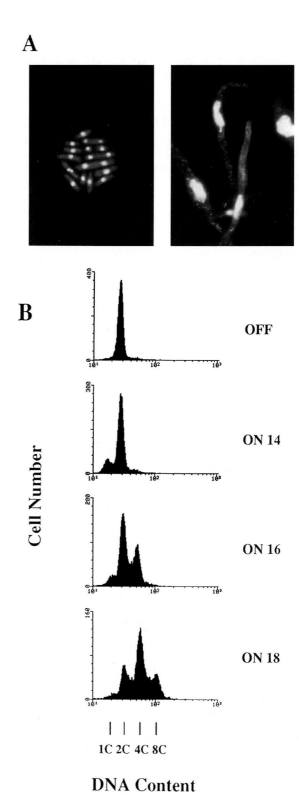

Fig. 1. *rum1⁺* overexpression induces over-replication. (A) *S. pombe leu1-32 h⁻* cells transformed with pREP3X-*rum1⁺*; promoter off (left), promoter on (right). (B) Time course of induction of *rum1⁺* up to 18 hours in the integrant strain. FACS analysis (1C, 2C, 4C, 8C peaks are indicated).

Table 1. Cell mass at S phase in wild type, *rum1Δ*, *wee1-50* and *wee1-50 rum1Δ* and rum1 overexpressor

Strain	Cell mass at S phase
Wild type	1.49
rum1Δ	1.43
wee1-50	1.00
wee1-50 rum1Δ	0.82
rum1 OVP	1.65

rum1+ also acts as an inhibitor of mitotic entry. When *rum1+* is overexpressed the percentage of mitotic cells falls to zero and the p34^{cdc2}/p56^{cdc13} associated protein kinase activity is very low (Moreno and Nurse, 1994). Recent experiments indicate that the rum1 protein expressed and purified from *E. coli* acts directly as a very potent inhibitor of the p34^{cdc2}/p56^{cdc13} complex in vitro (J. Correa, S. Moreno and P. Nurse, unpublished results).

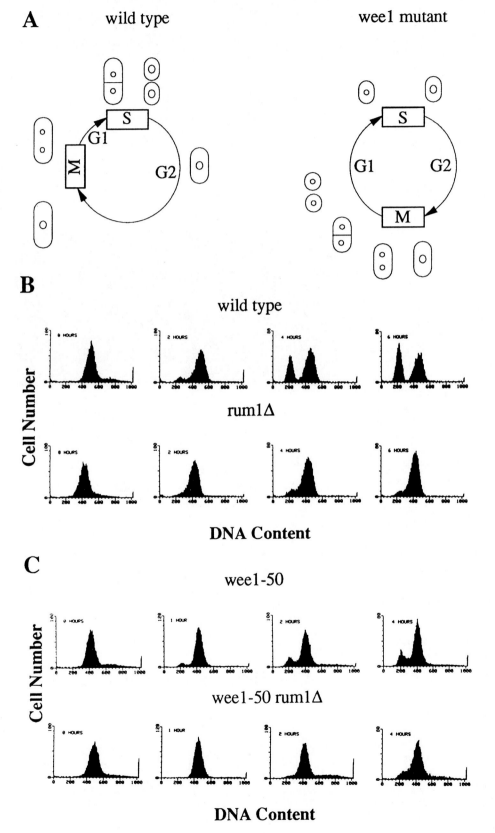

Fig. 2. rum1Δ mutants do not arrest in G$_1$ in response to nitrogen starvation or in combination with a wee1-50 mutant. (A) Cell cycle diagrams of wild-type and wee1 mutant strains. (B) FACS profile of the wild-type (upper) and *rum1Δ* (lower) strains after nitrogen starvation at 32°C. (C) FACS profile of a time course after shifting to 36°C a *wee1-50* (upper) and *wee1-50 rum1Δ* (lower) strain.

To demonstrate that cells can undergo DNA replication without intervening mitosis, we overexpressed *rum1*⁺ in a *cdc25-22* temperature-sensitive mutant. At the restrictive temperature these cells, arrested in G₂, were able to undergo multiple rounds of S-phase (Moreno and Nurse, 1994). However, the over-replication phenotype was blocked in temperature-sensitive mutants of *cdc2* or *cdc10* at 36°C (Moreno and Nurse, 1994). Since these two mutants block cell cycle progression through G₁ at Start, overreplicating cells with elevated *rum1*⁺ expression must pass Start before they can initiate each S-phase.

rum1⁺ inhibits cell cycle progression in G₁

If the *rum1*⁺ gene product acts as a transient inhibitor of G₁ progression, reducing the normal level of the *rum1*⁺ gene product should shorten the G₁ interval and reduce the cell mass at which S-phase takes place. Rapidly growing wild-type cells have no pre-Start G₁ interval because cells completing mitosis already have the cell mass required to pass Start (Fig. 2A). The pre-Start G₁ interval is extended in small cells, such as nitrogen starved cells or in *wee1* mutants, which divide at reduced cell mass (Fig. 2A). Reducing the normal level of the *rum1*⁺ gene product should therefore decrease the G₁ interval in these small cells, but have little effect in rapidly growing wild-type cells.

As expected, deleting the *rum1*⁺ gene has no effect on rapidly growing wild-type cells, but a dramatic effect is seen when these cells are nitrogen starved. When wild-type cells are nitrogen starved there is an accumulation of cells blocked in G₁ (Fig. 2B). In contrast, cells deleted for *rum1*⁺ show no extension of G₁ (Fig. 2B). This is not due to cells failing to divide after shifting into medium lacking nitrogen, as the cell number increase in the two cultures is identical (data not shown). The failure to extend G₁ is because the small cells initiate S-phase immediately after cell division. These cells were also found to be sterile, probably because conjugation requires G₁ arrest at Start after nitrogen starvation.

A dramatic effect is also seen when *rum1*⁺ is deleted in the temperature-sensitive *wee1-50* mutant. Two hours after shift to 36°C, *wee1-50* cells begin to accumulate in G₁ but no such accumulation was seen in *wee1-50* cells deleted for *rum1*⁺ (Fig. 2C). The G₁ interval observed in a *wee1-50* strain is eliminated when *rum1*⁺ is deleted. Therefore *rum1*⁺ must encode a major element that determines the length of G₁ in these small cells. In the absence of the *rum1*⁺ gene product the requirement to attain a critical cell mass before passing Start is reduced. This was verified by measuring the protein/DNA ratio, which was reduced by 18% when *rum1*⁺ was deleted and increased by 65% when *rum1*⁺ was over-produced (Table 1, values are calculated with respect to the values obtained for a *wee1* mutant after two hours at 36°C). In the absence of *rum1*⁺, *wee1-50* cells undergo Start and initiate S phase as soon as they complete mitosis.

rum1⁺ defines a cell as being in G₁ pre-Start

The above results suggested that the *rum1*⁺ gene product may be required to define a cell as being in the pre-Start G₁-phase of the cell cycle. If this is so, cells lacking *rum1*⁺ should be unable to block in this interval of the cell cycle. This was investigated by deleting *rum1*⁺ in the *cdc10-129* mutant and in a *cdc2-M26* mutant. The *cdc10*⁺ gene encodes a transcription factor that is required for cells to pass Start and activate the

transcription of a number of S-phase genes (Lowndes et al., 1992). When a *cdc10-129* culture is shifted to 36°C, most cells are initially post-Start and so proceed to divide once before arresting, resulting in a cell number doubling. But *cdc10-129* cells deleted for *rum1*⁺ continue to divide further (Moreno and Nurse, 1994). Analysis of a synchronous culture of the *cdc10-129 rum1Δ* mutant showed that cells were unable to remain arrested at the pre-Start interval, and underwent mitosis and cell division even though S-phase had not take place, resulting in a 'cut' phenotype (Fig. 3A). A similar experiment was performed with a *cdc2-M26* strain deleted for *rum1*⁺. Most *cdc2ts* mutant alleles cause arrest in G₁ and G₂ upon shift to the restrictive temperature, though the G₁ block is transient and leaks through after several hours. *cdc2-M26* is unusual in that the block in G₁ is very tight and cells can be arrested before Start for at least 12 hours. A *cdc2-M26 rum1Δ* double mutant does not remain arrested in pre-Start G₁, however, it blocks

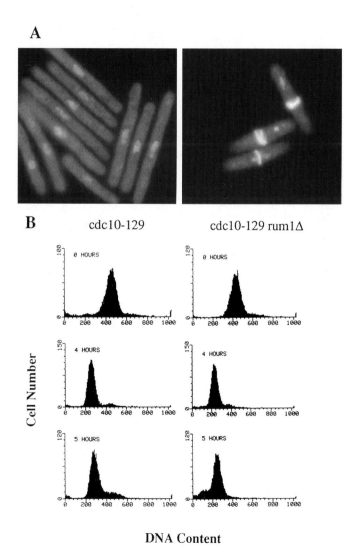

Fig. 3. *cdc10-129* at the restrictive temperature blocks G₁ progression at START. (A) Microscopic appearance of *cdc10-129* (right) and *cdc10-129 rum1Δ* (left) 5 and 7 hours, respectively, after the shift from 25 to 36°C. Cells were doubled-stained with DAPI and calcofuor. (B) FACS analysis of cdc10-129 (left) and cdc10-129 rum1Δ (right) after shift from 25°C to 36°C.

very transiently in G_1, and all cells have passed Start and completed S-phase by 4 hours (K. Labib, S. Moreno and P. Nurse, in preparation). This confirms that cells lacking *rum1+* are unable to remain in a pre-Start G_1 state, and also suggests a close interaction between cdc2 and rum1 in G_1.

Since *rum1+* is important to prevent entry into mitosis from pre-Start G_1 we tested whether it was required during S-phase to prevent entry into mitosis. We found that addition of hydroxyurea to wild-type and *rum1+*-deleted cells was identical in effect (Moreno and Nurse, 1994). Cell division stopped and cells became elongated with no mitotic features.

These experiments indicate that the *rum1+* gene product defines a cell as being in the pre-Start G_1 interval. When *rum1+* is deleted then a cell blocked in this interval cannot recognise this situation and proceeds with the program of cell division. But if the same cells are allowed to proceed into the post-Start G_1 interval where progression is blocked using hydroxyurea, then the cell now recognises this situation and prevents mitosis and cell division, suggesting that different checkpoint controls must be operative in the G_1 interval, one prior to Start involving *rum1+* and a second post-Start, which does not involve *rum1+* (Moreno and Nurse, 1994).

The rum1 protein

The *rum1+* gene potentially encodes a protein of 25 kDa (Moreno and Nurse, 1994). This gene product contains several interesting motifs: there is a putative bipartite nuclear localisation signal suggesting the protein may be targeted to the nucleus, as well as potential phosphorylation sites for both the cdc2 and MAP protein kinases, located in the amino terminus of the protein, that might be important for cell cycle regulation.

DISCUSSION

Three aspects of *rum1+* gene function are involved in regulating the pre-Start G_1 interval. Firstly, it acts as a major element determining the length of G_1. It functions as a transient inhibitor of S-phase onset, delaying Start until the cell has attained a critical minimal mass. When *rum1+* is deleted this mass is reduced and when *rum1+* is overexpressed this mass is increased. The only other class of genes known to affect the length of G_1 are the G_1-cyclins of *S. cerevisiae* and vertebrate cells. Dominant mutants in CLN genes shorten the G_1 interval in budding yeast (Sudbery et al., 1980; Nash et al., 1988; Cross, 1988; Hadwiger et al., 1989). This is analogous to the effects of *rum1+*, except that G_1 cyclins act positively whilst *rum1+* acts negatively. In mammalian cells ectopic expression of cyclins D or E also shortens the G_1 interval (Ohtsubo and Roberts, 1993; Quelle et al., 1993).

Secondly, *rum1+* also influences the need to complete mitosis before a cell can undergo Start and initiate the next S-phase. When *rum1+* is overexpressed in G_2, cells can proceed to Start and initiate a new round of DNA replication in the absence of mitosis. The checkpoint control that monitors whether mitosis has been completed is disturbed in these cells. This phenomenon may occur naturally during endoreduplication in certain tissues in multicellular organisms, such as salivary glands of *Drosophila* (Smith and Orr-Weaver, 1991).

Thirdly, the *rum1+* gene product defines the cell as being in

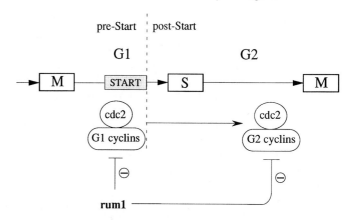

Fig. 4. Passage through START and entry into mitosis are brought about by the G_1 and G_2 forms of p34^{cdc2}, respectively. The *rum1+* gene product inhibits p34^{cdc2} in G_1 until the cell mass required for START is attained. On attainment of the required minimal cell mass the inhibitory effect of the *rum1+* gene product is lost allowing START to take place and p34^{cdc2} to be converted to the G_2 form. In the absence of the *rum1+* gene product START and S-phase occur prematurely at a reduced cell mass and the G_2 form of p34^{cdc2} can be generated even if cells are not allowed to complete START, resulting in premature mitosis.

the pre-Start G_1 interval, and restrains such a cell from undergoing mitosis. When *rum1+* is overexpressed, onset of mitosis is inhibited, and when *rum1+* is deleted cells that normally block at Start can proceed with the cell division program and undergo mitosis even though S-phase has not taken place. Fission yeast cells, arrested in late G_1 post-Start or in S-phase, send a signal that blocks p34^{cdc2} function at mitosis (Enoch and Nurse, 1991). This signal may be generated by the assembly of replication complexes post-Start, and is mediated via inhibitory phosphorylation of a residue of tyrosine 15 in the p34^{cdc2} protein kinase (Enoch et al., 1992). Cells prior to Start are unlikely to have assembled replication complexes, and so a separate checkpoint mechanism restraining mitosis in pre-Start cells is required; we propose a role for *rum1+* in such a control. Separate mechanisms restraining mitosis before and after Start are further suggested by the fact that mutants such as cdc2-3w, lacking the post-Start checkpoint, are still able to arrest cell cycle progression pre-Start without entering mitosis (Enoch and Nurse, 1991).

Based on the above discussion and recent biochemical experiments, we propose that rum1 might be an inhibitor of the cell cycle machinary acting in a similar way to FAR1 (Chang and Herskowitz, 1990) and p40 (Mendenhall et al., 1987; Mendenhall, 1993) in *Saccharomyces cerevisiae,* or p21^{CIP1} (Wade Harper et al., 1993; Xiong et al., 1993) and p27^{KIP1} (Polyak et al., 1994) in animal cells (Fig. 4). In G_1, when cells are too small to undergo Start, p34^{cdc2} is inactivated by the *rum1+* gene product until the critical mass is attained. This inhibition of the G_1 form of p34^{cdc2} automatically prevents conversion into the G_2 form and thus blocks mitotic onset. Once the critical mass is reached the *rum1+* inhibitory effect is lost and the cell executes Start and proceeds to S-phase. At the same time p34^{cdc2} is converted to the G_2 form but is restrained from bringing about mitosis by a new checkpoint control, activated by the assembly of replication complexes, working through p34^{cdc2} tyrosine 15 phosphorylation.

Cells lacking the *rum1*$^+$ inhibitor cannot delay Start until the correct critical mass is attained, explaining why G$_1$ is not extended in small cells deleted for *rum1*$^+$. A cell arrested prior to Start in the absence of the *rum1*$^+$ gene product cannot block the conversion of p34^{cdc2} to the G$_2$ form, and as a consequence the cell undergoes premature mitosis. If the *rum1*$^+$ gene product is present at high levels in a G$_2$ cell, this results in a potent inhibition of p34^{cdc2}/p56^{cdc13} and cells never enter mitosis. However these cells can undergo S-phase when cells attain the critical cell mass.

The presence of potential MAP kinase phosphorylation sites suggests an interaction with MAP kinase homologues in fission yeast, perhaps analogous to the regulation of FAR1 in response to pheromone action in budding yeast. Such interaction could delay G$_1$ progression in the presence of *S. pombe* pheromones.

We dedicate this paper to Professor Murdoch Mitchison. He helped to initiate the study of the cell cycle problems that are the subject of this article, and has continued to influence our thinking. We thank Dr Bruce Edgar for his kind gift of the cDNA library and his help at the initial stages of this work and all the members of our groups for many discussions and ideas during the course of this work. This project was supported by ICRF, SERC, the MRC, the EC, EMBO, the Worshipful Company of Bakers, and the DGICYT.

REFERENCES

Bostock, C. J. (1970). DNA synthesis in the fission yeast *Schizosaccharomyces pombe*. *Exp. Cell Res.* **60**, 16-26.

Bueno, A. and Russell, P. (1993). Two fission yeast B-type cyclins, *cig2* and *cdc13*, have different functions in mitosis. *Mol. Cell. Biol.* **13**, 2286-2297.

Caligiuri, M. and Beach, D. (1993). Sct1 functions in partnership with *cdc10* in a transcriptional complex that activates cell cycle 'start' and inhibits differentiation. *Cell* **72**, 607-619.

Chang, F. and Herskowitz, I. (1990). Identification of a gene necessary for cell cycle arrest by a negative growth factor of yeast: *FAR1* is an inhibitor of a G$_1$ cyclin, *CLN2*. *Cell* **63**, 999-1011.

Connolly, T. and Beach, D. (1994). Interaction between the *cig1* and *cig2* B-type cyclins in the fission yeast cell cycle. *Mol. Cell. Biol.* **14**, 768-776.

Cross, F. (1988). *DAF1*, a mutant gene affecting size control, pheromone arrest and cell cycle kinetics of *S. cerevisiae*. *Mol. Cell. Biol.* **8**, 4675-4684.

Enoch, T. and Nurse, P. (1991). Coupling M phase and S phase: controls maintaining the dependence of mitosis on chromosome replication. *Cell* **65**, 921-923.

Enoch, T., Gould, K. L. and Nurse, P. (1992). Mitotic checkpoint control in fission yeast. *Cold Spring Harbor Symp. Quant. Biol.* **56**, 409-416.

Forsburg, S. L. and Nurse, P. (1991). Identification of a G$_1$-type cyclin *puc1*$^+$ in the fission yeast *Schizosaccharomyces pombe*. *Nature* **351**, 245-8.

Gendimenico, G. J., Bouquin, P. L. and Tramposch, K. M. (1988). Diphenylamine-colorimetric method for DNA assay - a shortened procedure by incubating samples at 50°C. *Anal. Biochem.* **173**, 45-48.

Hadwiger, J. A., Wittenberg, C., Richardson, H. E., De Barros Lopes, M.

and Reed, S. I. (1989). A family of cyclin homologs that control the G$_1$ phase in yeast. *Proc. Nat. Acad. Sci. USA* **86**, 6255-6259.

Hartwell, L. (1974). *Saccharomyces cerevisiae* cell cycle. *Bacteriol. Rev.* **38**, 164-198.

Lowndes, N. F., Mcinerny, C. J., Johnson, A. L., Fantes, P. A. and Johnston, L. (1992). Control of DNA synthesis genes in fission yeast by the cell-cycle gene *cdc10*$^+$. *Nature* **355**, 449-53.

Mendenhall, M. D., Jones, C. A. and Reed, S. I. (1987). Dual regulation of the yeast CDC28-p40 protein kinase complex: cell cycle, pheromone, and nutrient limitation effects. *Cell* **50**, 927-35.

Mendenhall, M. D. (1993). An inhibitor of p34^{CDC28} protein-kinase activity from *Saccharomyces-cerevisiae*. *Science* **259**, 216-219.

Moreno, S., Klar, A. and Nurse, P. (1991). Molecular genetic analysis of fission yeast *Schizosaccharomyces pombe*. *Meth. Enzymol.* **194**, 795-23.

Moreno, S. and Nurse, P. (1994). Regulation of progression through the G$_1$ phase of the cell cycle by the *rum1*$^+$ gene. *Nature* **367**, 236-242.

Nash, R., Tokiwa, G., Anand, S., Erickson, K. and Futcher, A. B. (1988). The *WHI1*$^+$ gene of *S. cerevisiae* tethers cell division to cell size and is a cyclin homolog. *EMBO J.* **7**, 4335-4346.

Nasmyth, K., Nurse, P. and Fraser, R. (1979). The effect of cell mass on the cell cycle timing and duration of S-phase in fission yeast. *J. Cell Sci.* **39**, 215-233.

Nurse, P. (1975). Genetic control of cell size at cell division in yeast. *Nature* **256**, 547-551.

Nurse, P. and Thuriaux, P. (1977). Controls over the timing of DNA replication during the cell cycle of fission yeast. *Exp. Cell. Res.* **107**, 365-75.

Nurse, P. (1981). Genetic control of the yeast cell cycle. In *The Fungal Nucleus*. pp. 331-345. Cambridge University Press, Cambridge, UK.

Nurse, P. and Bisset, Y. (1981). Cell cycle gene required in G1 for commitment to cell division and in G2 for control of mitosis in fission yeast. *Nature* **292**, 558-560.

Obara-Ishihara, T. and Okayama, H. (1994). B type cyclins controls conjugation in the fission yeast *S. pombe*. *EMBO J.* **13**, 1863-1872.

Ohtsubo, M. and Roberts, J. M. (1993). Cyclin-dependent regulation of G$_1$ in mammalian fibroblasts. *Science* **259**, 1908-1912.

Polyak, K., Kato, J., Solomon, M. K., Sherr, C. J., Massague, J., Roberts, J. M. and Koff, A. (1994). p27^{KIP1}, a cyclin-cdk inhibitor, links transforming growth factor-β and contact inhibition to cell cycle arrest. *Genes Dev.* **8**, 9-22.

Quelle, D. E., Ashmun, R. A., Shurtleff, S. A., Kato, J., Bar-Sagi, D., Roussel, M. F. and Sherr, C. J. (1993). Overexpression of mouse D-type cyclins accelerates G$_1$ phase in rodent fibroblasts. *Genes Dev.* **7**, 1559-1571.

Sambrook, J., Fritsch, E. and Maniatis, T. (1989). *Molecular Cloning: a Laboratory Manual*. Second edition. Cold Spring Harbor Laboratory Press, Cold Spring Harbor, NY.

Sazer, S. and Sherwood, S. W. (1990). Mitochondrial growth and DNA synthesis occur in the absence of nuclear DNA replication in fission yeast. *J. Cell Sci.* **97**, 509-516.

Smith, A. V. and Orr-Weaver, T. L. (1991). The regulation of the cell-cycle during *Drosophila* embryogenesis - the transition to polyteny. *Development* **112**, 997-1008.

Sudbery, P. E., Goodey, A. R. and Carter, B. L. A. (1980). Genes which control cell proliferation in the yeast *Saccharomyces cerevisiae*. *Nature* **288**, 401-404.

Tanaka, K., Okazaki, K., Okazaki, N., Ueda, T., Sugiyama, A., Nojima, H. and Okayama, H. (1992). A new *cdc*-gene required for S-phase entry of *Schizosaccharomyces-pombe* encodes a protein similar to the *cdc10*$^+$ and *swi4*-gene products. *EMBO J.* **11**, 4923-4932.

Wade-Harper, J., Adami, G. R., Wei, N., Keyomarski, K. and Elledge, S. J. (1993). The p21 cdk-Interacting Protein Cip1 is a potent inhibitor of G$_1$ cyclin-dependent kinases. *Cell* **75**, 805-816.

Xiong, Y., Zhang, H. and Beach, D. (1993). Subunit rearrangements of the cyclin-dependent kinases is associated with cellular transformation. *Genes Dev.* **7**, 1572-1583.

Journal of Cell Science, Supplement 18, 69-73 (1994)
Printed in Great Britain © The Company of Biologists Limited 1994

G₁ control in mammalian cells

Steven I. Reed, Eric Bailly, Vjekoslav Dulic, Ludger Hengst, Dalia Resnitzky and Joyce Slingerland

Department of Molecular Biology, MB-7, The Scripps Research Institute, 10666 North Torrey Pines Road, La Jolla, CA 92037, USA

SUMMARY

Cyclin-dependent kinases (Cdks) control the major cell cycle transitions in eukaryotic cells. On the basis of a variety of experiments where cyclin function either is impaired or enhanced, D-type cyclins as well as cyclins E and A have been linked to G_1 and G_1/S phase roles in mammalian cells. We therefore sought to determine if agents that block the G_1/S phase transition do so at the level of regulating the Cdk activities associated with these cyclins. A variety of conditions that lead to G_1 arrest were found to correlate with accumulation of G_1-specific Cdk inhibitors, including treatment of fibroblasts with ionizing radiation, treatment of epithelial cells with TGF-β, treatment of HeLa cells with the drug lovastatin, and removal of essential growth factors from a variety of different cell types. Mechanistically, inhibition of Cdks was found to involve the stoichiometric binding of Cdk inhibitor proteins. p21[Waf1/Cip1] was associated with DNA damage induced arrest while p27[Kip1]/p28[Ick1] accumulated under a variety of antiproliferative conditions.

Key words: cell cycle, G_1, cyclin, Cdk

INTRODUCTION

Understanding of the eukaryotic cell cycle has been revolutionized by the discovery that all of the major regulatory points are controlled by a class of protein kinases known as cyclin-dependent kinases, or Cdks (for reviews see Sherr, 1993; Reed, 1992; Pines and Hunter, 1991). The functional paradigm of these kinases is that they are composed of a catalytic subunit that has no intrinsic activity and a requisite positive regulatory subunit known as a cyclin. In simple eukaryotic organisms such as yeast, a single Cdk catalytic subunit interacts with numerous different classes of cyclin to mediate diverse cell cycle phase transitions. In mammalian cells, the regulatory environment is complicated by the presence of multiple Cdks (Meyerson et al., 1992) as well as cyclins (Xiong and Beach, 1991; Lew and Reed, 1992). It has been our goal to elucidate the roles of these kinases and cyclins in the regulation of the G_1 to S phase transition.

RESULTS AND DISCUSSION

G₁ cyclins

A number of lines of evidence implicate three types of cyclin in G_1 and S phase functions. Cyclins D1 and E were identified on the basis of their ability to rescue a deficiency of G_1 cyclin function in the simple eukaryote yeast (Lew et al., 1991; Xiong et al., 1991; Koff et al., 1991). At the same time, the cyclin D1 cDNA was isolated on the basis of the growth factor inducibility of the corresponding mRNA (Matsushime et al., 1991) and because of its location at a chromosomal breakpoint associated with malignancy (Motokura et al., 1991; Withers et al., 1991).

After the identification of cyclin D1, two other closely related cyclins, D2 and D3, were identified on the basis of their homology to cyclin D1 (Matsushime et al., 1991). Patterns of expression suggested that cyclins D and E were associated with G_1 and/or G_1/S phase functions (Dulic et al., 1992; Koff et al., 1992; Baldin et al., 1993; Won et al., 1992). Finally, cyclin A, shown to accumulate beginning at the G_1/S phase boundary, was suggested to have a potential role during S phase (Pines and Hunter, 1990).

Several lines of evidence confirm G_1 or G_1/S phase roles for these three classes of cyclin. Antibody microinjection experiments using IgGs specific for cyclins A and D1 have demonstrated that these cyclins are required for initiation or progression through S phase (Girard et al., 1991; Pagano et al., 1992; Zindy et al., 1992; Baldin et al., 1993; Quelle et al., 1993). Similar experiments using cyclin E-specific antibodies have been unsuccessful, possibly for technical reasons (G. Mondesert and S. Reed, unpublished). However, cyclin E has been shown to be essential for entry into S phase in *Drosophila* (Knoblich et al., 1994), suggesting an essential S phase initiation function in mammalian cells as well. Conversely, constitutive expression of these three cyclins can lead to premature entry into S phase, suggesting that they control functions that are rate-limiting for passage through G_1 into S phase (Ohtsubo and Roberts, 1993; Quelle et al., 1993; Resnitzky et al., 1994; D. Resnitzky and S. Reed, unpublished; Table 1). However, expression of no cyclin alone appears to be able to advance the G_1/S phase to the degree that G_1 can be eliminated. This suggests either that several individual rate-limiting transitions within G_1 are controlled by different cyclins or that compartments exist within the G_1 interval that cannot be influenced by the action of cyclin-dependent kinases.

Table 1. Effect of cyclin E and cyclin D1 on asynchronous cells versus cells emerging from quiescence

Clone	% G1 in asynchronous populations		Length of G1 in asynchronous populations (h)		Decrease in length of G1 in asynchronous populations (h)	Decrease in length of G0/G1 after serum starvation/ stimulation (h)
	+tet	−tet	+tet	−tet		
D5	48.4	41.8	6.78	5.85	0.93±0.17	4.7±0.7
D3	44.1	39.9	6.17	5.58	0.53±0.11	3.1±1.1
E2	52.2	39.9	7.31	5.59	1.72±0.04	2.5±0.9
E19	49.2	36.9	6.89	5.17	1.72±0.18	1.7±0.7

The percentage of G1 cells in asynchronous populations was determined by flow cytometric analysis and was used with the population doubling time to determine the length of the G1 phase. The relative lengths of G0/G1 in populations emerging from quiescence was determined by direct measurement using flow cytometric analysis to monitor entry into S phase. In all experiments, comparisons were based on cultures growing in the presence of tetracycline (cyclins repressed) versus in the absence of tetracycline (cyclins repressed) (Resnitzky et al., 1994). Clones D5 and D3 are Rat1 fibroblasts expressing human cyclin D1 and clones E2 and E19 express human cyclin E.

It is of interest to note that whereas constitutive expression of cyclins D1 and E have a more profound effect on advance of S phase in cells emerging from quiescence as compared to cycling cells, expression of cyclin E confers an equivalent S phase advance in either circumstance, suggesting participation in distinct pathways (Resnitzky et al., 1994; Table 1).

Finally, with the demonstration that mammalian cells contain a number of different Cdk catalytic subunits, it was important to establish which combinations of G1 cyclins and catalytic subunits contribute to the activities described above. Although a large number of combinatorial possibilities have been detected, the biologically critical complexes for G1/S-phase functions appear to be cyclins A and E combined with catalytic subunit Cdk2 (Pines and Hunter, 1990; Dulic et al., 1992; Koff et al., 1992) and D type cyclins combined with Cdk4 (Matsushime et al., 1992; see Fig. 1).

Targets of cyclin-dependent kinase action

Of all the potential targets for the G1 cyclin-dependent kinases, the retinoblastoma susceptibility gene product, pRb is the one most often invoked to explain regulation of the G1/S phase transition. It is known that pRb inhibits cell cycle progression when in a hypophosphorylated form and that phosphorylation reverses these inhibitory functions (Buchkovich et al., 1989; Chen et al., 1989; DeCaprio et al., 1992; Ludlow et al., 1993; Mihara et al., 1989). A mounting body of evidence suggests that the inhibitory function of pRb is based on the ability of hypophosphorylated pRb to sequester some members of a family of essential transcription factors known together as E2F (Helin et al., 1992; Kaelin et al., 1992; Nevins, 1992). Phosphorylation of pRb is thought to lead to the release of transcription-competent E2F. Furthermore, the in vivo phosphorylation sites on pRb correspond to Cdk consensus phosphorylation sites and a variety of Cdks have been shown to be capable of phosphorylating pRb in vitro (Lees et al., 1991; Lin et al., 1991; Kato et al., 1993). The most compelling evidence for an in vivo role for Cdks in pRb phosphorylation comes from experiments in SAOS-2 osteosarcoma cells where ectopic expression of pRb caused G1 arrest but co-expression of pRb with either cyclin D, E or A did not (Hinds et al., 1992; Ewen et al., 1993). It could be shown that, concomitant with the release from G1 arrest, pRb became hyperphosphorylated. These data suggest that all of the proposed G1 and G1/S phase Cdk activities have the capacity to phosphorylate pRb directly

or to stimulate its phosphorylation by other protein kinases in vivo. These experiments have the caveat, however, that both pRb and cyclins are highly overexpressed, perhaps imbuing them with abnormal properties. Therefore the issue of which Cdks (cyclins and catalytic subunits) actually contribute to pRb phosphorylation under normal cellular growth circumstances remains to be resolved. It is noteworthy that D-type cyclins contain motifs that allow them to bind directly to pRb, presumably facilitating the direction of kinase activity toward this potential substrate (Ewen et al., 1993; Dowdy et al., 1993).

Several other proteins with Rb-like physical proterties have been identified. p107 and p130 have structural homology with pRb, can bind viral oncoproteins, as can pRb, and can bind E2F as well (Ewen et al., 1991; Hannon et al., 1993). However the relationship of these proteins to cell cycle control is less well understood than that of pRb. High levels of expression of p107 in some cell types confer G1 arrest, suggesting an inhibitory role similar to that of pRb (Zhu et al., 1993). The relationship of cell cycle control to sequestration of E2F is less clear. Although p107 and p130 bind E2F, it appears that different isoforms are involved relative to pRb (Lees et al., 1993). The roles of these isoforms have not yet been elucidated nor has the relationship between phosphorylation of p107 and p130 and release of E2F. However, it has been shown that cyclin

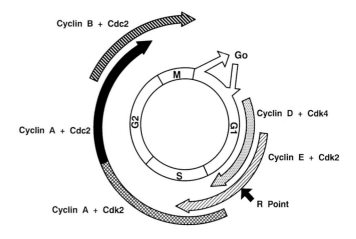

Fig. 1. The roles and temporal participation of various cyclins and cyclin-dependent kinases in the mammalian cell cycle.

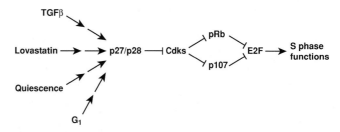

Fig. 2. The functions of p53 and p21 in mediating cell cycle control in response to DNA damage. DNA damage incurred from external sources such as ionizing radiation (IR) or internal sources, such as the transition to senescence, leads to elevation of p53 levels. p53 promotes elevated expression of p21, which in turn inhibits G₁ Cdks. This ultimately has the effect of inhibiting functions essential for S phase, notably the the release of E2F isoforms from antagonists such as pRb and p107.

Fig. 3. Mediation of cell cycle control by p27/p28. A variety of conditions, including response to TGFβ (epithelial cells), treatment with lovastatin, starvation for serum or contact inhibition, and passage through the G₁ phase of the cell cycle, lead to accumulation of the Cdk inhibitor p27^{Kip1}/p28^{Ick1}. As with p21, this is likely to prevent the release of the essential S phase transcription factor E2F.

E/Cdk2 is included in p107/E2F complexes in late G₁ and early S phase whereas cyclin A/Cdk2 is in similar complexes during S phase and G₂ (Lees et al., 1992). This suggests a regulatory role for cyclin E and cyclin A in regulation of p107 functions. If p107 functions analogously to pRb, then cyclin E/Cdk2 may control release of E2F isoforms associated with p107 by direct phosphorylation of p107. Other potential targets of G₁ Cdks are proteins directly involved in initiation of DNA replication, such as origin binding proteins. However, these remain to be identified before this idea can be explored.

The Role(s) of Cdk inhibitors

In budding yeast, developmental control of the cell cycle occurs at G₁ and is implemented at the level of controlling G₁-specific Cdks (Reed, 1992). Therefore, investigation of G₁ control in mammalian cells has focused on G₁ Cdks, as well (Sherr, 1993). Several model systems have been explored including the effects of DNA damage (Dulic et al., 1994), negative growth factors (Koff et al., 1993; Polyak et al., 1994; Slingerland et al., 1994), antiproliferative drugs (Hengst et al., 1994) and growth factor deprivation (Dulic et al., 1994; Hengst et al., 1994; Polyak et al., 1994; Slingerland et al., 1994). A common theme has emerged, namely that G₁ control in response to a variety of signals is mediated at the level of proteins that inhibit the kinase activities of Cdks via stoichiometric binding (Dulic et al., 1994; Hengst et al., 1994; Polyak et al., 1994; Slingerland et al., 1994).

When human diploid fibroblasts are synchronized by growth to confluence followed by replating, they can be prevented from entering S phase by high doses of ionizing radiation such as γ-rays (Little and Nagasawa, 1985). Unirradiated cells enter S phase at approximately 18 hours after release from contact inhibition. Cells blocked in G₁ were found to accumulate normal levels of cyclin E and D1 and to form normal levels of cyclin E/Cdk2 and cyclin D1/Cdk4 complexes. However, these complexes were found not to be active (Dulic et al., 1994). It was shown that cyclin/Cdk complexes under these conditions contained a heat stable Cdk inhibitory protein whose presence was dependent on the wild-type status of the tumor suppressor p53. Further investigation indicated that this inhibitor corresponded to p21$^{Waf1/Cip1}$ (El-Deiry et al., 1993; Harper et al., 1993; Xiong et al., 1993; Gu et al., 1993), shown to be a p53-inducible Cdk inhibitor (Dulic et al., 1994). These data establish a p53-dependent signal transduction pathway linking DNA damage to cell cycle control (Fig. 2). The loss of genome

stability in response to negation of p53 function is likely to arise from the uncoupling of cell cycle control from DNA damage responses. This is likely to be an important modality in the transition to malignancy. Similar data have been obtained for senescent fibroblasts (Dulic et al., 1993) where DNA damage signals have been invoked to explain the block to proliferation.

The response of epithelial cells to epithelial antiproliferative agent, TGF-β, is phenomenologically similar to the response to DNA damage. In human breast epithelial cells presynchronized by growth factor depletion and refeeding, and then treated with TGF-β, cyclin E accumulates on schedule, associates with Cdk2, but cyclin/Cdk complexes are inactive (Slingerland et al., 1994). Similarly, in the situation with ionizing radiation, a heat stable Cdk inhibitor could be detected in lysates from TGF-β treated cells (Slingerland et al., 1994; E. Bailly and S. Reed, unpublished). However it is unlikely that this inhibitor is p21$^{Waf1/Cip1}$. Similar studies on mink lung epithelial cells suggest that the inhibitor induced by treatment with TGF-β is a 27/28 kDa protein that is distinct from p21 (Polyak et al., 1994). This protein has been alternately designated p27^{Kip1} and p28^{Ick1}.

p27/p28 accumulates under a number of conditions associated with G₁ arrest of the cell cycle (Fig. 3). HeLa cells treated with the drug lovastatin, which confers G₁ arrest, accumulate p27/p28 in inactive cyclin/Cdk complexes (Hengst et al., 1994). Since p27/p28 is heat stable, it can be released from these complexes by boiling. p27/p28 also accumulates in fibroblasts and epithelial cells deprived of essential growth factors (Hengst et al., 1994). It has also been shown to fluctuate through the cell cycle in proliferating cells, with maximal levels in mid-G₁ (Hengst et al., 1994). Finally, like p21, it has been shown to have the ability to bind and inhibit a broad spectrum of Cdks (Hengst et al., 1994). These data suggest that a variety of conditions that confer G₁ arrest in mammalian cells lead to the production or maintenance of a Cdk inhibitor, p27/p28 that has the capacity to arrest the cell cycle in G₁. In addition, this inhibitor fluctuates through the cell cycle, presumably to prevent premature activation of Cdks during the G₁ interval. Finally, p27/p28 and p21 appear to play complementary roles in cell cycle control mediating the antiproliferative responses associated with distinct signals. In particular, p21 seems to be associated with responses to DNA damage, whereas p27/p28 appears to mediate a more general antiproliferative response.

In summary, the primary motif of cell cycle regulation in G_1 appears to be through the action of cell cycle inhibitory proteins that bind to and inhibit Cdks by a stoichiometric mechanism. This is distinct from control of the G_2/M phase transition, which is mediated primarily at the level of negative phosphorylation of the Cdk1 catalytic subunit (Gould and Nurse, 1989). One possible reason for the prevalence of broad spectrum Cdk inhibitors in G_1 control is that it would allow coordinate control of several distinct Cdks thought to collaborate in progression through G_1 to S phase. It is not yet clear whether p21 and p27/p28 define all of the Cdk inhibitors involved in cell cycle control or whether they are only the first members of a larger family to be identified.

REFERENCES

Baldin, V., Lukas, J., Marcote, M. J., Pagano, M. and Draetta, G. (1993). Cyclin D1 is a nuclear protein required for cell cycle progression in G_1. *Genes Dev.* **7**, 812-821.

Buchkovich, K., Duffy, L. A. and Harlow, E. (1989). The retinoblastoma protein is phosphorylated during specific phases of the cell cycle. *Cell* **58**, 1097-1105.

Chen, P.-L., Scully, P., Shew, J.-Y., Wang, J. Y. J. and Lee, W.-H. (1989). Phosphorlylation of the retinoblastoma gene product is modulated during the cell cycle and cellular differentiation. *Cell* **58**, 1193-1198.

DeCaprio, J. A., Furukawa, Y., Ajchenbaum, F., Griffin, J. D. and Livingston, D. (1992). The retionblastoma-susceptibility gene product becomes phosphorylated in multiple stages during cell cycle entry and progression. *Proc. Nat. Acad. Sci. USA* **89**, 1795-1798.

Dowdy, S. F., Hinds, P. W., Louie, K., Reed, S. I., Arnold, A. and Weinberg, R. A. (1993). Physical interaction of the retinoblastoma protein with human D cyclins. *Cell* **73**, 499-511.

Dulic, V., Lees, E. and Reed, S. I. (1992). Association of human cyclin E with a periodic G_1-S phase protein kinase. *Science* **257**, 1958-1961.

Dulic, V., Drullinger, L. F., Lees, E., Reed, S. I. and Stein, G. H. (1993). Alternate regulation of G_1 cyclins in senescent human fibroblasts: Accumulation of inactive cyclin D1/Cdk2 and cyclin E/Cdk2 complexes. *Proc. Nat. Acad. Sci. USA* **90**, 11034-11038.

Dulic, V., Kaufmann, W. K., Wilson, S. J., Tlsty, T. D., Lees, E., Harper, J. W., Elledge, S. J. and Reed, S. I. (1994). p53-dependent inhibition of cyclin-dependent kinase activities in human fibroblasts during radiation-induced G_1 arrest. *Cell* **76**, 1013-1023.

El-Deiry, W. S., Tokino, R., Velculescu, V. E., Levy, D. B., Parsons, R., Trent, J. M., Lin, D., Mercer, W. E., Kinzler, K. W. and Vogelstein, B. (1993). WAF1, a potential mediator of p53 tumor suppression. *Cell* **75**, 817-825.

Ewen, M. E., Xing, Y., Lawrence, J. B. and Livingston, D. M. (1991). Molecular cloning, chromosomal mapping, and expression of the cDNA for p107, a retinoblastoma gene product-related protein. *Cell* **66**, 1155-1164.

Ewen, M. E., Sluss, H. K., Sherr, C. J., Matsushime, H., Kato, J.-Y. and Livingston, D. M. (1993). Functional interactions of the retinoblastoma protein with mammalian D-type cyclins. *Cell* **73**, 487-497.

Girard, F., Strausfeld, U., Fernandez, A. and Lamb, N. (1991). Cyclin A is required for the onset of DNA replication in mammalian fibroblasts. *Cell* **67**, 1169-1179.

Gould, K. and Nurse, P. (1989). Tyrosine phosphorylation of the fission yeast cdc2+ protein kinase regulates entry into mitosis. *Nature* **342**, 39-45.

Gu, Y., Turck, C. W. and Morgan, D. O. (1993). Inhibition of Cdk2 activity in vivo by an associated 20K regulatory subunit. *Nature* **366**, 707-710.

Hannon, G. J., Demetrick, D. and Beach, D. (1993). Isolation of the Rb-related p130 through its interaction with CDK2 and cyclins. *Genes Dev.* **7**, 2378-2391.

Harper, J. W., Adami, G. R., Wei, N., Kayomarsi, K. and Elledge, S. J. (1993). The p21-Cdk-interacting protein, Cip1 is a potent inhibitor of G_1 cyclin-dependent kinases. *Cell* **75**, 805-816.

Helin, K., Lees, J. A., Vidal, M., Dyson, N., Harlow, E. and Fattaey, A. (1992). A cDNA encoding a pRB-binding protein with properties of the transcription factor E2F. *Cell* **70**, 337-350.

Hengst, L., Dulic, V., Slingerland, J. M., Lees, E. and Reed, S. I. (1994). A cell cycle regulated inhibitor of cyclin dependent kinases. *Proc. Nat. Acad. Sci. USA* **91**, 5291-5295.

Hinds, P. W., Mittnacht, S., Dulic, V., Arnold, A., Reed, S. I. and Weinberg, R. A. (1992). Regulation of retinoblastoma protein functions by ectopic expression of human cyclins. *Cell* **70**, 993-1006.

Kaelin, W. G., Jr, Krek, W., Sellers, W. R., DeCaprio, J. A., Ajchenbaum, F., Fuchs, C. S., Chittenden, T., Li, Y., Farnham, P. J., Blanar, M. A., Livingston, D. M. and Flemington E. K. (1992). Expression cloning of a cDNA encoding a retinoblastoma-binding protein with E2F-like properties. *Cell* **70**, 351-364.

Kato, J.-Y., Matsushime, H., Hiebert, S. W., Ewen, M. E. and Sherr, C. J. (1993). Direct binding of cyclin D to retinoblastoma gene product (pRb) and pRb phosphorylation by the cyclin D-dependent kinase CDK4. *Genes Dev.* **7**, 331-342.

Knoblich, J. A., Sauer, K., Jones, L., Richardson, H., Saint, R. and Lehner, C. F. (1994). Cyclin E controls progression through S phase and its down regulation during Drosophila embryogenesis is required for the arrest of cell proliferation. *Cell* **77**, 107-120.

Koff, A., Cross, F., Fisher, A., Schumacher, J., Leguellec, K., Philippe, M. and Roberts, J. M. (1991). Human cyclin E, a new cyclin that interacts with two members of the cdc2 gene family. *Cell* **66**, 1217-1228.

Koff, A., Giordano, A., Desai, D., Yamashita, K., Harper, J. W., Elledge, S., Nishimoto, T., Morgan, D. O., Franza, R. B. and Roberts, J. M. (1992). Formation and activation of a cyclin E-Cdk2 complex during the G_1 phase of the human cell cycle. *Science* **257**, 1689-1694.

Koff, A., Ohtsuki, M., Polyak, K., Roberts, J. M. and Massague, J. (1993). Negative regulation of G_1 in mammalian cells: Inhibition of cyclin E-dependent kinase by TGF-β. *Science* **260**, 536-539.

Lees, J. A., Buchkovich, K. J., Marshak, D. R., Anderson, C. W. and Harlow, E. (1991). The retinoblastoma protein is phosphorylated on multiple sites by human cdc2. *EMBO J.* **10**, 4279-4290.

Lees, E., Faha, B., Dulic, V., Reed, S. I. and Harlow, E. (1992). Cyclin E/cdk2 and cyclin A/cdk2 kinases associate with p107 and E2F in a termporally distinct manner. *Genes Dev.* **6**, 1874-1885.

Lees, J. A., Saito, M., Vidal, M., Valentine, M., Look, T., Harlow, E., Dyson, N. and Helin, K. (1993). The retinoblastoma protein binds to a family of E2F transcription factors. *Mol. Cell Biol.* **13**, 7813-7825.

Lew, D. J., Dulic, V. and Reed, S. I. (1991). Isolation of three novel human cyclins by rescue of G_1 cyclin (Cln) function in yeast. *Cell* **66**, 1197-1206.

Lew, D. J. and Reed, S. I. (1992). A proliferation of cyclins. *Trends Cell Biol.* **2**, 77-81.

Lin, B. T.-Y., Gruenwald, S. Morla, A. O., Lee, W.-H. and Wang, J. Y. J. (1991). Retinoblastoma cancer suppressor gene product is a substrate of the cell cycle regulator of cdc2 kinase. *EMBO J.* **10**, 857-864.

Little, J. B. and Nagasawa, H. (1985). Effect of confluent holding on potentially lethal damage repair, cell cycle progression, and chromosomal aberrations in human normal and ataxia-telangiectasia fibroblasts. *Radiat. Res.* **101**, 81-93.

Ludlow, J. W., DeCaprio, J. A., Huang, C.-M., Lee, W.-H., Paucha, E. and Livingston, D. M. (1989). SV40 large T antigen binds preferentially to an underphosphorylated member of the retinoblastoma susceptibility gene product family. *Cell* **56**, 57-65.

Matsushime, H., Roussel, M. F., Ashmun, R. A. and Sherr, C. J. (1991). Colony-stimulating factor 1 regulates novel cyclins during the G_1 phase of the cell cycle. *Cell* **65**, 701-713.

Matsushime, H., Ewen, M. E., Strom, D. K., Kato, J.-Y., Hanks, S. K., Roussel, M. F. and Sherr, C. J. (1992). Identification and properties of an atypical catalytic subunit (p34^{PSKJ3}/cdk4) for mammalian D type G_1 cyclins. *Cell* **71**, 323-334.

Meyerson, M, Enders, G. H., Wu, C., Su, L., Gorka, C., Nelson, C., Harlow, E. and Tsai, L. (1992). A family of human cdc2-related kinases. *EMBO J.* **11**, 2909-2917.

Mihara, K., Cao, X. R., Yen, A., Chandler, S., Driscoll, B. Murphree, A. L. T'ang, A. and Fung, Y. K. (1989). Cell cycle-dependent regulation of phosphorylation of the human retinoblastoma gene product: *Science* **246**, 1300-1303.

Motokura, T., Bloom, T., Kim, H. G., Juppner, H., Ruderman, J. V., Kronenberg, H. M. and Arnold, A. (1991). A novel cyclin encoded by a Bcl1-linked candidate oncogene. *Nature* **350**, 512-515.

Nevins, J. R. (1992). E2F: A link between the Rb tumor suppressor protein and viral oncoproteins. *Science* **258**, 424-429.

Ohtsubo, M. and Roberts, J. M. (1993). Cyclin-dependent regulation of G_1 in mammalian cells. *Science* **259**, 1908-1912.

Pagano, M., Pepperkok, R., Verde, F., Ansorge, W. and Draetta, G. (1992).

Cyclin A is required at two points in the human cell cycle. *EMBO J.* **11**, 961-971.

Pines, J. and Hunter, T. (1990). Human cyclin A is adenovirus E1A-associated p60 and behaves differently from cyclin B. *Nature* **346**, 760-763.

Pines, J. and Hunter, T. (1991). Cyclin-dependent kinases: a new cell cycle motif? *Trends Cell Biol.* **1**, 117-121.

Polyak, K., Kato, J.-Y., Solomon, M. J., Sherr, C. J., Massague, J., Roberts, J. M. and Koff, A. (1994). p27^{Kip1}, a cyclin-Cdk inhibitor, links transforming growth factor-β and contact inhibition to cell cycle arrest. *Genes Dev.* **8**, 9-22.

Quelle, D. E., Ashmun, R. A., Shurtleff, S. A., Kato, J.-Y., Bar-Sagi, D., Roussel, M. F. and Sherr, C. J. (1993). Overexpression of mouse D-type cyclins accelerates G₁ phase in rodent fibroblasts. *Genes Dev.* **7**, 1559-1571.

Reed, S. I. (1992). The role of p34 kinases in the G₁ to S phase transition. *Annu. Rev. Cell Biol.* **8**, 529-561.

Resnitzky, D., Gossen, M., Bujard, H. and Reed, S. I. (1994). Acceleration of the G₁/S phase transition by expression of cyclins D1 and E using an inducible system. *Mol. Cell. Biol.* **14**, 1669-1679.

Sherr, C. J. (1993). Mammalian G₁ cyclins. *Cell* **73**, 1059-1065.

Slingerland, J. M., Hengst, L., Pan, C.-H., Alexander, D., Stampfer, M. R. and Reed, S. I. (1994). A novel inhibitor of cylicn/Cdk activity detected in TGF-β arrested epithelial cells. *Mol. Cell. Biol.* **14**, 3683-3694.

Withers, D. A., Harvey, R. C., Faust, J. B., Melnyk, O., Carey, K. and Meeker, T. C. (1991). Characterization of a candidate *bcl1-1* gene. *Mol. Cell. Biol.* **11**, 4846-4853.

Won, K.-A., Xiong, Y., Beach, D. and Gilman, M. Z. (1992). Growth-regulated expression of D-type cyclin genes in human diploid fibroblasts. *Proc. Nat. Acad. Sci. USA* **89**, 9910-9914.

Xiong, Y. and Beach, D. (1991). Population explosion in the cyclin family. *Curr. Biol.* **1**, 362-364.

Xiong, Y., Connolly, T., Futcher, B. and Beach, D. (1991). Human D-type cyclin. *Cell* **65**, 691-699.

Xiong, Y., Hannon, G. J., Zhang, H., Casso, D., Kobayashi R. and Beach, D. (1993). p21 is a universal inhibitor of cyclin kinases. *Nature* **366**, 701-704.

Zhu, L., van de Heuvel, S., Helin, K., Fattaey, A., Ewen, M. E., Livingston, D., Dyson, N. and Harlow E. (1993). Inhibition of cell proliferation by p107, a relative of the retinoblastoma protein. *Genes Dev.* **7**, 1111-1125.

Zindy, F., Lamas, E., Chenivesse, X., Sobczak, J., Wang, J., Fesquet, D. Henglein, B. and Brechot, C. (1992). Cyclin s is required in phase in normal epithelial cells. *Biochem. Biophys. Res. Commun.* **182**, 1144-1154.

Journal of Cell Science, Supplement 18, 75-79 (1994)
Printed in Great Britain © The Company of Biologists Limited 1994

The role of cdc25 in checkpoints and feedback controls in the eukaryotic cell cycle

Ingrid Hoffmann and Eric Karsenti

Cell Biology Programme, European Molecular Biology Laboratory, Meyerhofstr. 1, D-69117 Heidelberg, Germany

SUMMARY

Major checkpoints that gate progression through the cell cycle function at the G_1/S transition, entry into mitosis and exit from mitosis. Cells use feedback mechanisms to inhibit passage through these checkpoints in response to growth control signals, incomplete DNA replication or spindle assembly. In many organisms, transition points seem to involve regulation of the activity of cyclin-dependent kinases (cdks) not only through their interactions with various cyclins, but also by phosphorylation-dephosphory-lation cycles acting on the kinase activity of the cdks. These phosphorylation cycles are modulated by the regulation of the opposing kinases and phosphatases that act on cdks and form feedback loops. In this article, we discuss the role of positive and negative feedback loops in cell cycle timing and checkpoints, focusing more specifically on the regulation of the dual specificity cdc25 phosphatase.

Key words: cdk, cdc25, cell cycle, phosphorylation, feedback control

INTRODUCTION

The past five years have seen a prodigious advance in our understanding of how the cell cycle is regulated. Separate lines of studies in different organisms, like yeast, flies, frogs and cultured mammalian cells have converged, allowing identification of the molecular mechanisms controlling the cell cycle, the so-called 'cell cycle engine'. Key components of the cell-cycle engine are members of the cyclin-dependent kinase (cdks) family. These kinases are complexes between a catalytic subunit (a member of the cdk family) and a regulatory subunit (a cyclin). It has become clear that many, if not all, eukaryotic cells contain multiple forms of this kinase, some concerned with commitment to the cell cycle, others with S phase, and yet others with various aspects of mitosis. The best character-ized of these kinases is maturation promoting factor (MPF), a complex of p34^{cdc2} (cdk1) and cyclinB. The activation of MPF results in entry into mitosis and its inactivation in exit from mitosis. Cdc2 kinase activity is regulated through its association with cyclins and by reversible phosphorylation events (Draetta and Beach, 1988; Draetta et al., 1988; Gautier et al., 1989; Morla et al., 1989). The phosphorylation of cdc2 on Tyr15 (in vertebrates also Thr14) negatively regulates kinase activity. Phosphorylation on Thr161/167 is required for tight association with cyclin and activity of the kinase (Ducommun et al., 1991; Gould et al., 1991; Krek and Nigg, 1991; Solomon et al., 1992). The residues whose phosphorylation is significant for vertebrate cdc2 activity seem to be conserved throughout the family of cyclin-dependent kinases and the regulation of the phosphorylation of these residues in various cdks may be similar to what has been described for cdc2 (Meyerson et al., 1992).

We begin to understand how these phosphorylation reactions are used to generate checkpoints at the G_1/S and G_2/M transitions, when the cell makes decisions about progression through the division cycle. In this review we report recent knowledge accumulated on the biochemistry of the control of these critical transitions. We try to show that beyond the apparent diversity of players, there might be a functional homogeneity in the molecular mechanisms involved in decision making at the G_1/S, G_2/M and M/G_1 transitions.

MITOTIC FEEDBACK CONTROLS

Many of the genes controlling entry into mitosis were first identified in the fission yeast *Schizosaccharomyces pombe*. They involve at least four gene functions acting together in a network. A schematic illustration of the control of mitosis in eukaryotic cells is shown in Fig. 1. The product of the *cdc2*$^+$ gene in fission yeast, p34, is essential for entry into mitosis. The *nim1*$^+$ and *wee1*$^+$/*mik1*$^+$ (Russell and Nurse, 1987a,b; Feilotter et al., 1991; Lundgren et al., 1991) gene products, which encode serine/threonine protein kinases are negative regulators of cdc2 gene function whereas the *cdc25*$^+$ gene product, which encodes a protein phosphatase is a positive regulator (Russell and Nurse, 1986). The balance between these two pathways regulates cdc2 function and advances or delays onset of mitosis (Fantes, 1979; Russell and Nurse, 1986, 1987a,b). The wee1 protein kinase catalyzes the phosphorylation of cdc2 at Tyr15 (McGowan, 1993; Parker et al., 1992) and inhibits the activation of the kinase. The *nim1*$^+$ (*cdr1*) gene product is a putative protein kinase (Russell and Nurse, 1987b; Feilotter et al., 1991) that negatively regulates wee1 (Coleman

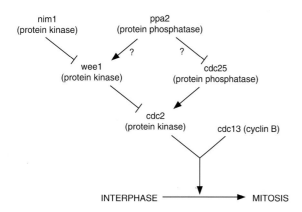

Fig. 1. Genes involved in the control of entry into mitosis in *Schizosaccharomyces pombe*.

et al., 1993; Wu and Russell, 1993). The cdc25 phosphatase removes the inhibitory phosphate from the Tyr15 residue of $p34^{cdc2}$ (Kumagai and Dunphy, 1991; Gautier et al., 1991; Millar et al., 1991a; Lee et al., 1992). The timing of entry into mitosis seems, therefore, to be largely determined by the temporal control of the phosphorylation of the Tyr15 residue on $p34^{cdc2}$. In the end, this timing must be determined by changes in the balance between the activities of wee1 and cdc25.

Entry into mitosis is regulated by a positive feedback loop

In human cells, three homologues of the fission yeast cdc25 protein have been identified, denoted cdc25A, B and C (Sadhu et al., 1990; Galaktionov and Beach, 1991). The protein level of cdc25C does not vary greatly during the cell cycle (Millar et al., 1991b; Kumagai and Dunphy, 1992; Izumi et al., 1992), but this protein undergoes phosphorylation and activation during mitosis in HeLa cells (Hoffmann et al., 1993; Kumagai and Dunphy, 1992; Izumi et al., 1992). Depletion of cdc2 and cyclinB from mitotic extracts using specific antibodies showed that the phosphorylation and activation of cdc25C was dependent on active cdc2/cyclinB complex, and purified cdc2/cyclinB kinase was shown to catalyze directly the phosphorylation of cdc25C at sites identical to those observed in vivo (Hoffmann et al., 1993). This creates a positive feedback loop that may be responsible for the rapid activation of cdc2/cyclinB at the onset of mitosis (Fig. 2). Similar results in *Xenopus* have been reported by Izumi and Maller (1993), who also showed that the cdc25C phosphatase is inactivated if mutations are introduced at the consensus cdc2 phosphorylation sites present in the cdc25 protein.

The question of how the loop is initiated is still unresolved (Hoffmann et al., 1993). One interesting possibility is that the phosphatase that keeps cdc25C dephosphorylated and inactive in interphase is not constitutively active and that its down regulation is required for entry into mitosis. Cdc25C is dephosphorylated and inactivated by a type 2A phosphatase (PP-2A) that is down regulated during mitosis (Clarke et al., 1993; Kumagai and Dunphy, 1992). It is possible that in vivo, the positive feedback loop controlling the activation of cdc2/cyclinB fires when signals coming from the DNA repli-

cation machinery or from the state of chromatin organization lead to inhibition of the type 2A phosphatase that dephosphorylates cdc25C (Clarke et al., 1993) (Fig. 2). The timing of cdc2 kinase activation at this check point may also involve regulation of the wee1 pathway (Smythe and Newport, 1992; see also Atherton-Fessler et al., 1993, for a recent review). We propose that the existence of a positive feedback loop regulating the activation of cdc2 kinase at the onset of mitosis provides both a timing device that adjusts the rate of cdc2 kinase activation and a switch on which sensory mechanisms can act to determine when cdc2 kinase should activate. The reversibilty of phosphorylation-dephosphorylation reactions is perfectly suited to build this kind of regulatory network (Novak and Tyson, 1993). These functions may not be essential in all organisms and at all times during development (Edgar et al., 1994), but they are certainly important in many cases to synchronize the successive events of the cell cycle. Interestingly, it has been reported that the Tyr phosphorylation pathway is not functional in budding yeast (Sorger and Murray, 1992; Amon et al., 1992) and in this organism, the boundary between S phase and mitosis is not very clear to say the least (Nurse, 1985). So it is perhaps not surprising that the Tyr phosphorylation pathway is deficient. In fact this may be taken as an argument supporting the idea that positive feedback loops are essential to create sharp boundaries between two cell cycle phases.

Exit from mitosis is regulated by a negative feedback loop

Exit from metaphase requires inactivation of MPF, which follows cyclin degradation (Murray, 1992). This process is triggered by active cdc2 kinase, which activates the cyclin degradation machinery (at least in *Xenopus* egg extracts (Félix et al., 1990) (Fig. 3). The signal for cyclin degradation is given only when cdc2 kinase activity reaches a threshold that corresponds roughly to the mitotic level of cdc2 kinase activity. Moreover, there is a lag of about 10 minutes between the time when cdc2 kinase activity has reached the threshold and the time when cyclin is degraded (Félix et al., 1990). This creates a negative feedback loop that can be used to time the length of mitosis. The enzyme(s) responsible for the recognition of cyclin and initiation of its proteolysis have not been identified. There is evidence implicating a ubiquitin-dependent protease in cyclin degradation (Glotzer et al., 1990; Hershko et al., 1991). It is not clear, however, whether poly-ubiquitination is the sole signal for cyclin destruction. The biochemical route of ubiquitinated cyclin destruction is also unknown, although the multifunctional proteasome is likely to be involved. Therefore, it is still difficult to propose a mechanism accounting for the requirement of a threshold level of cdc2 kinase activity to induce cyclin degradation and for the lag observed before cyclin is actually degraded. The threshold and lag suggest anyway that a switch built of cdc2 kinase and an opposing phosphatase acting on a substrate essential for cyclin degradation is involved. The lag may also involve complex ubiquitination rates in addition to phosphorylation cycles. Other feedback loop mechanisms may also be important in the inactivation of MPF as, for example, the activation of the Thr161 phosphatase. All available data, however, indicate that dephosphorylation of cdc2 on Thr161 occurs concomitantly with cyclin degradation (Draetta, 1993). It seems that the feedback

Fig. 2. Positive feedback loops at the G₁/S and G₂/M transition. The existence of a positive feedback loop at the G₂/M transition has been demonstrated (see text). This involves the increase in activity of cdc25C after its phosphorylation by the active cyclin B/cdc2 kinase. This leads to an increased rate of cdc2 activation. When fully active, the cdc2/cyclinB induces entry into M-phase. We have shown recently that cdc25A is phosphorylated and activated by cyclinE/cdk2 during S phase, suggesting that there is another positive feedback loop at this transition, built as described in the model. This remains speculative however, because we have not demonstrated yet that cyclinE/cdk2 is an in vivo substrate for the phosphorylated form of cdc25A. CyclinE/cdk2 is probably important to induce S phase. We think that both loops are important to generate sharp and irreversible cell cycle transitions and to provide switches on which cell cycle signals can impinge to allow or forbid progression in the next phase of the cycle.

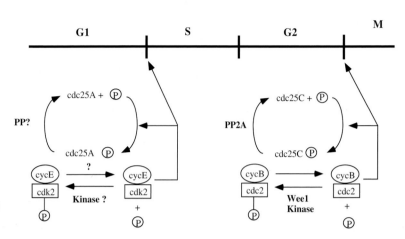

loop of cdc2 kinase on cyclin degradation could very well contain a switch on which sensors detecting misaligned chromosomes or badly assembled spindles could act to block cyclin degradation.

In summary, the oscillator driving the mitotic cycle is based on a succession of positive and negative feedback loops. These loops can act as timing devices to determine the length of the cell cycle phases they control and as switches on which sensors can impinge to adjust the period of the oscillator to the rate of DNA replication and spindle assembly. The building blocks of these loops appear to be couples of kinases and phosphatases that oppose each other by acting on specific substrates.

G₁/S FEEDBACK CONTROLS

The proliferation of all eukaryotic cells is primarily regulated by a decision that occurs during the G₁ phase of the cell cycle - to remain in the cell cycle and divide or to withdraw from the cell cycle and adopt an alternative cell fate (Pardee, 1989). In budding yeast this decision, called START, is the physio-

logical process whereby specific extracellular and intracellular signals combine to promote either cell cycle progression or cell cycle arrest and preparation for conjugation (Reed, 1991; Pringle and Hartwell, 1981). Proliferation of mammalian fibroblasts is also regulated by mitogenic signals during the G₁ phase of the cell cycle, and cells can switch between quiescence and proliferation at a unique point in G₁ (Pardee, 1989). Experiments in a number of model systems support the idea that, like yeast, higher eukaryotes require a cdk for the completion of G₁ and the onset of DNA replication.

A positive feedback loop for cyclin transcription in budding yeast

The apparently simple picture of a cyclin-kinase complex assembling at START belies a complicated array of cyclins and cdks that function during G₁ and S phases. The budding yeast G₁ cyclins CLN1, 2 and 3, all activate the CDC28 kinase at START. In the absence of all three CLNs, the cell cycle arrests at START (Richardson et al., 1989). While CLN1 and CLN2-associated kinase activities fluctuate during the cell cycle, CLN3/CDC28 activity does not, suggesting that it might have

Fig. 3. Regulation of MPF activity by feedback loops during the cell cycle. Two feedback loops seem to produce the rapid activation and inactivation of MPF. The positive feedback loop is triggered by the phosphorylation of cdc25. Activation of a ubiquitin-dependent proteolytic pathway is part of the negative feedback loop.

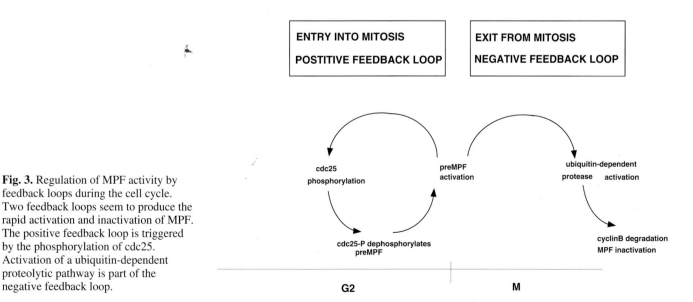

a different function (Tyers et al., 1993). Another family, composed of B-type cyclins encoded by CLB1, 2, 3 and 4 genes, is necessary for the formation and function of the mitotic apparatus (Fitch et al., 1992; Richardson et al., 1992; Surana et al., 1991). CLB5 and CLB6, encoding another pair of B-type cyclins have a function in S phase (Epstein and Cross, 1992; Schwob and Nasmyth, 1993).

Much of the order and timing of cell cycle events seems to be determined by transcriptional control, involving positive feedback loops. A postive feedback loop has been invoked to explain the appearance of CLN1 and CLN2 proteins in late G_1. It has been proposed that in daughter cells, CLN/CDC28 kinase activates a transcription factor, SBF, which in turn activates CLN1 and CLN2 transcription, thereby closing the loop by further activating CDC28 (Ogas et al., 1991; Dirick and Nasmyth, 1991). The existence of a positive feedback loop may help to understand the apparent irreversibility of START, which might be determined by the transition from low to high CLN-dependent kinase activity (Nasmyth, 1993).

Feedback controls regulating G_1 and S phases in mammalian cells

Cell cycle progression in vertebrates seems also to be driven by successive waves of cyclins. The regulation of SBF is similar to that of the mammalian transcription factor E2F. Both are involved in the activation of gene expression during late G_1 or early S phase (Pagano et al., 1992; Devoto et al., 1992). In vertebrate cells, progression through the cell cycle is blocked by the binding of retinoblastoma protein (Rb) to E2F (Chellappan et al., 1991). This block is released when Rb is phosphorylated and dissociated from E2F by a cdk/G_1 cyclin. The free E2F induces transcription of both early and delayed response genes including G_1 cyclin genes. Thus, progression through the restriction point in mammalian cells may also be regulated by an autocatalytic positive feedback loop acting at the transcriptional level.

Regulation of the G_1 to S phase transition may also involve positive feedback loops regulating the kinase activity of cdks at the post-translational level. In human cells, the cdk2 kinase is involved in the regulation of S phase progression when associated with cyclinA (Pagano et al., 1993). Its activity is negatively regulated by tyrosine (and probably also threonine) phosphorylation (Gu et al., 1992), suggesting that cdk2/cyclinA activation also requires dephosphorylation by cdc25 (Gu et al., 1992). Recently, we found that human cdc25A is phosphorylated and activated during S phase (Hoffmann et al. 1994, unpublished data). However, cdc25A phosphorylation and activation does not seem to be mediated by cdk2/cyclinA but rather by the cdk2/cyclinE complex. We still do not know what is the physiological substrate of cdc25A (cdk2/cyclinA or cdk2/cyclinE). However, these results strongly suggest that a positive feedback loop acting on the phosphorylation level of cdk2 associated to cyclinE and cyclinA plays an important role in the temporal control of the G_1/S transition and maybe in the progression through S phase (Fig. 2).

Why should such a level of regulation exist during G_1/S and maybe even during S phase progression? The positive feedback loop involving cdc25C at the G_2/M transition, seems to be a switch capable of sensing the state of DNA replication and therefore to tie entry into mitosis to the end of DNA replica-

tion. The situation is obviously very different during late G_1 and early S phase where the cdc25A-positive feedback loop would be operating. Our favorite hypothesis is that this loop senses late G_1 events, like centrosome duplication, or the level of components essential for the initiation of DNA replication. Cdc25A may also be involved in regulating the successive activation of cdk2/cyclinE and cdk2/cyclinA. Alternatively, it may simply be used to produce a sharp timing of cdk2 activation at the onset of S phase.

CONCLUSION

Although the actors involved at each cell cycle transition point vary (G_1 and mitotic cyclins, G_1 and mitotic cdks), it seems that similar basic principles govern each transition: feedback loops. Beyond the identification of specific kinases and phosphatases, if we are to understand the logic of the cell cycle, we have to understand the kinetics of cdk activation and inactivation. We have to understand how the positive and negative feedback loops function to generate irreversible transition points. We also have to understand how such loops provide switches to be acted upon by sensory devices, allowing the cell to decide whether to go or not to go one step further in the cycle.

The authors thank U. W. Hoffmann Rohrer and G. Simos for their comments on the manuscript.

REFERENCES

Amon, A., Surana, U., Muroff, I. and Nasmyth, K. (1992). Regulation of p34CDC28 tyrosine phosphorylation is not required for entry into mitosis in S. cerevisiae. *Nature* **355**, 368-371.

Atherton-Fessler, S., Hanning, G. and Piwnica-Worms, H. (1993). Reversible tyrosine phosphorylation and cell cycle control. *Semin. Cell Biol.* **4**, 433-442.

Chellappan, S. P., Hiebert, S., Mudryi, M., Horowitz, J. M. and Nevins, J. R. (1991). The E2F transcription factor is a cellular target for the Rb protein.

Clarke, P., Hoffmann, I., Draetta, G. and Karsenti, E. (1993). Dephosphorylation of cdc25-C by a type-2A protein phosphatase: specific regulation during the cell cycle in *Xenopus* egg extracts. *Mol. Biol. Cell* **4**, 397-411.

Coleman, T. R., Tang, Z. and Dunphy, W. G. (1993). Negative regulation of the wee1 protein kinase by direct action of the nim1/cdr1 mitotic inducer. *Cell* **72**, 919-929.

Devoto, S. H., Mudryi, M., Pines, J., Hunter, T. and Nevins, J. (1992). A cyclin A-protein kinase complex possesses sequence-specific DNA binding activity: p33cdk2 is a component of the E2F-cyclin A complex. *Cell* **68**, 167-176.

Dirick, L. and Nasmyth, K. (1991). The role of SWI4 and SWI6 in the activity of G1 cyclins in yeast. *Nature* **66**, 995-1013.

Draetta, G. and Beach, D. (1988). p34 protein kinase, a human homolog of the yeast cell cycle control proteins encoded by cdc2+ and CDC28. *Cancer Cells* **6**, 259-263.

Draetta, G., Piwnica-Worms, H., Morrison, D., Druker, B., Roberts, T. and Beach, D. (1988). Human cdc2 protein kinase is a major cell-cycle regulated tyrosine kinase substrate. *Nature* **336**, 738-44.

Draetta, G. (1993). cdc2 activation: the interplay of cyclin binding and Thr161 phosphorylation. *Trends Cell Biol.* **3**, 287-289.

Ducommun, B., Brambilla, P., Felix, M.-A., Franza, B. R. J., Karsenti, E. and Draetta, G. (1991). cdc2 phosphorylation is required for its interaction with cyclin. *EMBO J.* **10**, 3311-3319.

Edgar, B., Sprenger, F., Duronio, R., Leopold, P. and O´Farrell, P. (1994). Distinct molecular mechanisms regulate cell cycle timing at successive stages of *Drosophila* embryogenesis. *Genes Dev.* **8**, 440-452.

Epstein, C. and Cross, F. (1992). CLB5: a novel B cyclin from budding yeast with a role in S phase. *Genes Dev.* **6**, 2021-2034.

Fantes, P. A. (1979). Epistatic gene interactions in the control of division in fission yeast. *Nature* **279**, 428.

Feilotter, H., Nurse, P. and Young, P. G. (1991). Genetic and molecular analysis of *cdr1/nim1* in *Schizosaccharomyces pombe*. *Genetics* **127**, 309-318.

Félix, M. A., Labbé, J. C., Dorée, M., Hunt, T. and Karsenti, E. (1990). Cdc2-kinase triggers cyclin degradation in interphase extracts of amphibian eggs. *Nature* **346**, 379-382.

Fitch, I., Dahmann, C., Surana, U., Amon, A., Nashmit, K., Goetsch, L., Byers, B. and Futcher, B. (1992). Characterization of four B-type cyclin genes of the budding yeast *Saccharomyces cerevisiae*. *Mol. Biol. Cell* **3**, 805-818.

Galaktionov, K. and Beach, D. (1991). Specific activation of cdc25 tyrosine phosphatase by B-type cyclins: evidence for multiple roles of mitotic cyclins. *Cell* **67**, 1181-1194.

Gautier, J., Matsukawa, T., Nurse, P. and Maller, J. (1989). Dephosphorylation and activation of Xenopus p34cdc2 protein kinase during the cell cycle. *Nature* **339**, 626-629.

Gautier, J., Solomon, M. J., Booher, R. N., Bazan, J. F. and Kirschner, M. W. (1991). cdc25 is a specific tyrosine phosphatase that directly activates p34cdc2. *Cell* **67**, 197-211.

Glotzer, M., Murray, A. and Kirschner, M. (1990). Cyclin is degraded by the ubiquitin pathway. *Nature* **349**, 132-138.

Gould, K. L., Moreno, S., Owen, D. J., Sazer, S. and Nurse, P. (1991). Phosphorylation at Thr167 is required for *Schizosaccharomyces pombe* p34^{cdc2} function. *EMBO J.* **10**, 3297-309.

Gu, Y., Rosenblatt, J. and Morgan, D. O. (1992). Cell cycle regulation of cdk2 activity by phosphorylation of Thr160 and Tyr15. *EMBO J.* **11**, 3995-4005.

Hershko, A., Ganoth, D., Pehrson, J., Palazzo, R. and Cohen, L. (1991). Methylated ubiquitin inhibits cyclin degradation in clam embryo extracts. *J. Biol. Chem.* **266**, 16376-16379.

Hoffmann, I., Clarke, P. R., Marcote, M., J.,, Karsenti, E. and Draetta., G. (1993). Phosphorylation and activation of human cdc25-C by cdc2-cyclin B and its involvement in the self-amplification of MPF at mitosis. *EMBO J.* **12**, 53-63.

Izumi, T., Walker, D. and Maller, J. (1992). Periodic changes in phosphorylation of the *Xenopus* cdc25 phosphatase regulates its activity. *Mol. Biol. Cell* **3**, 927-939.

Izumi, T. and Maller, J. (1993). Elimination of cdc2 phosphorylation sites in the cdc25 phosphatase blocks initiation of M-phase. *Mol. Biol. Cell* **4**, 1337-1350.

Krek, W. and Nigg, E. (1991). Differential phosphorylation of vertebrate p34^{cdc2} kinase at the G1/S and G2/M transitions of the cell cycle: identification of major phosphorylation sites. *EMBO J.* **10**, 305-316.

Kumagai, A. and Dunphy, W. (1991). The cdc25 protein controls tyrosine dephosphorylation of the cdc2 protein in a cell-free system. *Cell* **64**, 903-914.

Kumagai, A. and Dunphy, W. G. (1992). Regulation of the cdc25 protein during the cell cycle in Xenopus extracts. *Cell* **70**, 139-151.

Lee, M. S., Ogg, S., Xu, M., Parker, L., Donoghue, D., Maller, J. and Piwnica-Worms, H. (1992). cdc25 encodes a protein phosphatase that dephosphorylates cdc2. *Mol. Biol. Cell* **3**, 73-84.

Lundgren, K., Walworth, N., Booher, R., Dembski, M., Kirschner, M. and Beach, D. (1991). *mik1* and *wee1* cooperate in the inhibitory tyrosine phosphorylatin of cdc2. *Cell* **64**, 1111-1122.

McGowan, C. H. and Russell, P. (1993). Human wee1 kinase inhibits cell division by phosphorylationg p34cdc2 exclusively on Tyr15. *EMBO J.* **12**, 75-85.

Meyerson, M., Enders, G. H., Wu, C.-L., Su, L.-K., Gorka, C., Nelson, C., Harlow, E. and Tsai, L.-H. (1992). A family of human cdc2-related protein kinases. *EMBO J.* **11**, 2909-2917.

Millar, J., McGowan, C. H., Lenaers, G., Jones, R. and Russell, P. (1991a). p80cdc25 mitotic inducer is the tyrosine phosphatase that activates p34cdc2 kinase in fission yeast. *EMBO J.* **10**, 4301-4309.

Millar, J. B. A., Blevitt, J., Gerace, L., Sadhu, K., Featherstone, C. and Russell, P. (1991b). p55^{cdc25} is a nuclear protein required for initiation of mitosis in human cells. *Proc. Nat. Acad. Sci. USA.* **88**, 10500-10504.

Morla, A., Draetta, G., Beach, D. and Wang, J. Y. J. (1989). Reversible tyrosine phosphorylation of cdc2: Dephosphorylation accompanies activation during entrance into mitosis. *Cell* **58**, 193-203.

Murray, A. W. (1992). Creative blocks: cell-cycle checkpoints and feedback controls. *Nature* **359**, 599-604.

Nasmyth, K. (1993). Control of the yeast cell cycle by the CDC28 protein kinase. *Curr. Biol.* **5**, 166-179.

Novak, B. and Tyson, J. J. (1993). Numerical analysis of a comprehensive model of M-phase control in *Xenopus* oocyte extracts and intact embryos. *J. Cell Sci.* **106**, 1153-1168.

Nurse, P. (1985). Cell cycle control genes in yeast. *Trends Cell Biol.* **1**, 51-55.

Ogas, J., Andrews, B. and Herskowitz, I. (1991). Transcriptional activation of CLN1, CLN2 and a putative new G1 cyclin (HCS26) by SWI4, a positive regulator of G1-specific transcription. *Cell* **66**, 1015-1026.

Pagano, M., Draetta, G. and Jansen-Durr, P. (1992). Association of cdk2 kinase with the transcription factor E2F during S phase. *Science* **255**, 1144-1147.

Pagano, M., Pepperkok, R., Lukas, J., Baldin, V., Ansorge, W., Bartek, J. and Draetta, G. (1993). Regulation of the human cell cycle by the cdk2 protein kinase. *J. Cell Biol.* **121**, 101-111.

Pardee, A. B. (1989). G1 events and regulation of cell proliferation. *Science* **246**, 603-614.

Parker, L., Atheron-Fessler, S. and Piwnica-Worms, H. (1992). p107^{wee1} is a dual-specific kinase that phosphorylates p34^{cdc2} on tyrosine 15. *Proc. Nat. Acad. Sci.* **89**, 2917-2921.

Pringle, J. R. and Hartwell, L. H. (1981). The Saccharomyces cerevisiae cell cycle. In *The Molecular Biology of the Yeast* Saccharomyces. *Life Cycle and Inheritance* (ed. J. N. Strathern, E. W. Jones and J. R. Broach), pp. 97-142. Cold Spring Harbour Laboratory Press, Cold Spring Harbour, New York.

Reed, S. (1991). G₁-specific cyclins: in search of an S-phase promoting factor. *Trends Genet.* **7**, 95-99.

Richardson, H., Wittenberg, K., Cross, F. and Reed, S. (1989). An essential G1 function for cyclin-like proteins in yeast. *Cell* **59**, 1127-1133.

Richardson, H., Lew, D. J., Henze, M., Sugimoto, K. and Reed, S. (1992). Cyclin-B homologs in *Saccharomycaes cerevisiae* function in S phase and in G2. *Genes Dev.* **6**, 2021-2034.

Russell, P. and Nurse, P. (1986). *cdc25+* functions as an inducer in the mitotic control of fission yeast. *Cell* **45**, 145-53.

Russell, P. and Nurse, P. (1987a). The mitotic inducer *nim1+* functions in a regulatory network of protein kinase homologs controlling the initiation of mitosis. *Cell* **49**, 569-576.

Russell, P. and Nurse, P. (1987b). Negative regulation of mitosis by *wee1+*, a gene encoding a protein kinase homolog. *Cell* **49**, 559-567.

Sadhu, K., Reed, S. I., Richardson, H. and Russell, P. (1990). Human homolog of fission yeast *cdc25* is predominantly expressed in G1. *Proc. Nat. Acad. Sci. USA* **87**, 5139-5143.

Schwob, E. and Nasmyth, K. (1993). CLB5 and CLB6, a new pair of B cyclins involved in S phase and mitotic spindle formation in *S. cerevisiae*. *Genes Dev.* **7**, 1160-1175.

Smythe, C. and Newport, J. W. (1992). Coupling of mitosis to the completion of S-phase in Xenopus occurs via modulation of the tyrosine kinase that phosphorylates p34^{cdc2}. *Cell* **68**, 787-797.

Solomon, N., Lee, T. and Kirschner, M. W. (1992). Role of phosphorylation in p34cdc2 activation: identification of an activating kinase. *Mol. Biol. Cell* **3**, 13-27.

Sorger, P. K. and Murray, A. W. (1992). S-phase feedback control in budding yeast independent of tyrosine phosphorylation of p34^{CDC28}. *Nature* **355**, 365-368.

Surana, U., Robitsch, H., Price, C., Schuster, T., Fitch, I., Futcher, A. B. and Nasmyth, K. (1991). The role of CDC28 and cyclins during mitosis in the budding yeast S. cerevisiae. *Cell* **65**, 145-161.

Tyers, M., Tokiwa, G. and Futcher, B. (1993). Comparison of the *S. cerevisiae* G1 cyclins: Cln3 may be an upstream activator of Cln1, Cln2 and other cyclins. *EMBO J.* **12**, 1955-1968.

Wu, L. and Russell, P. (1993). Nim1 kinase promotes mitosis by inactivating wee1 tyrosine kinase. *Nature* **363**, 738-741.

Journal of Cell Science, Supplement 18, 81-87 (1994)
Printed in Great Britain © The Company of Biologists Limited 1994

pRB, p107 and the regulation of the E2F transcription factor

Nicholas Dyson

Laboratory of Molecular Oncology, Massachusetts General Hospital Cancer Center, Building 149, 13th Street, Charlestown, MA 02129, USA

SUMMARY

Small DNA tumor viruses, such as adenovirus, encode proteins that deregulate the cell cycle. These proteins are potent transforming agents when tested in standard oncogenic assays. For adenovirus the best characterized viral oncoproteins are the early region 1A (E1A) products. Mutational studies have shown that E1A's oncogenic ability is determined primarily by its ability to bind to certain cellular proteins and interfere with their function. One of these cellular targets for E1A is the product of the retinoblastoma tumor suppressor gene, pRB. pRB is a negative regulator of cell proliferation, and its inactivation has been shown to be an important oncogenic step in the development of many human cancers. In adenovirus-mediated transformation, E1A binds to pRB and inactivates it, thus functionally mimicking the loss of pRB often seen in human tumors.

There is now compelling evidence to suggest that pRB regulates transcription at specific phases of the cell cycle by physically associating with key transcription factors. The best characterized target of pRB is the transcription factor E2F. The interaction of pRB and E2F leads to the inhibition of E2F-mediated transactivation. Most of the genes that are known to be controlled by E2F have key roles in the regulation of cell proliferation. During cell cycle progression, phosphorylation of pRB appears to change its conformation and E2F is released. In pathogenic settings E2F transactivation is not regulated by pRB binding. In human tumors with mutations in the retinoblastoma gene, functional pRB is absent and hence can no longer inhibit E2F activity. During adenovirus transformation, E1A binds to pRB and displaces E2F. In both these cases, E2F is released from pRB-mediated regulation at inappropriate times. The activation of these E2F-responsive genes may lead to the stimulation of cell proliferation. While we do not know whether E2F is the only target for pRB action, this work has formed a general picture of how tumor suppressor gene products such as pRB can control specific transcriptional events and act as negative regulators of cell growth.

Recent experiments have shown that E2F represents the combined activity of an extensive series of protein complexes. There are at least five genes that encode E2F polypeptides, and probably several more have yet to be identified. The E2F transcription factor is a heterodimer composed of two related polypeptides, one encoded by a member of the E2F gene family and the other by a member of the DP family. Intriguingly DP and E2F genes are also found in *Drosophila* and these may provide alternative approaches to the investigation of E2F function. In mammalian cells E2F/DP heterodimers are regulated, at least in part, by the formation of many larger complexes. E2F is found in separate complexes with pRB, p107/cyclin A/cdk2 or p107/cyclin E/cdk2, and additional complexes exist that have yet to be fully characterized. These E2F complexes are detected at specific points of the cell cycle and appear to provide different elements of E2F regulation.

Key words: pRB, p107, E2F transcription factor, regulation

pRB AND p107 ARE CELLULAR TARGETS FOR E1A-MEDIATED TRANSFORMATION

The E1A proteins are the first viral proteins to be synthesized during adenovirus infection (Lewis and Mathews, 1980; Nevins, 1981). Although these proteins are multifunctional, their overall function is to alter infected cells, changing their metabolism for a state more conducive for viral propagation. When E1A is studied by itself in the absence of other viral functions, it proves to be a potential nuclear oncoprotein. These activities are thought to drive cell cycle progression into S phase, where viral DNA synthesis can begin.

The regions of E1A that enable it to drive cell cycle progression correspond closely to the regions that are essential for E1A's oncogenic properties (Howe et al., 1990; Howe and Bayley, 1992). These regions include several domains that allow the interaction with cellular proteins (Whyte et al., 1989). There are two major classes of interaction, one with a cellular protein known as p300 and one with a group of related proteins that include pRB, p107, and p130. These two classes of interaction can be distinguished by the regions on E1A that make the contacts with the cellular proteins. Binding to p300 requires the amino-terminal regions of E1A between residues 1 and 76, while binding to pRB, p107, and p130 requires two independent interaction domains encompassing residues 35-60 and 120 to 127 (Whyte et al., 1989; Giordano et al., 1991a,b). Mutations in either region, which destroy the ability of E1A to bind to these cellular proteins, destroy E1A's ability to act as an oncogene.

Analysis of E1A's binding to pRB, p107, and p130 has

shown that these proteins are found in separate complexes, with E1A using similar sequences to bind to each protein independently. Adenovirus is not the only DNA tumor virus that encodes proteins that can bind to these cellular proteins. Both the polyomaviruses, best represented by SV40, and the human papillomaviruses encode proteins that bind to pRB and p107 (DeCaprio et al., 1988; Dyson et al., 1989a,b, 1992; Ewen et al., 1989). In vitro binding experiments suggest that these viral proteins will also bind to p130. Large T antigens of the polyomaviruses and the E7 proteins of human papillomaviruses show structural homologies to E1A in the regions that are needed to bind to pRB and p107 (Stabel, 1985; Figge et al., 1988; Phelps et al., 1988). In these viruses too, the pRB- and p107-binding regions are important for the viral proteins to act as oncogenes (Ewen et al., 1989; Munger et al., 1989; Larose et al., 1990). Thus, it appears that many small DNA viruses target cellular proteins such as p107 and pRB and that these interactions are an integral part of the oncogenic properties of their early products.

THE RETINOBLASTOMA TUMOR SUPPRESSOR GENE

The *RB-1* gene was the first tumor suppressor gene to be isolated and recognized for its involvement with human cancer. Inactivation of both copies of the *RB-1* gene has been found in 100% of retinoblastomas, and the inheritance of a mutated *RB-1* allele has been shown to be the genetic lesion in familial retinoblastoma (reviewed by Weinberg, 1988, 1992). Following the isolation of the *RB-1* gene considerable effort was focused into determining the biochemical function of its protein product (pRB). Although initial progress was slow, discoveries made during the last two to three years have allowed the development of models for the function of pRB. Many lines of evidence indicate that pRB serves as a regulator of transcription factors. Several factors have been shown to bind to pRB, including c-myc, N-myc, E2F (also called DRTF1), elf1, PU1, myoD, myogenin, ATF2 and abl (Bandara and La Thangue, 1991; Chellappan et al., 1991; Rustgi et al., 1991; Kim et al., 1992; Gu et al., 1993; Hagemeier et al., 1993; Wang et al., 1993; Welch and Wang, 1993). Of these, the best studied is the transcription factor E2F, and the pRB/E2F interaction is discussed in more detail below. E2F-mediated transcription is inhibited by its association with pRB (Hiebert et al., 1992; Zamanian and La Thangue, 1992; Helin and Harlow, 1993). pRB binding has also been proposed to repress several other factors, including c-myc, N-myc, Elf-1, PU1 (Rustgi et al., 1991; Hagemeier et al., 1993; Wang et al., 1993). Although these complexes are less well studied than E2F, the available data suggests that these interactions have many similarities to the E2F/pRB complex. In other cases (ATF-2, MyoD and myogenin) the pRB interaction is less well understood but may be fundamentally different since the association is proposed to cause transcriptional activation (Kim et al., 1992; Gu et al., 1993; Wang et al., 1993).

The *RB-1* gene is the prototype for all tumor suppressor genes. Loss or mutation of both *RB-1* alleles is a key step in the tumorigenic progression of many human cancers (see, for example, Weinberg, 1990). This loss or inactivation of functional pRB removes an inhibitor to cell proliferation and

thereby promotes inappropriate division. Since E1A is a positively acting oncoprotein, the demonstration that pRB was one of the proteins bound to E1A led to a suggestion that E1A overcame pRB's negative regulatory role, mimicking the loss of pRB seen in many tumors (Whyte et al., 1988). Further work has shown that model to be correct.

A FAMILY OF POCKET PROTEINS - POTENTIAL CELL CYCLE REGULATORS

p107 was first identified through its interaction with the adenovirus early protein E1A (Yee and Branton, 1985; Harlow et al., 1986). The study of p107 has drawn further attention following the cloning of a partial cDNA by Ewen et al. (1991). This original clone represents the carboxy-terminal 90% of the full-length coding region for p107 recently isolated by Zhu et al. (1993). Many of the properties of p107, including how it interacted with E1A, suggested that it would be related to pRB. The sequence of the first p107 clone proved these suggestions correct (Ewen et al., 1991). p107 and pRB have 7 regions of recognizable sequence homology, the best homology showing 62% identity. Not surprisingly, a great deal of the homology was found in a region that corresponds to the binding site for E1A. This region, which has become known as the 'pocket', is composed of two essential segments separated by a 'spacer' region that is required for binding but whose sequence is irrelevant for interaction. In addition there is good homology in the carboxy-terminal region of pRB and p107.

The recent cloning of p130 has revealed that it is closely related to pRB and p107 (Hannon et al., 1993; Li et al., 1993; Mayol et al., 1993). The p130 protein also contains a pocket-domain structure that mediates its interaction with E1A. Sequence comparisons show that p130 and p107 are more closely related to one another than to pRB. This is most apparent in the comparisons of the spacer domains. Studies of p107 have shown that the spacer region contains a high-affinity binding site for the cyclin A/cdk2 and cyclin E/cdk2 kinases (Ewen et al., 1992; Faha et al., 1992, 1993) and analogous complexes may also exist for p130 (Hannon et al., 1993; Li et al., 1993). Although the spacer sequences of p107 and p130 are 44% identical neither sequence has any homology with the spacer domain of pRB and it appears that the stable association with cyclin-dependent kinases is a feature that distinguishes p107 and p130 from pRB. The function of these complexes are unknown; however, the stoichiometry is high. Up to 50% of the p107 found in the cell is associated with these cyclin/cdk complexes. This high level of interaction suggests that they are likely to play an important role in the action of p107 and p130.

Several approaches have been used to demonstrate that the reintroduction of pRB into tumor cells that lack a normal *RB-1* can cause cell cycle arrest (Goodrich et al., 1991; Hinds et al., 1992). Analogous experiments have shown that p107, when transiently expressed at high levels after transfection, can also cause cell cycle arrest (Zhu et al., 1993). In these experiments p107 was cotransfected with a second plasmid that expresses a cell surface marker that enables transfected cells to be identified after flow cytometry. Comparison between the growth suppression properties of pRB and p107 has enabled some initial conclusions to be drawn (Zhu et al., 1993). Many cell lines are unaffected by the overexpression of pRB and p107, even cell lines such as J82 that lack a functional *RB-1* gene. A few cell lines, however, appear to be sensitive to these proteins and expression causes cell cycle arrest. Saos-2 cells, an osteosarcoma cell line, respond to pRB and p107 in an similar manner and arrest in G_1. However, the responses are not identical in other cells. In C33A cells, the overexpression of p107 caused cell cycle arrest in G_1, but the expression of pRB did not. This was one of the first indications that pRB and p107 have distinguishable functional characteristics. A second feature of these experiments reinforced this suggestion. These differences are apparent in the ability of various other genes to overcome growth arrest in G_1 induced by pRB or p107. Hinds et al. (1992) have demonstrated that co-transfecting G_1 cyclins overcomes the pRB arrest. However, in similar conditions these cyclins had little effect on the p107 block (Zhu et al., 1993). Similarly the over-expression of the E2F-1 gene overcame the pRB block but had no effect on the p107 arrested cells. Conversely the adenovirus E1A protein, which binds to both pRB and p107, overcame the p107 arrest with considerably greater efficiency than the pRB arrest. These different rescue properties provided a further indication that pRB and p107 have related but distinct potential for growth arrest.

THE E2F TRANSCRIPTION FACTOR

The first clues to the biochemical role of pRB came from other viral studies looking at the activation of the E2 promoter of adenovirus. Following infection, the E2 promoter is transactivated by E1A. One of the regions of the promoter that allowed E1A transactivation was called E2F for E2 factor (Yee et al., 1987). Adenovirus E1A activates transcription from the E2 promoter by releasing active E2F from inhibitory complexes (Bagchi et al., 1993). When the regions of E1A that were needed to cause this transactivation were mapped they corresponded with the regions that were needed to bind to pRB, p107, and p130 (Raychaudhuri et al., 1991). Purified E2F was examined and shown to be physically associated with pRB (Bagchi et al., 1991; Chellappan et al., 1991). More recent work has shown that by binding to E2F, pRB is able to inhibit E2F-mediated transcription (Hiebert et al., 1992; Zamanian and La Thangue, 1992; Helin and Harlow, 1993). Thus, one role of pRB is to bind to E2F and inhibit transcription. E1A breaks apart this interaction and leads to the activation of E2F-mediated transcription.

Purification of E2F on DNA-affinity columns suggested that it was a heterogeneous factor and that DNA binding required at least two different components (Huber et al., 1993). This impression has been confirmed by the cloning of at least 5 genes encoding components of E2F (Helin et al., 1992; Kaelin et al., 1992; Shan et al., 1992; Girling et al., 1993; Ivey-Hoyle et al., 1993; Lees et al., 1993). These genes fall into two classes, termed E2F or DP, whose products heterodimerize to produce a DNA-binding complex capable of activating transcription from promoters containing E2F sites (Bandara et al., 1993; Helin et al., 1993). In transient transfections the products of any one of the E2F-1, E2F-2, and E2F-3 genes heterodimerize with either of the DP-1 or DP-2 encoded proteins producing a transcriptional activator (J. Lees and C.-L. Wu, personal communication). Northern analyses suggest that some of these genes may be differentially expressed, but no func-

tional differences between these complexes are known (Lees et al., 1993).

The cloning of E2F genes has allowed a detailed examination of the pRB/E2F interaction. pRB binds directly to the transactivation domain of E2F and represses its activity (Helin et al., 1994). This interaction appears to be regulated in several ways. One of the mechanisms of regulation appears to be at the level of protein phosphorylation. pRB contains several sites that are substrates for many of the cyclin-dependent kinases (cdks) that are active at discrete points of the cell cycle, and pRB becomes heavily phosphorylated as cells progress from G_1 into S phase (Buchkovich et al., 1989; Chen et al., 1989; DeCaprio et al., 1989; Mihara et al., 1989). Despite this, only the un- or underphosphorylated forms of pRB are found associated with E2F (Chellappan et al., 1991; Helin et al., 1992; Kaelin et al., 1992), thus the release of E2F from pRB may provide a temporal control to E2F activity.

POTENTIAL TARGETS FOR E2F

One of the outcomes of this regulation is that adenovirus infections lead to the activation of E2F-mediated transcription. While adenovirus has an early promoter that is activated by E2F, there are no E2F-responsive promoters in the polyomaviruses or the papillomaviruses. Therefore, the target promoters that are affected by viral proteins binding to pRB must be different for adenovirus. A potential answer to this problem comes from the demonstration that many cellular promoters that control genes involved in growth control also have E2F sites. These genes include those encoding c-myc, N-myc, b-myb, DNA polymerase-α, DHFR, thymidine kinase, thymidylate synthase, cdc2, and cyclin A (for a review see (Nevins, 1992; Helin and Harlow, 1993). In the c-myc, DHFR, b-myb, thymidine kinase, and cdc2 promoters the E2F sites have been shown to be essential for the transcriptional activation of these genes that occurs as serum-starved cells are stimulated to progress through the cell cycle (Blake and Azizkhan, 1989; Hiebert et al., 1989; Thalmeier et al., 1989; Dalton, 1992; Means et al., 1992; Lam and Watson, 1993). In this experimental system, the presence of a short element carrying 2 overlapping E2F sites has been shown to be sufficient for the temporal expression of the DHFR gene at the G_1 to S transition (Slansky et al., 1993). The view that emerges from these studies is that the transcription of a broad range of important growth-regulating genes appears to be regulated by E2F or E2F-related proteins.

Based on this information, the loss of pRB function is predicted to deregulate the transcription of E2F-responsive genes. The notion that this may contribute to the deregulation of cell cycle control is supported by several observations. First, the microinjection of E2F-1 protein stimulates DNA synthesis in quiescent cells (Johnson et al., 1993). Second, transfection of E2F-1 into WI38 fibroblasts inhibits cell cycle arrest upon serum withdrawal (Johnson et al., 1993). Third, the recent finding that Chinese hamster ovary cells are fully transformed by the cotransfection of E2F-1 and DP-1 (N. Heintz, personal communication). Fourth, the E2F-1 gene appears to undergo genetic rearrangements in some leukemias (Saito et al., 1994). All of these data point to an important role for E2F in the control of cell proliferation.

THERE ARE MANY E2F COMPLEXES

pRB is only one of several regulators of E2F. When extracts from various cell lines were tested for protein complexes that can bind specifically to E2F oligonucleotides, at least two major complexes were detected. One of these was identified as the pRB/E2F complex (Bandara and La Thangue, 1991; Chellappan et al., 1991). The other larger complex was originally demonstrated to contain cyclin A (Mudryj et al., 1991). The appearance of cyclin A in the complex prompted several labs to investigate whether other proteins might be found in this complex. Work from several groups showed that this E2F-binding complex contains p107, cyclin A, and cdk2 (Cao et al., 1992; Devoto et al., 1992; Shirodkar et al., 1992). Further analysis of p107/E2F showed that it actually contained two complexes, one with E2F/p107/cyclin A/cdk2 and one with E2F/p107/cyclin E/cdk2 (Lees et al., 1992). Surprisingly, these complexes exist in different stages of the cell cycle. The cyclin E/cdk2 version is found in G_1, while the cyclin A/cdk2 E2F/p107 complex is found in S phase.

Bandshift experiments using extracts from synchronized cells showed that serum-starved cells and cells that were early in G_1 phase contained E2F complexes that did not appear to contain either pRB or p107 (Mudryj et al., 1991; Shirodkar et al., 1992). Recently Cobrinik et al. (1993) have demonstrated that these complexes contain the p130 protein, and like p107, the p130/E2F complexes can also be formed with cyclin dependent kinases. By analogy with pRB, p107 and p130 may also be repressors of E2F activity. During adenovirus infection E1A dissociates all of the pRB-, p107-, and p130-E2F complexes and this correlates with the activation of E2F. Furthermore the transient overexpression of p107 has been shown to repress the activity of both endogenous and exogenous E2F (Schwarz et al., 1993; Zamanian and Thangue, 1993; Zhu et al., 1993).

The E2F complexes with p107 and p130 provide an added level of intrigue. Most of the E2F/p107 and E2F/p130 DNA-bound complexes contain stoichiometric levels of the cdks. These complexes provide a direct connection between the kinases that regulate cell cycle progression and the temporal expression of genes that are required for cell proliferation. It is widely speculated that this connection is important for the functions of both the kinases and E2F, but the consequence of the interaction is unclear. Many models have been proposed; examples are: that the complex targets the kinase to a DNA-bound substrate; that the complex targets the kinase to E2F/DP (conceivably it switches the factor on or off); that the kinase phosphorylates p107 or p130 and regulates the p107/E2F or p130/E2F interaction; that E2F/DP sequesters the kinase away from other substrates.

pRB AND p107 ASSOCIATE WITH DIFFERENT E2FS

Work in the last several months has emphasized the differences between pRB and p107. Analysis of the polypeptides that co-precipitate with p107 and pRB has revealed that DP-1 and DP-2 are associated with both pRB and p107 (Girling et al., 1993; C.-L. Wu and J. Lees, personal communication) but that the E2F components of the heterodimers differ (Dyson et al., 1993; Lees et al., 1993). The E2F polypeptides migrate differently on

SDS-PAGE and yield different patterns after partial proteolytic digestion. Furthermore, antibodies raised against the products of cloned E2F genes differ in their ability to recognize the pRB-associated and p107-associated E2F proteins. Polyclonal antisera specific for E2F-1, E2F-2 and E2F-3 all immunoprecipitate pRB-associated E2F but fail to recognize p107-associated E2F (Dyson et al., 1993; Lees et al., 1993). To date only one E2F-1 antibody, a pan-reactive anti-peptide antibody that was raised against the pRB-binding domain of E2F-1, has been found to immunoprecipitate both pRB- and p107-associated E2F polypeptides. These findings suggest that pRB and p107 regulate different forms of E2F. Thus, although p107 and pRB both associate with E2F they appear to provide different elements of the regulation. It is unclear whether pRB-E2F and p107-E2F regulate a single set of genes in different ways or whether they act on different E2F-responsive promoters

ADDITIONAL TIERS OF E2F REGULATION

Several lines of evidence suggest that there may be tiers of regulation in addition to the interactions mentioned above. Phosphorylation of E2F is likely to be one mechanism of control. Early studies of partially purified E2F indicated that DNA-binding activity was influenced by phosphorylation state and many of the E2F polypeptides undergo extensive modifications (Bagchi et al., 1989; Yee et al., 1989). It is also clear that the levels of E2F proteins are an additional point of regulation. Initial studies of E2F-1 have revealed that the level of E2F-1 mRNAs and proteins are under strong regulation during the cell cycle, as E2F-1 mRNA is not found in G_0 cells (Kaelin et al., 1992). Raychaudhuri et al. (1991) have shown that dissociation of E2F complexes by detergent treatment greatly increases the total amount of E2F-DNA binding activity, suggesting that the DNA-binding activity of E2F was regulated by protein association. These workers purified a subset of E2F/pRB complexes that were unable to bind to DNA (Bagchi et al., 1991) and identified an associated inhibitory factor that modulated the DNA-binding properties of E2F/pRB complexes (Ray et al., 1992). Although the E2F/pRB complexes are not predicted to have transactivating properties, they may play an important role in regulation of gene expression. Such a role was suggested by Weintraub et al. (1992) who observed that E2F sites can act as silencing elements in the presence of high levels of pRB.

There are also some indications that the phosphorylation of pRB may not be the only regulator of the pRB/E2F interaction. Experiments using synchronized cells suggest that some of the pRB/E2F complexes persist late into S-phase (Shirodkar et al., 1992; Schwarz et al., 1993) by which time the majority of pRB is heavily phosphorylated and the transcription of many of the proposed E2F-regulated genes has already been elevated. This may indicate that different complexes are regulated at different times or that E2F transactivation has occurred prior to the disappearance of the pRB/E2F complex, presumably at a time when the pRB/E2F complex is not fully dissociated by pRB phosphorylation. It has been known for several years that some cell lines (the F9 embryonal carcinoma cell line is probably the best studied example) have normal levels of E2F and pRB but lack any of the larger E2F complexes (La Thangue et al., 1990). It has been suggested that these cells contain an E1A-like activity that inhibits the pRB/E2F interaction, although the nature of this activity is unknown.

E2F GENES IN *DROSOPHILA*

All this supports the notion that the normal regulation of E2F in mammalian cells is a highly complex process, and it is clear that the E2F/pRB complex is only one aspect of an intricate network of controls. Currently, many groups are studying the biochemistry of E2F complexes. However, many of the fundamental questions about E2F function have yet to be addressed and a full investigation of E2F regulation will require both genetic and biochemical approaches.

To complement ongoing biochemical studies of E2F we have isolated E2F and DP genes from *Drosophila* and demonstrated that they are functional homologs of the human E2F genes in transactivation (Dynlacht et al., 1994). Both of the genes have been localized to regions of the *Drosophila* genome that have been extensively studied. If mutation of these genes leads to a clear phenotype then it may be possible to use genetic approaches to study the E2F pathway. Such a system may provide a unique opportunity to investigate the composition of the E2F pathway and its function. In particular it would be interesting to determine whether the E2F pathway is essential for viability and to investigate the role of E2F in normal development.

I thank Ed Harlow for his support, Jackie Lees and Chin-Lee Wu for communication of data prior to publication, Li-Huei Tsai for help with the writing of this manuscript, and members of the Molecular Biology Laboratory for stimulating discussions.

REFERENCES

Bagchi, S., Raychaudhuri, P. and Nevins, J. R. (1989). Phosphorylation-dependent activation of the adenovirus-inducible E2F factor in a cell-free system. *Proc. Nat. Acad. Sci. USA* **86**, 4352-4356.

Bagchi, S., Raychaudhuri, P. and Nevins, J. R. (1990). Adenovirus E1A proteins can dissociate heteromeric complexes involving the E2F transcription factor: a novel mechanism fpr E1A trans-activation. *Cell* **62**, 659-669.

Bagchi, S., Weinmann, R. and Raychaudhuri, P. (1991). The retinoblastoma protein copurifies with E2F-I, an E1A-regulated inhibitor of the transcription factor E2F. *Cell* **65**, 1063-1072.

Bandara, L. R. and La Thangue, N. B. (1991). Adenovirus E1a prevents the retinoblastoma gene product from complexing with a cellular transcription factor. *Nature* **351**, 494-497.

Bandara, L. R., Buck, V. M., Zamanian, M., Johnston, L. H. and La Thangue, N. B. (1993). Functional synergy between DP-1 and E2F-1 in the cell cycle-regulating transcription factor DRTF1/E2F. *EMBO J.* **12**, 4317-4324.

Blake, M. C. and Azizkhan, J. C. (1989). Transcription factor E2F is required for efficient expression of the hamster dihydrofolate reductase gene in vitro and in vivo. *Mol. Cell. Biol.* **9**, 4994-5002.

Buchkovich, K., Duffy, L. A. and Harlow, E. (1989). The retinoblastoma protein is phosphorylated during specific phases of the cell cycle. *Cell* **58**, 1097-1105.

Cao, L., Faha, B., Dembski, M., Tsai, L.-H., Harlow, E. and Dyson, N. (1992). Independent binding of the retinoblastoma protein and p107 to the transcription factor E2F. *Nature* **355**, 176-179.

Chellappan, S., Hiebert, S., Mudryj, M., Horowitz, J. and Nevins, J. (1991). The E2F transcription factor is a cellular target for the RB protein. *Cell* **65**, 1053-1061.

Chen, P.-L., Scully, P., Shew, J.-Y., Wang, J. and Lee, W.-H. (1989). Phosphorylation of the retinoblastoma gene product is modulated during the cell cycle and cellular differentiation. *Cell* **58**, 1193-1198.

Cobrinik, D., Whyte, P., Peeper, D. S., Jacks, T. and Weinberg, R. A.

(1993). Cell-cycle specific association of E2F with the p130 E1A-binding protein.

Dalton, S. (1992). Cell cycle regulation of the human cdc2 gene. *EMBO J.* **11**, 1797-1804.

DeCaprio, J. A., Ludlow, J. W., Figge, J., Shew, J. Y., Huang, C. M., Lee, W. H., Marsilio, E., Paucha, E. and Livingston, D. M. (1988). SV40 large tumor antigen forms a specific complex with the product of the retinoblastoma susceptibility gene. *Cell* **54**, 275-283.

DeCaprio, J. A., Ludlow, J. W., Lynch, D., Furukawa, Y., Griffin, J., Piwnica-Worms, H., Huang, C. M. and Livingston, D. M. (1989). The product of the retinoblastoma susceptibility gene has properties of a cell cycle regulatory element. *Cell* **58**, 1085-1095.

Devoto, S. H., Mudryj, M., Pines, J., Hunter, T. and Nevins, J. R. (1992). A cyclin A-protein kinase complex possesses sequence-specific DNA binding activity: p33cdk2 is a component of the E2F- cyclin A complex. *Cell* **68**, 167-176.

Dynlacht, B. D., Brook, A., Dembski, M. S., Yenush, L. and Dyson, N. (1994). Transactivation and DNA-binding by Drosophila E2F and DP. *Proc. Nat. Acad. Sci. USA* **81**, 6359-6363.

Dyson, N., Buchkovich, K., Whyte, P. and Harlow, E. (1989a). The cellular 107K protein that binds to adenovirus E1A also associates with the large T antigens of SV40 and JC virus. *Cell* **58**, 249-255.

Dyson, N., Howley, P. M., Munger, K. and Harlow, E. (1989b). The human papilloma virus-16 E7 oncoprotein is able to bind to the retinoblastoma gene product. *Science* **243**, 934-937.

Dyson, N., Guida, P., Munger, K. and Harlow, E. (1992). Homologous sequences in adenovirus E1A and human papillomavirus E7 proteins mediate interaction with the same set of cellular proteins. *J. Virol.* **66**, 6893-6902.

Dyson, N., Dembski, M., Fattaey, A., Nguwu, C., Ewen, M. and Helin, K. (1993). Analysis of p107-associated proteins; p107 associates with a form of E2F that differs from pRB associated E2F-1. *J. Virol.* **67**, 7641-7647.

Ewen, M. E., Ludlow, J. W., Marsilio, E., DeCaprio, J. A., Millikan, R. C., Cheng, S. H., Paucha, E. and Livingston, D. M. (1989). An N-terminal transformation-governing sequence of SV40 large T antigen contributes to the binding of both p110Rb and a second cellular protein, p120. *Cell* **58**, 257-67.

Ewen, M. E., Xing, Y., Lawrence, J. B. and Livingston, D. M. (1991). Molecular cloning, chromosomal mapping, and expression of the cDNA for p107, a retinoblastoma gene product-related protein. *Cell* **66**, 1155-1164.

Ewen, M., Faha, B., Harlow, E. and Livingston, D. (1992). Interaction of p107 with cyclin A independent of complex formation with viral oncoproteins. *Science* **255**, 85-87.

Faha, B., Ewen, M., Tsai, L.-H., Livingston, D. and Harlow, E. (1992). Interaction between human cyclin A and adenovirus E1A-associated p107 protein. *Science* **255**, 87-90.

Faha, B. F., Harlow, E. and Lees, E. M. (1993). The adenovirus E1A-associated kinase consists of cyclin E/p33cdk2 and cyclin A/p33cdk2. *J. Virol.* **67**, 2456-2465.

Figge, J., Webster, T., Smith, T. F. and Paucha, E. (1988). Prediction of similar transforming regions in simian virus 40 large T, adenovirus E1A, and myc oncoproteins. *J. Virol.* **62**, 1814-1818.

Giordano, A., Lee, J. H., Scheppler, J. A., Herrmann, C., Harlow, E., Deuschule, U., Beach, D. and Franza B. R. (1991a). Cell cycle regulation of histone H1 kinase activity associated with the adenoviral protein E1A. *Science* **253**, 1271-1275.

Giordano, A., McCall, C., Whyte, P. and Franza, B. R. (1991b). Human cyclin A and the retinoblastoma protein interact with similar but distinguishable sequences in the adenovirus E1A gene product. *Oncogene* **6**, 481-486.

Girling, R., Partridge, J. F., Bandara, L. R., Burden, N., Totty, N. F., Hsuan, J. J. and La Thangue, N. B. (1993). A new component of the transcription factor DRTF1/E2F. *Nature* **362**, 83-87.

Goodrich, D. W., Wang, N. P., Qian, Y.-W., Lee, E. Y.-H. P. and Lee, W.-H. (1991). The retinoblastoma gene product regulates progression through the G1 phase of the cell cycle. *Cell* **67**, 293-302.

Gu, W., Schneider, J. W., Condorelli, G., Kaushai, S., Mahdavi, V. and Nadal-Ginard, B. (1993). Interaction of myogenic factors and the retinoblastoma protein mediates muscle cell commitment and differentiation. *Cell* **72**, 309-324.

Hagemeier, C., Bannister, A. J., Cook, A. and Kouzarides, T. (1993). The activation domain of transcription factor PU.1 binds the retinoblastoma (RB) protein and the transcription factor TFIID *in vitro*: RB shows sequence similarity to TFIID and TFIIB. *Proc. Nat. Acad. Sci. USA* **90**, 1580-1584.

Hannon, G. J., Demetrick, D. and Beach, D. (1993). Isolation of the Rb-related p130 through its interaction with CDK2 and cyclins. *Genes Dev.* **7**, 2378-2391.

Harlow, E., Whyte, P., Franza, B. J. and Schley, C. (1986). Association of adenovirus early-region 1A proteins with cellular polypeptides. *Mol. Cell. Biol.* **6**, 1579-1589.

Helin, K., Harlow, E. and Fattaey, A. R. (1993). Inhibition of E2F-1 transactivation by direct binding of the retinoblastoma protein. *Mol. Cell. Biol.* **13**, 6501-6508.

Helin, K., Lees, J. A., Vidal, M., Dyson, N., Harlow, E. and Fattaey, A. (1992). A cDNA encoding a pRB-binding protein with properties of the transcription factor E2F. *Cell* **70**, 337-350.

Helin, K., Wu, C., Fattaey, A., Lees, J., Dynlacht, B., Ngwu, C. and Harlow, E. (1993). Heterodimerization of the transcription factors E2F-1 and DP-1 leads to cooperative transactivation. *Genes Dev.* **7**, 1850-1861.

Helin, K. and Harlow, E. (1993). The retinoblastoma protein as a transcriptional repressor. *Trends Cell Biol.* **3**, 43-46.

Hiebert, S. W., Lipp, M. and Nevins, J. R. (1989). E1A-dependent trans-activation of the human MYC promoter is mediated by the E2F factor. *Proc. Nat. Acad. Sci. USA* **86**, 3594-3598.

Hiebert, S. W., Chellappan, S. P., Horowitz, J. M. and Nevins, J. R. (1992). The interaction of pRb with E2F inhibits the transcriptional activity of E2F. *Genes Dev.* **6**, 177-185.

Hinds, P. W., Mittnacht, S., Dulic, V., Arnold, A., Reed, S. I. and Weinberg, R. A. (1992). Regulation of retinoblastoma protein functions by ectopic expression of human cyclins. *Cell* **70**, 993-1006.

Howe, J. A., Mymryk, J. S., Egan, C., Branton, P. E. and Bayley, S. T. (1990). Retinoblastoma growth suppressor and a 300-kDa protein appear to regulate cellular DNA synthesis. *Proc. Nat. Acad. Sci. USA* **87**, 5883-5887.

Howe, J. A. and Bayley, S. (1992). Effects of Ad5 E1A mutant viruses on the cell cycle in relation to the binding of cellular proteins including the retinoblastoma protein and cyclin A. *Virology* **186**, 15-24.

Huber, H. E., Edwards, G., Goodhart, P. J., Patrick, D. R., Huang, P. S., Ivey-Hoyle, M., Barnett, S. F., Oliff, A. and Heimbrook, D. C. (1993). Transcription factor E2F binds DNA as a heterodimer. *Proc. Nat. Acad. Sci. USA* **90**, 3525-3529.

Ivey-Hoyle, M., Conroy, R., Huber, H., Goodhart, P., Oliff, A. and Heinbrook, D. C. (1993). Cloning and characterization of E2F-2, a novel protein with the biochemical properties of transcription factor E2F. *Mol. Cell Biol.* **13**, 7802-7812.

Johnson, D. G., Schwartz, J. K., Cress, W. D. and Nevins, J. R. (1993). Expression of transcription factor E2F1 induces quiescent cells to enter S phase. *Nature* **365**, 349-352.

Kaelin, W. G., Krek, W., Sellers, W. R., DeCaprio, J. A., Ajchanbaum, F., Fuchs, C. S., Chittenden, T., Li, Y., Farnham, P. J., Blanar, M. A., Livingston, D. M. and Flemington, E. K. (1992). Expression cloning of a cDNA encoding a retinoblastoma-binding protein with E2F-like properties. *Cell* **70**, 351-364.

Kim, S.-J., Wagner, S., Liu, F., O'Reilly, M. A., Robbins, P. D. and Green, M. R. (1992). Retinoblastoma gene product activates expression of the human TGF-β2 gene through transcription factor ATF-2. *Nature* **358**, 331-334.

La Thangue, N. B., Thimmappaya, B. and Rigby, P. W. J. (1990). The embryonal carcinoma stem cell E1a-like activity involves a differentiation-regulated transcription factor. *Nucl. Acids Res.* **18**, 2929-2938.

Lam, E. W.-F. and Watson, R. J. (1993). An E2F-binding site mediates cell-cycle regulated repression of mouse B-myb transcription. *EMBO J.* **12**, 2705-2713.

Larose, A., St-Onge, L. and Bastin, M. (1990). Mutations in polyomavirus large T affecting immortalization of primary rat embryo fibroblasts. *Virology* **176**, 98-105.

Lees, E., Faha, B., Dulic, V., Reed, S. I. and Harlow, E. (1992). Cyclin E/cdk2 and cyclin A/cdk2 kinases associate with p107 and E2F in a temporally distinct manner. *Genes Dev.* **6**, 1874-1885.

Lees, J. A., Saito, M., Vidal, M., Valentine, M., Look, T., Harlow, E., Dyson, N. and Helin, K. (1993). The retinoblastoma protein binds to a family of E2F transcription factors. *Mol. Cell Biol.* **13**, 7813-7825.

Lewis, J. B. and Mathews, M. B. (1980). Control of adenovirus early gene expression: a class of immediate early products. *Cell* **21**, 303-13.

Li, Y., Graham, C., Lacy, S., Duncan, A. M. V. and Whyte, P. (1993). The adenovirus E1A-associated 130-kD protein is encoded by a member of the retinoblastoma gene family and physically interacts with cyclins A and E. *Genes Dev.* **7**, 2366-2377.

Mayol, X., Grana, X., Baldi, A., Sang, N., Hu, Q. and Giordano, A. (1993). Cloning of a new member of the retinoblastoma gene family (pRb2) which binds to the E1A transforming domain. *Oncogene* **8**, 2561-6.

Means, A. L., Slansky, J. E., McMahon, S. L., Knuth, M. W. and Farnham,

P. J. (1992). The HIP binding site is required for growth regulation of the dihydrofolate reductase promoter. *Mol. Cell. Biol.* **12**, 1054-1063.

Mihara, K., Cao, X. R., Yen, A., Chandler, S., Driscoll, B., Murphree, A. L., T'Ang, A. and Fung, Y. K. (1989). Cell cycle-dependent regulation of phosphorylation of the human retinoblastoma gene product. *Science* **246**, 1300-1303.

Mudryj, M., Devoto, S. H., Hiebert, S. W., Hunter, T., Pines, J. and Nevins, J. R. (1991). Cell cycle regulation of the E2F transcription factor involves an interaction with cyclin A. *Cell* **65**, 1243-1253.

Munger, K., Werness, B. A., Dyson, N., Phelps, W. C., Harlow, E. and Howley, P. M. (1989). Complex formation of human papillomavirus E7 proteins with the retinoblastoma tumor suppressor gene product. *EMBO J.* **8**, 4099-105.

Nevins, J. R. (1981). Mechanism of activation of early viral transcription by the adenovirus E1A gene product. *Cell* **26**, 213-220.

Nevins, J. R. (1992). E2F; A link betwen the Rb Tumor suppressor protein and viral oncoproteins. *Science* **258**, 424-429.

Phelps, W. C., Yee, C. L., Munger, K. and Howley, P. M. (1988). The human papillomavirus type 16 E7 gene encodes transactivation and transformation functions similar to those of adenovirus E1A. *Cell* **53**, 539-47.

Ray, S., Arroyo, K. M., Bagchi, S. and Raychaudhuri, P. (1992). Identification of a 60-kilodalton Rb-binding protein that allows the RB-E2F complex to bind to DNA. *Mol. Cell. Biol.* **12**, 4327-4333.

Raychaudhuri, P., Bagchi, S., Devoto, S. H., Kraus, V. B., Moran, E. and Nevins, J. R. (1991). Domains of the adenovirus E1A protein that are required for oncogenic activity are also required for dissociation of E2F transcription factor complexes. *Genes Dev.* **5**, 1200-1211.

Rustgi, A. K., Dyson, N. J. and Bernards, R. (1991). Amino-terminal domains of c-*myc* and N-*myc* proteins mediate binding to the retinoblastoma gene product. *Nature* **352**, 541-544.

Saito, M., Helin, K., Valentine, M., Griffith, B., Willman, C., Harlow, E. and Look, T. (1994). Amplification of the E2F-1 transcription factor gene in the HEL erythroleukemia cell line. *Blood* (in press).

Schwarz, J. K., Devoto, S. H., Smith, E. J., Chellappan, S. P., Jakoi, L. and Nevins, J. R. (1993). Interactions of the p107 and Rb proteins with E2F during the cell proliferation response. *EMBO J.* **12**, 1013-1020.

Shan, B., Zhu, X., Chen, P.-L., Durfee, T., Yang, Y., Sharp, D. and Lee, W.-H. (1992). Molecular cloning of cellular genes encoding retinoblastoma-associated proteins: identification of a gene with properties of the transcription factor E2F. *Mol. Cell. Biol.* **12**, 5620-5631.

Shirodkar, S., Ewen, M., DeCaprio, J. A., Morgan, D., Livingston, D. and Chittenden, T. (1992). The transcription factor E2F interacts with the retinoblastoma product and a p107-cyclin A complex in a cell cycle-regulated manner. *Cell* **68**, 157-166.

Slansky, J., Li, Y., Kaelin, W. G. and Farnham, P. J. (1993). A protein synthesis-dependent increase in E2F1 mRNA correlates with growth regulation of the dihydrofolate reductase promoter. *Mol. Cell. Biol.* **13**, 1610-1618.

Stabel, S., Argos, P. and Philipson, K. (1985). The release of growth arrest by microinjection of adenovirus E1A DNA. *EMBO J.* **4**, 2329-2336.

Thalmeier, K., Synovzik, H., Mertz, R., Winnacker, E.-L. and Lipp, M. (1989). Nuclear factor E2F mediates basic transcription and trans-activation by E1a of the human MYC promoter. *Genes Dev.* **3**, 527-536.

Wang, C.-J., Petryniak, B., Thompson, C. B., Kaelin, W. G. and Leiden, J. M. (1993). Regulation of the Ets-related transcription factor Elf-1 by binding to the retinoblastoma protein. *Science* **260**, 1130-1135.

Weinberg, R. A. (1988). Finding the anti-oncogene. *Sci. Am.* **259**, 44-51.

Weinberg, R. A. (1990). The retinoblastoma gene and cell growth control. *Trends Biochem. Sci.* **15**, 199-202.

Weinberg, R. A. (1992). The retinoblastoma gene and gene product. In *Tumour Suppressor Genes, the Cell Cycle and Cancer*. pp. 43-57. New York, Cold Spring Harbor Laboratory Press.

Weintraub, S. J., Prater, C. A. and Dean, D. C. (1992). Retinoblastoma protein switches the E2F site from positive to negative element. *Nature* **358**, 259-261.

Welch, P. J. and Wang, J. Y. J. (1993). A C-terminal protein-binding domain in the retinoblastoma protein regulates nuclear c-abl tyrosine kinase in the cell cycle. *Cell* **75**, 779-790.

Whyte, P., Buchkovich, K. J., Horowitz, J. M., Friend, S. H., Raybuck, M., Weinberg, R. A. and Harlow, E. (1988). Association between an oncogene and an anti-oncogene: the adenovirus E1A proteins bind to the retinoblastoma gene product. *Nature* **334**, 124-129.

Whyte, P., Williamson, N. M. and Harlow, E. (1989). Cellular targets for transformation by the adenovirus E1A proteins. *Cell* **56**, 67-75.

Yee, S. P. and Branton, P. E. (1985). Detection of cellular proteins associated with human adenovirus type 5 early region 1A polypeptides. *Virology* **147**, 142-153.

Yee, A. S., Reichel, R., Kovesdi, I. and Nevins, J. R. (1987). Promoter interaction of the E1A-inducible factor E2F and its potential role in the formation of a multi-component complex. *EMBO J.* **6**, 2061-2068.

Yee, A. S., Raychaudhuri, P., Jakoi, L. and Nevins, J. R. (1989). The adenovirus-inducible factor E2F stimulates transcription after specific DNA binding. *Mol. Cell Biol.* **9**, 578-585.

Zamanian, M. and La Thangue, N. B. (1992). Adenovirus E1A prevents the retinoblastoma gene product from repressing the activity of a cellular transcription factor. *EMBO J.* **11**, 2603-2610.

Zamanian, M. and Thangue, N. B. L. (1993). Transcriptional repression by the Rb-related protein p107. *Mol. Biol. Cell* **4**, 389-396.

Zhu, L., van den Heuvel, S., Helin, K., Fattaey, A., Ewen, M., Livingston, D., Dyson, N. and Harlow, E. (1993). Inhibition of cell proliferation by p107, a relative of the retinoblastoma protein. *Genes Dev.* **7**, 1111-1125.

Journal of Cell Science, Supplement 18, 89-96 (1994)
Printed in Great Britain © The Company of Biologists Limited 1994

The D-type cyclins and their role in tumorigenesis

Gordon Peters

Imperial Cancer Research Fund Laboratories, PO Box 123, 44 Lincoln's Inn Fields, London WC2A 3PX, UK

SUMMARY

The D-type cyclins are expressed during the progression from G_0/G_1 to S phase in the mammalian cell cycle. There is considerable evidence that they contribute to the development of specific cancers, both in humans and in mouse models. For example, cyclin D1 can be activated by chromosomal translocation, DNA amplification and retroviral integration. Cyclins D1, D2 and D3 preferentially associate with two closely related members of the cyclin-dependent kinase family, Cdk4 and Cdk6 and the various complexes are each capable of phosphorylating the retinoblastoma gene product (pRb), at least in vitro. This suggests that the growth promoting effects of the D-cyclins may be manifest via their interactions with tumour suppressor genes.

Key words: cell cycle, cyclin-dependent kinase, cyclins D1, D2 and D3, Cdk4 and Cdk6, DNA amplification, chromosome 11q13, chromosome translocation, retroviral integration, breast cancer, centrocytic lymphoma, PRAD1, CCND1, BCL1, retinoblastoma gene, DNA tumour virus

INTRODUCTION

The discovery of cyclin D1, first reported in 1991, is a striking example of convergent research where several groups, working independently on quite different aspects of biology, found themelves studying the same gene. Some were investigating the regulation of the cell cycle (Lew et al., 1991; Xiong et al., 1991), some were looking for genes induced by specific cytokines (Matsushime et al., 1991), while others were trying to identify oncogenes associated with specific cancers (Motokura et al., 1991; Withers et al., 1991; Schuuring et al., 1992). It is hardly surprising therefore that the D-cyclins have generated enormous interest over the last few years but such is the pace of these activities that the recorded information does not always concur. As well as summarizing the general features of the D-cyclins and the evidence linking them to cancer, this short review will try to distil some order from the recent literature and advance some speculative views as to the possible functions of these proteins.

REGULATION OF THE CELL CYCLE BY CYCLIN-DEPENDENT KINASES

In higher eukaryotes, cell division is regulated by a cyclical series of events in which two protein families play leading roles. The first are the cyclins, the classic example of which was discovered by its marked accumulation and destruction in synchrony with the cell division cycle (Evans et al., 1983). The second are the cyclin-dependent kinases (Cdks), for which the prototype is the 34 kDa serine/threonine kinase encoded by the cdc2 gene in Schizosaccharomyces pombe and the related CDC28 gene in Saccharomyces cerevisiae (reviewed by Norbury and Nurse, 1992; Reed, 1992). As the recently adopted Cdk nomenclature implies (see for example Meyerson et al., 1992), the active enzyme complexes are formed by a partnership between a regulatory cyclin and a catalytic kinase subunit.

Historically, much of this information was gleaned from genetic analyses of the cell division cycle in yeast and studies on oocyte maturation in marine invertebrates and amphibia. These pioneering studies led to a model for the regulation of mitosis by the cyclin B/cdc2 complex in which kinase activity is 'switched on' by specific dephosphorylation of the catalytic subunit and 'switched off' by the rapid destruction of the cyclin (Norbury and Nurse, 1992; Reed, 1992; Solomon, 1993). This paradigm appears to be conserved in all eukaryotes and although the players may be different the same principles are probably relevant to other critical phases of the cell cycle. For example, the G_1/S transition in Saccharomyces cerevisiae is regulated by a group of G_1 cyclins, termed CLN1, 2 and 3, acting in conjunction with the CDC28 kinase (reviewed by Reed, 1992). Not surprisingly, the picture appears more complex in mammalian cells, where the numbers of potential Cdks and cyclins have expanded dramatically, and the details are just beginning to be unravelled.

The identification of new members of the cyclin family was largely stimulated by the search for mammalian equivalents of the yeast CLN genes in complementation assays (Koff et al., 1991; Lew et al., 1991; Xiong et al., 1991). Cyclins C, D1 and E were all identified in this way but in hindsight it seems that the assay may have been scoring the presence of a so-called 'cyclin box', a region of sequence homology that is conserved in all cyclins (Fig. 1) and is probably critical in the interaction between cyclins and their respective kinase partners (Kobayashi et al., 1992; Lees and Harlow, 1993). The other notable characteristic of cyclins is their rapid turnover. In cyclins A and B, this is mediated by a motif near the amino terminus that appears

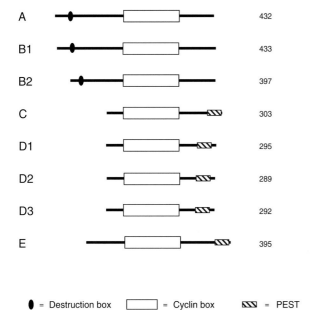

= Destruction box   [ ] = Cyclin box   = PEST

Fig. 1. The mammalian cyclin family. The figure depicts 8 of the known cyclin-related polypeptides identified in human cells, designated A through E as indicated. The number of amino acid residues in each protein is shown on the right. The open box locates the region of homology termed the cyclin box. Other symbols show the presence of protein destabilization elements.

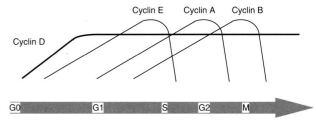

Fig. 2. The mammalian cell cycle. The phases of the cell cycle are shown in a linear form for cells leaving the resting G_0 state and entering the division cycle. DNA synthesis and mitosis occur, respectively, in the S and M phases, separated by two gap phases, G_1 and G_2. The curves above the line are a highly schematized impression of the levels of various cyclin proteins at different phases of the cycle.

to target the protein for destruction via the ubiquitin pathway (Glotzer et al., 1991) whereas cyclins C, D and E have so-called PEST sequences near their carboxy termini (Fig. 1). Although such concentrations of proline, glutamic acid, serine and threonine residues are thought to contribute to protein instability (Rogers et al., 1986), their significance to cyclin turnover has yet to be confirmed experimentally.

Protein stability is clearly important for controlling the levels of the different cyclins throughout the cell cycle but only cyclins A, B and E show the classical periodic fluctuations that gave the family its name. Significantly, the levels of these proteins and their associated kinase activities peak in a distinct temporal order as illustrated in Fig. 2. A relatively cohesive model can thus be formulated in which specific cell cycle transitions are regulated by the consecutive action of these cyclin/kinase complexes (Fig. 2). In this scheme, the cyclin E/Cdk2 complex regulates events at the G_1/S transition (Dulic et al., 1992; Koff et al., 1992; Ohtsubo and Roberts, 1993; Tsai et al., 1993), cyclinA/Cdk2 operates in S and G_2 (Girard et al., 1991; Walker and Maller, 1991; Pagano et al., 1992; Tsai et al., 1993), and cyclin B/cdc2 orchestrates mitosis (Norbury and Nurse, 1992; Reed, 1992). However, this is clearly an oversimplification since the partnerships between cyclins and Cdks are not monogamous. For example cyclin A can form active complexes with either Cdk1 (i.e. cdc2) or Cdk2 and, as discussed in more detail below, the latter can be found associated with cyclins A, E or D.

THE D-TYPE CYCLINS

The D-cyclins form a distinct subset within the cyclin family based on structural and functional criteria. Although the genes

map to different chromosomes (Inaba et al., 1992; Xiong et al., 1992a), they encode proteins that are between 57 and 62% identical in pairwise comparisons and absolutely conserved at 140 residues spread throughout the respective molecules (Fig. 3). Similarity to other cyclins is restricted to the cyclin box domain, and the D-cyclins are particularly well conserved in the amino-terminal half of this region. It was sequence relatedness that pointed to the existence of cyclins D2 and D3, by cross-hybridization with cyclin D1 probes (Matsushime et al., 1991), and the other members of the family were not uncovered by the various strategies that led to the discovery of cyclin D1.

As alluded to above, cyclin D1 was among a number of human cDNA clones that were able to complement for CLN activity in yeast (Lew et al., 1991; Xiong et al., 1991). It was also isolated as a 'delayed-early' gene in cytokine-stimulated mouse macrophages by differential screening of cDNA clones (Matsushime et al., 1991). In this system, the expression of cyclin D1 is dependent on the presence of CSF-1 and reaches a maximum in late G_1 phase. Subsequent studies have shown that the expression of all three D-cyclins can be regulated by cytokines but the results and their interpretation are rather inconsistent (Matsushime et al., 1991; Cocks et al., 1992; Motokura et al., 1992; Surmacz et al., 1992; Won et al., 1992; Ajchenbaum et al., 1993; Jansen-Dürr et al., 1993; Musgrove et al., 1993; Sewing et al., 1993; Winston and Pledger, 1993). Perhaps the most contentious issue is whether the levels of the RNAs and/or proteins actually cycle, but some of the confusion undoubtedly reflects the way that cells were synchronised and analysed in different labs. Our own findings suggest that while cyclin D1, for example, accumulates significantly in G_1 in serum-stimulated fibroblasts, it does not undergo the dramatic fluctuations that are characteristic of cyclins A and B. Other groups report similar conclusions but suggest that there are more subtle fluctuations and that the protein, which is normally found in the cell nucleus, may become redistributed during S phase (Baldin et al., 1993; Sewing et al., 1993; Lukas et al., 1994).

Clearly, much remains to be learned about the regulation of cyclin D expression and the balance between synthesis and degradation of both transcripts and proteins. The interplay of positive and negative inputs from the signal transduction pathways has yet to be fully explored and there is currently no obvious explanation for the need for three closely related

	Chromosome	RNA	Protein	Molecular weight
CCND1	11q13	4.5 kb	295 aa	33,729 Da
CCND2	12p13	~7 kb	289 aa	33,045 Da
CCND3	6p21	2.2 kb	292 aa	32,482 Da

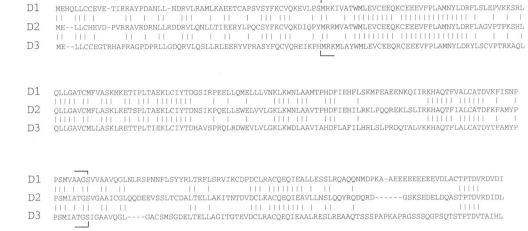

D1 MEHQLLCCEVE-TIRRAYPDANLL-NDRVLRAMLKAEETCAPSVSYFKCVQKEVLPSMRKIVATWMLEVCEEQKCEEEVFPLAMNYLDRFLSLEPVKKSRL
      || ||| || || | || || || ||||| | | |||||| | | | ||| ||||||||||||| ||||||||||||||||| ||||||||
D2 ME--LLCHEVD-PVRRAVRDRNLLRDDRVLQNLLTIEERYLPQCSYFKCVQKDIQPYMRRMVATWMLEVCEEQKCEEEVFPLAMNYLDRFLAGVPTPKSHL
      || ||| || || || || ||| |||||| | |||||| ||| ||||| ||||||||||||||||||||||||||||||||| ||
D3 ME--LLCCEGTRHAPRAGPDPRLLGDQRVLQSLLRLEERYVPRASYFQCVQREIKPHMRKMLAYWMLEVCEEQRCEEEVFPLAMNYLDRYLSCVPTRKAQL

D1 QLLGATCMFVASKMKETIPLTAEKLCIYTDGSIRPEELLQMELLLVNKLKWNLAAMTPHDFIEHFLSKMPEAEENKQIIRKHAQTFVALCATDVKFISNP
      ||||| || |||| || |||||||||||| | ||| | || || | |||||| ||| ||||||| || | || |||||| |||||||| | |
D2 QLLGAVCMFLASKLKETSPLTAEKLCIYTDNSIKPQELLEWELVVLGKLKWNLAAVTPHDFIEHILRKLPQQREKLSLIRKHAQTFIALCATDFKFAMYP
      ||||| || |||| | || || |||||||| | | || || ||||| ||| ||| ||||| | || || |||||| ||||||| ||||
D3 QLLGAVCMLLASKLRETTPLTIEKLCIYTDHAVSPRQLRDWEVLVLGKLKWDLAAVIAHDFLAFILHRLSLPRDQTALVKKHAQTFLALCATDYTFAMYP

D1 PSMVAAGSVVAAVQGLNLRSPNNFLSYYRLTRFLSRVIKCDPDCLRACQEQIEALLESSLRQAQQNMDPKA-AEEEEEEEEEVDLACTPTDVRDVDI
      ||||| | || || || || || | ||| |||||||||| |||||||| | | |||||
D2 PSMIATGSVGAAICGLQQDEEVSSLTCDALTELLAKITNTDVDCLKACQEQIEAVLLNSLQQYRQDQRD------GSKSEDELDQASTPTDVRDIDL
      ||| |||| ||| || || || || |||||| || |||||||||| ||| |||| | ||| | |||||
D3 PSMIATGSIGAAVQGL----GACSMSGDELTELLAGITGTEVDCLRACQEQIEAALRESLREAAQTSSSPAPKAPRGSSSQGPSQTSTPTDVTAIHL

Fig. 3. The human D-type cyclins. The chromosomal locations and transcript sizes for the human D-cyclin genes, *CCND1*, *CCND2* and *CCND3* are indicated along with the characteristics and primary sequences of the encoded proteins, in single letter amino acid code. Vertical lines identify conserved residues and the square brackets delineate the so-called cyclin box.

genes. Many cell types express two and occasionally all three members of the family and few clear patterns have yet become apparent. Perhaps it is significant that, despite sporadic reports to the contrary, we have yet to identify a cell line that does not express at least some levels of cyclin D3 whereas cells lacking either D1 or D2 are much more common (unpublished observations).

CHROMOSOMAL REARRANGEMENTS AFFECTING CYCLIN D1

The other line of research that led to the identification of the D-cyclins was the search for oncogenes associated with specific genetic alterations. Most of the evidence relates to cyclin D1 and although largely circumstantial, it is becoming increasingly persuasive. As indicated in Fig. 4, the gene for cyclin D1 (*CCND1*) maps to the karyotypically defined band q13 on the long arm of human chromosome 11, a region known to be the site of tumour-specific chromosomal abnormalities. For example, some cases of benign parathyroid adenoma show a clonal inversion of chromosome 11 that places the cyclin D1 gene on 11q13 adjacent to regulatory elements of the parathyroid hormone gene on 11p15 (Arnold et al., 1989; Motokura et al., 1991). Although the frequency of this rearrangement in parathyroid adenomas is quite low, its clonality and the resultant increase in cyclin D1 expression are strongly suggestive of a role in the disease (Rosenberg et al., 1991a). It was through this association that the name *PRAD1* was coined, whereas earlier reports referred to the anonymous locus designation D11S287. Both names appear in the recent literature but are essentially synonymous for *CCND1*.

A different and more frequent rearrangement of 11q13 has been observed in B-cell neoplasms, particularly centrocytic lymphoma and multiple myeloma. In this t(11;14)(q13;q32) translocation, a reciprocal exchange occurs between chromosome 11q13 and the Ig heavy chain locus on 14q32 (Erikson et al., 1984; Tsujimoto et al., 1984), exactly analogous to the translocations that activate *MYC* in Burkitt's lymphoma and *BCL2* in follicular lymphoma. When the translocation breakpoint was cloned, and designated *BCL1*, it was naturally assumed that a nearby gene would be activated by juxtaposition to the Ig enhancer. As it turns out, the nearest gene is *CCND1*, which is located some 120 kb distal to the original breakpoint cluster (Withers et al., 1991; Brookes et al., 1992) but it is now clear that the breaks can occur at multiple sites within the intervening DNA (see for example Williams et al., 1992; de Boer et al., 1993). Nevertheless, the original expectations are fulfilled in that the translocation results in increased transcription of the cyclin D1 gene (Rosenberg et al., 1991b; Seto et al., 1992). Although such findings have led to references to the 'BCL1 gene', this is a potential source of confusion since the originally defined *BCL1* probe is quite distant from the *CCND1* gene.

AMPLIFICATION OF CYCLIN D1

The distinction between *BCL1* and *CCND1* becomes relevant in considering the other chromosomal abnormality that affects cyclin D1, DNA amplification. It has been widely documented that a significant subset of human breast cancers and squamous cell carcinomas show amplification of markers at 11q13, whereas this amplicon is rarely observed in other tumour types (reviewed by Lammie and Peters, 1991; Fantl et al., 1993). The amplification was originally detected using probes for two known oncogenes in the region, *FGF3* and *FGF4*, often in conjunction with the *BCL1* translocation breakpoint probe. We

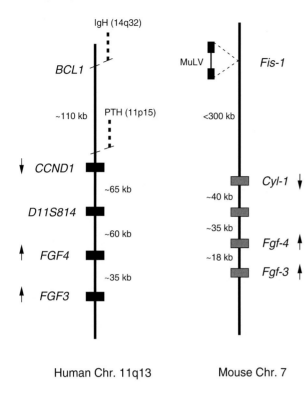

Human Chr. 11q13   Mouse Chr. 7

Fig. 4. Chromosomal perturbations that affect cyclin D1. Syntenic regions of human chromosome 11 and mouse chromosome 7 are depicted in which the shaded boxes represent known CpG islands. The distances between these loci were established by a combination of cosmid walking and pulsed field gel electrophoresis. The islands corresponding to the cyclin D1 gene (*CCND1* and *Cyl-1*), and to *FGF3* and *FGF4* are as indicated and the arrows refer to the transcriptional orientation of the gene. The originally defined translocation breakpoints on human chromosome 11q13, in parathyroid adenomas and B-cell lymphomas, and the MuLV integration locus *Fis-1* on mouse chromosome 7 are as indicated.

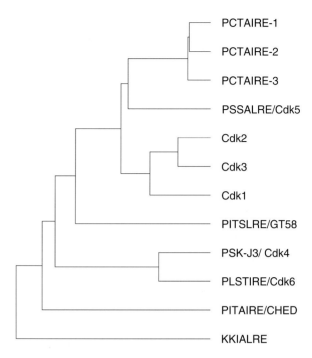

Fig. 5. Evolutionary tree of known CDC-2 related polypeptides. An evolutionary tree was constructed from the published sequences of 12 human proteins that show homology with p34^{cdc2} (Hanks et al., 1988; Bunnell et al., 1990; Lapidot-Lifson et al., 1992; Matsushime et al., 1992; Meyerson et al., 1992; Okuda et al., 1992). The region of each protein that aligns with residues 11 to 230 inclusive of human CDC2, were subjected to pairwise comparisons and the percentage divergence converted into a linear distance using the Intelligenetics GeneWorks software.

now know that *CCND1* (alias D11S287) maps between *BCL1* and *FGF4* (Brookes et al., 1992) and is therefore a consistent component of the amplicon, a fact that was reported before the true nature of the gene became apparent (Lammie et al., 1991). More importantly, *CCND1* is expressed at relatively low levels in normal breast epithelium and its expression is elevated upon DNA amplification (Lammie et al., 1991; Buckley et al., 1993; Gillett et al., 1994). Since this is not true for either *FGF3* or *FGF4*, which remain silent in the adult mammary gland, cyclin D1 is currently the best candidate for the key oncogene on the amplified DNA (Fantl et al., 1993).

The only point of contention is that *CCND1* is not the only expressed gene affected by the amplification (Schuuring et al., 1992, 1993), leading to suggestions that there may be more than one focus for amplification in the 11q13 region (Gaudray et al., 1992). Thus, in some tumours, the *BCL1* probe appears to be more highly amplified than *CCND1*, while in others the converse is true. As we have argued elsewhere (Fantl et al., 1993; Gillett et al., 1994), it is difficult to interpret these observations without a better understanding of the function of cyclin D1, since it may have both positive and negative effects on proliferation depending on the cell type or level of expression achieved (see below). Whatever the resolution of these issues,

it is now possible to detect the amplification of the *CCND1* gene at the protein level, by staining tumour sections with cyclin D1 antibodies (Jiang et al., 1993b; Gillett et al., 1994). This should greatly facilitate the analysis of clinical material and there are preliminary indications that the frequency of over expression of cyclin D1 may be much higher than concluded from DNA analyses. Thus, in our own study, approximately one in three breast tumours stained above normal for cyclin D1 (Gillett et al., 1994). As these are almost exclusively tumours that are positive for oestrogen receptor, staining for cyclin D1 holds considerable promise for refining the classification of breast cancers and may well have prognostic significance.

VIRAL ACTIVATION OF CYCLINS D1 AND D2

The final piece of evidence connecting D-cyclins and tumorigenesis is their activation by tumour viruses. For example, both the cyclin D1 and D2 genes are transcriptionally activated by the nearby integration of murine leukaemia virus in mouse T-lymphomas (Lammie et al., 1992; Hanna et al., 1993). For cyclin D1, the insertions occur at the previously defined *Fis-1* locus on mouse chromosome 7 in a region that is a direct parallel of 11q13 (see Fig. 4). Although the exact distance between *Fis-1* and the cyclin D1 gene has not been established, it seems reasonable to conclude that proviral insertions at *Fis-1* are functionally analogous to translocations at *BCL1*

(Lammie et al., 1992). With cyclin D2 on the other hand, the insertions occur adjacent to the gene and the genomic DNA was cloned independently as a common site of viral integration, termed *Vin-1* (Hanna et al., 1993). To date, there are no obvious parallels for *Vin-1* disruption in human tumours. However, we have noted one potential link between cyclin D2 and lymphomagenesis in that the immortalisation of primary B-lymphocytes by Epstein-Barr virus is accompanied by transcriptional activation of cyclin D2 (Palmero et al., 1993; Sinclair et al., 1994). We are currently exploring the possiblity that this is a direct effect of viral gene expression and a key step in the immortalisation process.

INTERACTION OF D-CYCLINS AND CDKS

Apart from one isolated case of hepatitis-B virus integration into the cyclin A gene (Wang et al., 1990), none of the other cyclins have yet been implicated in tumorigenesis. Does this mean that there is something fundamentally different about the D-cyclins? An obvious question is whether they interact with catalytic subunits in the same way as cyclins A, B and E, and several groups set out to determine the kinase partners for cyclins D1, D2 and D3. The strategies used were dictated by the availability of cDNA clones and specific antisera to potential candidates but the most significant outcome was the demonstration that a 33 kDa protein kinase designated PSK-J3 (now renamed Cdk4) is a major partner for the D-cyclins (Matsushime et al., 1992; Xiong et al., 1992b). PSK-J3 had been isolated previously in a general screen for new kinases and was recognised as a distant cousin of cdc2 (Hanks et al., 1988). However, its close association with the D-cyclins not only solved some of the mysteries surrounding this kinase but provided encouraging evidence that the cyclin/kinase paradigm might be extended to new members of the respective families. For example, the growing list of cdc2-related sequences in the literature included a 38 kDa protein, originally referred to as PLSTIRE, that is very closely related to Cdk4 (see Fig. 5). We and others have recently shown that this protein, now designated Cdk6, also associates with the D-cyclins (Bates et al., 1994a; Meyerson and Harlow, 1994). Thus, just as the D-cyclins form a distinct subset of the cyclin family, so Cdk4 and Cdk6 form a distinct subset of the Cdk family, and appear to interact exclusively with the D-cyclins. All six possible pairings can be detected by immunoprecipitation of cell lysates (Bates et al., 1994b).

These are not the only interactions observed for the D-cyclins; Xiong et al. (1992b) reported that in primary human fibroblasts, cyclin D1 can be associated with Cdk2 and yet another member of the family designated Cdk5. The significance of the latter remains uncertain but the association with Cdk2 clearly demands some explanation, since this is also a partner for cyclins A and E. A possible clue may be that it is the hypophosphorylated and hence inactive form of Cdk2 that is found associated with cyclin D1 (Dulic et al., 1993; Bates et al., 1994a). A further clue may be that this complex accumulates as primary cells undergo senescence (Dulic et al., 1993; Lucibello et al., 1993). It is therefore conceivable that cyclin D1 performs two contrasting functions, as a positive regulator of Cdk4 and Cdk6 and as a negative regulator that sequesters Cdk2 in an inactive form. Our inability to detect the cyclin D1/Cdk2 complex in tumour cell lines (Bates et al., 1994a) and its absence in transformed cells (Xiong et al., 1993) would therefore tie in with an escape from senescence. If the recently described p21 protein is also part of this complex (El-Deiry et al., 1993; Harper et al., 1993; Xiong et al., 1993; Noda et al., 1994), this would provide an additional arm to p53-mediated cell cycle arrest.

The notion that the D-cyclins may have double lives could of course explain why some functional experiments have produced paradoxical results. For example, transfection of cells with vectors expressing D-cyclins from constitutive or inducible promoters has been shown to accelerate the G_1/S transition, exactly as one might expect for over-expression of a G_1 cyclin (Ando et al., 1993; Jiang et al., 1993a; Quelle et al., 1993; Resnitzky et al., 1994). However, at least one published and several anecdotal reports testify to the toxicity of the D-cyclins in transfection assays (Quelle et al., 1993). This would make some sense if cyclin D is having contrasting influences depending on its Cdk partner. It might also explain why early attempts to demonstrate the oncogenic potential of cyclin D1 by DNA transfection were unrewarding, yet if the appropriate levels are achieved then it can cooperate with *RAS* in transforming primary rodent cells (Hinds et al., 1994; Lovec et al., 1994). Finally, such considerations might explain why the over-expression of cyclin D1 as a result of DNA amplification is not always as dramatic as one might expect and why in some tumours there appear to be rearrangements that down-regulate cyclin D1 expression from the amplified DNA (Gillett et al., 1994).

INTERACTION BETWEEN THE D-CYCLINS AND pRB

The evidence that D-cyclins can interact with Cdks and can accelerate cell cycle progression raises an obvious question - what are the substrates for the multiple kinase combinations? Perhaps the most attractive candidates and certainly the current favourites are the product of the retinoblastoma gene, pRb and its close relative p107. As discussed elsewhere in this volume, pRb is known to act as a negative regulator of G_1 progression, leading to a relatively robust model in which the inactivation of pRb by phosphorylation is a critical step in permitting entry into S phase. A number of studies have shown that pRb can be phosphorylated by various cyclin/Cdk combinations (Lees et al., 1991; Lin et al., 1991; Hinds et al., 1992; Hu et al., 1992) but the timing of the initial phosphorylation events have encouraged the idea that the D-cyclins may be involved. Certainly, the phosphorylation of pRb can be demonstrated in vitro using mixtures of the D-cyclins and Cdk2, Cdk4 or Cdk6 expressed in insect cells using baculovirus vectors (Matsushime et al., 1992; Ewen et al., 1993; Kato et al., 1993; Meyerson and Harlow, 1994). However, it has proved much more difficult to detect such activities in immunoprecipitates from cycling cells (Matsushime et al., 1994; Meyerson and Harlow, 1994) and there are still some puzzling features about the specificities of the different complexes. It would seem strange that all six complexes involving D-cyclins, Cdk4 and Cdk6 are doing exactly the same thing.

Despite these reservations, it does seem very likely that the function of the D-cyclins is somehow connected to pRb, if for no other reason than the presence of a sequence feature near their amino termini that suggests they may interact directly with pRb (Dowdy et al., 1993). This is the LxCxE motif that is common to the SV40 T-antigen, adenovirus E1A, and human papilloma virus E7 proteins, each of which is thought to bind to and functionally inactivate pRb. For the respective DNA tumour viruses this would have the advantage of promoting entry into S-phase, a prerequisite for viral DNA replication. For the D-cyclins, it raises the possibility, albeit unlikely, that they can inactivate pRb by direct binding and displacement of associated transcription factors. Supportive evidence for this idea has been reported, based on the reversal of pRb-induced cell cycle arrest in SAOS-2 cells (Hinds et al., 1992), but it remains curious that cyclin D1 can apparently achieve this effect without concomitant phosphorylation of pRb, whereas cyclins D2 and D3 are thought to inactivate pRb by phosphorylation (Dowdy et al., 1993; Ewen et al., 1993). Either way, one can rationalise how the elevated expression of a D-cyclin in a tumour cell could accelerate G_1 progression.

However, there are a number of uncomfortable facets to such ideas, not least of which is the potential for functional redundancy implicit in the findings. Why should elevated expression of a D-cyclin be so critical to a cell that already expresses one of its close relatives? Moreover, tumour cells do not cycle more rapidly than normal cells and it would be much more attractive to postulate that the D-cyclins are in some way regulating exit from G_0 or the cell's ability to return to a G_0 state after completing mitosis. Finally, it seems clear that pRb is not the master regulator of all cell cycles so that it is premature to settle for pRb as the substrate for D-cyclin/kinases. As if matters were not already confusing enough, we have recently noted that, in cells in which pRb has been inactivated, either by DNA tumour virus infection or as a result of naturally occurring mutations, it is very difficult to detect associations between the D-cyclins and any of their kinase partners (Bates et al., 1994b). Taken at face value, the data suggest that the substrate for D-cyclin/Cdk complexes must be present for the active enzyme to be formed.

As in all rapidly advancing fields, it is almost impossible to draw all the published and soon to be published data into a cohesive picture. Models are being formulated, modified and discarded at an alarming rate as each new component appears on the scene. Within the last few months, two more players have entered the arena, the p21 protein that links p53 to the cyclin/Cdk framework (El-Deiry et al., 1993; Harper et al., 1993; Xiong et al., 1993; Noda et al., 1994) and p16, a specific inhibitor of Cdk4 (Serrano et al., 1993). Exciting times lie ahead.

REFERENCES

Ajchenbaum, F., Ando, K., DeCaprio, J. A. and Griffin, J. D. (1993). Independent regulation of human D-type cyclin gene expression during G_1 phase in primary T lymphocytes. *J. Biol. Chem.* **268**, 4113-4119.

Ando, K., Ajchenbaum-Cymbalista, F. and Griffin, J. D. (1993). Regulation of G_1/S transition by cyclins D2 and D3 in hematopoietic cells. *Proc. Nat. Acad. Sci. USA* **90**, 9571-9575.

Arnold, A., Kim, H. G., Gaz, R. D., Eddy, R. L., Fukushima, Y., Byers, M. G., Shows, T. B. and Kronenberg, H. M. (1989). Molecular cloning and chromosomal mapping of DNA rearranged with the parathyroid hormone gene in a parathyroid adenoma. *J. Clin. Invest.* **83**, 2034-2040.

Baldin, V., Likas, J., Marcotte, M. J., Pagano, M. and Draetta, G. (1993). Cyclin D1 is a nuclear protein required for cell cycle progression. *Genes Dev.* **7**, 812-821.

Bates, S., Bonetta, L., MacAllan, D., Parry, D., Holder, A., Dickson, C. and Peters, G. (1994a). CDK6 (PLSTIRE) and CDK4 (PSK-J3) are a distinct subset of the cyclin-dependent kinases that associate with cyclin D1. *Oncogene* **9**, 71-79.

Bates, S., Parry, D., Bonetta, L., Vousden, K., Dickson, C. and Peters, G. (1994b). Absence of cyclin D/cdk complexes in cells lacking functional retinoblastoma protein. *Oncogene* **9** (in press).

Brookes, S., Lammie, G. A., Schuuring, E., Dickson, C. and Peters, G. (1992). Linkage map of a region of human chromosome band 11q13 amplified in breast and squamous cell tumors. *Genes Chrom. Cancer.* **4**, 290-301.

Buckley, M. F., Sweeney, K. J. E., Hamilton, J. A., Sini, R. L., Manning, D. L., Nicholson, R. I., de Fazio, A., Watts, C. K. W., Musgrove, E. A. and Sutherland, R. L. (1993). Expression and amplification of cyclin genes in human breast cancer. *Oncogene* **8**, 2127-2133.

Bunnell, B. A., Heath, L. S., Adams, D. E., Lahti, J. M. and Kidd, V. J. (1990). Increased expression of a 58-kDa protein kinase leads to changes in the CHO cell cycle. *Proc. Nat. Acad. Sci. USA* **87**, 7467-7471.

Cocks, B. G., Vairo, G., Bodrug, S. E. and Hamilton, J. A. (1992). Suppression of growth factor-induced CYL1 cyclin gene expression by antiproliferative agents. *J. Biol. Chem.* **267**, 12307-12310.

de Boer, C. J., Loyson, S., Kluin, P. M., Kluin-Nelemans, H. C., Schuuring, E. and van Krieken, J. H. J. M. (1993). Multiple breakpoints within the *BCL-1* locus in B-cell lymphoma: rearrangements of the cyclin D1 gene. *Cancer Res.* **53**, 4148-4152.

Dowdy, S. F., Hinds, P. W., Louie, K., Reed, S. I., Arnold, A. and Weinberg, R. A. (1993). Physical interaction of the retinoblastoma protein with human D cyclins. *Cell* **73**, 499-511.

Dulic, V., Lees, E. and Reed, S. I. (1992). Association of human cyclin E with a periodic G_1-S phase protein kinase. *Science* **257**, 1958-1961.

Dulic, V., Drullinger, L. F., Lees, E., Reed, S. I. and Stein, G. H. (1993). Altered regulation of G_1 cyclins in senescent human diploid fibroblasts: accumulation of inactive cyclin E-Cdk2 and cyclin D1-Cdk2 complexes. *Proc. Nat. Acad. Sci. USA* **90**, 11034-11038.

El-Deiry, W. S., Tokino, T., Velculescu, V. E., Levy, D. B., Parsons, R., Trent, J. M., Lin, D., Mercer, W. E., Kinzler, K. W. and Vogelstein, B. (1993). *WAF1*, a potential mediator of p53 tumor suppression. *Cell* **75**, 817-825.

Erikson, J., Finan, J., Tsujimoto, Y., Nowell, P. C. and Croce, C. M. (1984). The chromosome 14 breakpoint in neoplastic B cells with the t(11;14) translocation involves the immunoglobulin heavy chain locus. *Proc. Nat. Acad. Sci. USA* **81**, 4144-4148.

Evans, T., Rosenthal, E. T., Youngblom, J., Distel, D. and Hunt, T. (1983). Cyclin: a protein specified by maternal mRNA in sea urchin eggs that is destroyed at each cleavage division. *Cell* **33**, 389-396.

Ewen, M. E., Sluss, H. K., Sherr, C. J., Matsushime, H., Kato, J. and Livingston, D. M. (1993). Functional interactions of the retinoblastoma protein with mammalian D-type cyclins. *Cell* **73**, 487-497.

Fantl, V., Smith, R., Brookes, S., Dickson, C. and Peters, G. (1993). Chromosome 11q13 abnormalities in human breast cancer. *Cancer Surveys* **18**, 77-94.

Gaudray, P., Szepetowski, P., Escot, C., Birnbaum, D. and Theillet, C. (1992). DNA amplification at 11q13 in human cancer: from complexity to perplexity. *Mutat. Res.* **276**, 317-328.

Gillett, C., Fantl, R., Fisher, C., Bartek, J., Dickson, C., Barnes, D. and Peters, G. (1994). Amplification and overexpression of cyclin D1 in breast cancer detected by immunohistochemical staining. *Cancer Res.* **54** (in press).

Girard, F., Stausfeld, U., Fernandez, A. and Lamb, N. J. C. (1991). Cyclin A is required for the onset of DNA replication in mammalian fibroblasts. *Cell* **67**, 1169-1179.

Glotzer, M., Murray, A. W. and Kirschner, M. W. (1991). Cyclin is degraded by the ubiquitin pathway. *Nature* **349**, 132-138.

Hanks, S. K., Quinn, A. M. and Hunter, T. (1988). The protein kinase family: conserved features and phylogeny of the catalytic domains. *Science* **241**, 42-52.

Hanna, Z., Janowski, M., Tremblay, P., Jiang, X., Milatovich, A., Francke, U. and Jolicoeur, P. (1993). The *Vin-1* gene, identified by provirus insertional muatgenesis, is the cyclin D2. *Oncogene* **8**, 1661-1666.

Harper, J. W., Adami, G. R., Wei, N., Keyomarsi, K. and Elledge, S. J. (1993). The p21 Cdk-interacting protein Cip1 is a potent inhibitor of G_1 cyclin-dependent kinases. *Cell* **75**, 805-816.

Hinds, P. W., Mittnacht, S., Dulic, V., Arnold, A., Reed, S. I. and Weinberg, R. A. (1992). Regulation of retinoblastoma protein functions by ectopic expression of human cyclins. *Cell* **70**, 993-1006.

Hinds, P. W., Dowdy, S. F., Eaton, E. N., Arnold, A. and Weinberg, R. A. (1994). Function of a human cyclin gene as an oncogene. *Proc. Nat. Acad. Sci. USA* **91**, 709-713.

Hu, Q., Lees, J. A., Buchkovich, K. J. and Harlow, E. (1992). The retinoblastoma protein physically associates with the human cdc2 kinase. *Mol. Cell Biol.* **12**, 971-980.

Inaba, T., Matsushime, H., Valentine, M., Roussel, M. F., Sherr, C. J. and Look, A. T. (1992). Genomic organization, chromosomal localization, and independent expression of human cyclin D genes. *Genomics* **13**, 565-574.

Jansen-Dürr, P., Meichle, A., Steiner, P., Pagano, M., Finke, K., Botz, J., Wessbacher, J., Draetta, G. and Eilers, M. (1993). Differential modulation of cyclin gene expression by MYC. *Proc. Nat. Acad. Sci. USA* **90**, 3685-3689.

Jiang, W., Kahn, S. M., Zhou, P., Zhang, Y.-J., Cacace, A. M., Infante, A. S., Doi, S., Santella, R. M. and Weinstein, I. B. (1993a). Overexpression of cyclin D1 in rat fibroblasts causes abnormalities in growth control, cell cycle progression and gene expression. *Oncogene* **8**, 3447-3457.

Jiang, W., Zhang, Y.-J., Kahn, S. M., Hollstein, M. C., Santella, R. M., Lu, S.-H., Harris, C. C., Montesano, R. and Weinstein, I. B. (1993b). Altered expression of the cyclin D1 and retinoblastoma genes in human esophageal cancer. *Proc. Nat. Acad. Sci. USA* **90**, 9026-9030.

Kato, J., Matsushime, H., Hiebert, S. W., Ewen, M. E. and Sherr, C. J. (1993). Direct binding of cyclin D to the retinoblastoma gene product (pRb) and pRb phosphorylation by the cyclin D-dependent kinase CDK4. *Genes Dev.* **7**, 331-342.

Kobayashi, H., Stewart, E., Poon, R., Adamczewski, J. P., Gannon, J. and Hunt, T. (1992). Identification of the domains in cyclin A required for binding to, and activation of, p34cdc2 and p32cdk2 protein kinase subunits. *Mol. Biol. Cell* **3**, 1279-1294.

Koff, A., Cross, F., Fisher, A., Schumacher, J., Leguellec, K., Philippe, M. and Roberts, J. M. (1991). Human cyclin E, a new cyclin that interacts with two members of the *CDC2* gene family. *Cell* **66**, 1217-1228.

Koff, A., Giordano, A., Desai, D., Yamashita, K., Harper, J. W., Elledge, S., Nishimoto, T., Morgan, D. O., Franza, B. R. and Roberts, J. M. (1992). Formation and activation of a cyclin E-cdk2 complex during the G1 phase of the human cell cycle. *Science* **257**, 1689-1694.

Lammie, G. A., Fantl, V., Smith, R., Schuuring, E., Brookes, S., Michalides, R., Dickson, C., Arnold, A. and Peters, G. (1991). D11S287, a putative oncogene on chromosome 11q13, is amplified and expressed in squamous cell and mammary carcinomas and linked to BCL-1. *Oncogene* **6**, 439-444.

Lammie, G. A. and Peters, G. (1991). Chromosome 11q13 abnormalities in human cancer. *Cancer Cells* **3**, 413-420.

Lammie, G. A., Smith, R., Silver, J., Brookes, S., Dickson, C. and Peters, G. (1992). Proviral insertions near cyclin D1 in mouse lymphomas: a parallel for BCL1 translocations in human B-cell neoplasms. *Oncogene* **7**, 2381-2387.

Lapidot-Lifson, Y., Patinkin, D., Prody, C. A., Ehrlich, G., Seidman, S., Ben-Aziz, R., Benseler, F., Eckstein, F., Zakut, H. and Soreq, H. (1992). Cloning and antisense oligodeoxynucleotide inhibition of a human homolog of *cdc2* required in hematopoiesis. *Proc. Nat. Acad. Sci. USA* **89**, 579-583.

Lees, E. M. and Harlow, E. (1993). Sequences within the conserved cyclin box of human cyclin A are sufficient for binding to and activatin of cdc2 kinase. *Mol. Cell. Biol.* **13**, 1194-1201.

Lees, J. A., Buchkovich, K. J., Marshak, D. R., Anderson, C. W. and Harlow, E. (1991). The retinoblastoma protein is phosphorylated on multiple sites by human cdc2. *EMBO J.* **10**, 4279-4290.

Lew, D. J., Dulic, V. and Reed, S. I. (1991). Isolation of three novel human cyclins by rescue of G1 cyclin (Cln) function in yeast. *Cell* **66**, 1197-1206.

Lin, B. T.-Y., Gruenwald, S., Morla, A. O., Lee, W.-H. and Wang, J. Y. J. (1991). Retinoblastoma cancer suppressor gene product is a substrate of the cell cycle regulator cdc2 kinase. *EMBO J.* **10**, 857-864.

Lovec, H., Sewing, A., Lucibello, F. C., Müller, R. and Möröy, T. (1994). Oncogenic activity of cyclin D1 revealed through cooperation with Ha-*ras*: link between cell cycle control and malignant transformation. *Oncogene* **9**, 323-326.

Lucibello, F. C., Sewing, A., S, B., Bürger, C. and Müller, R. (1993). Deregulation of cyclins D1 and E and suppression of cdk2 and cdk4 in senescent human fibroblasts. *J. Cell Sci.* **105**, 123-133.

Lukas, J., Pagano, M., Staskova, Z., Draetta, G. and Bartek, J. (1994). Cyclin D1 protein oscillates and is essential for cell cycle progression in human tumour cell lines. *Oncogene* **9**, 707-718.

Matsushime, H., Roussel, M. F., Ashmun, R. A. and Sherr, C. J. (1991). Colony-stimulating factor 1 regulates novel cyclins during the G1 phase of the cell cycle. *Cell* **65**, 701-713.

Matsushime, H., Ewen, M. E., Strom, D. K., Kato, J.-Y., Hanks, S. K., Roussel, M. F. and Sherr, C. J. (1992). Identification and properties of an atypical catalytic subunit (p34PSK-J3/cdk4) for mammalian D type G1 cyclins. *Cell* **71**, 323-334.

Matsushime, H., Quelle, D. E., Shurtleff, S. A., Shibuya, M., Sherr, C. J. and Kato, J.-Y. (1994). D-type cyclin-dependent kinase activity in mammalian cells. *Mol. Cell. Biol.* **14**, 2066-2076.

Meyerson, M., Enders, G. H., Wu, C.-L., Su, L.-K., Gorka, C., Nelson, C., Harlow, E. and Tsai, L.-H. (1992). A family of human cdc2-related protein kinases. *EMBO J.* **11**, 2909-2917.

Meyerson, M. and Harlow, E. (1994). Identification of G1 kinase activity for cdk6, a novel cyclin D partner. *Mol. Cell. Biol.* **14**, 2077-2086.

Motokura, T., Bloom, T., Kim, H. G., Jüppner, H., Ruderman, J. V., Kronenberg, H. M. and Arnold, A. (1991). A novel cyclin encoded by a *bcl1*-linked candidate oncogene. *Nature* **350**, 512-515.

Motokura, T., Keyomarsi, K., Kronenberg, H. M. and Arnold, A. (1992). Cloning and characterization of human cyclin D3, a cDNA closely related in sequence to the PRAD1/cyclin D1 proto-oncogene. *J. Biol. Chem.* **267**, 20412-20415.

Musgrove, E. A., Hamilton, J. A., Lee, C. S. L., Sweeney, K. J. E., Watts, C. K. W. and Sutherland, R. L. (1993). Growth factor, steroid, and steroid antagonist regulation of cyclin gene expression associated with changes in T-47D human breast cancer cell cycle progression. *Mol. Cell Biol.* **13**, 3577-3587.

Noda, A., Ning, Y., Venable, S. F., Pereira-Smith, O. M. and Smith, J. R. (1994). Cloning of senescent cell-derived inhibitors of DNA synthesis using an expression screen. *Exp. Cell Res.* **211**, 90-98.

Norbury, C. and Nurse, P. (1992). Animal cell cycles and their control. *Annu. Rev. Biochem.* **61**, 441-470.

Ohtsubo, M. and Roberts, J. M. (1993). Cyclin-dependent regulation of G1 in mammalian fibroblasts. *Science* **259**, 1908-1912.

Okuda, T., Cleveland, J. L. and Downing, J. R. (1992). *PCTAIRE-1* and *PCTAIRE-3*, two members of a novel *cdc2/CDC28*-related protein kinase gene family. *Oncogene* **7**, 2249-2258.

Pagano, M., Pepperhok, R., Verde, F., Ansorge, W. and Draetta, G. (1992). Cyclin A is required at two points in the human cell cycle. *EMBO J.* **11**, 961-971.

Palmero, I., Holder, A., Sinclair, A. J., Dickson, C. and Peters, G. (1993). Cyclins D1 and D2 are differentially expressed in human B-lymphoid cell lines. *Oncogene* **8**, 1049-1054.

Quelle, D. E., Ashmun, R. A., Shurtleff, S. A., Kato, J.-Y., Bar-Sagi, D., Roussel, M. F. and Sherr, C. J. (1993). Overexpression of mouse D-type cyclins accelerates G1 phase in rodent fibroblasts. *Genes Dev.* **7**, 1559-1571.

Reed, S. I. (1992). The role of p34 kinases in the G1 to S-phase transition. *Annu. Rev. Cell Biol.* **8**, 529-561.

Resnitzky, D., Gossen, M., Bujard, H. and Reed, S. I. (1994). Acceleration of the G1/S phase transition by expression of cyclins D1 and E with an inducible system. *Mol. Cell. Biol.* **14**, 1669-1679.

Rogers, S., Wells, R. and Rechsteiner, M. (1986). Amino acid sequences common to rapidly degraded proteins: the PEST hypothesis. *Science* **234**, 364-368.

Rosenberg, C. L., Kim, H. G., Shows, T. B., Kronenberg, H. M. and Arnold, A. (1991a). Rearrangement and overexpression of D11S287E, a candidate oncogene on chromosome 11q13 in benign parathyroid tumors. *Oncogene* **6**, 449-453.

Rosenberg, C. L., Wong, E., Petty, E. M., Bale, A. E., Tsujimoto, Y., Harris, N. L. and Arnold, A. (1991b). *PRAD1*, a candidate *BCL1* oncogene: mapping and expression in centrocytic lymphoma. *Proc. Nat. Acad. Sci. USA* **88**, 9638-9642.

Schuuring, E., Verhoeven, E., Mooi, W. J. and Michalides, R. J. A. M. (1992). Identification and cloning of two overexpressed genes, U21B31/*PRAD*1 and EMS1, within the amplified chromosome 11q13 region in human carcinomas. *Oncogene* **7**, 355-361.

Schuuring, E., Verhoeven, E., Litvinov, S. and Michalides, R. J. A. M. (1993). The product of the *EMS1* gene, amplified and overexpressed in human carcinomas, is homologous to a v-*src* substrate and is located in cell-substratum contact sites. *Mol. Cell. Biol.* **13**, 2891-2898.

Serrano, M., Hannon, G. J. and Beach, D. (1993). A new regulatory motif in cell-cycle control causing specific inhibition of cyclin D/CDK4. *Nature* **366**, 704-707.

Seto, M., Yamamoto, K., Iida, S., Akao, Y., Utsumi, K. R., Kubonishi, I., Miyoshi, I., Ohtsuki, T., Yawata, Y., Namba, M., Motokura, T., Arnold, A., Takahashi, T. and Ueda, R. (1992). Gene rearrangement and overexpression of *PRAD1* in lymphoid malignancy with t(11;14)(q13;q32) translocation. *Oncogene* **7**, 1401-1406.

Sewing, A., Bürger, C., Brüsselbach, S., Schalk, C., Lucibello, F. C. and Müller, R. (1993). Human cyclin D1 encodes a labile nuclear protein whose synthesis is directly induced by growth factors and suppressed by cyclic AMP. *J. Cell Sci.* **104**, 545-554.

Sinclair, A. J., Palmero, I., Peters, G. and Farrell, P. J. (1994). EBNA-2 and EBNA-LP cooperate to cause G_0 to G_1 transition during immortalisation of resting human B-lymphocytes by Epstein-Barr virus. *EMBO J.* **13**, 3321-3328.

Solomon, M. J. (1993). Activation of the various cyclin/cdc2 protein kinases. *Curr. Opin. Cell Biol.* **5**, 180-186.

Surmacz, E., Reiss, K., Sell, C. and Baserga, R. (1992). Cyclin D1 messenger RNA is inducible by platelet-derived growth factor in cultured fibroblasts. *Cancer Res.* **52**, 4522-4525.

Tsai, L.-H., Lees, E., Faha, B., Harlow, E. and Riabowol, K. (1993). The cdk2 kinase is required for the G_1-to-S transition in mammalian cells. *Oncogene* **8**, 1593-1602.

Tsujimoto, Y., Yunis, J., Onorato-Showe, L., Erikson, J., Nowell, P. C. and Croce, C. M. (1984). Molecular cloning of the chromomal breakpoint of B-cell lymphomas and leukemias with the t(11;14) chromosome translocation. *Science* **224**, 1403-1406.

Walker, D. H. and Maller, J. L. (1991). Role for cyclin A in the dependence of mitosis on completion of DNA replication. *Nature* **354**, 314-317.

Wang, J., Chenivesse, X., Henglein, B. and Bréchot, C. (1990). Hepatitis B virus integration in a cyclin A gene in a hepatocellular carcinoma. *Nature* **343**, 555-557.

Williams, M. E., Swerdlow, S. H., Rosenberg, C. L. and Arnold, A. (1992). Characterization of chromosome 11 translocation breapoints at the *bcl*-1 and *PRAD1* loci in centrocytic lymphoma. *Cancer Res. (suppl.)* **52**, 5541s-5544s.

Winston, J. T. and Pledger, W. J. (1993). Growth factor regulation of cyclin D1 mRNA expression through protein synthesis-dependent and -independent mechanisms. *Mol. Biol. Cell* **4**, 1133-1144.

Withers, D. A., Harvey, R. C., Faust, J. B., Melnyk, O., Carey, K. and Meeker, T. C. (1991). Characterization of a candidate *bcl*-1 gene. *Mol. Cell. Biol.* **11**, 4846-4853.

Won, K.-A., Xiong, Y., Beach, D. and Gilman, M. Z. (1992). Growth-regulated expression of D-type cyclin genes in human diploid fibroblasts. *Proc. Nat. Acad. Sci. USA* **89**, 9910-9914.

Xiong, Y., Connolly, T., Futcher, B. and Beach, D. (1991). Human D-type cyclin. *Cell* **65**, 691-699.

Xiong, Y., Menninger, J., Beach, D. and Ward, D. C. (1992a). Molecular cloning and chromosomal mapping of *CCND* genes encoding human D-type cyclins. *Genomics* **13**, 575-584.

Xiong, Y., Zhang, H. and Beach, D. (1992b). D type cyclins associate with multiple protein kinases and the DNA replication and repair factor PCNA. *Cell* **71**, 505-514.

Xiong, Y., Hannon, G. J., Zhang, H., Casso, D., Kobayashi, R. and Beach, D. (1993). p21 is a universal inhibitor of cyclin kinases. *Nature* **366**, 701-704.

Xiong, Y., Zhang, H. and Beach, D. (1993). Subunit rearrangement of the cyclin-dependent kinases is associated with cellular transformation. *Genes Dev.* **7**, 1572-1583.

Journal of Cell Science, Supplement 18, 97-104 (1994)
Printed in Great Britain © The Company of Biologists Limited 1994

Structure and function of SH2 domains

Luc E. M. Marengere[1,2] and Tony Pawson[1,2]

[1]Division of Molecular and Developmental Biology, Samuel Lunenfeld Research Institute, Mount Sinai Hospital, 600 University Avenue, Toronto, Ontario M5G 1X5, Canada
[2]Department of Molecular and Medical Genetics, University of Toronto, Ontario M5S 1A8, Canada

SUMMARY

In order for cells to respond to their environment, a series of regulated molecular events has to take place. External signalling molecules bind to cellular receptors and thereby trigger the activation of multiple intracellular pathways, which modify cellular phenotypes. The cell-surface receptors for a wide range of polypeptide hormones possess protein tyrosine kinase activity, which is induced by binding of the appropriate extracellular ligand. Tyrosine phosphorylation can act as a molecular switch, by initiating the recruitment of cytoplasmic effector molecules containing Src homology (SH) 2 domains, to activated receptors. These SH2-containing proteins, in turn, regulate intracellular signalling pathways. Here, we discuss the role of tyrosine phosphorylation in triggering signalling pathways, as well as the functions of SH2 domains, which mediate these events through phosphotyrosine-dependent protein-protein interactions.

Key words: protein tyrosine kinase, signal transduction

RECEPTOR PROTEIN TYROSINE KINASES

Receptor protein tyrosine kinases (RPTKs) are membrane-spanning molecules, which function as regulators of cell growth and differentiation. RPTKs contain an extracellular ligand-binding domain, a transmembrane element, and an intracellular catalytic region. The extracellular portion is characterized by specific motifs such as cysteine-rich sequences, immunoglobulin-like loops, fibronectin repeats, and others, which are apparently involved in growth factor binding. The transmembrane domain is hydrophobic and plays a crucial role in receptor dimerization, while the intracellular region contains the tyrosine kinase domain and non-catalytic sequences that, following RPTK activation, serve as transphosphorylation substrates (Yarden and Ullrich, 1988; Ullrich and Schlessinger, 1990; van der Geer and Hunter, 1994). These characteristics are common to all RPTKs, but specific features can vary, such as the type of repeats in the extracellular domain, or the structure of the kinase domain, and these differences have been used to define subfamilies of RPTKs (Fig. 1) (van der Geer and Hunter, 1994). For example, receptors such as the epidermal growth factor receptor (EGFR), the platelet-derived growth factor receptor (PDGFR), the insulin receptor (IR), the nerve growth factor receptor (NGFR), and the fibroblast growth factor receptor (FGFR) constitute five subfamilies of RPTK. The EGFR, PDGFR, NGFR, and FGFR vary mostly in their extracellular ligand-binding domains, although the PDGFR has an additional kinase insert within its catalytic domain, while the IR has a different receptor architecture altogether (Fig. 1).

RPTK activation is achieved in the following fashion: binding of the growth factor to the extracellular portion of a RPTK induces receptor dimerization, and stimulates kinase activity, thereby permitting intermolecular autophosphorylation, which largely occurs within non-catalytic intracellular sequences. Mitogenic responses mediated by activated RPTKs are dependent upon receptor tyrosine kinase activity. Receptors in which the kinase domain is mutated and rendered inactive can no longer induce a mitogenic signal in response to growth factor stimulation. The importance of tyrosine kinase activity has also been shown in vivo. Loss-of-function (LOF) mutations in genes encoding RPTKs, such as *c-kit, torso, der, sevenless*, and *let23* drastically affect development of distinct species, such as the mouse, *Drosophila*, and *Caenorhabditis elegans* (Pawson and Bernstein, 1990). LOF mutations in the mouse *kit* gene affect hair pigmentation, hematopoiesis, and fertility depending on the severity of the mutated allele (Russel, 1979; Reith et al., 1990). The most severe *kit* allele, known as W^{42}, induces a substitution of an aspartic acid within the kinase domain, thought to be the catalytic base, leading to a complete loss of tyrosine kinase activity. In *Drosophila*, mutations in the *torso* tyrosine kinase gene affect terminal embryonic structure development (Nusslein-Volhard et al., 1987); while LOF mutations in the *Drosophila* gene *der*, affect head and central nervous system development (Schejter and Shilo, 1989; Price et al., 1989). The *sevenless* LOF mutation specifically affects the development of photoreceptor cell R7, which normally differentiates into a neuronal retinal cell (Tomlinson et al., 1987). In *C. elegans*, *let23* mutations affect the development of the vulval precursor cells, which contribute to the formation of the hermaphrodite vulva (Ferguson et al., 1987; Aroian et al., 1991). Consistent with this view, gain-of-function (GOF) mutations in *let23*, which positively affect its tyrosine kinase activity, contribute to an increase in differentiated vulval precursor cells, and lead to the formation of multiple vulvae.

The identification of cell-surface receptors for growth

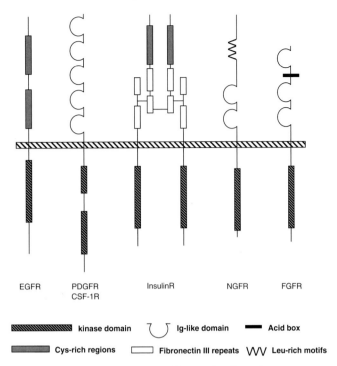

EGFR   PDGFR   InsulinR   NGFR   FGFR
CSF-1R

▨ kinase domain   ⌒ Ig-like domain   ▬ Acid box

▬ Cys-rich regions   ▭ Fibronectin III repeats   ⋁⋁ Leu-rich motifs

Fig. 1. Schematic representation of five subfamilies of receptor protein tyrosine kinases.

factors with intrinsic tyrosine kinase activity, and the discovery of the role of these receptors in cell growth, differentiation, and development have triggered great interest in determining their mechanism of action.

SIGNALLING MOLECULES

The initial molecular event mediated by RPTKs after binding their ligand is autophosphorylation and stimulation of tyrosine phosphorylation of cellular proteins. Stimulation of quiescent fibroblasts by PDGF is accompanied by autophosphorylation of the PDGFR and increased tyrosine-phosphorylation of cellular proteins (Kazlauskas and Cooper, 1989). The PDGFR kinase domain contains an insertion relative to the other tyrosine kinases, termed the kinase insert (Fig. 1), which together with other sites on the PDGFR intracellular domain, become tyrosine-phosphorylated. Autophosphorylation sites on the human βPDGFR also serve as docking sites for signalling molecules. Phosphatidylinositol (PI) 3′-kinase activity associates specifically with tyrosine-phosphorylated sites within the kinase insert of the activated βPDGFR. This association is dependent on tyrosine phosphorylation (Kazlauskas and Cooper, 1989; Coughlin et al., 1989). The binding of PI3′-kinase to the βPDGFR was mapped to tyrosine residues 740 and 751 (Y^{740} and Y^{751}) within the kinase insert, and substituting these residues for phenylalanine was shown to abolish the ability of the PDGFR to bind PI3′-kinase (Kazlauskas and Cooper, 1990; Escobedo et al., 1991). The PDGFR binds other signalling molecules, including p21ras GTPase-activating protein (GAP), phospholipase C-γ (PLCγ1), and the Syp phosphotyrosine phosphatase. These interactions involve the SH2 domain(s) of the signalling molecules and specific receptor

phosphotyrosine sites. The SH2-containing proteins become tyrosine-phosphorylated as a consequence of binding to the activated PDGFR (Molloy et al., 1989; Meisenhelder et al., 1989; Kazlauskas et al., 1990; Kaplan and Cooper, 1990; Morrison et al., 1990; Kazlauskas et al., 1993). In addition, members of the Src family of cytoplasmic tyrosine kinases, as well as Shc and Nck, all of which contain SH2 domains, can also bind the activated PDGFR (Kypta et al., 1990; Mori et al., 1993; Nishimura et al., 1993; Yokote et al., 1994). The colony-stimulating factor 1 receptor (CSF-1R) (Fig. 1) can induce proliferation of mouse fibroblasts engineered to express the receptor, in response to CSF-1. Consistent with the view that activated RPTKs, which have undergone tyrosine-autophosphorylation, can bind signalling molecules, the activated CSF-1R associates with PI3′-kinase, and Grb2 in a phosphotyrosine-dependent fashion (Downing et al., 1989; Reedijk et al., 1990, 1992; van der Geer and Hunter, 1993).

The IR has a similar mechanism for activating effector molecules upon insulin stimulation. Although the IR has tyrosine kinase activity, SH2-containing signalling molecules do not associate directly with the activated receptor. Activation of the IR leads to autophosphorylation and to tyrosine-phosphorylation of the insulin receptor substrate (IRS) 1, which in turn binds SH2-containing signalling molecules, such as PI3′-kinase, Grb2, Syp and Nck (Lavan et al., 1992; Myers et al., 1992; Yamamoto et al., 1992; Backer et al., 1992; Kuhne et al., 1993; Lee et al., 1993; Tobe et al., 1993; Pronk et al., 1994). The association of effector molecules with specific tyrosine-phosphorylated sites on activated RPTKs suggests a general mechanism by which RPTKs couple to intracellular signalling molecules.

SH2 BINDING

Receptor autophosphorylation acts as a switch to induce physical association between activated receptor and signalling molecules. Although these signalling proteins vary in their catalytic activities, structures, and cellular functions, they all share a common region termed the SH2 domain. The SH2 domain was initially identified as a common 100 amino acid sequence in the Src and Fps oncoproteins (Sadowski et al., 1986; Pawson, 1988). SH2 domains are highly conserved (approximately 35% identical amongst all SH2 domains), associate specifically with phosphotyrosine in a sequence-dependent manner, and are found in one or two copies in many cytoplasmic signalling molecules (Pawson and Gish, 1992). These SH2-containing proteins can be classified into two groups; the first group includes signalling proteins that contain intrinsic catalytic activity, and includes the Src, Fps and Abl families of intracellular tyrosine kinases, PLCγ1 and 2, GAP and tyrosine-specific phosphatases such as the SH2-containing tyrosine phosphatase Syp, amongst others. The second group includes molecules such as Grb2, SHC, Nck, Crk and the p85 subunit of PI3′-kinase, which do not have detectable intrinsic catalytic activity, but apparently function as molecular adaptors to couple RPTKs to signalling proteins that themselves may lack SH2 domains (Fig. 2).

The SH2 domains of proteins such as GAP, PLCγ1, PI3′-kinase, and Src were shown to be directly involved in protein-protein interactions with activated receptors. The binding sites of these and other SH2-containing molecules have been

Group 1:

SH2/SH3-containing proteins with enzymatic activity

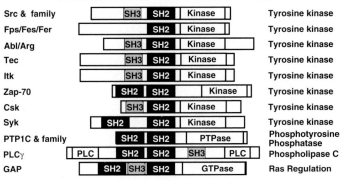

Src & family	SH3 SH2 Kinase	Tyrosine kinase
Fps/Fes/Fer	SH2 Kinase	Tyrosine kinase
Abl/Arg	SH3 SH2 Kinase	Tyrosine kinase
Tec	SH3 SH2 Kinase	Tyrosine kinase
Itk	SH3 SH2 Kinase	Tyrosine kinase
Zap-70	SH2 SH2 Kinase	Tyrosine kinase
Csk	SH3 SH2 Kinase	Tyrosine kinase
Syk	SH2 SH2 Kinase	Tyrosine kinase
PTP1C & family	SH2 SH2 PTPase	Phosphotyrosine Phosphatase
PLCγ	PLC SH2 SH2 SH3 PLC	Phospholipase C
GAP	SH2 SH3 SH2 GTPase	Ras Regulation

Group 2:

SH2/SH3-containing proteins without intrinsic enzymatic activity

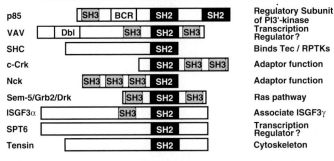

p85	SH3 BCR SH2 SH2	Regulatory Subunit of PI3'-kinase
VAV	Dbl SH3 SH2 SH3	Transcription Regulator ?
SHC	SH2	Binds Tec / RPTKs
c-Crk	SH2 SH3 SH3	Adaptor function
Nck	SH3 SH3 SH3 SH2	Adaptor function
Sem-5/Grb2/Drk	SH3 SH2 SH3	Ras pathway
ISGF3α	SH3 SH2	Associate ISGF3γ
SPT6	SH2	Transcription Regulator ?
Tensin	SH2	Cytoskeleton

Fig. 2. Structures of SH2-containing proteins. These molecules are divided into two groups: Group 1 includes proteins with intrinsic catalytic activity, while Group 2 includes proteins without intrinsic catalytic activity, serving an adaptor function, coupling RPTKs to downstream effector molecules. The catalytic activities, and adaptor functions are listed on the right. Kinase, the tyrosine kinase domain; PTPase, the phosphotyrosine phosphatase domain; PLC, the phospholipase domain; GTPase, Ras GTPase-activating domain; BCR, the G-binding protein Rac/Rho GTPase-activating domain; Dbl, a guanine-nucleotide exchange domain.

precisely mapped on several receptors. For example, Src, PI3'-kinase, GAP, Syp, and PLCγ1 bind tyrosine-phosphorylated sites Y^{579}/Y^{581}, Y^{740}/Y^{751}, Y^{771}, Y^{1009}, and Y^{1021}, respectively, on the PDGFR (Fig. 3). These SH2-binding sites were mapped using two main approaches. The first approach involves in vivo expression of the wild-type (wt) receptor, or variant forms of the receptor in which specific tyrosine phosphorylation sites are substituted with phenylalanine. These receptor-expressing cells are then stimulated with the appropriate ligand necessary for receptor activation. The wt or mutant receptors are immunoprecipitated and assayed for the presence of specific co-immunoprecipitated SH2-containing proteins. In the case of the PDGFR, specific receptor autophosphorylation sites are required for binding of defined SH2-containing proteins. In vitro, the autophosphorylated receptor can bind SH2 signalling proteins. These interactions can be efficiently competed by short tyrosine-phosphorylated peptides corresponding to specific receptor autophosphorylation sites. Together these approaches have identified specific receptor-binding sites for SH2-containing molecules (Kazlauskas and Cooper, 1989, 1990; Molloy et al., 1989; Downing et al., 1989; Kaplan et al., 1990; Morrison et al., 1990; Anderson et al., 1990; Escobedo et al., 1991; Fantl et al., 1992; Kashishian et

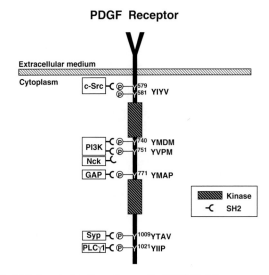

Fig. 3. SH2 domain binding sites on the PDGFR. The sequences C-terminal to the autophosphorylated tyrosine binding sites are indicated on the left of the receptor, in single letter amino acid code.

al., 1992; Kazlauskas et al., 1992, 1993; van der Geer et al., 1993).

The ability of SH2 domains to mediate phosphotyrosine-dependent interactions is not limited to receptors. For example, GAP, Grb2, Src, and other signalling proteins can also associate, via their SH2 domain(s) with tyrosine-phosphorylated cytoplasmic molecules (Moran et al., 1990; Koch et al., 1991; Lowenstein et al., 1992; Schaller et al., 1992; Cobb et al., 1994). This was demonstrated by the ability of v-Crk and v-Abl SH2 domains to bind a spectrum of tyrosine-phosphorylated proteins in solution, and in filter-binding assays (Matsuda et al., 1990; Mayer and Hanafusa, 1990; Mayer et al., 1991, 1992). The N-terminal SH2 domain of GAP was also shown to bind predominantly tyrosine-phosphorylated proteins p62 and p190 in vivo and in vitro (Moran et al., 1990; Marengere and Pawson, 1992). These proteins have been suggested to have RNA-binding ability, and a GTPase activity towards the small GTP-binding protein Rho, respectively (Wong et al., 1992; Settleman et al., 1992a,b). These experiments revealed that binding to phosphotyrosine-containing sites is a fundamental property of all SH2 domains.

SH2 SPECIFICITY

As noted above, autophosphorylated growth factor receptors possess multiple phosphotyrosine sites that bind to distinct SH2 domains (Fig. 3) (Fantl et al., 1992; Rotin et al., 1993; Mohammadi et al., 1991; Reedijk et al., 1990, 1992). The systematic mapping of p85α, GAP, and PLCγ1 binding site(s) on the PDGFR and CSF-1R has suggested that the sequence C-terminal to the phosphotyrosine regulates SH2-binding specificity (van der Geer and Hunter, 1993; Mohammadi et al., 1991; Cantley et al., 1991; Panayotou et al., 1992; Kashishian et al., 1992; Kazlauskas et al., 1992). For example, binding sites for the SH2-containing p85 protein on the polyoma virus middle T-antigen, PDGFR, CSF-1R, c-Kit, and IRS-1 have the consensus sequence pTyr-(Met/Val)-(Asp/Glu/Pro)-(Met)

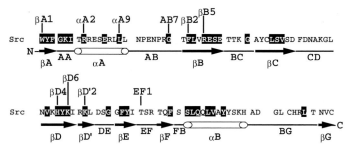

Fig. 4. Sequence of the Src SH2 domain with conserved residues highlighted, and respective positions indicated above. The locations of the α-helices, β-sheets and loops are indicated below according to the nomenclature developed by Eck et al. (1993).

depicted in single letter code as [pY(M/V)-(D/E/P)-(M)] (Escobedo et al., 1991; Auger et al., 1992; McGlade et al., 1992; Backer et al., 1992). Furthermore, the p85 SH2 domains can bind to phosphopeptides containing the consensus sequence pYM/V-X-M with high affinity (Felder et al., 1993; Panayotou et al., 1993). Based on the data for the p85 SH2 domain-selectivity, a degenerate phosphopeptide library screen was developed in order to determine the specificity of individual SH2 domains (Songyang et al., 1993, 1994). Initially, the p85 SH2 domains expressed as fusion proteins were incubated with phosphopeptides, containing the sequence GDGpTyrX^{+1}X^{+2}X^{+3}SPLLL (single letter amino acid code), where X represents a degenerate position at the +1, +2, and +3 residues. The p85 N- and C-terminal SH2 domains selected amino acid motifs very similar to the consensus binding sites in the physiological targets mentioned above. Consequently, the assay was expanded to other SH2 domains, in order to investigate their respective potential specificity (Songyang et al., 1993, 1994).

Based on their binding specificity, SH2 domains can be classified into two groups (Songyang et al., 1994). The first group selects mostly hydrophilic residues at the two residues C-terminal to the phosphotyrosine (the +1 and +2 positions), and a hydrophobic residue at +3. The second group preferentially selects hydrophobic residues. (Songyang et al., 1993, 1994).

The ability of this assay to predict SH2-binding sequences implies that SH2 domain can independently select for phosphotyrosine and residues at the +1, +2, and +3 positions. This selection must therefore be performed by residues strategically located within the SH2 domain, which specifically interact with these positions. Evidence of SH2 domain binding-specificity was first provided by structural analysis of the v-Src SH2 domain complexed to the pYEEI peptide, and will be discussed in the next section.

SH2 STRUCTURE

NMR solutions of the uncomplexed Abl SH2, and p85α N-SH2 domains provided information about the overall topology of these modular domains, which comprise a central β-sheet flanked by two α-helices (Overduin et al., 1992; Booker et al., 1992).

The X-ray structures of v-Src SH2 and Lck SH2 domains complexed to the high affinity peptide EPQpY^{0}E^{+1}E^{+2}I^{+3}PIYL (pYEEI) added information about SH2 interactions with phos-

photyrosine and the +1Glu, +2Glu, and +3Ile residues within the phosphopeptide (Waksman et al., 1993; Eck et al., 1993). Following the structural analysis of these domains, a new nomenclature was adopted for SH2 residues based on secondary structures (see Fig. 4). X-ray crystallographic structures were also of higher resolution, showing two clefts; the first being the phosphotyrosine-binding site, and the second, a hydrophobic-binding pocket for the +3 residue. Both pockets are flexible; the phosphotyrosine-binding pocket closes upon association with phosphotyrosine, while the hydrophobic pocket opens after interaction with the +3 residue. As expected, well-conserved residues within the SH2 domains form the hydrophobic core and the phosphotyrosine-binding pocket, while the more variable residues are involved in interactions with the +1 to +3 residues, and therefore in conferring specificity. The phosphotyrosine moiety is stabilized mostly via interactions with ArgαA2, ArgβB5, and LysβD6, which contact the phenyl ring and the phosphate group. Residues within the BC loop also stabilize the phosphotyrosine structure through interactions with the terminal phosphate oxygens.

In contrast to the phosphotyrosine-binding site, the +1 and +2Glu residues lie on the surface of the SH2 domain. The +1Glu forms ionic interactions with TyrβD5 and LysβD3, while the +2Glu is stabilized by ionic interactions via water molecules with ArgβD′1, LysβD6 and the carbonyl oxygen of the +1Glu. The hydrophobic binding pocket specific for the +3Ile is formed by residues in the EF and BG loops, and engulfs the +3Ile. We have recently shown that changing the Thr at the EF1 position of the Src SH2 domain to Trp markedly alters its binding specificity and biological behaviour (Marengere et al., 1994).

The interior of the binding pocket is lined by helix αB, while the edges are formed by the EF and BG loops, and the βD strand. More specifically, IleβE4, TyrβD5, TyrαA9, LeuBG4, GlyBG3 and ThrEF1 are residues that directly interact with the +3Ile and may therefore be important in determining specificity at that position. These amino acids vary amongst SH2 domains, consistent with the possibility that they are major determinants in SH2 specificity, at least at the +3 position. The Src and Lck SH2 structures have identified one specific type of SH2/phosphopeptide interaction, in which the phosphopeptide can be represented as a two-pronged plug (the prongs being formed by phosphotyrosine and the +3Ile sidechain), while the SH2 domain is a socket with two accommodating holes.

The NMR structure of the PLCγ1 C-terminal SH2 (C-SH2) domain complexed to DNDpY^{0}I^{+1}I^{+2}P^{+3}LPDPK (termed pYIIP) phosphopeptide, has shown a second class of SH2 binding-specificity (Pascal et al., 1994). The PLCγ1 C-SH2 domain shares some topological features with the complexed Src/Lck SH2 domains, such as the hydrophobic core and the concentration of basic residues near the phosphotyrosine-binding pocket. Interestingly, the PLCγ1 C-SH2 domain differs with respect to its phosphotyrosine-stabilizing interactions, SH2-binding surface for positions C-terminal to the phosphotyrosine, and its additional ability to contact the phosphopeptide +4, +5, and +6 positions.

Also in contrast to the +3-binding pocket of the Src SH2 domain, the PLCγ1 C-SH2 domain binding surface, has an extended hydrophobic groove in which the +1, +3 and +5 residues are buried. One factor contributing to this difference in binding surface is the SH2 position βD5, which is a Tyr in Src SH2 domain, but a Cys in the PLCγl C-SH2 domain. TyrβD5 in the Src SH2 domain interacts with the BG loop, and pinches that segment of the binding surface, closing the hydrophobic groove, and thereby forcing the +1 and +2 residues to bind at the surface of the SH2 domain. The other major difference between SH2 structures is the ability of the PLCγl C-SH2 domain to associate with the +4, +5, and +6 positions of the phosphopeptide. Although 85% of the NMR-detected interactions were between the SH2 domain and the phosphotyrosine +1, +2, and +3 positions, interactions between the +4Leu, +5Pro, and +6Asp of the phosphopeptide were also detected, mostly with SH2 residues within the EF and BG loops. SH2 binding to the +4, +5, and +6 residues may confer optimal binding affinity towards a physiological target.

Another example of an SH2 domain binding to a phospho-tyrosine-containing sequence, is provided by the structural analysis of the Syp N-terminal SH2 domain (N-SH2) complexed to high affinity peptides (Lee et al., 1994). The Syp N-SH2 domain displays some unique features, while other facets resemble either the Src SH2 or the PLCγl C-SH2 domain structures. For example, the Gly at αA2, which replaces the Arg found at αA2 in the Src/Lck and PLCγl C-SH2 domains, does not contact the phosphotyrosine moiety. Instead, the invariant ArgβB5 of the Syp N-SH2 domain interacts with both the phenyl ring and the phosphate group terminal oxygens. In contrast to the PLCγl C-SH2 domain structure, no additional basic residues are found to bind the phosphotyrosine, which might compensate for the absence of the ArgαA2.

As found in the PLCγl C-SH2, IleβD5 of the Syp N-SH2 domain does not interact with the BG loop and is important for forming a hydrophobic binding channel in which the +1, +2, and +3 positions are deeply buried. Also consistent with this type of binding surface topology, Syp N-SH2 domain residues interact weakly with the +4 peptide residue, and tightly with the +5 residue. Although SH2 domains are well-conserved and display very similar backbone conformations, they vary in the details of their phosphotyrosine-binding pockets, and in their binding surfaces for the peptide residues C-terminal to the phosphotyrosine.

A growing body of evidence shows that residues both N-terminal of the phosphotyrosine, and C-terminal to +3 can affect SH2 binding-specificity. The ability of p85α N-SH2 to bind a phosphopeptide representing the IRS-1 Tyr[628] binding site, was investigated by systematically substituting peptide positions −4 to +5, relative to the phosphotyrosine, with benzoylphenyl-lalanine (Bpa) (Williams and Shoelson, 1993). Most changes had little effect on binding affinity but Bpa substitution for +1Met and +3Met greatly reduced the affinity of the p85α N-SH2 domain for these altered peptides. It was also shown that Bpa-substitution at positions −1 and +4 decreased the affinity of the p85α N-SH2 domain for these peptides. The −1 and +4 positions were cross-linked, upon photoactivation of the Bpa complex, to residues within the α-helix A and BG loop, respectively, contributing to the overall affinity. These data are consistent with the NMR structure of PLCγl C-SH2 and the X-ray crystallographic structure of Syp N-SH2, which observed interactions between +4, +5, and +6 peptide positions, and residues within EF and BG loops (Pascal et al., 1994; Lee et al., 1994).

GENETIC EVIDENCE FOR THE ROLE OF SH2 DOMAINS IN SIGNAL TRANSDUCTION - SH2 DOMAINS REGULATE DEVELOPMENTAL PATHWAYS

The first genetic evidence describing a role for SH2 domains in development was provided by the *C. elegans* gene *sex myoblasts abnormal (sem)-5* (Clark et al., 1992). Disruptions within the *sem-5* gene affect hermaphrodite vulval development, and proper migration of sex myoblasts. *sem-5* mutations also affect the clear (clr) 1 phenotype, and larval viability (Horvitz and Sternberg, 1991).

The *sem-5* gene encodes a protein containing almost exclusively SH3 and SH2 domains (Fig. 2), and mutations affecting development map to these domains (Clark et al., 1992). A substitution at position BC1, within the BC loop of the SH2 domain, affects vulval development, sex myoblast migration, and the clr-1 phenotype, while a substitution at position BC2 affects the clr-1 phenotype and has a very minimal effect on vulval development. The BC1 mutation induces a substitution of the well-conserved Glu residue for Lys, while the BC2 mutation affects a more variable residue (Ser for Asn), possibly explaining the minimal effect on developmental processes compared to the BC1 mutation. A third mutation disrupts a splice acceptor site, and likely generates a null allele. This mutation results in a high level of larval lethality, and severe suppression of vulval development, sex myoblast migration and the clr-1 phenotype.

The *Drosophila downstream of receptor kinase (drk)* gene, which is homologous to the *C. elegans* gene *sem-5*, is required for proper differentiation of the R7 photoreceptor cell, leading to normal eye development. *drk* is also required for pupal viability, and is apparently involved in signalling pathways downstream of multiple receptor tyrosine kinases, including sevenless, the *Drosophila* EGFR homologue and torso (Olivier et al., 1993; Simon et al., 1993; Doyle and Bishop, 1993). Mutant alleles of *drk*, *E(sev)2B* and *Su(Sev^{s11})R1*, were initially identified by their effect on eye development (Simon et al., 1991), and later mapped as point mutations affecting well-conserved SH2 residues αA2 (substitution of Arg for His) and βD6 (substitution of His for Tyr) involved in phosphotyrosine binding (Olivier et al., 1993). Transheterozygous combinations of these mutant alleles result in pupal lethality (Olivier et al., 1993). Genetically, *drk* lies upstream of *son-of-sevenless (sos)*, which encodes a guanine nucleotide exchange factor for Ras (Simon et al., 1991). The SH3 domains of drk were shown to bind directly to the proline-rich tail of Sos (Olivier et al., 1993). drk therefore provides a direct link between activated receptors and Sos, which is able to directly convert Ras into the active GTP-bound state. These mutations affect the ability of the drk SH2 domain to bind activated receptor tyrosine kinases, thereby blocking signalling cascades and directly altering cellular responses (Olivier et al., 1993).

SH3 DOMAIN

Many signalling proteins that couple activated RPTKs to intracellular signalling events, contain single or multiple copies of SH3 domains, which can often be found in the same molecule as SH2 domains. SH3 domains are also well-conserved regions of approximately 50-75 residues, with no known catalytic function, that are found both in signalling molecules with intrinsic catalytic activities and in adaptor proteins (Fig. 2) (Pawson, 1988; Gish and Pawson, 1992; Pawson and Gish, 1992). SH3 domains specifically recognize and bind with high affinity to proline-rich sequences. This was first demonstrated from the identification of the SH3-binding protein (3BP) 1, cloned from an expression library, using the SH3 domain of the tyrosine kinase c-Abl (Cicchetti et al., 1992). The c-Abl SH3 domain-binding site was later mapped to a proline-rich sequence within the C-terminal region of 3BP1. This SH3-binding site was further refined to a ten amino acid proline-rich motif with the sequence APTMPPPLPP (Ren et al., 1993). Furthermore, a second c-Abl SH3 domain binding protein was identified and termed 3BP2 (Ren et al., 1993). The binding site for c-Abl SH3 domain on 3BP2 was localized to the sequence PPAYPPPPVP (Ren et al., 1993). This suggested a binding specificity for SH3 domains and a role in signal transduction by mediating protein-protein interactions.

Genetic analyses of the mammalian Grb2 homologues *Drosophila* drk and *C. elegans* Sem-5 proteins, have revealed a role for SH3 domains in the conserved signalling pathway that couples activated receptor to Ras (Clark et al., 1992; Olivier et al., 1993). As discussed previously, mutations within the SH2 domains of drk and Sem-5, have defined their role in mediating signalling in both species. In *C. elegans*, Sem-5 SH3 mutations also disrupt normal signalling, and cause severe defects in vulval induction, sex myoblast migration, clr-1 suppression, and larval viability, showing a role for SH3 domains in cellular signalling (Clark et al., 1992). In contrast to mutations in the N-terminal SH3 domain of Sem-5, a substitution of Gly201 for Arg in the Sem-5 C-terminal SH3 domain, only results in a minor clr-1 suppression. This suggests that the N-terminal SH3 domain might play a more crucial role than the C-terminal SH3 domain in mediating proper signalling in this pathway. These genetically identified pathways, and the role played by drk and Sem-5 signalling molecules, were substantiated by biochemical studies in mammalian cells with their homologue Grb2 and mSos1/mSos2 (Lowenstein et al., 1992; Bowtell et al., 1992). As with drk, the SH3 domains of Grb2 form a stable cytoplasmic complex by binding the proline-rich sequences in the C terminus of the guanine nucleotide releasing protein mSos1 and mSos2 (the mouse homologues of *Drosophila* Son-of-sevenless). Upon activation and autophosphorylation of the EGFR, the Grb2-mSos1 complex binds directly to the receptor through recognition of binding site pYINQ (Tyr[1068]) by the Grb2 SH2. As a consequence, it is hypothesized that mSos1 becomes co-localized with p21ras, and catalyses the exchange of GDP for GTP, activating p21ras and its signalling pathway (Pawson and Schlessinger, 1993; Gale et al., 1993; Rozakis-Adcock et al., 1993; Li et al., 1993; Buday and Downward, 1993; Egan et al., 1993). SH3 domains apparently have many other functions that are beyond the scope of this article. In particular, they are implicated in the subcellular localization of proline-rich proteins, and in the organization of signalling complexes.

In summary, SH2 and SH3 domains regulate a network of protein-protein interactions that are important for signalling downstream of receptors associated with tyrosine kinase activity.

REFERENCES

Anderson, D., Koch, C. A., Grey, L., Ellis C., Moran, M. F. and Pawson, T. (1990). Binding of SH2 domains of phospholipase Cγ1, GAP, and Src to activated growth factor receptors. *Science* **250**, 979-982.

Aroian, R. V. and Sternberg, P. W. (1991). Multiple functions of *let-23*, a *Caenorhabditis elegans* receptor tyrosine kinase gene required for vulval induction. *Genetics* **128**, 251-267.

Auger, K., Carpenter, C. L., Shoelson, S. E., Piwnica-Worms, H. and Cantley, L. C. (1992). Polyoma virus middle-T antigen-pp60c-src complex associates with purified phosphatidylinositol 3-kinase in vitro. *J. Biol. Chem.* **267**, 5408-5415.

Backer, J., Myers M. G. Jr, Shoelson, S. E., Chin, D. J., Sun, Z. J., Miralpeix, M., Hu, P., Margolis, B., Skolnik, E. Y., Schlessinger, J. and White, M. F. (1992). Phosphatidylinositol 3′-kinase is activated by association with IRS-1 during insulin stimulation. *EMBO J.* **11**, 3469-3479.

Booker, G. W., Breeze, A. L., Downing, A. K., Panayotou, G., Gout, I., Waterfield, M. D. and Campbell, I. D. (1992). Structure of an SH2 domain of the p85α subunit of phosphatidylinositol-3-kinase. *Nature* **358**, 684-687.

Bowtell, D., Fu, P., Simon, M. and Senior, P. (1992). Identification of murine homologues of the *Drosophila sos of sevenless* gene: potential activators of Ras. *Proc. Nat. Acad. Sci. USA* **89**, 6511-6515.

Buday, L. and Downward, J. (1993). Epidermal growth factor regulates p21ras through the formation of a complex of receptor, Grb2 adapter protein, and Sos nucleotide exchange factor. *Cell* **73**, 611-620.

Cantley, L. C., Auger, K. R., Carpenter, C., Duckworth, B., Graziani, A., Kapeller, R. and Soltoff, S. (1991). Oncogenes and signal transduction. *Cell* **64**, 281-302.

Cicchetti, P., Mayer, B. J., Thiel, G. and Baltimore, D. (1992). Identification of a protein that binds to the SH3 region of Abl and is similar to Bcr and GAP-rho. *Science* **257**, 803-806.

Clark, S. G., Stern, M. J. and Horvitz, H. R. (1992). *C. elegans* cell-signalling gene *sem-5* encodes a protein with SH2 and SH3 domains. *Nature* **356**, 340-344.

Cobb, B. S., Schaller, M. D., Leu, T. H. and Parsons, J. T. (1994). Stable association of pp60src and pp59fyn with the focal adhesion-associated protein tyrosine kinase, pp125FAK. *Mol. Cell. Biol.* **14**, 147-155.

Coughlin, S. R., Escobedo, J. A. and Williams, L. T. (1989). Role of phosphatidylinositol kinase in PDGF receptor signal transduction. *Science* **243**, 1191-1194.

Doyle, H. J. and Bishop, J. M. (1993). Torso, a receptor tyrosine kinase required for embryonic pattern formation, shares susbstrates with the Sevenless and EGF-R pathways in *Drosophila*. *Genes Dev.* **7**, 633-646.

Downing, J. R., Margolis, B. L., Zilberstein, A., Ashmun, R. A., Ullrich, A., Sherr, C. S. and Schlessinger, J. (1989). Phospholipase C-γ, a substrate for PDGF receptor kinase, is not phosphorylated on tyrosine during the mitogenic response to CSF-1. *EMBO J.* **8**, 3345-3350.

Eck, M. J., Shoelson, S. E. and Harrison, S. C. (1993). Recognition of a high-affinity phosphotyrosyl peptide by the Src homology-2 domain of p56lck. *Nature* **362**, 87-91.

Egan, S. E., Giddings, B. W., Brooks, M. W., Buday, L., Sizeland, A. M. and Weinberg, R. A. (1993). Association of Sos Ras exchange protein with Grb2 is implicated in tyrosine kinase signal transduction and transformation. *Nature* **363**, 45-51.

Escobedo, J. A., Kaplan, D. R., Kavanaugh, W. M., Turck, C. W. and Williams, L. T. (1991). A phosphatidylinositol-3 kinase binds to platelet-derived growth factor receptors through a specific receptor sequence containing phosphotyrosine. *Mol. Cell. Biol.* **11**, 1125-1132.

Fantl, W. T., Escobedo, J. A., Martin, G. A., Turck, C. W., del Rosario, M., McCormick, F. and Williams, L. T. (1992). Distinct phosphotyrosines on a growth factor receptor bind to specific molecules that mediate different signalling pathways. *Cell* **69**, 413-423.

Felder, S., Zhou, M., Hu, P., Urena, J., Ullrich, A., Chaudhuri, M., White, M., Shoelson, S. E. and Schlessinger, J. (1993). SH2 domains exhibit high-affinity binding to tyrosine-phosphorylated peptides yet also exhibit rapid dissociation and exchange. *Mol. Cell. Biol.* **13**, 1449-1455.

Ferguson, E. L., Sternberg, P. W. and Horwitz, H. R. (1987). A genetic pathway for the specification of the vulval cell lineages of *Caenorhabditis elegans*. *Nature* **326**, 259-267.

Gale, N. W., Kaplan, S., Lowenstein, E. J., Schlessinger, J. and Bar-Sagi, D. (1993). Grb2 mediates the EGF-dependent activation of guanine nucleotide exchange on Ras. *Nature* **363**, 88-92.

Horvitz, H. R. and Sternberg, P. W. (1991). Multiple intercellular signalling systems control the development of the *Caenorhabditis elegans* vulva. *Nature* **351**, 535-541.

Kaplan, D. R., Morrison, D. K., Wong, G., McCormick, F. and Williams, L. T. (1990). PDGF β-receptor stimulates phosphorylation of GAP and association of GAP with a signalling complex. *Cell* **61**, 125-133.

Kashishian, A., Kazlauskas, A. and Cooper, J. A. (1992). Phosphorylation sites in the PDGF receptor with different specificities for binding GAP and PI3 kinase in vivo. *EMBO J.* **11**, 1373-1382.

Kazlauskas, A. and Cooper, J. A. (1989). Autophosphorylation of the PDGF receptor in the kinase insert region regulates interactions with cell proteins. *Cell* **58**, 1121-1133.

Kazlauskas, A. and Cooper, J. A. (1990). Phosphorylation of the PDGF receptor β subunit creates a tight binding site for phosphatidylinositol 3 kinase. *EMBO J.* **9**, 3279-3286.

Kazlauskas, A., Kashishian, A., Cooper, J. A. and Valius, M. (1992). GTPase-activating protein and phosphatidylinositol 3-kinase bind to distinct regions of the platelet-derived growth factor receptor beta subunit. *Mol. Cell. Biol.* **12**, 2534-2544.

Kazlauskas, A., Feng, G.-S., Pawson, T. and Valius, M. (1993). The 64-kDa protein that associates with the platelet-derived growth factor receptor β subunit via Tyr-1009 is the SH2-containing phosphotyrosine phosphatase Syp. *Proc. Nat. Acad. Sci. USA* **90**, 6939-6942.

Koch, C. A., Anderson, D., Moran, M. F., Ellis, C. and Pawson, T. (1991). SH2 and SH3 domains: elements that control interactions of cytoplasmic signalling proteins. *Science* **252**, 668-674.

Kuhne, M. R., Pawson, T., Lienhard, G. E. and Feng, G.-S. (1993). The insulin receptor substrate 1 associates with the SH2-containing phosphotyrosine phosphatase Syp. *J. Biol. Chem.* **268**, 11479-11481.

Kypta, R. M., Goldberg, Y., Ulug, E. T. and Courtneidge, S. A. (1990). Association between the PDGF receptor and members of the *src* family of tyrosine kinases. *Cell* **62**, 481-492.

Lavan, B. E., Kuhne, M. R., Garner, C. W., Anderson, D., Reedijk, M., Pawson, T. and Lienhard, G. E. (1992). The association of insulin-elicited phosphotyrosine proteins with *src* homology 2 domains. *J. Biol. Chem.* **267**, 11631-11636.

Lee, C.-H., Li, W., Nishimura, R., Zhou, M., Batzer, A. G., Myers M. G. Jr, White, M. F., Schlessinger, J. and Skolnik, E. Y. (1993). Nck associates with the SH2 domain-docking protein IRS-1 in insulin-stimulated cells. *Proc. Nat. Acad. Sci. USA* **90**, 11713-11717.

Lee, C.-H., Kominos, D., Jacques, S., Margolis, B., Schlessinger, J., Shoelson, S. E. and Kuriyan, B. (1994). Crystal structures of peptide complexes of the N-terminal SH2 domain of the Syp tyrosine phosphatase. *Curr. Biol.* **2**, 423-438.

Li, N., Batzer, A., Daly, R., Yajnik, V., Skolnik, E., Chardin, P., Bar-Sagi, D., Margolis, B. and Schlessinger, J. (1993). Guanine-nucleotide-releasing factor hSos1 binds to Grb2 and links receptor tyrosine kinases to Ras signalling. *Nature* **363**, 85-88.

Lowenstein, E. J., Daly, R. J., Batzer, A. G., Li, W., Margolis, B., Lammers, R., Ullrich, A., Skolnik, E. Y., Bar-Sagi, D. and Schlessinger, J. (1992). The SH2 and SH3 domain-containing protein Grb2 links receptor tyrosine kinases to ras signalling. *Cell* **70**, 431-442.

Marengere, L. E. M. and Pawson, T. (1992). Identification of residues in GTPase-activating protein Src homology 2 domains that control binding to tyrosine phosphorylated growth factor receptors and p62. *J. Biol. Chem.* **267**, 22779-22786.

Marengere, L. E. M., Songyang, Z., Gish, G. D., Schaller, M. D., Parsons, J. T., Stern, M. J., Cantley, L. C. and Pawson, T. (1994). SH2 domain specificity and activity modified by a single residue. *Nature* **369**, 502-505.

Matsuda, M., Mayer, B. J., Fukui, Y. and Hanafusa, H. (1990). Binding of transforming protein, p47gag-crk, to a broad range of phosphotyrosine-containing proteins. *Science* **248**, 1537-1539.

Mayer, B. J. and Hanafusa, H. (1990). Mutagenic analysis of the *v-crk* oncogene: requirement for SH2 and SH3 domains and correlation between increased cellular phosphotyrosine and transformation. *J. Virol.* **64**, 3581-3589.

Mayer, B. J., Jackson, P. K. and Baltimore, D. (1991). The non-catalytic src homology region 2 segment of *abl* tyrosine kinase binds to tyrosine-phosphorylated cellular proteins with high affinity. *Proc. Nat. Acad. Sci. USA* **88**, 627-631.

Mayer, B. J., Jackson, P. K., Van Etten, R. A. and Baltimore, D. (1992). Point mutations in the *abl* SH2 domain coordinately impair phosphotyrosine binding *in vitro* and transforming activity *in vivo*. *Mol. Cell. Biol.* **12**, 609-618.

McGlade, C. J., Ellis, C., Reedijk, M., Anderson, D., Mbamalu, G., Reith, A., Panayotou, G., End, P., Bernstein, A., Kazlauskas, A., Waterfield, M.

D. and Pawson, T. (1992). SH2 domains of the p85α subunit of phosphatidylinositol 3-kinase regulate binding to growth factor receptors. *Mol. Cell. Biol.* **12**, 991-997.

Meisenhelder, J., Suh, P.-G., Rhee, S. G. and Hunter, T. (1989). Phospholipase C-γ is a substrate for the PDGF and EGF receptor protein-tyrosine kinases in vivo and in vitro. *Cell* **57**, 1109-1122.

Mohammadi, M., Honegger, A. M., Rotin, D., Fischer, R., Bellot, F., Li, W., Dionne, C. A., Jaye, M., Rubenstein, M. and Schlessinger, J. (1991). A tyrosine-phosphorylated carboxy-terminal peptide of the fibroblast growth factor receptor (Flg) is a binding site for the SH2 domain of phospholipase Cγ 1. *Mol. Cell. Biol.* **11**, 5068-5078.

Molloy, C. J., Bottaro, D. P., Fleming, T. P., Marshal, M. S., Gibbs, J. B. and Aaronson, S. A. (1989). PDGF induction of tyrosine phosphorylation of GTPase activating protein. *Nature* **342**, 711-714.

Moran, M. F., Koch, C. A., Anderson, D., Ellis, C., England, L., Martin, G. S. and Pawson, T. (1990). Src homology region 2 domains direct protein-protein interactions in signal transduction. *Proc. Nat. Acad. Sci. USA* **87**, 8622-8626.

Mori, S. M., Ronnstrand, L., Yokote, K., Engstrom, A., Courtneidge, S. A., Claesson-Welsh, L. and Heldin, C.-H. (1993). Identification of two juxtamembrane autophosphorylation sites in the PDGF β-receptor: involvement in the interaction with Src family tyrosine kinases. *EMBO J.* **12**, 2257-2264.

Morrison, D. K., Kaplan, D. R., Rhee, S. G. and Williams, L. T. (1990). Platelet-derived growth factor (PDGFR)-dependent association of phospholipase C-γ with the PDGF receptor signaling complex. *Mol. Cell. Biol.* **10**, 2359-2366.

Myers, M. G., Backer, J. M., Sun, X. J., Shoelson, S., Hu, P., Schlessinger, J., Yoakim, M., Schaffhausen, B. and White, M. F. (1992). IRS-1 activates phosphatidylinositol 3'-kinase by associating with *src* homology 2 domains of p85. *Proc. Nat. Acad. Sci. USA* **89**, 10350-10354.

Nishimura, R., Li, W., Kashishian, A., Mondino, A., Zhou, M., Cooper, J. A. and Schlessinger, J. (1993). Two signalling molecules share a phosphotyrosine-containing binding site in the platelet-derived growth factor receptor. *Mol. Cell. Biol.* **13**, 6889-6896.

Nusslein-Volhard, C., Frohnhofer, H. G. and Lehman, R. (1987). Determination of anteroposterior polarity in *Drosophila*. *Science* **238**, 1675-1681.

Olivier, J. P., Raabe, T., Henkemeyer, M., Dickson, B., Mbamalu, G., Margolis, B., Schlessinger, J., Hafen, E. and Pawson, T. (1993). A Drosophila SH2-SH3 adaptor protein implicated in coupling the sevenless tyrosine kinase to an activator of ras guanine nucleotide exchange, Sos. *Cell* **73**, 179-191.

Overduin, M., Rios, C., Mayer, B., Baltimore, D. and Cowburn, D. (1992). Three-dimensional solution structure of the src homology 2 domain of c-abl. *Cell* **70**, 697-704.

Panayotou, G., Bax, B., Gout, I., Federwisch, M., Wroblowski, B., Dhand, R., Fry, M. J., Blundell, T. L., Wollmer, A. and Waterfield, M. D. (1992). Interaction of the p85 subunit of PI 3-kinase and its N-terminal SH2 domain with a PDGF receptor phosphorylation site: structural features and analysis of conformational changes. *EMBO J.* **11**, 4261-4272.

Panayotou, G., Gish, G. D., End, P., Truong, O., Gout, I., Dhand, R., Fry, M. J., Hiles, I., Pawson, T. and Waterfield, M. (1993). Interactions between SH2 domains and tyrosine-phosphorylated platelet-derived growth factor β-receptor sequences: analysis of kinetic parameters by a novel biosensor-based approach. *Mol. Cell. Biol.* **13**, 3567-3576.

Pascal, S. M., Singer, A. U., Gish, G. D., Yamazaki, T., Shoelson, S. E., Pawson, T., Kay, L. E. and Forman-Kay, J. D. (1994). NMR structure of an SH2 domain of phospholipase C-γ1 complexed with a high-affinity binding peptide. *Cell* **77**, 461-472.

Pawson, T. (1988). Non-catalytic domains of cytoplasmic protein tyrosine kinases: regulatory elements in signal transduction. *Oncogene* **3**, 491-495.

Pawson, T. and Bernstein, A. (1990). Receptor tyrosine kinases: genetic evidence for their role in *Drosophila* and mouse development. *Trends Genet* **6**, 350-356.

Pawson, T. and Gish, G. D. (1992). SH2 and SH3 domains: from structure to function. *Cell* **71**, 359-362.

Pawson, T. and Schlessinger, J. (1993). SH2 and SH3 domains. *Curr. Biol.* **3**, 434-442.

Price, J. V., Clifford, R. J. and Schupbach, T. (1989). The maternal ventralizing locus *torpedo* is allelic to *faint little ball*, an embryonic lethal, and encodes the *Drosophila* EGF receptor homolog. *Cell* **56**, 1085-1092.

Pronk, G. J., de Vries-Smits, A. M. M., Buday, L., Downward, J., Maassen, J. A., Medema, R. H. and Bos, J. L. (1994). Involment of Shc in insulin- and epidermal growth factor-induced activation of p21ras. *Mol. Cell. Biol.* **14**, 1575-1581.

Reedijk, M., Liu, X. and Pawson, T. (1990). Interactions of phosphatidylinositol kinase, GTPase-activating protein (GAP), and GAP-associated proteins with the colony-stimulating factor 1 receptor. *Mol. Cell. Biol.* **10**, 5601-5608.

Reedijk, M., Liu, X., van der Geer, P., Letwin, K., Waterfield, M. D., Hunter, T. and Pawson, T. (1992). Tyr721 regulates specific binding of the CSF-1 receptor kinase insert to PI 3′-kinase SH2 domains: a model for SH2-mediated receptor-target interactions. *EMBO J.* **11**, 1365-1372.

Reith, A. D., Rottapel, R., Giddens, E., Brady, C., Forrester, L. and Bernstein, A. (1990). *W* mutant mice with mild or severe developmental defects contain distinct point mutations in the kinase domain of the *c-kit* receptor. *Genes Dev.* **4**, 390-400.

Ren, R., Mayer, B. J., Cicchetti, P. and Baltimore, D. (1993). Identification of a ten-amino acid proline-rich SH3 binding site. *Science* **259**, 1157-1161.

Rotin, D., Margolis, B., Mohammadi, M., Daly, R. J., Daum, G., Li, N., Fischer, E. H., Burgess, W. H., Ullrich, A. and Schlessinger, J. (1993). SH2 domains prevent tyrosine dephosphorylation of the EGFR: identification of Tyr992 as the high-affinity binding site for SH2 domains of phospholipase C-γ. *EMBO J.* **11**, 559-567.

Rozakis-Adcock, M., Fernley, R., Wade, J., Pawson, T. and Bowtell, D. (1993). The SH2 and SH3 domains of mammalian Grb2 couple the EGF receptor to the Ras activator mSos1. *Nature* **363**, 83-85.

Russel, E. S. (1979). Hereditary anemias of the mouse: a review for geneticists. *Advan. Genet.* **20**, 357-459.

Sadowski, I., Stone, J. C. and Pawson, T. (1986). A non-catalytic domain conserved among cytoplasmic protein-tyrosine kinases modifies the kinase function and transforming activity of fujinami sarcoma virus p130gag-fps. *Mol. Cell. Biol.* **6**, 4396-4408.

Schaller, M. D., Borgman, C. A., Cobb, B. S., Vines, R. R., Reynolds, A. B. and Parsons, J. T. (1992). pp125FAK, a structurally distinctive protein-tyrosine kinase associated with focal adhesions. *Proc. Nat. Acad. Sci. USA* **89**, 5192-5196.

Schejter, E. D. and Shilo, B.-Z. (1989). The Drosophila EGF receptor homolog (DER) gene is allelic to faint little ball, a locus essential for embryonic development. *Cell* **56**, 1093-1104.

Settleman, J., Narasimhan, V., Foster, L. C. and Weinberg, R. A. (1992a). Molecular cloning of cDNAs encoding the GAP-associated protein p190: implications for a signalling pathway from ras to the nucleus. *Cell* **69**, 539-549.

Settleman, J., Albright, C. F., Foster, L. C. and Weinberg, R. A. (1992b). Association between GTPase activators for Rho and Ras families. *Nature* **359**, 153-154.

Simon, M. A., Bowtell, D. D. L., Dodson, G. S., Laverty, T. R. and Rubin, G. M. (1991). Ras1 and a putative guanine nucleotide exchange factor perform crucial steps in signalling by the Sevenless protein tyrosine kinase. *Cell* **67**, 701-716.

Simon, M. A., Dodson, G. S. and Rubin, G. M. (1993). An SH3-SH2-SH3 protein is required for p21ras activation and binds to Sevenless and Sos proteins in vitro. *Cell* **73**, 169-177.

Songyang, Z., Shoelson, S. E., Chaudhuri, M., Gish, G. D., Pawson, T., Haser, W. G., King, F., Roberts, T., Ratnofsky, S., Lechleider, R. J., Neel, B. G., Birge, R. B., Fajardo, J. E., Chou, M. M., Hanafusa, H., Schaffhausen, B. and Cantley, L. C. (1993). SH2 domains recognize specific phosphopeptide sequences. *Cell* **72**, 1-20.

Songyang, Z., Shoelson, S. E., McGlade, C. J., Olivier, P., Pawson, T., Bustelo, R. X., Hanafusa, H., Yi, T., Ren, R., Baltimore, D., Ratnofsky, S., Feldman, R. A. and Cantley, L. C. (1994). Specific motifs recognized by the SH2 domains of csk, 3BP2, fes/fps, Grb2, SHPTP1, SHC, Syk and vav. *Mol. Cell. Biol.* **14**, 2777-2785.

Tobe, K., Matuoka, K., Tamemoto, H., Ueki, K., Kaburagi, Y., Asai, S., Noguchi, T., Matsuda, M., Tanaka, S., Hattori, S., Fukui, Y., Akanuma, Y., Yasaki, Y., Takenawa, T. and Kadowaki, T. (1993). Insulin stimulates association of insulin receptor substrate-1 with the protein abundant Src homology/growth factor receptor bound protein-2. *J. Biol. Chem.* **268**, 11167-11171.

Tomlinson, A., Bowtell, D. D. L., Hafen, E. and Rubin, G. M. (1987). Localisation of the sevenless protein, a putative receptor for positional information, in the eye imaginal disc of Drosophila. *Cell* **51**, 143-150.

Ullrich, A. and Schlessinger, J. (1990). Signal transduction by receptors with tyrosine kinase activity. *Cell* **61**, 203-212.

van der Geer, P. and Hunter, T. (1993). Mutation of Tyr697, a Grb2-binding site, and Tyr721, a PI 3-kinase binding site, abrogates signal transduction by the murine CSF-1 receptor expressed in Rat-2 fibroblasts. *EMBO J.* **12**, 5161-5172.

van der Geer, P. and Hunter, T. (1994). Receptor protein-tyrosine kinases and their signal transduction pathways. *Annu. Rev. Cell Biol.* (in press).

Waksman, G., Shoelson, S. E., Pant, N., Cowburn, D. and Kuriyan, J. (1993). Binding of a high affinity phosphotyrosyl peptide to the Src SH2 domain: crystal structures of the complexed and peptide-free forms. *Cell* **72**, 779-790.

Williams, K. P. and Shoelson, S. E. (1993). A photoaffinity scan maps regions of the p85 SH2 domain involved in phosphoprotein binding. *J. Biol. Chem.* **268**, 5361-5364.

Wong, G., Muller, O., Clark, R., Conroy, L., Moran, M. F., Polakis, P. and McCormick, F. (1992). Molecular cloning and nucleic acid binding properties of the GAP-associated tyrosine phosphoprotein p62. *Cell* **69**, 551-558.

Yamamoto, K., Altschuler, D., Wood, E., Horlick, K., Jacobs, S. and Lapetina, E. G. (1992). Association of phosphorylated insulin-like growth factor-1 receptor with the SH2 domains of phosphatidylinositol 3-kinase p85. *J. Biol. Chem.* **267**, 11337-11343.

Yarden, Y. and Ullrich, A. (1988). Growth factor receptor tyrosine kinases. *Annu. Rev. Biochem.* **57**, 443-478.

Yokote, K., Mori, S., McGlade, J., Pawson, T., Heldin, C.-H. and Claesson-Welsh, L. (1994). Direct interaction between Shc and the Platelet-derived growth factor β-receptor. *J. Biol. Chem.* **269**, 15337-15343.

Journal of Cell Science, Supplement 18, 105-108 (1994)
Printed in Great Britain © The Company of Biologists Limited 1994

Signal transduction by the macrophage-colony-stimulating factor receptor (CSF-1R)

Martine F. Roussel

St Jude Children's Research Hospital, Memphis, Tennessee, USA

SUMMARY

The macrophage-specific colony-stimulating factor 1 (CSF-1 or M-CSF) is required throughout the G_1 phase of the cell cycle to regulate both immediate and delayed early responses necessary for cell proliferation. These are triggered by the binding of the growth factor to the colony-stimulating factor 1 receptor and the activation of its intrinsic tyrosine-specific protein kinase. Phosphorylation of the colony-stimulating factor 1 receptor on specific tyrosine residues enables it to bind directly to cytoplasmic effector proteins, which in turn relay receptor-induced signals through multiple-signal transduction pathways. The activity of p21*ras* as well as transcription factors of the *ets* gene family appears to be required for colony-stimulating factor 1 to induce the c-*myc* gene, and the latter response is essential to ensure cell proliferation. Genes within the *fos/jun* or activator protein 1 family are targeted via a parallel and independently regulated signal transduction pathway. The continuous requirement for colony-stimulating factor 1 after the immediate early response is initiated indicates that expression of additional delayed early response genes, although contingent on previously induced gene products, might also depend on colony-stimulating factor 1-induced signals. Among the growth factor-regulated delayed early response genes are D-type G_1 cyclins, which play an important role in cell-cycle progression.

Key words: CSF-1, CSF-1R, signal transduction

INTRODUCTION

Macrophage colony-stimulating factor (M-CSF or CSF-1) is a lineage-restricted growth factor that regulates proliferation, differentiation, and survival of monocytes, macrophages, and, their early bone-marrow progenitors (Sherr and Stanley, 1990). It is a homodimeric glycoprotein produced by fibroblasts and mesenchymal cells in biologically active secreted and membrane-bound forms (Rettenmier and Roussel, 1988). CSF-1-deficient mice (op/op) develop osteoporosis because they lack the ability to produce osteoclasts, which are macrophage-derived. Nevertheless, this defect can be corrected by CSF-1 administration (Wiktor-Jedrzejczak et al., 1990). CSF-1 is also involved in placental and fetal development (Pollard et al., 1987; Regenstreif and Rossant, 1989).

CSF-1 mediates its effects by binding to a single high-affinity transmembrane glycoprotein receptor (CSF-1R) with intrinsic tyrosine kinase activity (Roussel and Sherr, 1993). CSF-1R, the *fms* proto-oncogene (Sherr, 1988; Rohrschneider and Woolford, 1992) is a member of a growth factor receptor family that includes the platelet-derived growth factor receptors (PDGF-R, A and B), stem cell factor receptor (c-*kit*), and *flk2/flt3* proteins (Claesson-Welsh et al., 1989; Matsui et al., 1989; Qiu et al., 1988; Mathews et al., 1991). Each of these receptors is characterized by a unique kinase insert (KI) domain, which can serve as an anchor for several signaling proteins.

Growth factor binding and subsequent activation of the receptor trigger a series of events that ultimately leads to mitosis. Removal of growth factors results in cell cycle arrest, while prolonged starvation leads to cell death by apoptosis. However, restimulation by specific growth factors or serum following short periods (12-18 hours) of growth factor deprivation allows re-entry into the cell cycle and initiates the expression of a series of immediate early genes (including *fos*, *jun* and *myc*). Transcription of delayed early genes follows. These includes the G_1 D-type cyclins and their catalytic partners, which play an important role in G_1 progression and initiation of DNA synthesis (Sherr, 1993).

CSF-1R SIGNAL TRANSDUCTION

Ectopic expression of the human CSF-1R into naïve murine cell lines, including fibroblasts and IL-3-dependent myeloid cells, enables them to respond mitogenically to human CSF-1 and mimic macrophage signaling (Roussel and Sherr, 1989; Kato et al., 1989; Kato and Sherr, 1990). Transduction of the human CSF-1R gene into the murine fibroblast cell line NIH-3T3, rendered the cells dependent on human CSF-1 for growth and abrogated their requirement for PDGF, insulin growth factor (IGF), and epidermal growth factor (EGF) (Roussel and Sherr, 1989). Although fibroblasts secrete CSF-1, the murine growth factor binds with low affinity to the human CSF-1R and is unable to activate the receptor's intrinsic tyrosine kinase, thereby precluding an autocrine loop. Hence, the transduced cells can divide indefinitely in chemically-defined medium with human CSF-1 as the sole growth factor present. This enables us to study the immediate and early responses triggered by the interaction of CSF-1 with its receptor in the absence of other stimuli. Further, these CSF-1R-transduced fibroblasts express an equivalent number of PDGF receptors, which can serve as a control in CSF-1 signal transduction studies.

On binding CSF-1, the receptor undergoes dimerization, activation of its intrinsic tyrosine kinase, and phosphorylation *in trans* of specific tyrosine residues: at amino acid 561, on the cytoplasmic side of the transmembrane domain (S. A. Court-neidge et al., unpublished results); at amino acids 699, 708 and 723, in the kinase insert domain, and at amino acid 809 in the core kinase domain (Clark et al., 1992; Shurtleff et al., 1990; Roussel et al., 1990). These phosphotyrosine residues then serve as 'magnets' for anchorage and activation of *src* homology-2 (SH2) motif-containing cytoplasmic effector proteins. The effectors, which may also be phosphorylated, are thought to transmit mitogenic signals. Several SH2-containing proteins bind to members of the CSF-1R family with diverse affinities (for review see Cantley et al., 1991; Koch et al., 1991; Songyang et al., 1993). They include: (1) phospholipase C-γ1 (PLCγ1) (Anderson et al., 1990); (2) GTPase activating protein (GAP) (Reedijk et al., 1990); (3) *src* family proteins (*src*, *fyn* and *yes*)(Courtneidge et al., 1993); (4) the *sem5*/GRB2 gene product, a 25 kDa adaptor that constitutively binds and activates the *ras* guanine nucleotide exchange factor SOS-1 (Lowenstein et al., 1992; Clark et al., 1992; Bowtell et al., 1992); (5) SHC, another adaptor protein (Pelicci et al., 1992); and (6) the 85 kDa subunit of phosphotidylinositol 3 kinase (PI-K3) (Cantley et al., 1991).

Unlike the activated form of the PDGF-receptor, which associates with most of the above effectors, CSF-1R binds relatively few signal transducing proteins. It interacts with the *src* family of tyrosine kinases (Courtneidge et al., 1993), as well as PI-3K (Shurtleff et al., 1990) and GRB2 (Van der Geer and Hunter, 1990), the binding sites for which have been mapped to the KI domain at Tyr723 and 699, respectively (Van der Geer et al., 1990). However, binding and activation of *src* family kinases by CSF-1R requires phosphorylation of the receptor on both Tyr809 and on Tyr561 (Courtneidge and Roussel, unpublished results; Courtneidge et al., 1993). To date, no other SH2-containing cytoplasmic effector has been shown to interact directly with the activated CSF-1R. This would be analogous to the situation for the activated insulin receptor (Tobe et al., 1993).

Mutating specific tyrosine residues in CSF-1R selectively affected different pathways required for mitogenic signaling. Deletion of the receptor's entire kinase domain does not significantly affect v-*fms* transformation or CSF-1-induced cell proliferation suggesting that tyrosines 699, 708 and 723 (which occur in the PI3-K and GRB2 binding sites), are not essential for mitogenesis (Shurtleff et al., 1990). In contrast, substituting phenylalanine for tyrosine at amino acid 809 severely inhibited CSF-1R-induced cell growth. Cells expressing the mutant receptor were blocked early in G$_1$ (Roussel et al., 1994), failing to grow in chemically-defined medium that contains CSF-1 or to form colonies in agar, despite retaining wild-type kinase activity and PI3K binding capability (Roussel et al., 1990).

The role of *src* family kinases in CSF-1R signaling

The *src* family kinases, *src*, *fyn* and *yes*, are activated as a result of their association, via their SH2 domains, with phosphotyrosine residue 809 of CSF-1R (Courtneidge et al., 1993). Substitution of Tyr809 for phenylalanine prevents efficient binding and subsequent activation of *src*, suggesting that P-Tyr809 and its flanking sequences play an essential role in CSF-1 proliferation. Microinjection of an antibody (anti-*cst*-1) recognizing all three of the above *src* kinases, inhibited S phase entry as measured by BrdU incorporation into DNA. This inhibition was maximal when CSF-1R wild-type-expressing cells were injected between 0 and 6 hours after re-entry into the cell cycle. However, the antibody had no effect when injected after mid-G$_1$. This suggests that activation of the *src* kinase family is critical and essential for CSF-1 signaling early in G$_1$, but dispensable, several hours prior to S phase commitment (W. Roche, M. Koegl, M. F. Roussel and S. A. Courtneidge, unpublished results).

CSF-1R signaling and *ras*

CSF-1 induces an increase in guanine nucleotide triphosphate (GTP) bound to p21*ras* in cells expressing wild-type CSF-1R (Gibbs et al., 1990). Indeed, microinjection of anti-p21[ras] antibodies inhibits v-*src*, v-*fms* and v-*ras* transformation (Stacey et al., 1991). GAP, a downstream regulator of *ras* activity, inhibits CSF-1-mediated proliferation as demonstrated by overexpression of the full-length or merely the catalytic domain of *ras* GAP (Bortner et al., 1991). GAP neither binds to CSF-1R nor undergoes tyrosine phosphorylation in proliferating macrophages (Reedijk et al., 1990), suggesting that signaling through p21*ras* might be mediated by an unknown adaptor, or by GRB2, binding to the activated receptor. However, GRB2 was found to bind to Tyr699, which we showed was not required for mitogenic signaling in NIH-3T3 fibroblasts (Van der Geer and Hunter, 1990; Shurtleff et al., 1990). Indeed, in cells harboring the CSF-1R(Phe809) mutant, we were unable to detect an active form of *ras* (J. Nathan Davis and M. F. Roussel, unpublished results), which suggests that CSF-1R activation of *ras* requires phosphorylation of Tyr809 and, potentially, other unmapped tyrosine-phosphorylated residues, and/or the binding of as yet uncharacterized signaling effector proteins.

The immediate early gene response

A single point mutation in CSF-1R substituting phenylalanine for tyrosine at codon 809 inhibits the mitogenic response to CSF-1 (Roussel et al., 1990). Transcription of the immediate early-response genes, c-*fos* and *jun*B, are induced, whereas c-*myc* expression is considerably reduced. However, ectopic expression of c-*myc* restored CSF-1-dependent proliferation indicating that c-*myc* function appears essential for CSF-1-dependent cell growth (Roussel et al., 1991). Further, these data suggest that mitogenic signaling by CSF-1R is mediated minimally by two independent pathways: one leading to c-*fos* and *jun*B transcription, and the other leading to c-*myc* transcription. The importance of these two signaling pathways in mitogenesis, particularly the c-*myc* pathway, has been demonstrated for other growth factor receptors, including the IL-2 receptor β chain (IL-2Rβ) (Shibuya et al., 1992), and the epidermal growth factor receptor (EGF-R) in the myeloid cell line, BAF-BO3 (Shibuya et al., 1992), as well as for the *bcr-abl* oncogene (Sawyers et al., 1992). NIH-3T3 cells expressing CSF-1R (Phe809) can, therefore, be used as a genetic trap to identify cellular signaling molecules specifically involved in the *myc* pathway or which can bypass the requirement for *myc* transcription.

The activity of p21*ras* is required for the CSF-1R proliferative response by stimulating transcription from promoter elements containing binding sites recognized by the *ETS* family of transcription factors (Reddy et al., 1992). Enforced expression in CSF-1R-containing NIH-3T3 cells of the DNA-binding domain (DBD) of a human *ETS*-2 gene lacking a trans-activation domain suppresses their CSF-1 responsiveness but does not affect the expression of c-*fos* and c-*jun*, immediate early genes. However, cells bearing CSF-1R (Phe809), have impaired c-*myc* expression. Ectopic expression of the c-*myc* gene overrides this suppressive effect and resensitizes the cells to CSF-1 (Langer et al., 1992). Conversely, cells expressing the CSF-1R (Phe809) can be complemented by the enforced expression of several *ETS* family members, including *ETS*-1, and *ETS*-2 (Roussel et al., 1994; Langer et al., 1992), *fli-1* and EWS-*fli-1* (M. F. Roussel and J. Ghysdael, unpublished results), as well as *elf-1* (J. N. Davis and M. F. Roussel, unpublished results). However, these cells grow more slowly in CSF-1 than those expressing wild-type CSF-1R, suggesting either that: (1) *ETS* transcription factors must signal via the *myc* pathway to be fully active; or (2) other members of the *ETS* family are involved in the regulation of CSF-1-induced *myc* expression. Indeed, *ETS*-1 and *ETS*-2 transactivate reporter genes driven by the human and mouse c-*myc* promoters through a binding site that overlaps an E2F-1 site, required for E1A and serum-induced c-*myc* expression (Roussel et al., 1994). Although E2F-1 and *ETS* proteins share structural similarities in their DNA-binding domain and interact with similar consensus DNA-binding sites, E2F-1 and *ETS*-1 do not form heterodimers in vitro and do not transactivate c-*myc* synergistically (Roussel et al., 1994). These data suggest that E2F-1 and *ETS* factors may independently regulate c-*myc* through the same binding sites but at different times following growth factor stimulation.

Deregulation of the c-*myc* proto-oncogene is a hallmark of Ewing sarcoma (ES), a childhood bone and soft tissue tumor associated with a reciprocal translocation t(11;22)(q24;q12), which results in a fusion mRNA formed from the 5′ end of the gene on derivative (22) (EWS) and the 3′ DNA-binding portion of the *fli-1*, gene from chromosome 11. A member of the *ETS* family, *fli-1* is rearranged and overexpressed in 75% of erythroleukemias induced in newborn mice infected with the replication-competent Friend leukemia virus (Ben-David et al., 1991). In line with the elevated expression of c-*myc*, EWS-*fli-1* has been found to upregulate the activity of a human c-*myc* promoter/reporter construct (Bailly et al., 1994).

FUTURE PERSPECTIVES

Cells expressing the CSF-1R mutants offer a unique system to dissect different signal transduction pathways that mediate mitogenicity in response to CSF-1. Appropriately engineered cell lines should enable us to identify the cellular effectors that relay signals through these specific pathways.

Because cells expressing the CSF-1R (Phe809) can survive in the presence of CSF-1 without proliferating, they can be used as a genetic trap to identify regulators that govern cell cycle entry and progression in response to CSF-1. Complementation of the signaling-defective CSF-1R (Phe809) has already proven to be an effective means of identifying genes in the *myc* pathway. This strategy could also pinpoint genes downstream of *myc* that are essential for CSF-1R-induced mitogenesis such as the D-type cyclins.

My thanks to Drs Charles J. Sherr, J. Nathan Davis, John L. Cleveland and Scott W. Hiebert, as well as the many colleagues who contributed data originating in my laboratory. I also thank Dr Michael Ostrowski and his co-workers who initiated the GAP and *ETS* dominant suppression studies; Dr Sara Courtneidge and the members of her laboratory for their studies of the role of the *src* family kinases in CSF-1R signaling; and Dr Jacques Ghysdael for graciously providing *ETS*-family reagents and for helpful comments. This laboratory is supported in part by the National Institute of Health, grant CA56819 and by the CORE grant, CA21765. I also gratefully acknowledge the support of the American Lebanese Syrian Associated Charities (ALSAC) of St Jude Children's Research Hospital.

REFERENCES

Anderson, D., Koch, C. A., Grey, L., Ellis, C., Moran, M. F. and Pawson, T. (1990). Binding of SH2 domains of phospholipase γ1, GAP and *src* to activated growth factor receptors. *Science* 250, 979-982.

Bailly, R., Bosselut, R., Zucman, J., Cormier, F., Delattre, O. and Roussel, M. (1994). DNA binding and transcriptional activation properties of the EWS-FLI-1 fusion protein resulting from the t(11;22) translocation in Ewing sarcoma. *Mol. Cell. Biol.* (in press).

Ben-David, Y., Giddens, E. B., Letwin, K. and Bernstein, A. (1991). Erythroleukemia induction by Friend murine leukemia virus: Insertional activation of a new member of the *ets* gene family Fli-1, closely linked to c-*ets*-1. *Genes Dev.* 5, 908-918.

Bortner, D. M., Ulivi, M., Roussel, M. F. and Ostrowski, M. C. (1991). The carboxy-terminal catalytic domain of GTPase-activating protein inhibits nuclear signal transduction and morphological transformation mediated by the CSF-1 receptor. *Genes Dev.* 5, 1777-1785.

Bowtell, D., Fu, P., Simon, M. and Senior, P. (1992). Identification of murine homologues of the *Drosophila* Son of Sevenless gene: Potential activators of *ras*. *Proc. Nat. Acad. Sci. USA* 89, 6511-6515.

Cantley, L. C., Auger, K. R., Carpenter, C., Duckworth, B., Graziani, A., Kapeller, R. and Soltoff, S. (1991). Oncogenes and signal transduction. *Cell* 64, 281-302.

Claesson-Welsh, L., Eriksson, A., Westermark, B. and Heldin, C. H. (1989). cDNA cloning and expression of the human A-type platelet-derived growth factor (PDGF) receptor establishes structural similarity to the B-type PDGF receptor. *Proc. Nat. Acad. Sci. USA* 86, 4917-4921.

Clark, S. G., Stern, M. J. and Horvitz, H. R. (1992). *C. elegans* cell signaling gene *sem*-5 encodes a protein with SH2 and SH3 domains. *Nature* 356, 340-344.

Courtneidge, S. A., Dhand, R., Pilat, D., Twamley, G. M., Waterfield, M. D. and Roussel, M. F. (1993). Activation of SRC family kinases by colony stimulating factor-1, and their association with its receptor. *EMBO J.* 12, 943-950.

Gibbs, J. B., Marshall, M. S., Scolnick, E. M., Dixon, R. A. F. and Vogel, U. S. (1990). Modulation of guanine nucleotides bound to *ras* in NIH-3T3 cells by oncogenes, growth factors, and GAP. *J. Biol. Chem.* 265, 20437-20442.

Kato, J. Y., Roussel, M. F., Ashmun, R. A. and Sherr, C. J. (1989). Transduction of human colony stimulating factor-1 receptor into interleukin-3-dependent mouse myeloid cells induces both CSF-1-dependent and factor-independent growth. *Mol. Cell. Biol.* 9, 4069-4073.

Kato, J. Y. and Sherr, C. J. (1990). Human colony-stimulating factor 1 (CSF-1) receptor confers CSF-1 responsiveness to interleukin-3-dependent 32DCL3 mouse myeloid cells and abrogates differentiation in response to granulocyte CSF. *Blood* 75, 1780-1787.

Koch, C. A., Anderson, D., Moran, M. F., Ellis, C. and Pawson, J. (1991). SH2 and SH3 domains: elements that control interactions of cytoplasmic signaling proteins. *Science* **252**, 668-674.

Langer, S. J., Bortner, D. M., Roussel, M. F., Sherr, C. J. and Ostrowski, M. C. (1992). Mitogenic signaling by colony-stimulating factor 1 and *ras* is suppressed by the *ets*-2 DNA-binding domain and restored by *myc* overexpression. *Mol. Cell. Biol.* **12**, 5355-5362.

Lowenstein, E. J., Daly, R. J., Batzer, A. G., Li, W., Margolis, B., Lammers, R., Ullrich, A., Skolnik, E. Y., Bar-Sagi, D. and Schlessinger, J. (1992). The SH2 and SH3 domain-containing protein GRB2 links receptor tyrosine kinases to *ras* signaling. *Cell* **70**, 431-442.

Mathews, W., Jordan, C. T., Wiegand, G. W., Pardoll, D. and Lemischka, I. R. (1991). A receptor tyrosine kinase specific to hematopoietic stem and progenitor cell-enriched populations. *Cell* **65**, 1143-1152.

Matsui, T., Heideran, M., Miki, T., Popescu, N., La Rochelle, W., Kraus, M., Pierce, J. and Aaronson, S. A. (1989). Isolation of a novel receptor cDNA establishes the existence of two PDGF receptor genes. *Science* **243**, 800-804.

Pelicci, G., Lanfrancone, L., Grignani, F., McGlade, J., Cavallo, F., Forni, G., Nicoletti, I., Pawson, P. and Pellici, P. G. (1992). A novel transforming protein (SHC) with an SH2 domain is implicated in mitogenic signal transduction. *Cell* **70**, 93-104.

Pollard, J. W., Bartocci, A., Arceci, R., Orlofsky, A., Ladner, M. B. and Stanley, E. R. (1987). Apparent role of the macrophage growth factor, CSF-1, in placental development. *Nature* **330**, 484-486.

Qiu, F. H., Ray, P., Brown, K., Barker, P. E., Jhanwar, S., Ruddle, F. H. and Besmer, P. (1988). Primary structure of c-*kit*: Relationship with the CSF-1/PDGF receptor kinase family oncogenic activation of v-*kit* involves deletion of extracellular domain and C terminus. *EMBO J.* **7**, 1003-1011.

Reddy, A. S., Langer, S. J., Colman, M. and Ostrowski, M. C. (1992). An enhancer element responsive to *ras* and *fms* signaling pathways is composed of two distinct nuclear factor binding sites. *Mol. Endocrinol.* **6**, 1051-1060.

Reedijk, M., Liu, X. and Pawson, T. (1990). Interactions of phosphatidylinositol kinase, GTPase-activating protein (GAP), and GAP-associated proteins with the colony-stimulating factor 1 receptor. *Mol. Cell. Biol.* **10**, 5601-5608.

Regenstreif, L. J. and Rossant, J. (1989). Expression of the c-*fms* proto-oncogene and of the cytokine, CSF-1, during mouse embyogenesis. *Dev. Biol.* **133**, 284-294.

Rettenmier, C. W. and Roussel, M. F. (1988). Differential processing of colony-stimulating factor-1 precursors encoded by two human cDNAs. *Mol. Cell. Biol.* **8**, 5026-5034.

Rohrschneider, L. R. and Woolford, J. F. (1992). Structural and functional comparison of viral and cellular *fms*. *Semin. Virol.* **2**, 385-395.

Roussel, M. F. and Sherr, C. J. (1989). Mouse NIH/3T3 cells expressing human CSF-1 receptors overgrow in serum-free medium containing human CSF-1 as their only growth factor. *Proc. Nat. Acad. Sci. USA* **86**, 7924-7927.

Roussel, M. F., Shurtleff, S. A., Downing, J. R. and Sherr, C. J. (1990). A point mutation at tyrosine 809 in the human colony-stimulating factor 1 receptor impairs mitogenesis without abrogating tyrosine kinase activity,

association with phosphatidylinositol 3-kinase, or induction of *fos* and *jun*B genes. *Proc. Nat. Acad. Sci. USA* **87**, 6738-6742.

Roussel, M. F., Cleveland, J. L., Shurtleff, S. A. and Sherr, C. J. (1991). *Myc* rescue of a mutant CSF-1 receptor impaired in mitogenic signalling. *Nature* **353**, 361-363.

Roussel, M. F. and Sherr, C. J. (1993). Signal transduction by the macrophage colony-stimulating factor receptor. *Curr. Opin. Hematol.* **1**, 11-18.

Roussel, M. F., Davis, J. N., Cleveland, J. L., Ghysdael, J. and Hiebert, S. W. (1994). Dual control of *myc* expression through a single DNA binding site targeted by *ets* family proteins and E2F-1. *Oncogene* **9**, 405-415.

Sawyers, C. L., Callahan, W. and Witte, O. N. (1992). Dominant negative *MYC* blocks transformation by *ABL* oncogenes. *Cell* **70**, 901-910.

Sherr, C. J. (1988). The role of the CSF-1 receptor gene (c-*fms*) in cell transformation. *Leukemia* **2**, 132-142.

Sherr, C. J. and Stanley, E. R. (1990). Colony stimulating factor-1. In *Peptide Growth Factors and their Receptors* (ed. M. B. Sporn and A. B. Roberts), pp. 667-698. Springer-Verlag, Heidelberg,

Sherr, C. J. (1993). Mammalian G1 cyclins. *Cell* **73**, 1059-1065.

Shibuya, H., Yoneyama, M., Ninomiya-Tsuji, J., Matsumoto, K. and Taniguchi, T. (1992). IL-2 and EGF receptors stimulate the hematopoietic cell cycle via different signaling pathways: Demonstration of a novel role for c-*myc*. *Cell* **70**, 57-67.

Shurtleff, S. A., Downing, J. R., Rock, C. O., Hawkins, S. A., Roussel, M. F. and Sherr, C. J. (1990). Structural features of the colony-stimulating factor 1 receptor that affect its association with phosphatidylinositol 3-kinase. *EMBO J.* **9**, 2415-2421.

Songyang, A., Shoelson, S. E., Chandhuri, M., Gish, G., Pawson, T., Haser, W. G., King, F., Roberts, T., Ratnofsky, S., Lechleider, R. J., Neel, B. G., Birge, R. B., Fajardo, J. E., Chou, M. M., Hanafusa, H., Shaffhuaser, B. and Cantley, L. C. (1993). SH2 domains recognize specific phosphopeptide sequences. *Cell* **72**, 767-778.

Stacey, D. W., Roudebush, M., Day, R., Mosser, S. D., Gibbs, J. B. and Feig, L. A. (1991). Dominant inhibitory Ras mutants demonstrate the requirement for Ras activity in the action of tyrosine kinase oncogenes. *Oncogene* **6**, 2297-2304.

Tobe, K., Matuoka, K., Tamemoto, H., Ueki, K., Kaburagi, Y., Asai, S., Noguchi, T., Matsuda, M., Tanaka, S., Hattori, S., Fukui, Y., Akanuma, Y., Yazaki, Y., Takenawa, T. and Kadowaki, T. (1993). Insulin stimulates association of insulin receptor substrate-1 with the protein abundant Src homology/growth factor receptor-bound protein 2. *J. Biol. Chem.* **268**, 11167-11171.

Van der Geer, P. and Hunter, T. (1990). Identification of tyrosine 706 in the kinase insert as the major colony-stimulating factor 1 (CSF-1)-stimulated autophosphorylation site in the CSF-1 receptor in a murine macrophage cell line. *Mol. Cell. Biol.* **10**, 2991-3002.

Wiktor-Jedrzejczak, W., Bartocci, A., Ferrante, A. W., Jr, Ahmed-Ansari, A., Sell, K. W., Pollard, J. W. and Stanley, E. R. (1990). Total absence of colony-stimulating factor 1 in the macrophage-deficient osteopetrotic (*op/op*) mouse. *Proc. Nat. Acad. Sci. USA* **87**, 4828-4832.

Journal of Cell Science, Supplement 18, 109-113 (1994)
Printed in Great Britain © The Company of Biologists Limited 1994

Focal adhesion kinase: structure and signalling

J. Thomas Parsons[1],*, **Michael D. Schaller[1]**, **Jeffrey Hildebrand[1]**, **Tzeng-Horng Leu[1]**, **Alan Richardson[1]** and **Carol Otey[2]**

[1]Department of Microbiology and [2]Anatomy and Cell Biology, Health Sciences Center, University of Virginia, Charlottesville, VA 22908, USA

*Author for correspondence

SUMMARY

Studies on the attachment and spreading of cells in culture have provided valuable insights into the mechanisms by which cells transmit information from the outside to the inside of the cell. This brief review considers recent information on the role of focal adhesion-associated protein tyrosine kinases in integrin-regulated cell signalling.

Key words: integrin, paxillin, focal adhesion kinase

INTRODUCTION

Cell adhesion and motility play a central role in a diverse array of cellular events, including cellular differentiation, development and cancer (Albelda and Buck, 1990; Hynes, 1992). An experimental entry into the study of the molecular events triggering cell adhesion comes from the analysis of cell attachment and spreading, a process that is driven by the formation of molecular structures called focal adhesions. Focal adhesions (also referred to as focal contacts) are points of close apposition between the cell membrane and the extracellular matrix (ECM), which is comprised of proteins such as collagen, fibronectin or vitronectin (Burridge et al., 1988; Luna and Hitt, 1992). The structural organization of focal adhesions is complex. Integrins, heterodimeric transmembrane receptors comprised of α and β subunits (Albelda and Buck, 1990; Hynes, 1992) bridge the cell membrane, the extracellular ligand-binding domains engaging the ECM on the outside of the cell and the short cytoplasmic tails interacting with the cytoplasmic cytoskeleton. Thus, integrins physically link the ECM to the cytoplasmic actin cytoskeletal network and may function to transmit signals from the extracellular matrix to the cytoplasm (Turner and Burridge, 1991; Schwartz, 1992). The actual linkage between integrin cytoplasmic tails and actin bundles or stress fibers appears to be mediated by an intricate structure comprised of focal adhesion-associated proteins. Considerable evidence suggests that at least two of these focal adhesion-associated proteins, talin and α-actinin, interact directly with the cytoplasmic domain of β integrin subunits (Tapley et al., 1989a; Otey et al., 1990). Both talin and α-actinin have also been shown to bind to the actin-binding protein vinculin, supporting the idea that protein-protein interactions are responsible in large part for the ordered structure of the focal adhesion (Burridge et al., 1988).

Several lines of evidence point to the importance of tyrosine phosphorylation in the formation and organization of focal adhesions. In cells transformed by the tyrosine kinase oncogene pp60[src], two focal adhesion-associated proteins, tensin and paxillin, are highly phosphorylated on tyrosine (Turner et al., 1990; Davis et al., 1991). In addition, in Src-transformed cells, other focal adhesion proteins, talin, vinculin and β_1 integrin subunits have been reported to be tyrosine phosphorylated, albeit at low stoichiometry (Sefton and Hunter, 1981; DeClue and Martin, 1987; Tapley et al., 1989b). Thus the dramatic alterations in cytoskeletal structure induced by Src transformation may be due in part to the tyrosine phosphorylation of focal adhesion-associated proteins. In normal cells, immunofluorescence analysis with antibodies to phosphotyrosine reveals prominent staining of focal adhesions, indicating the presence of significant levels of tyrosine phosphorylated proteins (Maher et al., 1985; Burridge et al., 1988). The attachment and spreading of rodent fibroblasts in culture leads to the increased tyrosine phosphorylation of both paxillin and tensin (Burridge et al., 1992; Bockholt and Burridge, 1993), while treatment of cells with inhibitors of protein tyrosine kinases blocks spreading of fibroblasts in culture (Burridge et al., 1992).

Studies from our own laboratory have led to the identification of a major pp60[src] substrate, of M_r 125,000 (pp125), which localizes to focal adhesions of normal adherent chicken embryo cells (Schaller et al., 1992). The isolation and characterization of cDNA clones encoding pp125 revealed that pp125 was a novel protein tyrosine kinase, which we designated focal adhesion kinase, or pp125[FAK]. Clues to the function of pp125[FAK] come from numerous studies showing that the tyrosine phosphorylation of pp125[FAK] is increased as a consequence of either the engagement of integrins with the extracellular matrix, for example the attachment and spreading of embryo fibroblasts onto a fibronectin matrix (Guan et al., 1991; Burridge et al., 1992; Schaller et al., 1993) or the cross-linking of surface integrins with integrin-specific antibodies (Kornberg et al., 1991, 1992). In addition, activation of fibrinogen-dependent platelet aggregation also induces tyrosine phosphorylation of pp125[FAK] in vivo and an increase in pp125[FAK] tyrosine kinase activity in vitro (Lipfert et al., 1992). Thus, the increased tyrosine phosphorylation of pp125[FAK] appears to be closely coupled with binding and activation of cell surface integrin receptors. In this brief review, we consider recent experimental data indicating that pp125[FAK] plays a role in regulating cellular events leading to the assembly of focal adhesions. In addition, we speculate on the possible role of pp125[FAK] in cellular signalling via pathways that modulate or control cellular gene expression.

THE BASIC FAKS: FUNCTIONAL DOMAINS OF pp125[FAK]

To date, pp125[FAK] homologues have been identified in mouse, human and *Xenopus* (Hanks et al., 1992; Andre and Becker-Andre, 1993; Whitney et al., 1993; M. Hens and D. DeSimone, personal communication). The structure of the pp125[FAK] in each of these species is highly conserved and is distinct from all other known protein tyrosine kinases. The catalytic domain exhibits most of the structural hallmarks of a typical tyrosine kinase, however, in the case of pp125[FAK] the catalytic domain is flanked by two non-catalytic domains that exhibit little sequence similarity to other proteins (or gene products) present in the existing data bases (Fig. 1). FAK is expressed in most cell lines and tissues examined to date (Hanks et al., 1992; Andre and Becker-Andre, 1993; Turner et al., 1993). In some cells the carboxyl-terminal domain of pp125[FAK] is expressed autonomously as a 41,000 M_r protein (called FRNK - FAK-related non-kinase; Schaller et al., 1993). In avian cells and tissues, FRNK is encoded by an alternatively processed 2.4 kb mRNA (Schaller et al., 1993). A similar sized mRNA has been detected in human tissues, but it remains to be determined if this mRNA encodes p41[FRNK]. A notable feature of pp125[FAK] structure is the absence of SH2 and SH3 domains, domains present in the Src family of kinases and other cytoplasmic protein tyrosine kinases, as well as many protein components of receptor-directed signalling pathways (reviewed by Pawson and Gish, 1992). In most SH2-containing proteins, the SH2 domains appear to direct protein-protein interactions, promoting stable interactions with unique phosphotyrosine-containing peptide sequence motifs (Pawson and Gish, 1992;

Songyang et al., 1993). SH3 domains also appear to mediate protein-protein interactions, directing binding to proteins with proline-rich peptide sequence motifs (Ren et al., 1993). The lack of SH2 and SH3 domains in pp125[FAK] suggests that FAK may play a role in cell signalling distinct from previously characterized non-receptor protein tyrosine kinases. In addition, as we will discuss below, it is likely that the non-catalytic domains of pp125[FAK] participate in directing the protein-protein interactions that regulate and control pp125[FAK] function.

THE 'INS AND OUTS' OF THE FOCAL ADHESION: SEQUENCES THAT TARGET pp125[FAK] TO FOCAL ADHESIONS

Little information is available as to how focal adhesion-associated proteins are directed to the existing or newly formed focal adhesions. The first clues as to how pp125[FAK] is targeted to focal adhesions came from the analysis of a series of deletion mutations within the amino- and carboxyl-terminal non-catalytic domains (Hildebrand et al., 1993). Deletion of sequences between residues 853 and 1012 greatly diminished the translocation of retrovirally expressed FAK protein to the focal adhesions of chicken embryo cells grown in culture. In contrast, deletion of sequences within the amino-terminal non-catalytic domain or small deletions within a region of the C-terminal domain proximal to the kinase domain had no effect on the efficient localization of pp125[FAK] to focal adhesions. These data indicate that residues 853 to 1012 comprise a targeting sequence (termed the 'focal adhesion targeting' or 'FAT' sequence) necessary for the efficient localization of pp125[FAK] to focal adhesions (Fig. 2). Further evidence for the importance of the FAT sequence comes from studies analyzing hybrid proteins comprised of unmyristylated, cytosolic pp60[src] fused to a polypeptide containing residues 853 to 1052 of pp125[FAK]. Immunofluorescence staining of chicken embryo cells infected with a retrovirus encoding the Src-FAT fusion protein showed efficient localization of Src-FAT protein to focal contacts, providing additional evidence that FAT sequences direct the translocation of pp125[FAK] to focal adhesions.

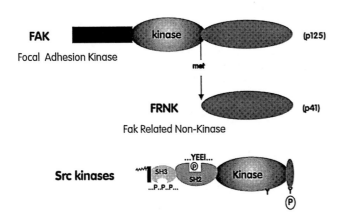

Fig. 1. A comparison of the structure of pp125[FAK] and the Src family kinase, pp60[src]. See text for detail.

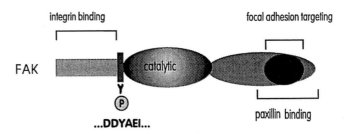

Fig. 2. Functional domains of the focal adhesion kinase, pp125[FAK]. Genetic and biochemical studies described in the text have led to the identification of domains within pp125[FAK]. Integrin binding is localized to the amino terminal domain, whereas interactions with the focal adhesion-associated protein, paxillin, and targeting to the focal adhesion is mediated by sequences present in the carboxyl-terminal domain.

MORE THAN FAT: THE CARBOXYL-TERMINAL NON-CATALYTIC DOMAIN DIRECTS THE BINDING OF pp125[FAK] TO THE FOCAL ADHESION PROTEIN PAXILLIN

Recent evidence indicates that within the cell there is a direct interaction between pp125[FAK] and the focal adhesion-associated protein paxillin. Immunoprecipitation of pp125[FAK] from extracts of cells expressing wild-type pp125[FAK] demonstrates the efficient co-immunoprecipitation of pp125[FAK] and paxillin (M. Schaller, J. Hildebrand and J. T. Parsons, unpublished observations). The stable association of these two proteins was not observed when cells expressing FAK mutants lacking the FAT sequence or mutants lacking the C-terminal 11 residues of pp125[FAK] were subjected to a similar analysis. Parallel in vitro experiments using glutathione S-transferase fused to FAK peptides containing sequences present in residues 687 to 1052 confirmed that paxillin could efficiently bind to sequences present in the carboxyl-terminal non-catalytic domain of pp125[FAK] (J. Hildebrand, M. Schaller and J. T. Parsons, unpublished observations). Furthermore, the binding to paxillin appears to be direct, since isotopically labelled GST-FAK bound to paxillin immobilized on a filter matrix (a 'south-western' blot). A careful analysis of a series of GST fusion proteins containing deletions of residues within the carboxyl-terminal domains shows that paxillin binding was functionally distinct from sequences necessary for focal adhesion targeting, although sequences required for paxillin binding appear to overlap, in part, the sequences required for focal adhesion targeting (Fig. 2). These results provide evidence for a role for the carboxyl-terminal non-catalytic domain of pp125[FAK] in both the localization of pp125[FAK] to focal adhesions as well as directing the binding of pp125[FAK] to a potential cellular substrate.

HOW DO INTEGRINS SIGNAL FAK: THE AMINO-TERMINAL NON-CATALYTIC DOMAIN DIRECTS THE BINDING OF pp125[FAK] TO THE CYTOPLASMIC DOMAINS OF β INTEGRINS

The cell adhesion-dependent activation of pp125[FAK] tyrosine phosphorylation suggests that integrins may directly regulate, in some fashion, the activation of pp125[FAK] kinase activity. Previous experiments by Otey et al. (1990) showed that the interactions of focal adhesion proteins and integrin cytoplasmic domains can be analyzed in vitro. The focal adhesion-associated protein, α-actinin, binds in vitro to synthetic peptides mimicking the 47 amino acid cytoplasmic domain of the β_1 integrins. A similar experimental approach reveals that pp125[FAK] also binds efficiently to peptides mimicking the complete cytoplasmic domain of β_1 and β_3 integrins (M. Schaller, C. Otey and J. T. Parsons, unpublished observations). Further, analysis of pp125[FAK] binding to a set of four overlapping peptides comprising the total cytoplasmic domain sequence of β_1 shows that pp125[FAK] interacts preferentially with a peptide sequence representative of the first 13 residues adjacent to the transmembrane domain of β_1 (Fig. 3). Binding of pp125[FAK] to peptide-containing beads can be blocked by preincubation with excess soluble peptide and pp125[FAK] does not bind to beads containing a 'scrambled' short peptide. To determine where in pp125[FAK] the integrin peptide-binding sequences resides, individual domains of pp125[FAK] were expressed in *Escherichia coli* and used in the in vitro binding assay. Significant binding activity was observed with peptides derived from the amino-terminal non-catalytic domain, whereas no binding activity was observed with peptides derived from the carboxyl-terminal region of pp125[FAK]. These data argue convincingly that pp125[FAK] is capable of directly binding to integrin cytoplasmic domain sequences in vitro. Interestingly a comparison of the sequences of individual β cytoplasmic domains shows a a high degree of sequence conservation within sequences corresponding to the β_1 pp125[FAK]-binding regions (Fig. 3). Whether such sequences direct the binding of pp125[FAK] and integrins in vivo, whether pp125[FAK] interacts with different β integrins via a conserved sequence motif, and how such interactions regulate pp125[FAK] activity are issues under current investigation.

WHERE'S THE PHOSPHOTYROSINE? THE MAJOR AUTOPHOSPHORYLATION SITE OF pp125[FAK] IS TYR[397], A HIGH AFFINITY BINDING SITE FOR pp60[src] AND p59[fyn]

In Src-transformed cells the tyrosine phosphorylation of pp125[FAK] is increased several fold, an observation that lead to its original identification as a Src-substrate (Kanner et al., 1990). In these cells the majority (>80%) of pp125[FAK] is stably associated with pp60[src] (Cobb et al., 1994). Genetic experi-

		pp125[FAK] binding
SP1	KLLMIIH**D**RR**E**FA	+++
SP2	FAKFEKEKMNAKW	–
SP3	KWDTGENPIYKSA	–
SP4	AVTT----VV-NPKYEGK	–
β1	KLLMIIH**D**RR**E**FAKFEKEKMNAKWDTGENPIYKSAVTT----VV-NPKYEGK	+++
β2	KALIHLS**D**LR**E**YRRFEKEKLKSQWNN-DNPIFKSATTT----VM-NPKFAES	NT
β3	KLLITIH**D**RK**E**FAKFEEERARAKWDTANNPIYKEATST----FT-NITYRGT	+++
β5	KLLVTIH**D**RR**E**FAKFQSERSRARYEMASNPIYRKPISTHTVDFTFNKSYNGTVD	NT
β6	KLLVSFH**D**RK**E**VAKFEAERSKAKWQTGTNPLYRGSTST----FK-NVTYKHREKQKVDLSTDC	NT
β7	RLSVEIY**D**RR**E**YSRFEKEQQQLNWKQDSNPIYKSAITTTI-----NPRFQEADSPTL	NT

Fig. 3. Comparison of the sequences of the cytoplasmic domains of β integrins. SP1-4 denote the sequences of four short peptides that together comprise the complete sequence of β_1 cytoplasmic domain. (+++) denotes significant binding of pp125[FAK], (–) denotes little detectable binding; NT, not tested.

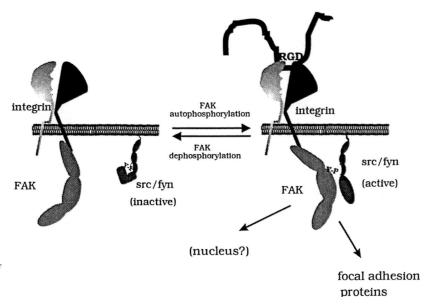

Fig. 4. Model for the integrin-dependent activation of pp125[FAK] and Src family kinases. See text for discussion.

focal adhesion proteins

ments using retroviruses expressing mutants of Src, as well as in vitro analysis of pp60[src]-pp125[FAK] complex formation, clearly indicate that the assembly of stable FAK-Src complexes requires both the SH2 domain of pp60[src] and the autophosphorylation site of pp125[FAK]. Peptide mapping experiments, coupled with site-directed mutagenesis of potential phosphorylation sites have identified the major site of pp125[FAK] autophosphorylation as Tyr[397] (Fig. 2) (Schaller et al., 1994). Mutation of Tyr[397] to Phe efficiently blocks pp60[src]-pp125[FAK] interactions in vivo and in vitro. Several features of the Tyr[397] autophosphorylation site are of interest. The position of Tyr[397] within pp125[FAK] distinguishes it from other receptor and non-receptor tyrosine kinases. In most instances tyrosine kinase autophosphorylation occurs at a highly conserved tyrosine within the catalytic domain (equivalent to Tyr[576] in pp125[FAK]; Tyr[416] in pp60[src]), within a kinase insert domain, which is a nonconserved insert found within the catalytic domains of some receptor protein tyrosine kinases (but not in pp125[FAK]) or distal to the catalytic domain at sites near the C terminus (a region found in many growth factor protein tyrosine kinases). Tyr[397] resides immediately amino-terminal to the catalytic domain, in relative proximity to the ATP-binding site. In addition Tyr[397] is embedded in the sequence DDYAEI, a sequence very similar to the consensus of a high-affinity Src SH2-binding peptide, YEEI (Songyang et al., 1993). These observations pose the possibility that in normal cells, integrin engagement may trigger autophosphorylation of pp125[FAK], which may, in turn, direct the translocation and concomitant activation of Src or other Src-like tyrosine kinases. Experimental support for such a model comes from the identification of pp125[FAK]-p59[fyn] complexes in extracts of normal adherent cultures of chicken embryo cells (Cobb et al., 1994).

SPECULATIONS, SPECULATIONS: A MODEL FOR pp125[FAK] SIGNALLING

One important function of the integrins is to translate extracellular cues into cytoplasmic signals, a function that is pre-

sumably important for the biological activities of integrins. On the basis of the data summarized above we are led to speculate that integrin engagement with the extracellular matrix may result in either the direct clustering of pp125[FAK], allosteric changes in pp125[FAK] or the stimulation of a regulator protein(s) that triggers pp125[FAK] activation. A direct consequence of such an activation step is the autophosphorylation of pp125[FAK] and generation of a high affinity binding site for Src and Src-family kinases. In normal cells the enzymatic activity of pp60[src] and pp59[fyn] is repressed through the action of a negative regulatory phosphorylation site at the C terminus of these kinases (Fig. 4). Phosphorylation of a highly conserved tyrosine within this region by a regulatory protein tyrosine kinase (Csk) is critical for down-regulation of catalytic activity (reviewed by Cooper and Howell, 1993). Current models for Src regulation suggest that the tyrosine phosphorylated C-terminal sequence binds in an intramolecular interaction to its own SH2 domain (Cantley et al., 1991; Cooper and Howell, 1993). The amino acid sequence flanking this C-terminal tyrosine does not resemble the consensus high affinity binding site and while a tyrosine phosphorylated C-terminal peptide can bind to the SH2 domain of pp60[src], it does so poorly (Songyang et al., 1993). In vitro, pp60[src] can be enzymatically activated by incubation with a synthetic phosphopeptide containing the consensus, high affinity, Src SH2-binding site, presumably by binding more efficiently to the SH2 domain than the regulatory C-terminal peptide (Liu et al., 1993). It is intriguing to speculate that autophosphorylation of Tyr[397] of pp125[FAK] may create a high affinity binding site for pp60[src] and pp59[fyn] and that these kinases may bind to pp125[FAK] resulting in the displacement of their C-termini from their SH2 domains. Thus, binding to pp125[FAK] may be a mechanism by which pp60[src] and pp59[fyn] are enzymatically activated in addition to a mechanism for the recruitment of these kinases to a highly localized site within the cell.

What might be the consequences of the activation of pp125[FAK] or the translocation-dependent activation of Src or Fyn? The adhesion-dependent increase in tyrosine phosphorylation of paxillin and tensin suggests that either or both of these focal adhesion proteins may be direct substrates for pp125^{FAK} or the pp125^{FAK}-Src/Fyn complex. The association of pp125^{FAK} and paxillin is interesting in this context and is consistent with the idea that pp125^{FAK} may play a direct role in bringing paxillin into the tyrosine kinase complex. It is interesting to speculate that activation of both pp125^{FAK} and Src/Fyn may be necessary for catalyzing the formation of focal adhesion assembly and for initiating signals that may direct the activation of other cellular signalling pathways. For example it is well established that cell adhesion and spreading can trigger the expression of cellular genes (Damsky and Werb, 1992). The association of pp125^{FAK} with either Src or Fyn may be sufficient to activate cellular signalling pathways that in turn lead to the activation of cellular genes. What these pathways are and how they function to regulate adhesion-dependent phenomena remain to be elucidated.

The studies from the author's laboratory were supported by NIH-NCI grants, P01 CA 40042, R37 CA 29243.

REFERENCES

Albelda, S. M. and Buck, C. A. (1990). Integrins and other cell adhesion molecules. *FASEB J.* **4**, 2868-2880.

Andre, E. and Becker-Andre, M. (1993). Expression of an N-terminally truncated form of human focal adhesion kinase in brain. *Biochem. Biophys. Res. Commun.* **190**, 140-146.

Bockholt, S. M. and Burridge, K. (1993). Cell spreading on extracellular-matrix proteins induces tyrosine phosphorylation of tensin. *J. Biol. Chem.* **268**, 14565-14567.

Burridge, K., Fath, K., Kelly, T., Nuckolls, G. and Turner, C. (1988). Focal adhesions: Transmembrane junctions between the extracellular matrix and the cytoskeleton. *Annu. Rev. Cell Biol.* **4**, 487-525.

Burridge, K., Turner, C. E. and Romer, L. H. (1992). Tyrosine phosphorylation of paxillin and pp125^{FAK} accompanies cell adhesion to extracellular matrix: a role in cytoskeletal assembly. *J. Cell Biol.* **119**, 893-903.

Cantley, L. C., Auger, K. R., Carpenter, C., Duckworth, B., Graziani, A., Kapeller, R. and Soltoff, S. (1991). Oncogenes and signal transduction. *Cell* **64**, 281-302.

Cobb, B. S., Schaller, M. D., Horng-Leu, Z. and Parsons, J. T. (1994). Stable association of pp60^{src} and p59^{fyn} with the focal adhesion-associated protein tyrosine kinase, pp125^{FAK}. *Mol. Cell. Biol.* **14**, 147-155.

Cooper, J. A. and Howell, B. (1993). The when and how of Src regulation. *Cell* **73**, 1051-1054.

Damsky, C. H. and Werb, Z. (1992). Signal transduction by integrin receptors for extracellular matrix: cooperative processing of extracellular information. *Curr. Opin. Cell. Biol.* **4**, 772-781.

Davis, S., Lu, M. L., Lo, S. H., Lin, S., Butler, J. A., Druker, B. J., Roberts, T. M., An, Q. and Chen, L. B. (1991). Presence of an SH2 domain in the actin-binding protein tensin. *Science* **252**, 712-715.

DeClue, J. E. and Martin, G. S. (1987). Phosphorylation of talin at tyrosine in Rous sarcoma virus-transformed cells. *Mol. Cell. Biol.* **7**, 371-378.

Guan, J.-L., Trevithick, J. E. and Hynes, R. O. (1991). Fibronectin/integrin interaction induces tyrosine phosphorylation of a 120-kDa protein. *Cell Regul.* **2**, 951-964.

Hanks, S. K., Calalb, M. B., Harper, M. C. and Patel, S. K. (1992). Focal adhesion protein tyrosine kinase phosphorylated in response to cell spreading on fibronectin. *Proc. Nat. Acad. Sci. USA* **89**, 8487-8489.

Hildebrand, J. D., Schaller, M. D. and Parsons, J. T. (1993). Identification of sequences required for the efficient localization of the focal adhesion kinase, pp125^{FAK}, to cellular focal adhesions. *J. Cell Biol.* **123**, 993-1005.

Hynes, R. O. (1992). Integrins: versatility, modulation, and signaling in cell adhesion. *Cell* **69**, 11-25.

Kanner, S. B., Reynolds, A. B., Vines, J. T. and Parsons, R. R. (1990). Monoclonal antibodies to tyrosine-phosphorylated protein substrates of oncogene-encoded tyrosine kinases. *Proc. Nat. Acad. Sci. USA* **87**, 3328-3332.

Kornberg, L. J., Earp, H. S., Turner, C. E., Prockop, C. and Juliano, R. L. (1991). Signal transduction by integrins: increased protein tyrosine phosphorylation caused by clustering of β1 integrins. *Proc. Nat. Acad. Sci. USA* **88**, 8392-8396.

Kornberg, L., Earp, H. S., Parsons, J. T., Schaller, M. and Juliano, R. L. (1992). Cell adhesion or integrin clustering increases phosphorylation of a focal adhesion-associated tyrosine kinase. *J. Biol. Chem.* **267**, 23439-23442.

Lipfert, L., Haimovich, B., Schaller, M. D., Cobb, B. S., Parsons, J. T. and Brugge, J. S. (1992). Integrin-dependent phosphorylation and activation of the protein tyrosine kinase pp125^{FAK} in platelets. *J. Cell Biol.* **119**, 905-912.

Liu, X., Brodeur, S. R., Gish, G., Zhou, S., Cantley, L. C., Laudano, A. P. and Pawson, T. (1993). Regulation of c-Src tyrosine kinase activity by the Src SH2 domain. *Oncogene* **8**, 1119-1126.

Luna, E. J. and Hitt, A. L. (1992). Cytoskeleton-plasma membrane interactions. *Science* **258**, 955.

Maher, P. A., Pasquale, E. B., Wang, J. Y. and Singer, S. J. (1985). Phosphotyrosine containing proteins are concentrated in focal adhesions and intercellular junctions in normal cells. *Proc. Nat. Acad. Sci. USA* **82**, 6576-6580.

Otey, C. A., Pavalko, F. M. and Burridge, K. (1990). An interaction between α-actinin and the β1 integrin subunit in vitro. *J. Cell Biol.* **111**, 721-729.

Pawson, T. and Gish, G. D. (1992). SH2 and SH3 domains: From structure to function. *Cell* **71**, 359-362.

Ren, R., Mayer, B. J., Cicchetti, P. and Baltimore, D. (1993). Identification of a ten-amino acid proline-rich SH3 binding site. *Science* **259**, 1157-1161.

Schaller, M. D., Borgman, C. A., Cobb, B. C., Reynolds, A. B. and Parsons, J. T. (1992). pp125^{FAK}, a structurally distinctive protein-tyrosine kinase associated with focal adhesions. *Proc. Nat. Acad. Sci. USA* **89**, 5192-5196.

Schaller, M. D., Borgman, C. A. and Parsons, J. T. (1993). Autonomous expression of a noncatalytic domain of the focal adhesion-associated protein tyrosine kinase pp125^{FAK}. *Mol. Cell. Biol.* **13**, 785-791.

Schaller, M. D., Hildebrand, J. D., Shannon, J. D., Fox, J. W., Vines, R. R. and Parsons J.T. (1994). Autophosphorylation of the focal adhesion kinase, pp125^{FAK}, directs SH2-dependent binding of pp60^{src}. *Mol. Cell. Biol.* **14**, 1680-1688.

Schwartz, M. A. (1992). Transmembrane signalling by integrins. *Trends Cell Biol.* **2**, 304-308.

Sefton, B. M. and Hunter, T. (1981). Vinculin: A cytoskeletal target of the transforming protein of Rous sarcoma virus. *Cell* **24**, 165-174.

Songyang, Z., Shoelson, S. E., Chaudhuri, M., Gish, G., Pawson, T., Haser, W. G., King, F., Roberts, T., Ratnofsky, S., Lechleider, R. J., Neel, B. G., Birge, R. B., Fajardo, J. E., Chou, M. M., Hanafusa, H., Schaffhausen, B. and Cantley, L. C. (1993). SH2 domains recognize specific phosphopeptide sequences. *Cell* **72**, 767-778.

Tapley, P., F. Horwitz, A., A. Buck, C., Burridge, K., Duggan, K., Hirst, R. and Rohrschneider, L. (1989a). Analysis of the avian fibronectin receptor (integrin) as a direct substrate for pp60v-src. *Oncogene* **4**, 325-333.

Tapley, P., Horwitz, A., Buck, C., Duggan, K. and Rohrschneider, L. (1989b). Integrins isolated from Rous sarcoma virus-transformed chicken embryo fibroblasts. *Oncogene* **4**, 325-333.

Turner, C. E. and Burridge, K. (1991). Transmembrane molecular assemblies in cell-extracellular matrix interactions. *Curr. Opin. Cell Biol.* **3**, 849-853.

Turner, C. E., Glenney, J. R. and Burridge, K. (1990). Paxillin: a new vinculin-binding protein present in focal adhesions. *J. Cell Biol.* **111**, 1059-1068.

Turner, C. E., Schaller, M. D. and Parsons, J. T. (1993). Tyrosine phosphorylation of the focal adhesion kinase pp125^{FAK} during development: relation to paxillin. *J. Cell Sci.* **105**, 637-645.

Whitney, G. S., Chan, P.-Y., Blake, J., Cosand, W. L., Neubauer, M. G., Aruffo, A. and Kanner, S. B. (1993). Human T and B lymphocytes express a structurally conserved focal adhesion kinase, pp125^{FAK}. *DNA Cell Biol.* **9**, 823-830.

Journal of Cell Science, Supplement 18, 115-119 (1994)
Printed in Great Britain © The Company of Biologists Limited 1994

Regulation and function of the MAP kinase cascade in *Xenopus* oocytes

Hidetaka Kosako[1,2], Yukiko Gotoh[1] and Eisuke Nishida[1,*]

[1]Department of Genetics and Molecular Biology, Institute for Virus Research, Kyoto University, Sakyo-ku, Kyoto 606-01, Japan
[2]Department of Biophysics and Biochemistry, Faculty of Science, University of Tokyo, Hongo, Tokyo 113, Japan

*Corresponding author

SUMMARY

In *Xenopus* oocytes, activation of MAP kinase occurs during meiotic maturation through a protein kinase cascade (the MAP kinase cascade), which is utilized commonly in various intracellular signaling pathways in eukaryotes. Studies with a neutralizing antibody against *Xenopus* MAP kinase kinase (MAPKK), a direct upstream activator for MAP kinase, have shown that the MAP kinase cascade plays a crucial role in both initiating oocyte maturation and inducing metaphase arrest.

Key words: MAP kinase, *Xenopus*, kinase cascade, MPF, oocyte maturation

INTRODUCTION

Mitogen-activated protein (MAP) kinases are serine/threonine kinases highly conserved throughout evolution and are activated commonly by various extracellular stimuli inducing mitogenesis or differentiation (reviewed by Cobb et al., 1991; Nishida and Gotoh, 1992; Pelech and Sanghera, 1992; Ruderman, 1993; Thomas, 1992). They are supposed to play a central role in intracellular signal transduction pathways. Full activation of MAP kinases requires phosphorylation of both tyrosine and threonine residues (Anderson et al., 1990). These phosphorylation sites have been determined to be located in the TEY sequence between kinase subdomains VII and VIII (Payne et al., 1991). A 45 kDa protein factor that can induce phosphorylation and activation of inactive MAP kinases in vitro was purified first from *Xenopus* unfertilized eggs (Matsuda et al., 1992) and subsequently from mammalian cells (Crews and Erikson, 1992; Nakielny et al., 1992b; Seger et al., 1992a; Shirakabe et al., 1992). This MAP kinase activating factor can undergo autophosphorylation on serine, threonine and tyrosine residues (Kosako et al., 1992; Nakielny et al., 1992b) and phosphorylate the kinase-deficient mutant of MAP kinase on tyrosine and threonine residues (Crews and Erikson, 1992; Kosako et al., 1993; Nakielny et al., 1992a; Seger et al, 1992a). Therefore, this factor is a dual specificity kinase and has been named MAP kinase kinase (MAPKK). cDNA cloning of MAPKK (Ashworth et al., 1992; Crews et al; 1992; Kosako et al., 1993; Seger et al., 1992b; Wu et al., 1993) revealed that MAPKK shows high similarities to several yeast protein kinases functioning in various signal transduction pathways such as the mating process and osmotic regulation. This suggests that the MAPKK/MAP kinase cascade functions universally in eukaryotic systems (reviewed by Errede and Levin, 1993; Nishida and Gotoh, 1993).

It has been shown that the activation of MAPKK and MAP kinase occurs during *Xenopus* oocyte maturation (Ferrell et al., 1991; Gotoh et al., 1991a,b; Matsuda et al., 1992; Posada et al.,

1991). Fully grown *Xenopus* oocytes (immature oocytes) are arrested at the first meiotic prophase. Exposure to progesterone induces the resumption of the meiotic process, leading to the production of the unfertilized egg, which is arrested at the second meiotic metaphase (metaphase II). The key event in this oocyte maturation process is thought to be the activation of maturation promoting factor (MPF), a complex of $p34^{cdc2}$ kinase and cyclin B, which is stored in immature oocytes as an inactive complex called pre-MPF (reviewed by Lohka, 1989; Maller, 1991; Nurse, 1990). MPF activity rises before germinal vesicle breakdown (GVBD), falls after metaphase I, and rises again and remains high during metaphase II. A cytostatic factor (CSF) is responsible for the metaphase II arrest with high MPF activity, and the product of the c-*mos* proto-oncogene, a 39 kDa serine/threonine protein kinase, is thought to be a component of CSF (Sagata et al., 1989). Translation of Mos is induced by progesterone and is necessary for meiosis I as well as for meiosis II and CSF arrest (Sagata et al., 1988). Moreover, bacterially expressed Mos protein can promote oocyte maturation when injected into immature oocytes without any hormonal stimulation and induce CSF arrest when injected into a two-cell embryo (Yew et al., 1992). Recent studies shed light on the roles of these four protein kinases (MPF, Mos, MAPKK and MAP kinase) during oocyte maturation process.

REGULATORY MECHANISM OF THE MAP KINASE CASCADE IN OOCYTE MATURATION

Activities of MAPKK and MAP kinase are elevated at about the same time as MPF during the course of oocyte maturation, remain high in unfertilized eggs and decrease to a basal level after fertilization (Ferrell et al., 1991; Gotoh et al., 1991a,b; Matsuda et al., 1992; Posada et al., 1991). Activation of MAPKK during this process is accompanied by its phosphorylation on threonine and serine residues (Kosako et al., 1992). Since MAPKK is deactivated by protein phosphatase 2A treatment in vitro (Gomez and

Cohen, 1991; Matsuda et al., 1992), MAPKK itself is thought to be activated by phosphorylation catalyzed by an upstream serine/threonine kinase(s), MAPKK kinase. Recent work has shown that MAPKK is phosphorylated on serine residues by MAPKK kinase and on threonine residues by its target kinase, MAP kinase (Matsuda et al., 1993; see Fig. 1). In the *Xenopus* MAPKK sequence there are two serine residues, S^{222} and S^{218}, located 9 and 13 amino acid residues upstream of the S(A)PE kinase motif, respectively. These two serine residues are conserved as serine or threonine residues among all the MAPKK homologs in vertebrates, *Drosophila* and yeasts. Site-directed mutagenesis studies have revealed that both or either of these serine residues may be important for activation of MAPKK by a variety of MAPKK kinases including Raf-1 (Gotoh et al., 1994). *Xenopus* MAPKK contains a single consensus sequence for phosphorylation by MAP kinase ($PST^{388}P$), and this sequence is conserved in mammalian and *Drosophila* MAPKK (Tsuda et al., 1993). A mutant MAPKK having threonine^{388} changed to alanine was not phosphorylated by MAP kinase purified from unfertilized eggs (Gotoh et al., 1994). This phosphorylation might have some regulatory role.

Recently, it has been revealed that Mos can work as a MAPKK kinase (Nebreda et al., 1993; Posada et al. 1993). Posada et al. (1993) showed that bacterially expressed Mos protein rapidly activates MAPKK and MAP kinase when injected into immature oocytes, and Nebreda and Hunt (1993) showed the activation of MAPKK and MAP kinase by adding recombinant Mos to cell-free extracts prepared from *Xenopus* immature oocytes. Both groups reported further that the recombinant Mos when expressed in *Escherichia coli* has no MAPKK kinase activity but it acquires the kinase activity after incubation with rabbit reticulocyte lysate (Posada et al., 1993) or with *Xenopus* egg extracts (Nebreda et al., 1993). Synthesis of Mos in response to progesterone may be responsible, at least in part, for activation of the MAPKK/MAP kinase cascade in oocyte maturation (Fig. 1).

On the other hand, it has been reported that the product of the *c-raf-1* proto-oncogene, a 74-76 kDa serine/threonine protein kinase, lies upstream of the MAPKK/MAP kinase cascade and functions as a MAPKK kinase in various signal transduction systems of mammals and *Drosophila* (Dent et al., 1992; Kyriakis et al., 1992; Howe et al., 1992; Tsuda et al., 1993). Since expression of dominant-negative Raf-1 inhibits progesterone-induced activation of MAP kinase in *Xenopus* oocytes (Fabian et al., 1993; Muslin et al., 1993), Raf-1 has been suggested to lie upstream of the MAP kinase cascade in the oocyte maturation process. However, activation of Raf-1 kinase as MAPKK kinase has not been demonstrated during oocyte maturation, and Ras, a putative direct upstream factor of Raf-1 (Moodie et al., 1993; Van Aelst et al., 1993; Vojtek et al., 1993; Zhang et al., 1993), is not supposed to be involved in progesterone-induced oocyte maturation (Deshpande and Kung, 1987). Thus, participation of Raf-1 in activation of the MAP kinase cascade during this process remains unclear (Fig. 1).

In yeasts, STE11, BCK1 and Byr2 are homologous serine/threonine protein kinases functioning upstream of each MAPKK homolog (STE7, MKK1/MKK2 and Byr1, respectively; reviewed by Errede and Levin, 1993; Nishida and Gotoh, 1993). A mammalian homolog of these putative yeast MAPKK kinases, termed MEKK, was shown to phosphorylate and activate MAPKK independently of Raf-1 (Lange-Carter et al., 1993). *Xenopus* MEKK has not been isolated yet, but bac-

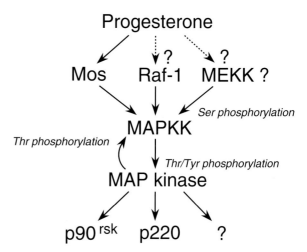

Fig. 1. Kinase cascade pathways resulting in MAP kinase activation during progesterone-induced oocyte maturation. Progesterone treatment induces synthesis of Mos protein, one of the MAPKK kinases. Whether other MAPKK kinases (Raf-1 and putative *Xenopus* MEKK) are activated by progesterone is unknown. These MAPKK kinases activate 45 kDa MAPKK by its serine phosphorylation (Gotoh et al., 1994). Then MAPKK (a dual specificity kinase) activates MAP kinase by phosphorylation on threonine and tyrosine residues. Activated MAP kinase phosphorylates several proteins, including MAPKK (an upstream kinase; Matsuda et al., 1993), p90^{rsk} (a downstream kinase; Sturgill et al., 1988) and p220 (a microtubule-associated protein; Shiina et al., 1992). It is likely that MAP kinase has other physiological substrates in maturing oocytes.

terially expressed STE11 protein can activate the MAP kinase cascade in cell-free extracts prepared from *Xenopus* immature oocytes (K. Takenaka et al., unpublished). Thus, MAPKK kinases other than Mos and Raf-1 could also function during oocyte maturation (Fig. 1).

Several groups have identified a family of mammalian dual specificity phosphatases that can specifically dephosphorylate and inactivate MAP kinase in vitro (reviewed by Nebreda, 1994). One of these phosphatases (3CH134 or CL100) is an immediate early gene product and is shown to be a physiological MAP kinase phosphatase by transient transfection studies (thus named MKP-1), suggesting a shut-off mechanism for the transient activation of MAP kinase in mitogenic stimulation (Sun et al., 1993). In *Xenopus* oocytes, the MAP kinase activity which is fully active during metaphase II arrest drops upon fertilization, but no gene expression occurs during early embryogenesis. Therefore, inactivation of MAP kinase after fertilization may occur by a different mechanism. Interestingly, a 47 kDa phosphatase purified from *Xenopus* eggs showed absolute specificity toward phosphotyrosine but not phosphothreonine of MAP kinase in vitro (Sarcevic et al., 1993). Regulation of this tyrosine phosphatase may provide an alternative mechanism for inactivation of MAP kinase.

FUNCTION OF THE MAP KINASE CASCADE IN *XENOPUS* OOCYTES

Requirement of the MAP kinase cascade for initiation of oocyte maturation

Recently, we prepared many polyclonal and monoclonal anti-

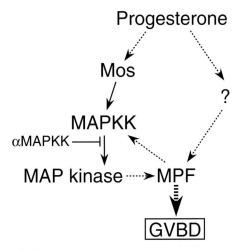

Fig. 2. A model for signal transduction pathways in oocyte maturation. This model proposes that progesterone-induced Mos, an essential protein for oocyte maturation, exerts its function through the MAPKK/MAP kinase cascade, resulting in MPF activation and GVBD. It is quite possible that other signaling pathways are required for progesterone-induced MPF activation.

bodies against bacterially expressed *Xenopus* 45 kDa MAPKK, one of which was found to be a neutralizing antibody that can specifically and efficiently inhibit *Xenopus* MAPKK activity in vitro (Kosako et al., 1994). This neutralizing antibody inhibited Mos- or okadaic acid-induced activation of MAP kinase when added to cell-free extracts prepared from *Xenopus* immature oocytes, suggesting that these agents activate MAP kinase through the 45 kDa MAPKK in a cell-free system. Furthermore, microinjection of this antibody into immature oocytes prevented progesterone- or Mos-induced activation of MAP kinase (Kosako et al., 1994). Our previous report showed that microinjection of the purified *Xenopus* MAPKK into immature oocytes resulted in rapid activation of endogenous MAP kinase (Matsuda et al., 1992). Thus, it is suggested that MAPKK, originally identified by its ability to activate MAP kinase in vitro, is the only direct activator of MAP kinase in *Xenopus* oocytes in vivo. Since there exist several putative MAPKK kinases (Raf-1, Mos and MEKK), MAPKK may function at a convergent point in various signaling pathways resulting in activation of MAP kinase (see Fig. 1).

The inhibition of activation of the MAP kinase cascade by microinjecting immature oocytes with the neutralizing antibody against MAPKK blocked the progesterone- or Mos-induced activation of MPF, as judged by inhibition of both GVBD and histone H1 kinase activation (Kosako et al., 1994). This suggests that the MAP kinase cascade plays a critical role in MPF activation during oocyte maturation and that there exists a signal transduction pathway consisting of Mos, MAPKK, MAP kinase and MPF (Fig. 2). The activated MAP kinase in this pathway may directly or indirectly regulate some proteins controlling MPF activity, such as cdc25, wee1 and CAK (reviewed by Solomon, 1993). However, whether MAP kinase activation is sufficient for MPF activation is unknown. It is possible that the MAP kinase cascade-independent pathways are also required for progesterone-induced MPF activation. It has been reported that p70[s6k], which is shown to be activated by mitogenic stimulation independently of the MAP kinase cascade in mammalian cultured cells (Ballou et

al., 1991), is rapidly activated by progesterone treatment in *Xenopus* oocytes (Lane et al., 1992). Other signaling pathways, such as inactivation of cAMP-dependent protein kinase, may also be necessary for progesterone-induced MPF activation (Daar et al., 1993).

We showed previously that purified MPF can activate MAPKK and MAP kinase when microinjected into immature oocytes or added to cell-free extracts prepared from interphase eggs (Gotoh et al., 1991b; Matsuda et al., 1992). Therefore, it is supposed that the MAPKK/MAP kinase cascade and MPF form a positive feedback loop (Fig. 2). This might explain the synchronous activation of MAP kinase and MPF during progesterone-induced oocyte maturation (Nebreda and Hunt, 1993).

Function of the MAP kinase cascade in CSF arrest

Mos, one of the MAPKK kinases, functions not only as an initiator of oocyte maturation but also as a component of cytostatic factor (CSF) that causes the natural arrest of unfertilized eggs in second meiotic metaphase (metaphase II arrest; Sagata et al., 1988, 1989). Recently, Haccard et al. (1993) reported that microinjection of thiophosphorylated MAP kinase (thiophosphorylated proteins are generally resistant to dephosphorylation by protein phosphatases) into one blastomere of a two-cell embryo induced metaphase arrest similar to that induced by Mos. This assay is the only index of CSF activity, and their result reveals that active MAP kinase is sufficient for metaphase arrest in *Xenopus* fertilized eggs. It is suggested that active MAP kinase in mature oocytes (unfertilized eggs) functions, downstream of Mos, to induce metaphase II arrest (Fig. 3). Interestingly, MAP kinase is deactivated before GVBD in clam oocytes that are not arrested at metaphase II (Shibuya et al., 1992a). We have shown by using the neutralizing antibody against MAPKK that the CSF activity of Mos is mediated by the MAP kinase cascade (H. Kosako, Y. Gotoh and E. Nishida, unpublished). Microinjection of bacterially expressed Mos protein into one blastomere of a two-cell embryo induced metaphase arrest as had been reported by Yew et al. (1992), but coinjection of Mos and the neutralizing antibody prevented the Mos-induced metaphase arrest. The previous report that Ras has CSF activity (Daar et al., 1991) may also be explained by Ras-induced activation of the MAP kinase cascade (Hattori et al., 1992; Itoh et al., 1993; Leevers and Marshall, 1992; Shibuya et al., 1992b; Fig. 3). Thus, the MAP kinase cascade is thought to play a pivotal role in both initiating oocyte maturation by hormonal stimulation and maintaining metaphase arrest in mature oocytes (Figs 2 and 3). The mechanism by which the same kinase cascade induces apparently different cellular responses is unclear, but MAP kinase may regulate, directly or indirectly, a factor(s) involved in both activation and stabilization of MPF.

PROSPECTS

In vertebrates, the MAP kinase cascade is activated downstream of several proto-oncogene products in various intracellular signal transduction pathways, but its significance for cellular function was unclear. The study utilizing the neutralizing antibody against *Xenopus* MAPKK has shown the physiological significance of the MAP kinase cascade in *Xenopus* oocyte maturation. However, target proteins of MAP kinase

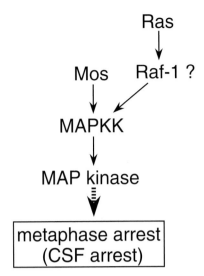

Fig. 3. A model for signal transduction pathways inducing metaphase arrest. This model proposes that the CSF activity of Mos is mediated by the MAP kinase cascade. The CSF activity of Ras may also be mediated by this kinase cascade probably through Raf-1, another MAPKK kinase.

during the oocyte maturation process have not been identified fully. It has been reported that MAP kinase phosphorylates a downstream kinase (p90[rsk] or S6 kinase II; Sturgill et al., 1988) and a microtubule-associated protein (p220; Shiina et al., 1992) present in *Xenopus* oocytes. Elucidation of a catalog of MAP kinase substrates and their function will increase our understanding of the function of the MAP kinase cascade not only in oocyte maturation but also in other cellular processes.

This work was supported by grants-in-aid from the Ministry of Education, Science and Culture of Japan, the Asahi Glass Foundation and the Toray Science Foundation.

REFERENCES

Anderson, N. G., Maller, J. L., Tonks, N. K. and Sturgill, T. W. (1990). Requirement for integration of signals from two distinct phosphorylation pathways for activation of MAP kinase. *Nature* **343**, 651-653.

Ashworth, A., Nakielny, S., Cohen, P. and Marshall, C. (1992). The amino acid sequence of a mammalian MAP kinase kinase. *Oncogene* **7**, 2555-2556.

Ballou, L. M., Luther, H. and Thomas, G. (1991). MAP2 kinase and 70K S6 kinase lie on distinct signalling pathways. *Nature* **349**, 348-350.

Cobb, M. H., Boulton, T. G. and Robbins, D. J. (1991). Extracellular signal-regulated kinases: ERKs in progress. *Cell Regul.* **2**, 965-978.

Crews, C. M., Alessandrini, A. and Erikson, R. L. (1992). The primary structure of MEK, a protein kinase that phosphorylates the *ERK* gene product. *Science* **258**, 478-480.

Crews, C. M. and Erikson, R. L. (1992). Purification of a murine protein-tyrosine/threonine kinase that phosphorylates and activates the *Erk-1* gene product: Relationship to the fission yeast *byr1* gene product. *Proc. Nat. Acad. Sci. USA* **89**, 8205-8209.

Daar, I., Nebreda, A. R., Yew, N., Sass, P., Paules, R., Santos, E., Wigler, M. and Vande Woude, G. F. (1991). The *ras* oncoprotein and M-phase activity. *Science* **253**, 74-76.

Daar, I., Yew, N. and Vande Woude, G. F. (1993). Inhibition of *mos*-induced oocyte maturation by protein kinase A. *J. Cell Biol.* **120**, 1197-1202.

Dent, P., Haser, W., Haystead, T. A. J., Vincent, L. A., Roberts, T. M. and Sturgill, T. W. (1992). Activation of mitogen-activated protein kinase kinase by v-Raf in NIH 3T3 cells and in vitro. *Science* **257**, 1404-1407.

Deshpande, A. K. and Kung, H.-F. (1987). Insulin induction of *Xenopus laevis* oocyte maturation is inhibited by monoclonal antibody against p21 *ras* proteins. *Mol. Cell. Biol.* **7**, 1285-1288.

Errede, B. and Levin, D. E. (1993). A conserved kinase cascade for MAP kinase activation in yeast. *Curr. Opin. Cell Biol.* **5**, 254-260.

Fabian, J. R., Morrison, D. K. and Daar, I. O. (1993). Requirement for Raf and MAP kinase function during the meiotic maturation of *Xenopus* oocytes. *J. Cell Biol.* **122**, 645-652.

Ferrell, J. E., Wu, M., Gerhart, J. C. and Martin, G. S. (1991). Cell cycle tyrosine phosphorylation of p34[cdc2] and a microtubule-associated protein kinase homolog in *Xenopus* oocytes and eggs. *Mol. Cell. Biol.* **11**, 1965-1971.

Gomez, N. and Cohen, P. (1991). Dissection of the protein kinase cascade by which nerve growth factor activates MAP kinases. *Nature* **353**, 170-173.

Gotoh, Y., Nishida, E., Matsuda, S., Shiina, N., Kosako, H., Shiokawa, K., Akiyama, T., Ohta, K. and Sakai, H. (1991a). In vitro effects on microtubule dynamics of purified *Xenopus* M phase-activated MAP kinase. *Nature* **349**, 251-254.

Gotoh, Y., Moriyama, K., Matsuda, S., Okumura, E., Kishimoto, T., Kawasaki, H., Suzuki, K., Yahara, I., Sakai, H. and Nishida, E. (1991b). *Xenopus* M phase MAP kinase: isolation of its cDNA and activation by MPF. *EMBO J.* **10**, 2661-2668.

Gotoh, Y., Matsuda, S., Takenaka, K., Hattori, S., Iwamatsu, A., Ishikawa, M., Kosako, H. and Nishida, E. (1994). Characterization of recombinant Xenopus MAP kinase kinases mutated at potential phosphorylation sites. *Oncogene* **9**, 1891-1898.

Haccard, O., Sarcevic, B., Lewellyn, A., Hartley, R., Roy, L., Izumi, T., Erikson, E. and Maller, J. L. (1993). Induction of metaphase arrest in cleaving *Xenopus* embryos by MAP kinase. *Science* **262**, 1262-1265.

Hattori, S., Fukuda, M., Yamashita, T., Nakamura, S., Gotoh, Y. and Nishida, E. (1992). Activation of mitogen-activated protein kinase and its activator by ras in intact cells and in a cell-free system. *J. Biol. Chem.* **267**, 20346-20351.

Howe, L. R., Leevers, S. J., Gomez, N., Nakielny, S., Cohen, P. and Marshall, C. J. (1992). Activation of the MAP kinase pathway by the protein kinase raf. *Cell* **71**, 335-342.

Itoh, T., Kaibuchi, K., Masuda, T., Yamamoto, T., Matsuura, Y., Maeda, A., Shimizu, K. and Takai, Y. (1993). A protein factor for ras p21-dependent activation of mitogen-activated protein (MAP) kinase through MAP kinase kinase. *Proc. Nat. Acad. Sci. USA* **90**, 975-979.

Kosako, H., Gotoh, Y., Matsuda, S., Ishikawa, M. and Nishida, E. (1992). *Xenopus* MAP kinase activator is a serine/threonine/tyrosine kinase activated by threonine phosphorylation. *EMBO J.* **11**, 2903-2908.

Kosako, H., Nishida, E. and Gotoh, Y. (1993). cDNA cloning of MAP kinase kinase reveals kinase cascade pathways in yeasts to vertebrates. *EMBO J.* **12**, 787-794.

Kosako, H., Gotoh, Y. and Nishida, E. (1994). Requirement for the MAP kinase kinase/MAP kinase cascade in *Xenopus* oocyte maturation. *EMBO J.* **13**, 2131-2138.

Kyriakis, J. M., App, H., Zhang, Z.-F., Banerjee, P., Brautigan, D. L., Rapp, U. and Avruch, J. (1992). Raf-1 activates MAP kinase-kinase. *Nature* **358**, 417-421.

Lane, H. A., Morley, S. J., Doree, M., Kozma, S. C. and Thomas, G. (1992). Identification and early activation of a *Xenopus laevis* p70[s6k] following progesterone-induced meiotic maturation. *EMBO J.* **11**, 1743-1749.

Lange-Carter, C. A., Pleiman, C. M., Gardner, A. M., Blumer, K. J. and Johnson, G. L. (1993). A divergence in the MAP kinase regulatory network defined by MEK kinase and Raf. *Science* **260**, 315-319.

Leevers, S. J. and Marshall, C. J. (1992). Activation of extracellular signal-regulated kinase, ERK2, by p21ras oncoprotein. *EMBO J.* **11**, 569-574.

Lohka, M. J. (1989). Mitotic control by metaphase-promoting factor and cdc proteins. *J. Cell Sci.* **92**, 131-135.

Maller, J. L. (1991). Mitotic control. *Curr. Opin. Cell Biol.* **3**, 269-275.

Matsuda, S., Kosako, H., Takenaka, K., Moriyama, K., Sakai, H., Akiyama, T., Gotoh, Y. and Nishida, E. (1992). *Xenopus* MAP kinase activator: identification and function as a key intermediate in the phosphorylation cascade. *EMBO J.* **11**, 973-982.

Matsuda, S., Gotoh, Y. and Nishida, E. (1993). Phosphorylation of *Xenopus* mitogen-activated protein (MAP) kinase kinase by MAP kinase kinase kinase and MAP kinase. *J. Biol. Chem.* **268**, 3277-3281.

Moodie, S. A., Willumsen, B. M., Weber, M. J. and Wolfman, A. (1993). Complexes of Ras•GTP with Raf-1 and mitogen-activated protein kinase kinase. *Science* **260**, 1658-1661.

Muslin, A. J., MacNicol, A. M. and Williams, L. T. (1993). Raf-1 protein kinase is important for progesterone-induced *Xenopus* oocyte maturation and acts downstream of mos. *Mol. Cell. Biol.* **13**, 4197-4202.

Nakielny, S., Cohen, P., Wu, J. and Sturgill, T. (1992a). MAP kinase activator from insulin-stimulated skeletal muscle is a protein threonine/tyrosine kinase. *EMBO J.* **11**, 2123-2129.

Nakielny, S., Campbell, D. G. and Cohen, P. (1992b). MAP kinase kinase from rabbit skeletal muscle. *FEBS Lett.* **308**, 183-189.

Nebreda, A. R., Hill, C., Gomez, N., Cohen, P. and Hunt, T. (1993). The protein kinase *mos* activates MAP kinase kinase in vitro and stimulates the MAP kinase pathway in mammalian somatic cells in vivo. *FEBS Lett.* **333**, 183-187.

Nebreda, A. R. and Hunt, T. (1993). The c-*mos* proto-oncogene protein kinase turns on and maintains the activity of MAP kinase, but not MPF, in cell-free extracts of *Xenopus* oocytes and eggs. *EMBO J.* **12**, 1979-1986.

Nebreda, A. R. (1994). Inactivation of MAP kinases. *Trends Biochem. Sci.* **19**, 1-2.

Nishida, E. and Gotoh, Y. (1992). Mitogen-activated protein kinase and cytoskeleton in mitogenic signal transduction. *Int. Rev. Cytol.* **138**, 211-238.

Nishida, E. and Gotoh, Y. (1993). The MAP kinase cascade is essential for diverse signal transduction pathways. *Trends Biochem. Sci.* **18**, 128-131.

Nurse, P. (1990). Universal control mechanism regulating onset of M-phase. *Nature* **344**, 503-508.

Payne, D. M., Rossomando, A. J., Martino, P., Erickson, A. K., Her, J.-H., Shabanowitz, J., Hunt, D. F., Weber, M. J. and Sturgill, T. W. (1991). Identification of the regulatory phosphorylation sites in pp42/mitogen-activated protein kinase (MAP kinase). *EMBO J.* **10**, 885-892.

Pelech, S. L. and Sanghera, J. S. (1992). Mitogen-activated protein kinases: versatile transducers for cell signaling. *Trends Biochem. Sci.* **17**, 233-238.

Posada, J., Sanghera, J., Pelech, S., Aebersold, R. and Cooper, J. A. (1991). Tyrosine phosphorylation and activation of homologous protein kinases during oocyte maturation and mitogenic activation of fibroblasts. *Mol. Cell. Biol.* **11**, 2517-2528.

Posada, J., Yew, N., Ahn, N. G., Vande Woude, G. F. and Cooper, J. A. (1993). Mos stimulates MAP kinase in *Xenopus* oocytes and activates a MAP kinase kinase in vitro. *Mol. Cell. Biol.* **13**, 2546-2553.

Ruderman, J. V. (1993). MAP kinase and the activation of quiescent cells. *Curr. Opin. Cell Biol.* **5**, 207-213.

Sagata, N., Oskarsson, M., Copeland, T., Brumbaugh, J. and Vande Woude, G. F. (1988). Function of c-*mos* proto-oncogene product in meiotic maturation in *Xenopus* oocytes. *Nature* **335**, 519-525.

Sagata, N., Watanabe, N., Vande Woude, G. F. and Ikawa, Y. (1989). The c-*mos* proto-oncogene product is a cytostatic factor responsible for meiotic arrest in vertebrate eggs. *Nature* **342**, 512-518.

Sarcevic, B., Erikson, E. and Maller, J. L. (1993). Purification and characterization of a mitogen-activated protein kinase tyrosine phosphatase from *Xenopus* eggs. *J. Biol. Chem.* **268**, 25075-25083.

Seger, R., Ahn, N. G., Posada, J., Munar, E. S., Jensen, A. M., Cooper, J. A., Cobb, M. H. and Krebs, E. G. (1992a). Purification and characterization of mitogen-activated protein kinase activator(s) from epidermal growth factor-stimulated A431 cells. *J. Biol. Chem.* **267**, 14373-14381.

Seger, R., Seger, D., Lozeman, F. J., Ahn, N. G., Graves, L. M., Campbell, J. S., Ericsson, L., Harrylock, M., Jensen, A. M. and Krebs, E. G. (1992b). Human T-cell mitogen-activated protein kinase kinases are related to yeast signal transduction kinases. *J. Biol. Chem.* **267**, 25628-25631.

Shibuya, E. K., Boulton, T. G., Cobb, M. H. and Ruderman, J. V. (1992a). Activation of p42 MAP kinase and the release of oocytes from cell cycle arrest. *EMBO J.* **11**, 3963-3975.

Shibuya, E. K., Polverino, A. J., Chang, E., Wigler, M. and Ruderman, J. V. (1992b). Oncogenic Ras triggers the activation of 42-kDa mitogen-activated protein kinase in extracts of quiescent *Xenopus* oocytes. *Proc. Nat. Acad. Sci. USA* **89**, 9831-9835.

Shiina, N., Moriguchi, T., Ohta, K., Gotoh, Y. and Nishida, E. (1992). Regulation of a major microtubule-associated protein by MPF and MAP kinase. *EMBO J.* **11**, 3977-3984.

Shirakabe, K., Gotoh, Y. and Nishida, E. (1992). A mitogen-activated protein (MAP) kinase activating factor in mammalian mitogen-stimulated cells is homologous to *Xenopus* M phase MAP kinase activator. *J. Biol. Chem.* **267**, 16685-16690.

Solomon, M. J. (1993). Activation of the various cyclin/cdc2 protein kinases. *Curr. Opin. Cell Biol.* **5**, 180-186.

Sturgill, T. W., Ray, L. B., Erikson, E. and Maller, J. L. (1988). Insulin-stimulated MAP-2 kinase phosphorylates and activates ribosomal protein S6 kinase II. *Nature* **334**, 715-718.

Sun, H., Charles, C. H., Lau, L. F. and Tonks, N. K. (1993). MKP-1 (3CH134), an immediate early gene product, is a dual specificity phosphatase that dephosphorylates MAP kinase in vivo. *Cell* **75**, 487-493.

Thomas, G. (1992). MAP kinase by any other name smells just as sweet. *Cell* **68**, 3-6.

Tsuda, L., Inoue, Y. H., Yoo, M.-A., Mizuno, M., Hata, M., Lim, Y.-M., Adachi-Yamada, T., Ryo, H., Masamune, Y. and Nishida, Y. (1993). A protein kinase similar to MAP kinase activator acts downstream of the Raf kinase in Drosophila. *Cell* **72**, 407-414.

Van Aelst, L., Barr, M., Marcus, S., Polverino, A. and Wigler, M. (1993). Complex formation between RAS and RAF and other protein kinases. *Proc. Nat. Acad. Sci. USA* **90**, 6213-6217.

Vojtek, A. B., Hollenberg, S. M. and Cooper, J. A. (1993). Mammalian Ras interacts directly with the serine/threonine kinase Raf. *Cell* **74**, 205-214.

Wu, J., Harrison, J. K., Vincent, L. A., Haystead, C., Haystead, T., Michel, H., Hunt, D., Lynch, K. R. and Sturgill, T. W. (1993). Molecular structure of a protein-tyrosine/threonine kinase activating p42 mitogen-activated protein (MAP) kinase: MAP kinase kinase. *Proc. Nat. Acad. Sci. USA* **90**, 173-177.

Yew, N., Mellini, M. L. and Vande Woude, G. F. (1992). Meiotic initiation by the *mos* protein in *Xenopus*. *Nature* **355**, 649-652.

Zhang, X.-F., Settleman, J., Kyriakis, J. M., Takeuchi-Suzuki, E., Elledge, S. J., Marshall, M. S., Bruder, J. T., Rapp, U. R. and Avruch, J. (1993). Normal and oncogenic p21[ras] proteins bind to the amino-terminal regulatory domain of c-Raf-1. *Nature* **364**, 308-313.

Journal of Cell Science, Supplement 18, 121-126 (1994)
Printed in Great Britain © The Company of Biologists Limited 1994

Specificity in recognition of phosphopeptides by src-homology 2 domains

Lewis C. Cantley[1,2] and Zhou Songyang[1,3]

[1]Department of Cell Biology, Harvard Medical School, Boston, MA 02115, USA
[2]Division of Signal Transduction, Beth Israel Hospital, Boston, MA 02115, USA
[3]Dept of Physiology, Tufts University School of Medicine, Boston, MA 02111, USA

SUMMARY

SH2 domains and SH3 domains, found in a number of protein-tyrosine kinases and substrates of protein-tyrosine kinases, provide specificity in downstream signaling. Both of these domains bind to relatively short linear sequences of peptides to provide specific interactions between proteins. The SH2 domains directly bind to phosphotyrosine residues of proteins in a specific sequence context. We have devised a phosphopeptide library technique that allows us to rapidly determine the sequence specificity of individual SH2 domains on the basis of amino acids selected at position +1, +2 and +3 C-terminal of the phosphotyrosine. The optimal motif for 22 distinct SH2 domains has been determined and used to predict likely sites of in vivo interaction. A second phosphopeptide library was devised in which the amino acids N-terminal of the phosphotyrosine were also varied. The residues N-terminal of phosphotyrosine had little influence on binding to the N-SH2 domain of the 85 kDa subunit of phosphoinositide 3-kinase. These results indicate that for this SH2 domain, specificity is determined by sequences carboxy-terminal of the phosphotyrosine moiety. Knowledge of the specificity of SH2 domains allows predictions about likely downstream targets on the basis of primary sequence of proteins. Some of these predictions will be discussed.

Key words: SH2 domain, SH3 domain, tyrosine kinase, phosphopeptide

INTRODUCTION

A breakthrough in understanding how protein-tyrosine kinases are regulated and specifically associate with downstream targets was provided by the discovery that SH2 and SH3 domains recognize specific short peptide sequences. These domains were originally pointed out by Tony Pawson as regions of homology conserved among cytosolic protein-tyrosine kinases that are not part of the kinase domain. As additional signaling proteins were found to contain SH2 and/or SH3 domains without protein kinase domains, it became clear that these domains have functions separate from the kinase domain. Later work from Pawson's laboratory and from Hanafusa's laboratory (Matsuda, 1990; Anderson, 1990; reviewed by Cantley et al., 1991) showed that SH2 domains mediate binding to heterologous proteins in a manner that depends on tyrosine phosphorylation of the target proteins. In fact, the binding could be blocked with phosphotyrosine indicating that the SH2 domain directly binds to the phosphotyrosine moiety of the proteins. In addition we noticed a short region of similarity between the sequence around a phosphotyrosine residue in polyoma middle t implicated in binding to phosphatidylinositol (PtdIns) 3-kinase (Whitman et al., 1985) and two tyrosine phosphorylation sites in the PDGF receptor implicated in binding this same enzyme (Kazlauskus and Cooper, 1989; Escobedo et al., 1991) that suggested a consensus site for binding of the PtdIns 3-kinase SH2 domains (phosphoTyr-Met/Val-Xxx-Met; Cantley et al., 1991). On the basis of these and other observations we suggested that SH2 domains from different signaling proteins bind phosphotyrosine in distinct sequence contexts such that the sequence immediately surrounding a site of tyrosine-phosphorylation dictates which SH2-containing protein will bind in vivo. This hypothesis has been supported by additional studies discussed below.

Like SH2 domains, SH3 domains recognize relatively short (10-12 amino acid) sequences of proteins or peptides. The abl SH3 domain was used to screen an expression library and cDNA clones of two proteins with regions rich in proline were isolated (Cicchetti et al., 1992). The proline-rich domains of the two proteins were shown to mediate the binding to the abl SH3 domain and a consensus sequence for binding to the abl SH3 domain was determined from studies with synthetic peptides (Ren et al., 1993). A number of other proteins with proline-rich regions have now been shown to bind to various SH3 domains. We discovered that in stimulated lymphocytes, the src-family members, p60[fyn] and p56[lck] utilize their SH3 domains to associate with PtdIns 3-kinase (Prasad et al., 1993; Kapeller et al., 1994). This association involves two proline-rich regions of the p85 regulatory subunit of PtdIns 3-kinase (Kapeller et al., 1994).

In this manuscript the results obtained using the phosphopeptide library to explore SH2 domains are discussed.

MATERIALS AND METHODS

Construction of peptide libraries

The phosphopeptide library with degeneracy carboxy-terminal of the phosphotyrosine was constructed as described by Songyang et al.

(1993). The sequence of the library mixture is GlyAspGly(phospho)TyrXxxXxxXxxSerProLeuLeuLeu where Xxx indicates all amino acids but Cys or Trp.

A second library with degeneracy amino-terminal of the phospho-Try was also made. This library has the sequence GlyAlaXxxXxxXxx(phospho)TyrXxxXxxXxxAlaLysLysLys where Xxx indicates all amino acids but Cys or Trp. The degeneracy of this library is 34,012,224.

GST-SH2 domains and affinity purification of peptides

cDNA clones of the various SH2 domains were expressed as glutathione S-transferase fusion proteins by expression in pGEX as described by Songyang et al. (1993). The GST-SH2 domain was harvested on glutathione beads and packed in a 1 ml syringe. The beads were washed with 1 ml PBS (150 mM NaCl, 3 mM KCl, 10 mM Na$_2$HPO$_4$, 2 mM KH$_2$PO$_4$, pH 7.2). The peptide mixture (~0.3 mg) was added to the column and allowed to stand for 10 minutes. The column was then quickly washed twice with 1 ml ice-cold PBS (containing 10 mg/ml blue dextran and 0.5% NP-40) and once with 1 ml ice-cold PBS (without blue dextran or detergent) using a plunger to force the solution through. Elution of the specifically associated peptides was accomplished with 200 μ l of 20 mM sodium phenylphosphate solution (pH 7.8). The solution was collected, concentrated by evaporation, and sequenced on the Applied Biosystems 477A protein sequencer.

RESULTS

We wished to test the hypothesis that SH2 domains provide specificity for downstream signaling by protein-tyrosine kinases because of their ability to distinguish between tyrosine-phosphorylated sites on the basis of the sequence immediately surrounding the phosphotyrosine. We had shown that relatively short phosphopeptides (as short as 6 amino acids) containing the motif phosphoTyr-Met-Pro-Met (based on Y315 of polyoma middle t) can bind to the N- or C-terminal SH2 domains of the p85 subunit of PtdIns 3-kinase in competition assays with K_i values of 5-20 nM (Auger et al., 1992; Carpenter et al., 1993). Scrambled phosphotyrosine-containing peptides bound orders of magnitude weaker. These results were consistent with studies done by Lewis Williams' laboratory using peptides based on sequences in the PDGF receptor (Fantl et al., 1992; Escobedo et al., 1991).

Despite these findings it was still not clear that phosphoTyr-Met/Val-Xxx-Met was the optimal sequence for binding to these SH2 domains since only a few amino acid replacements at the +1 and +3 positions were tested. In addition, no consensus motifs for the other ~30 SH2 domains known to exist had been determined.

In order to determine whether phosphoTyr-Met/Val-Xxx-Met is truly the optimal sequence for binding to the SH2 domains of p85, we constructed a partially degenerate phosphopeptide library. Every peptide in this library began with the sequence Gly-Asp-Gly-phosphoTyr-. The next three residues following the phosphotyrosine were degenerate such that all amino acids except Cys or Trp (left out because of problems in sequencing/disulfide bond formation) were present. In all peptides the C-terminal sequence was Ser-Pro-Leu-Leu-Leu. The Ser-Pro motif was added because it was detected downstream of many potential tyrosine-phosphorylation sites in proteins. The poly-Leu tail prevented wash-out during sequencing. The procedure for synthesis of this library and the

rational are discussed in detail in the Experimental Procedures of Songyang et al. (1993). The degeneracy of the library was $18^3 = 5832$ distinct peptides.

The N-terminal SH2 domain of p85 was expressed as a glutathione S-transferase fusion protein in bacteria, purified on glutathione beads and used to construct an affinity column. Washing and elution conditions were optimized using a radio-labeled phosphopeptide (^{125}I-labeled Arg-Glu-Asn-Glu-phosphoTyr-Met-Pro-Met-Ala-Pro-Gln-Ile-His) known to bind with high affinity to this SH2 domain. The column was then used to specifically retain peptides from the degenerate mixture that bound with highest affinity to the SH2 domain. (Phenylphosphate was used to elute the specifically-bound peptides.) Rather than attempt to separate distinct peptides in the mixture of affinity-purified peptides, we sequenced the complete mixture. Since in every case the phosphotyrosine is the 4th residue in the peptide, the relative abundance of the various amino acids detected at cycle 5 is an indication of the amino acid preference of this SH2 domain at the +1 site C-terminal of the phosphoTyr moiety. (The slight variation in relative abundance of the 18 amino acids at this cycle in the starting mixture was divided out). In this way we were able to show that the N-SH2 domain of p85 prefers Met, Val, Ile or Glu (in that order) at the +1 site and strongly prefers Met at the +3 site (Songyang et al., 1993). Little specificity was detected at the +2 site. These results were reassuring that the technique works since they agreed with the consensus sequence arrived at by comparing in vivo sites for binding of PtdIns 3-kinase (Cantley et al., 1991) and competition experiments done using synthetic phosphopeptides (Fantl et al., 1992; Carpenter et al., 1993).

We went on to use this library to determine the optimal motif for 21 additional SH2 domains (Songyang et al., 1993, 1994). We found that SH2 domains from src-family members all recognized a common motif (phosphoTyr-Glu-Glu-Ile) while each SH2 domain outside the src-family had a unique optimal motif. We synthesized a phosphopeptide based on this motif and showed that it has a very high affinity for the src SH2 domain. High affinity (10-50 nM K_d) was also demonstrated for the lck SH2 domain (Payne et al., 1993). Stephen Harrison's laboratory and John Kuriyan's laboratory used phosphopeptides based on this motif to form co-crystals with the lck (Eck et al., 1993) and src (Waksman et al., 1993) SH2 domains with the phosphoTyr-Glu-Glu-Ile peptides bound. The crystal structures revealed the regions of the SH2 domains that made contact with the side chains of the +1, +2 and +3 residues. These residues are summarized in Table 1. The amino acids selected at these positions could be rationalized based on the structure of the complex. Consistent with our finding that all src-family members bind the same optimal motif, the residues that made contact with the side chains were conserved in this family. In contrast, all other SH2 domains having one or more of the residues predicted to make contact with the side chains varied from the src structure. Thus, these results provide a clear structural explanation for the sequence specificity of SH2 domains. We also noted that the SH2 domains thus far known fall into 4 distinct groups on the basis of the residues at the peptide-binding sites (Songyang et al., 1993, 1994). General predictions about the likely motifs of SH2 domains can be made on the basis of which group they fall into.

This phosphopeptide library technique is extremely rapid.

Table 1. Phosphopeptide motifs for SH2 domains: residues predicted to interact with the side chains of the associated phosphopeptides

SH2 domain	+1	SRC-SH2 200 βD3	SRC-SH2 202 βD5	+2	SRC-SH2 205 βD'1	+3	SRC-SH2 202 βD5	SRC-SH2 214 βE4	SRC-SH2 215 EF1	SRC-SH2 230 αB9	SRC-SH2 237 BG4	
SRC	E	K	Y	E	R	**I**	Y	I	T	Y	L	
FYN	**E**	K	Y	**E**	R	**I**	Y	I	T	Y	L	
LCK	**E**	K	Y	E	R	**I**	Y	I	S	Y	L	GROUP 1A
FGR	**E**	K	Y	**E**	R	IV	Y	I	T	Y	L	
LYN		K	Y		R		Y	I	S	Y	L	
YES		K	Y		R		Y	I	T	Y	L	
HCK		K	Y		R		Y	I	S	Y	L	
Dsrc		K	Y		K		Y	L	S	Y	L	
SYK N		H	Y		E		Y	I	S	H	L	GROUP 1B
SYK C	QTE	L	Y	eqt	D	**L**	Y	I	P	Y	L	
ZAP70 C		Y	Y		S		Y	I	P	L	L	
TEC		R	Y		K		Y	L	A	H	L	
ATK		R	Y		C		Y	L	A	H	L	
ITK		K	Y		K		Y	V	A	H	L	
ABL	E	Y	Y	**N**	N	P	Y	V	S	H	L	
ARG		Y	Y		N		Y	V	T	H	L	
CSK	**T**	E	Y	n	M	mr	Y	I	D	Y	?	
CRK	D	S	Y	H	N	**P**	Y	A	G	Y	T?	
NCK	**D**	K	F	**E**	Q	**P**	F	I	G	Y	T?	
fes/fps	**E**	R	F	-	Q	vi	F	R	L	L	G	
ZAP70 N		H	F		E		F	I	A	Y	L	
SEM5	LV	Q	F	**N**	L	vp	F	L	W	H	R?	
DGBR2	y	Q	F	**N**	L	-	F	L	W	H	R?	
GRB2	qy	Q	F	**N**	L	y	F	L	W	H	R?	
GAP C		Q	F		C		F	M	G	Y	I?	
GAP N		N	F		I		F	I	G	Y	L?	
Tensin		R	F		T		F	?	?	H	?	
3BP2	**E**	R	Y	**N**	F	-	Y	E	G	Y	P?	
VAV	**M**	K	T	E	I	P	T	I	T	Y	?	GROUP 2
p85aN	MIVE	K	I	-	F	**M**	I	F	S	Y	A?	GROUP 3
p85bN		K	I		F		I	F	S	Y	A?	
p85aC	mli	K	C	-	N	**M**	C	F	A	Y	V?	
p85bC		K	C		Y		C	F	A	Y	V?	
PLC g1C	VI	K	C	IL	N	**PIV**	C	L	G	Y	Y?	
PLC g2C		K	C		Q		C	L	G	Y	Y?	
PLC g1N	**LIV**	Q	C	Ed	H	LIV	C	K	F	Y	L?	
PLC g2N		Q	C		R		C	K	Y	Y	L?	
SHPTP1 N	F	T	I	-	Q	**F**	I	D	L	Y	V	
SHPTP2 N	IV	T	I	-	Q	VI	I	D	L	Y	L	
CSW N		T	I		Q		I	D	L	Y	L	
SHPTP1 C		T	I		M		I	T	V	F	E	
SHC	EI	K	L	-	V	**ILM**	L	T	K	H	P?	
ShB		M	M		A		M	L	G	Y	?	GROUP 4
SHPTP2 C		T	V		R		V	D	V	Y	E	
CSW C		T	V		R		V	D	V	Y	E	
113 TF		F	A		P		A	L?	S?	Y	?	
91 TF		I	S		P		S	L?	Q?	Y	?	

Columns +1, +2 and +3 comprise the 1st, 2nd and 3rd residues C-terminal to P-tyrosine of the optimal phosphopeptide selected by each SH2 domain (e.g. P-YEEI for src SH2). SRC-SH2 200 and 202 indicate the residues of src (and residues at analogous positions of other SH2 domains) predicted to contact the +1 residue side chain of the associate peptide. SRC-SH2 205 is predicted to be near the +2 side chain and SRC 202, 214, 215 and 237 are predicted to form a hydrophobic pocket to bind the +3 residue side chain. The alignments were made on the basis of work by Waksman et al. (1992).

Bold letters indicate strong selection. Upper case without bold indicates medium selection. Lower case indicates weak selection. A hyphen indicates no selection. Motifs not yet determined or not submitted for publication are left blank.

Once the SH2 domain is expressed in bacteria as a GST-fusion protein it only requires 6 hours from the time of bacterial lysis until the affinity-selected peptide mixture is added to the micro sequencer. Each SH2 domain is evaluated at least twice from two different bacterial lysates to ensure reproducibility.

We also tested whether some SH2 domains may also be sensitive to the amino acids N-terminal of the phosphoTyr.

This does not appear to be the case for the SH2 domains of the p85 subunit of PtdIns 3-kinase. We constructed a library with the following sequence: Gly-Ala-Xxx-Xxx-Xxx-phosphoTyr-Xxx-Xxx-Xxx-Ala-Lys-Lys-Lys in which Xxx indicates all possible amino acids but Trp or Cys. The SH2 domains were used to affinity-purify optimal phosphopeptides from this library as before. For the p85 N-SH2 domain there was a slight

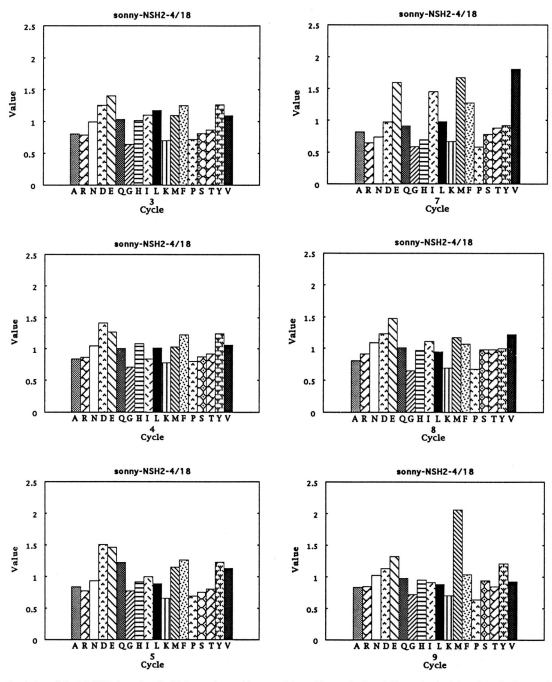

Fig. 1. The selectivity of the N-SH2 domain of p85 for amino acids at position, N-terminal and C-terminal of the phosphoTyr moiety of associated peptides. The GST-N-SH2 domain of p85 was used to affinity-purify peptides from a library with the sequence GAXXXpYXXXAKKK. The affinity-purified peptide mixture was sequenced and the data plotted as described by Songyang et al. (1993). The histogram in the top left corner indicates the relative amino acid abundance in the 3rd cycle of the sequence (the first degenerate position of the library) and the histogram under it represents the 4th cycle and etc. Cycle 6 (not shown) is phosphoTyr. Notice that significant selectivity is only observed at cycle 7 (the +1 position) and cycle 9 (the +3 position). Amino acids are indicated by single letter codes.

preference for Asp residues at the −1 and −2 positions but the major selection was still for Met/Val/Ile/Glu at +1 and for Met at +3 (Fig. 1). In this library, the sequences N-terminal of the phosphotyrosine and C-terminal from the region of degeneracy are different from those in the original library yet the same motif was selected, indicating that for the p85 N-SH2 domain the motif selected is not significantly affected by the residues outside the phosphoTyr-Xxx-Xxx-Xxx region.

DISCUSSION

Using a peptide library technique we have investigated the specificity of SH2 domains for linear sequences of phospho-Tyr-containing peptides. Twenty two distinct SH2 domains have been investigated using a library that varies the residues at positions +1, +2 and +3 amino acids carboxy-terminal of the phosphoTyr (Table 1). These SH2 domains can be distributed into 4 distinct groups on the basis of the amino acid at the βD5 position (Songyang et al., 1993). From the crystal structures of src and lck SH2 domains it is clear that this residue contacts the side chains of the amino acids +1 and +3 residues carboxy-terminal of the phosphoTyr (Eck et al., 1993; Waksman et al., 1993). In about half the known SH2 domains, this residue is either Tyr or Phe (Group I). Vav is the single known member of a group (Group II) in which βD5 is a Thr residue. Group III SH2 domains have a Cys or Ile at βD5 and the remaining SH2 domains have other residues at βD5.

The residue at βD5 is predictive of the type of phospho-peptide that will associate with the SH2 domain. For example, most Group I SH2 domains select peptides with the general motif phosphoTyr-Hydrophilic-Hydrophilic-Hydrophobic. In contrast most Group III SH2 domains select peptides with the sequence phosphoTyr-Hydrophobic-Xxx-Hydrophobic. Within these groups, the individual SH2 domains recognize specific sequences on the basis of diversity in the other residues that make up the +1, +2 and +3 binding sites. The possibility that additional contact is made between the SH2 domain and residues amino-terminal of the phosphoTyr-binding site was explored using the new library first described in this paper. The results with the N-SH2 domain of p85 indicate that this SH2 domain does not significantly interact with the side chains of residues amino-terminal of the phosphoTyr moiety. The fact that, using this library, a similar motif was observed to that observed with the original library in which only residues carboxy-terminal of phosphoTyr were varied (phosphoTyr-Val/Met/Ile/Glu-Xxx-Met; Fig 1 and Table 1) indicates that the procedure works. The results are in agreement with the crystal structures of Eck et al. (1993) and Waksman et al. (1993) in which the src and lck-SH2 domains had little contact with side chains of residues amino-terminal of the phosphoTyr moiety of the associated peptide.

Perhaps the most exciting outcome from determination of these motifs is the ability to predict likely sites in proteins for assembly of specific SH2 domain-containing proteins in vivo. For example, we correctly predicted the sites on the c-fms and c-kit receptor tyrosine kinases where PtdIns 3-kinase binds in vivo on the basis of the phosphoTyr-Met/Val-Xxx-Met motif (Cantley et al., 1991; Songyang et al., 1993). We also correctly predicted PtdIns 3-kinase-binding sites on proteins involved in B-cell and T-cell activation: CD19 (Tuveson et al., 1993) and CD 28 (Prasad et al., unpublished data) and on ERB B3 (Soltoff et al., 1994). Our peptide library results predicted that T-cell receptor Zeta, would be a good binding site for SHC and this was shown to occur in vivo (Ravichandran, 1993). Several other sites predicted by Songyang et al. (1993) have also been confirmed by us or other laboratories, including binding sites for sem5/grb-2 on the EGF receptor, SHPTP2 and on SHC (Pawson and Schlessinger, 1993).

It is now clear from these studies that specificity in signaling downstream of protein-tyrosine kinases is at least partially determined by the ability of SH2 domains to specifically interact with unique sites of tyrosine phosphorylation. In this way, by autophosphorylating on tyrosine residues that are within motifs optimal for the SH2 domains of PtdIns 3-kinase, PtdIns-PLC-g, ras-GAP, SHPTP2, and pp60[c-src], the PDGF receptor can specifically associate with these downstream targets (Fig. 2). The association with the receptor alone may activate some of these enzymes, as we have shown for PtdIns

PDGF Receptor Signal Transduction

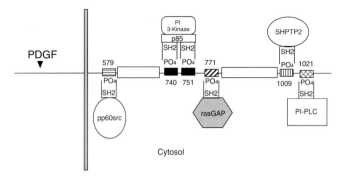

Fig. 2. A model for PDGF receptor interaction with cytosolic proteins bearing SH2 domains.

3-kinase (Carpenter et al., 1993). In most cases the associated proteins become phosphorylated on tyrosine. This tyrosine phosphorylation may regulate the activities of these proteins or provide binding sites for SH2 domains of yet additional signaling molecules.

This model raises the question of how much specificity in downstream signaling is mediated by the substrate specificity of the kinase domain of the protein-tyrosine kinase. It seems unlikely that the kinase domain will randomly phosphorylate any protein-tyrosine residue that is locally available and that specificity will be determined entirely by SH2 domain selection. In fact, the model that has arisen from studies of the PDGF receptor appears not to apply to many other receptors. For example, truncation or Tyr-Phe mutants of the EGF receptor that eliminate all the known autophosphorylation sites, including the binding sites for Grb-2, SHC, PLC-gamma and ras-GAP are not compromised in their ability to mediate EGF-dependent mitogenesis (Wells et al., 1990; Decker, 1993). These results indicate that some aspects of EGF receptor signaling are mediated directly by the kinase domain. We are currently using a peptide library technique to determine the specificity of kinase domains for linear peptide sequences. These results should provide further information about specificity in downstream signaling.

REFERENCES

Anderson, D., Koch, C. A., Grey, L., Ellis, C., Moran, M. F. and Pawson, T. (1990). Binding of SH2 domains of phospholipase C gamma 1, GAP, and Src to activated growth factor receptors. *Science* **250**, 979-82.

Auger, K. R., Carpenter, C. L. Shoelson, S. E., Piwnica-Worms, H. and Cantley, L. C. (1992). Polyoma virus middle T antigen/pp60[c-src] complex associates with purified phosphatidylinositol 3-kinase in vitro. *J. Biol. Chem.* **267**, 5408-5415.

Birge, R. B., Fajardo, J. E., Reichman, C., Shoelson, S. E., Songyang, Z., Cantley, L. C. and Hanafusa, H. (1993). Identification and characterization of a high-affinity interaction between v-Crk and tyrosine-phosphorylated paxillin in CT10-transformed fibroblasts. *Mol. Cell. Biol.* **13**, 4648-4656.

Cantley, L. C., Auger, K., Carpenter, C., Duckworth, B., Graziani, A., Kapeller, R. and Soltoff, S. (1991). Oncogenes and signal transduction. *Cell* **64**, 281-302.

Carpenter, C. L., Auger, K. R., Chaudhuri, M., Schaffhausen B., Schoelson, S. and Cantley, L. C. (1993). Phosphoinositide 3-kinase is activated by phosphopeptides that bind to the SH2 domains of the 85 kD subunit. *J. Biol. Chem.* **268**, 9478-9483.

Cicchetti, P., Mayer, B. J., Thiel, G. and Baltimore, D. (1992). Identification of a protein that binds to the SH3 region of Abl and is similar to Bcr and GAP-rho. *Science* **257**, 803-6.

Cobb, B. S., Schaller, M. D., Leu, T.-H. and Parsons, J. T. (1994). Stable association of pp60^{src} and pp59^{fyn} with the focal adhesion-associated protein tyrosine kinase, pp125^{Fak}. *Mol. Cell. Biol.* **14**, 147-155.

Courtneidge, S. A., Goutebroze, L., Cartwright, A., Heber, A., Scherneck, S. and Feunteun, J. (1991). Identification and characterization of the hamster polyomavirus middle T antigen. *J. Virol.* **65**, 3301-8.

Decker, S. J. (1993). *J. Biol. Chem.* **268**, 9176-9179.

Eck, M. J., Shoelson, S. E. and Harrison, S. C. (1993). Recognition of a high-affinity phosphotyrosyl peptide by the Src homology-2 domain of p56lck. *Nature* **362**, 87-91.

Escobedo, J. A., Kaplan, D. R., Kavanaugh, W. M., Turck, C. W. and Williams, L. T. (1991). A phosphatidylinositol-3 kinase binds to platelet-derived growth factor receptors through a specific receptor sequence containing phosphotyrosine. *Mol. Cell. Biol.* **11**, 1125-32.

Fantl, W. J., Escobedo, J. A., Martin, G. A., Turck, C. W., del, R. M., McCormick, F. and Williams, L. T. (1992). Distinct phosphotyrosines on a growth factor receptor bind to specific molecules that mediate different signaling pathways. *Cell* **69**, 413-23.

Fukui, Y. and Hanafusa, H. (1991). Requirement of phosphatidylinositol-3 kinase modification for its association with p60src. *Mol. Cell. Biol.* **11**, 1972-9.

Kapeller, R., Prasad, K. V. S., Janssen, O., Hou, W., Schaffhausen B. S., Rudd, C. E. and Cantley, L. C. (1994). Identification of two SH3-binding motifs in the regulatory subunit of phosphatidylinositol 3-kinase. *J. Biol. Chem.* **269**, 1927-1933.

Kazlauskas, A. and Cooper, J. A. (1989). Autophosphorylation of the PDGF receptor in the kinase insert region regulates interactions with cell proteins. *Cell* **58**, 1121-33.

Kim, J. W., Sim, S. S., Kim U.-H, Nishibe, S., Wahl, M. I., Carpenter, G. and Rhee, S. G. (1990). Tyrosine residues in bovine phospholipase C-g phosphorylated by the epidermal growth factor receptor in vitro. *J. Biol. Chem.* **265**, 3940-3943.

Liu, X., Brodeur, S. R., Gish, G., Songyang, Z., Cantley, L. C., Laudano, A. P. and Pawson, T. (1993). Regulation of c-Src tyrosine kinase activity by the Src SH2 domain. *Oncogene* **8**, 1119-26.

Marcote, M. J., Knighton, D. R., Basi, G., Sowadski, J. M., Brambilla, P., Draetta, G. and Taylor, S. S. (1993). A three-dimensional model of the Cdc2 protein kinase: localization of cyclin- and Suc1-binding regions and phosphorylation sites. *Mol. Cell. Biol.* **13**, 5122-31.

Matsuda, M., Mayer, B., Fukui, Y. and Hanafusa, H. (1990). Binding of transforming protein p47gag-crk to a broad range of phosphotyrosine-containing proteins. *Science* **248**, 1537-1539.

Mustelin, T. and Burn, P. (1993). Regulation of src family tyrosine kinases in lymphocytes. *Trends Biochem. Sci.* **18**, 215-220.

Pawson, T. and Gish, G. D. (1992). SH2 and SH3 domains: from structure to function. *Cell* **71**, 359-62.

Pawson, T. and Schlessinger, J. (1993). SH2 and SH3 domains. *Curr. Biol.* **3**, 434-442.

Payne, G., Shoelson, S. E., Gish, G. D., Pawson, T. and Walsh, C. T. (1993). Kinetics of p56lck and p60src Src homology 2 domain binding to tyrosine-phosphorylated peptides determined by a competition assay or surface plasmon resonance. *Proc. Nat. Acad. Sci. USA* **90**, 4902-6.

Prasad, K. V. S., Janssen, O., Kapeller, R., Raab, M., Cantley, L. C. and Rudd, C. E. (1993a). SRC-homology 3 domain of protein kinase p59^{fyn} mediates binding to phosphatidylinositol 3-kinase in T cells *Proc. Nat. Acad. Sci. USA* **90**, 7366-7370.

Prasad, K. V. S., Kapeller, R., Janssen, O., Repke, H., Duke-Cohan, J. S., Cantley, L. C. and Rudd, C. E. (1993b). Phosphatidylinositol 3-kinase and phosphatidylinositol 4-kinase binding to the CD4-p56lck complex: p56lck SH3 domain binding to PI 3-kinase but not PI 4-kinase. *Mol. Cell. Biol.* **13**, 7708-7717.

Pradsad, K. V., Cai, Y. C., Raab, M., Duckworth, B., Cantley, L., Shoelson, S. E., Rudd, C. E. (1994). T-cell antigen CD28 interact with the lipid kinase phosphatidylinositol 3-kinase by a cytoplasmic Tyr(p)-Met-Xaa-Met motif. *Proc. Nat. Acad. Sci. USA* **91**, 2834-2838.

Ravichandran, K. S., Lee, K. K., Songyang, Z., Cantley, L. C., Burn, P. and Burakoff, S. J. (1993). SHC interacts with the Zeta chain of the T cell receptor upon T cell activation. *Science* **262**, 902-905.

Ren, R., Mayer, B. J., Cicchetti, P. and Baltimore, D. (1993). Identification of a ten-amino acid proline-rich SH3 binding site. *Science* **259**, 1157-61.

Shoelson, S. E., Chatterjee, S., Chaudhuri, M. and White, M. F. (1992). YMXM motifs of IRS-1 define substrate specificity of the insulin receptor kinase. *Proc. Nat. Acad. Sci. USA* **89**, 2027-2031.

Soltoff, S. P., Carraway, K. L. III, Prigent, S. A., Gullick, W. G. and Cantley, L. C. (1994). ErbB3 is involved in the activation of phosphatidylinositol 3-kinase by epidermal growth factor. *Mol. Cell. Biol.* **14** (in press).

Songyang, Z., Shoelson, S. E., Chadhuri, M., Gish, G., Pawson, T., Haser, W. G., King, F., Roberts, T., Ratnofsky, S., Lechleider, R. J., Neel, B. G., Birge, R. B., Fajardom J. E., Chou, M. M., Hanafusa, H., Schaffhausen, B. and Cantley, L. C. (1993). SH2 domains recognize specific phosphopeptide sequences. *Cell* **72**, 767-778.

Songyang Z., Shoelson, S. E., McGlade, J., Olivier, P., Pawson, T., Bustelo, R. X., Barbacid, M., Sabe, H., Hanafusa, H., Yi, T., Ren, R., Baltimore, D., Ratnofsky, S., Feldman, R. A and Cantley, L. C. (1994). Specific motifs recognized by the SH2 domains of Csk, 3BP2, fps/fes, Grb-2, SHPTP1, SHC, Syk and Vav. *Mol. Cell. Biol.* **14** (in press).

Tuveson, D. A., Carter, R. H., Soltoff, S. P. and Fearon, D. T. (1993). CD19 of B Cells as a surrogate kinase insert region to bind Phosphatidylinositol 3-kinase. *Science* **260**, 986-989.

Wahl, M. I., Nishibe, S., Kim, J. W., Kim, H., Rhee, S. G. and Carpenter, G. (1990). Identification of two epidermal growth factor-sensitive tyrosine phosphorylation sites of phospholipase C-γ in intact HSC-1 cells. *J. Biol. Chem.* **265**, 3944-3948.

Waksman, G., Kominos, D., Robertson, S. C., Pant, N., Baltimore, D., Birge, R. B., Cowburn, D., Hanafusa, H., Mayer, B. J., Overduin, M., Resh, M. D. and Kuriyan, J. (1992). Crystal structure of the phosphotyrosine recognition domain SH2 of v-src complexed with tyrosine-phosphorylated peptides *Nature* **358**, 646-53.

Waksman, G., Shoelson, S. E., Pant, N., Cowburn, D. and Kuriyan, J. (1993). Binding of a high affinity phosphotyrosyl peptide to the Src SH2 domain: crystal structures of the complexed and peptide-free forms. *Cell* **72**, 779-90.

Wells, A., Welsh, J. B., Lazar, C. S., Wiley, H. S., Gill, G. N. and Rosenfeld, M. G. (1990). *Science* **247**, 962-964.

Whitman, M., Kaplan, D. R., Schaffhausen, B., Cantley, L. and Roberts, T. M. (1985). Association of phosphatidylinositol kinase activity with polyoma middle-T competent for transformation. *Nature* **315**, 239-242.

Journal of Cell Science, Supplement 18, 127-131 (1994)
Printed in Great Britain © The Company of Biologists Limited 1994

Signal transduction through the GTP-binding proteins Rac and Rho

Anne J. Ridley

Ludwig Institute for Cancer Research, University College/Middlesex Hospital Branch, 91 Riding House Street,
London W1P 8BT, UK

SUMMARY

Actin reorganization is an early response to many extra-cellular factors. In Swiss 3T3 fibroblasts, the Ras-related GTP-binding proteins Rho and Rac act as key signal trans-ducers in these responses: Rho is required for growth factor-induced formation of stress fibres and focal adhesions, whereas membrane ruffling is regulated by Rac proteins. Several proteins that act as GTPase activating proteins (GAPs) for Rho-related proteins have been iden-tified, and these could act either as targets or down-regu-lators of Rho or Rac in cells. In vitro, the GAP domain of p190 has a striking preference for Rho as a substrate, and when microinjected into Swiss 3T3 cells it inhibits stress fibre formation but not membrane ruffling induced by growth factors. BcrGAP acts on Rac but not Rho in vitro, and specifically inhibits membrane ruffling in vivo. Finally, RhoGAP acts preferentially on the Rho-related protein G25K/Cdc42Hs in vitro, but can inhibit Rho-mediated responses in vivo. These results suggest that p190, Bcr and RhoGAP play specific roles in signalling pathways through different Rho family members.

The mechanisms underlying Rho-regulated stress fibre formation have been investigated further by analysing the role of other signals known to be activated by lysophos-phatidic acid (LPA). Neither activation of PK-C, increased intracellular Ca^{2+}, decreased cAMP levels or Ras activa-tion appear to mediate stress fibre formation. However, LPA stimulates tyrosine phosphorylation of a number of proteins, including the focal adhesion kinase, pp125[FAK], and genistein, a tyrosine kinase inhibitor, prevents this increase in tyrosine phosphorylation. Genistein also inhibits LPA- and Rho-induced stress fibre formation, implying that a tyrosine kinase lies downstream of Rho in this signal transduction pathway.

Key words: Rho, Rac, GTPase, actin cytoskeleton, lysophosphatidic acid

INTRODUCTION

Rapid reorganization of the actin cytoskeleton is observed in cells in response to many extracellular factors. In fibroblasts, changes in two types of structure containing actin filaments, membrane ruffles and stress fibres, have been monitored fol-lowing addition of growth factors (Ridley and Hall, 1992). Membrane ruffles and lamellipodia are plasma membrane pro-trusions that contain a dense network of cross-linked actin fila-ments, while stress fibres are bundles of actin filaments contain-ing several other proteins including myosin, tropomyosin and α-actinin (Matsudaira, 1991; Stossel, 1993). At least one end of each stress fibre terminates at the plasma membrane in a focal adhesion, where integrins are clustered and link the extracellu-lar matrix to the actin cytoskeleton (Burridge et al., 1988).

There is increasing evidence that a number of small GTP-binding proteins are involved in signal transduction pathways at the plasma membrane. The prototype for this is Ras, which has been shown to be involved in regulating responses leading to proliferation or differentiation (Downward, 1990). More recently, it has been shown that two related proteins, Rac and Rho, are required for growth factor-induced actin reorganiza-tion, at least in fibroblasts (Ridley and Hall, 1992; Ridley et al., 1992). It was found that microinjection of activated Rac induced the formation of membrane ruffles, resembling the response of cells to growth factors such as PDGF and EGF.

Rho, on the other hand, stimulated the formation of stress fibres and focal adhesions, resembling the response to lysophospha-tidic acid (LPA), a component of serum. By inhibiting the function of endogenous Rho or Rac proteins, it was shown that Rac is required for growth factor-induced membrane ruffling, whereas Rho is required for stress fibre formation. Inhibition of Rho was achieved by microinjecting C3 transferase, an exoenzyme produced by *Clostridium botulinum* that ADP-ribosylates and inactivates Rho proteins. Rac was inhibited by microinjecting the dominant inhibitory protein N17 Rac1, which has amino acid 17 mutated from threonine to asparagine.

Interestingly, although activated Ras induces membrane ruffling in fibroblasts, normal Ras is not required for growth factor-induced actin reorganization in Swiss 3T3 cells (Ridley et al., 1992). In addition, Ras-induced membrane ruffling was found to be dependent on Rac activity. This suggests that in these cells at least one response to tyrosine kinase receptors, actin reorganization, is not dependent on Ras, and that receptors feed into multiple small GTP-binding proteins to induce different responses.

Two closely related *Rac* genes, *Rac*1 and *Rac*2, have been cloned, and three *Rho* genes, *Rho*A, *Rho*B and *Rho*C. Other Rho-related proteins in mammalian cells include G25K and its close homologue Cdc42Hs, RhoG and TC10 (Nobes and Hall, 1994). The three Rho proteins are ~80% homologous, and only differ signficantly from each other at the C terminus; whether these differences are functionally relevant is not clear. It is known, however, that the RhoB C-terminal sequences serve to target the protein predominantly to endosomes and lysosomes, whereas RhoA and RhoC C-terminal sequences target them to the plasma membrane and cytosol (Adamson et al., 1992).

Two lines of investigation have yielded further insight into the signal transduction pathways linking receptor activation to actin reorganization. First, the role of proteins, initially identified through their interaction with Rho or Rac in vitro, in regulating Rac- or Rho-dependent signalling in vivo has been studied. Second, the involvement of known signalling molecules or second messengers in regulating Rho- or Rac-mediated actin reorganization has been investigated.

PROTEINS INTERACTING WITH RHO AND RAC

Small GTP-binding proteins cycle between an active, GTP-bound form and an inactive, GDP-bound form. Extracellular signals are presumed to induce an increase in the amount of GTP-bound protein, and three mechanisms have been identified that could regulate this process: sequestration of the protein in an inactive complex with a GDI (guanine nucleotide dissociation inhibitor); stimulation of nucleotide exchange; and stimulation of GTP hydrolysis.

Little is known about the regulation of nucleotide exchange on Rac and Rho. The oncogene product Dbl has been shown to stimulate exchange on the related protein CDC42Hs, but is much less active on Rac (Hart et al., 1991). Several proteins with Dbl homology domains have been identified (Table 1; Nobes and Hall, 1994). As yet none of these proteins has been shown to have exchange factor activity on any member of the Rho family, although Ect2 has been shown to bind to Rac, Rho and Cdc42Hs (Miki et al., 1993). It is therefore possible that this domain represents a Rac/Rho interaction domain, and that only in the case of Dbl does this result in nucleotide exchange.

RhoGDI interacts with Rac, Rho and Cdc42Hs, inhibiting nucleotide exchange, GTP hydrolysis and interaction with GAPs (Nobes and Hall, 1994). In addition, it solubilizes the proteins from membranes, presumably by interacting with the hydrophobic prenyl groups attached to the C terminus of all Ras-related proteins (Isomura et al., 1991; Leonard et al., 1993). RhoGDI is therefore believed to sequester the proteins in an inactive, cytosolic form, and indeed in resting neutrophils it has been shown that Rac is predominantly cytosolic and bound to RhoGDI (Segal and Abo, 1993). Consistent with this model, microinjection of RhoGDI can inhibit Rho-dependent responses such as the formation of stress fibres (Miura et al., 1993).

Several proteins containing domains with GAP activity for Rho-related proteins have been identified and characterized, including RhoGAP, Bcr and p190 (Table 1; Hall, 1992; Boguski and McCormick, 1993). To determine whether these proteins exhibited any specificity in their GAP activity for different members of the Rho family, the GAP domains of each protein were tested for their relative GAP activities in vitro and following microinjection into Swiss 3T3 cells (Ridley et al., 1993). In vitro, at physiological ionic strength, RhoGAP was most effective as a GAP for G25K, while p190 acted on Rho, and Bcr acted on both Rac and G25K but not Rho (Table 2). When the domain of p190 was injected into Swiss 3T3 cells,

Table 1. Potential regulators of Rho-related proteins

(A) *Proteins with Dbl-homologous domains*

Dbl	Exchange factor activity for CDC42Hs
Bcr	Dbl domain in Bcr-Abl in some leukemias
Vav	Oncogene
Ect2	Oncogene
Sos	Exchange factor for Ras
RasGRF	Exchange factor for Ras

(B) *Guanine nucleotide dissociation inhibitors (GDIs)*

RhoGDI	Ubiquitous expression?
LyGDI	Lymphocytes
D4	Haemopoietic cells

(C) *Proteins with GAP domains*

RhoGAP	Active on Rho and G25K/Cdc42Hs
p190	Binds RasGAP
Bcr	Bcr-Abl fusion protein in leukemias
3BP-1	Binds SH3 domains
n-chimaerin	Brain-specific expression
β-chimaerin	Testis-specific expression
p85	Subunit of PI 3-kinase; no GAP activity shown

Table 2. Specificities of GAPs for Rac, Rho and G25K

GAP domain from:	In vitro GAP activity	Microinjected GAP domains
p190	Rho	Rho
Bcr	Rac/G25K	Rac
RhoGAP	G25K	Rho

The best substrate for each GAP domain was determined in vitro by testing their relative GAP activities on RhoA, Rac1 and G25K. In cells, the preference for Rho or Rac was determined by microinjecting each domain, and testing for its ability to inhibit either stress fibre formation or membrane ruffling (Ridley et al., 1993). It was not possible to determine their ability to act as GAPs for G25K in cells, as no measurable biological function of G25K has been described.

it caused the cells to round up in a similar manner to C3 transferase. In addition, it inhibited LPA- and serum-induced stress fibre formation but not PDGF-induced membrane ruffling (Table 2). These results suggest that in cells as well as in vitro p190 acts primarily as a GAP for Rho and not for Rac. In contrast, the GAP domain of Bcr inhibited PDGF-induced membrane ruffling but not LPA-induced stress fibre formation, indicating that Bcr acts as a GAP for Rac but not Rho in cells. RhoGAP, which acts primarily on G25K in vitro, inhibited stress fibre formation when microinjected into cells, but did not inhibit membrane ruffling. An action of growth factors dependent on G25K/Cdc42Hs has so far not been described, so it was not possible to analyse the ability of these GAPs to down-regulate G25K.

These results suggest that each GAP acts specifically in cells to downregulate either Rac or Rho, and therefore that the proteins are likely to act as components of one or other signal transduction pathway leading either to membrane ruffling or stress fibre formation. Whether they act merely as downregulators of Rac or Rho activity, or whether their GAP activity is normally linked in cells to their activation by Rho or Rac, is not known. It is interesting in this respect that both Bcr and p190 have other distinct domains with putative or known functions (Fig. 1). For example, Bcr has a domain with serine/threonine kinase activity (Maru and Witte, 1991), while

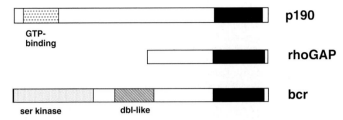

Fig. 1. Domain structures of GTPase activating proteins for Rac and Rho. Diagrammatic representations of the proteins RhoGAP, p190 and Bcr are shown to illustrate the relative positions of different domains; they are not to scale. See text for references.

p190 has a domain homologous to GTP-binding proteins and may therefore itself bind GTP (Settleman et al., 1992). It remains to be determined whether other members of the RhoGAP family also show activity on Rho or Rac in cells, and whether the GAPs tested so far act on other Rho-related proteins such as RhoG and TC10.

The best-characterized system so far involving a Rho-related protein is the NADPH oxidase of phagocytic cells, where Rac1 or Rac2 is required for activation of the complex at the plasma membrane (Segal and Abo, 1993). All of the components of this complex have been cloned, and NADPH oxidase activity can be reconstituted in vitro. This action of Rac is quite distinct from its ability to stimulate membrane ruffling, as the other components of the complex are not expressed in fibroblasts (Morel et al., 1991).

Recently, a serine/threonine kinase, p65^{PAK}, was identified by its ability to interact in vitro with Rac and Cdc42Hs bound to GTP. It was purified from brain extracts, leading to amino acid sequence and cDNA cloning (Manser et al., 1993). The kinase activity of p65^{PAK} is stimulated by Rac and Cdc42Hs, and it may therefore be a Rac/Cdc42Hs target, although at least in vitro it is activated by both proteins and therefore not a specific target.

SIGNAL TRANSDUCTION PATHWAYS REGULATING RHO-MEDIATED STRESS FIBRE FORMATION

LPA is the only extracellular factor tested so far that induces only stress fibre formation and not membrane ruffling in Swiss 3T3 cells. In addition, the second messengers generated in response to LPA have been characterized in detail in fibroblast cell lines (Moolenaar et al., 1992). The LPA response is therefore well-suited to analysis of the signal transduction pathways regulating stress fibre formation.

LPA is the simplest naturally occuring phospholipid, consisting of a glycerol backbone with a fatty acid esterified at position 1 and a phosphate at position 3. It appears to act primarily through a transmembrane receptor, and a putative receptor of approximately 39 kDa has been identified but not yet cloned (van der Bend et al., 1992). LPA is produced by activated platelets and is therefore present in serum, and several biological activities for LPA have been characterized (Table 3).

Early signals activated or generated by LPA in fibroblasts and other cell types are illustrated in Fig. 2. First, LPA activates a Pertussis toxin-sensitive G protein, leading to a decrease in intracellular cAMP levels and activation of Ras.

Table 3. Biological actions of LPA

Cell type	Activity
Fibroblast	DNA synthesis
	Stress fibre formation
	Focal adhesion formation
Platelet	Aggregation
Neuron	Growth cone retraction
Smooth muscle	Contraction
Dictyostelium	Chemotaxis

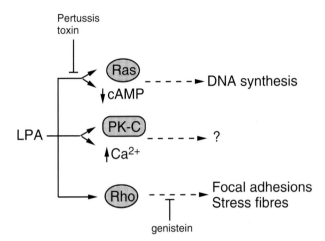

Fig. 2. Signalling pathways activated by LPA. LPA activates at least three distinct signalling pathways in fibroblasts. First, it activates a G$_i$ protein, leading to a decrease in cAMP levels, activation of Ras and downstream signals culminating in DNA synthesis. Second, it activates a phospholipase C, leading to stimulation of protein kinase C isoforms and release of Ca^{2+} from intracellular stores. Third, it activates a Rho-dependent pathway involving tyrosine phosphorylation of proteins, and leading to the formation of focal adhesions and stress fibres.

Neither of these signals were required for stress fibre formation, as the latter was not sensitive to Pertussis toxin (Ridley and Hall, 1994). In addition, neither increasing cAMP levels nor microinjection of neutralizing anti-Ras antibodies inhibited LPA-induced stress fibre formation (Ridley et al., 1992; Ridley and Hall, 1994). Second, LPA stimulates a phospholipase C leading to production of the second messengers inositol trisphosphate (IP$_3$) and diacylglycerol; the former stimulates release of Ca^{2+} from intracellular stores, whereas the latter activates protein kinase C (Moolenaar et al., 1992). Mimicking either or both of these responses did not stimulate stress fibre accumulation: the Ca^{2+} ionophore A23187 or the PK-C-activating phorbol ester PMA were used to mimic these signals. Third, LPA activates another, as yet undefined pathway, which is dependent on protein kinase activation (Jalink et al., 1993), and indeed LPA was found to stimulate the tyrosine phosphorylation of a number of proteins (Kumagai et al., 1993; Ridley and Hall, 1994). As mentioned above, LPA rapidly induces the formation of focal adhesions as well as stress fibres, and it has been shown previously that phosphotyrosine-containing proteins are located at focal adhesions in growing cells, using anti-phosphotyrosine antibodies (Maher et al., 1985; Burridge et al., 1992). We showed that LPA stimulated the accumulation of phosphotyrosine-containing proteins in focal adhesions very rapidly, within one minute of addition (Ridley and Hall, 1994). This process was dependent on endogenous Rho proteins as it was inhibited in cells microinjected with C3 transferase. Microinjected activated V14 RhoA similarly stimulated the clustering of phosphotyrosine-containing proteins at the ends of newly formed stress fibres.

To test whether the formation of stress fibres was dependent on tyrosine kinase activity, we used the kinase inhibitor genistein. This has been shown to inhibit several tyrosine kinases in vivo, and to act preferentially on tyrosine kinases compared to serine/threonine kinases such as protein kinase C or protein kinase A (Akiyama et al., 1987). Genistein inhibited both LPA- and Rho-induced stress fibre formation, and LPA-induced clustering of phosphotyrosine-containing proteins in focal adhesions. Genistein was clearly acting as a tyrosine kinase inhibitor in these cells, as at the same concentration of genistein, the increased tyrosine phosphorylation of several proteins induced by LPA and by bombesin was inhibited. Specifically, increased phosphorylation of pp125^{FAK} (focal adhesion kinase) was inhibited. pp125^{FAK} is a tyrosine kinase located in focal adhesions, which is activated by tyrosine phosphorylation following adhesion of fibroblasts to extracellular matrix proteins such as fibronectin (Schaller and Parsons, 1993). Interestingly, tyrosine phosphorylation of pp125^{FAK} is also stimulated by bombesin (Zachary et al., 1992), which induces stress fibre formation with a similar timecourse to LPA. Our data suggest that a tyrosine kinase acts downstream of Rho and is required for focal adhesion and stress fibre formation, although we cannot formally rule out the possibility that the primary target for genistein in this process is not a tyrosine kinase. Whether pp125^{FAK} plays a regulatory role in the formation of focal adhesions and/or stress fibres remains to be determined.

CONCLUSIONS

It has long been known that Ras is involved in early signal transduction events induced by a variety of extracellular factors. Over the past two years it has become clear that Ras-related proteins of the Rho subfamily are also involved in signal transduction. The plethora of signal transduction proteins and/or oncogene products recently shown to interact with Rho-related proteins indicates a fundamental role for these proteins in cellular responses. The available data suggest that in fibroblasts Rho is most likely to be involved in regulating cell adhesion to the extracellular matrix, and that stress fibres are formed as a consequence of this. In T cells it has been shown that C3 transferase inhibits integrin-mediated cell-cell interactions (Tominaga et al., 1993), suggesting that a more general role of Rho in various cell types could be to regulate integrin-mediated interactions. Rac, on the other hand, in regulating membrane ruffling and lamellipodia extension, is likely to be involved in cell motility responses.

REFERENCES

Adamson, P., Paterson, H. F. and Hall, A. (1992). Intracellular localization of the p21^{rho} proteins. J. Cell Biol. 119, 617-627.

Akiyama, T., Ishida, J., Nakagawa, S., Ogawara, H., Watanabe, S., Itoh, N., Shibuya, M. and Fukami, Y. (1987). Genistein, a specific inhibitor of tyrosine-specific protein kinases. J. Biol. Chem. 262, 5592-5595.

Boguski, M. S. and McCormick, F. (1993). Proteins regulating Ras and its relatives. Nature 366, 643-653.

Burridge, K., Fath, K., Kelly, T., Nuckolls, G. and Turner, C. (1988). Focal adhesions: transmembrane junctions between the extracellular matrix and the cytoskeleton. Annu. Rev. Cell Biol. 4, 487-525.

Burridge, K., Turner, C. E. and Romer, L. H. (1992). Tyrosine phosphorylation of paxillin and pp125FAK accompanies cell adhesion to extracellular matrix: a role in cytoskeletal assembly. J. Cell Biol. 119, 893-903.

Downward, J. (1990). The ras superfamily of small GTP-binding proteins. Trends Biochem. Sci. 15, 469-472.

Hall, A. (1992). Signal transduction through small GTPases - a tale of two GAPs. Cell 69, 389-391.

Hart, M. J., Eva, A., Evans, T., Aaronson, S. A. and Cerione, R. A. (1991). Catalysis of guanine nucleotide exchange on the CDC42Hs protein by the dbl oncogene product. Nature 354, 311-314.

Kumagai, N., Morii, N., Fujisawa, K., Nemoto, Y. and Narumiya, S. (1993). ADP-ribosylation of rho p21 inhibits lysophosphatidic acid-induced protein tyrosine phosphorylation and phosphatidylinositol 3-kinase activation in cultured Swiss 3T3 cells. J. Biol. Chem. 268, 24535-24538.

Isomura, M., Kikuchi, A., Ohga, N. and Takai, Y. (1991). Regulation of binding of rhoB p20 to membranes by its specific regulatory protein, GDP dissociation inhibitor. Oncogene 6, 119-124.

Jalink, K., Eichholtz, T., Postma, F. R., van Corven, E. J. and Moolenaar, W. H. (1993). Lysophosphatidic acid induces neuronal shape changes via a novel, receptor-mediated signaling pathway: similarity to thrombin action. Cell Growth Diff. 4, 247-255.

Leonard, D., Hart, M. J., Platko, J. V., Eva, A., Henzel, W., Evans, T. and Cerione, R. A. (1993). The identification and characterization of a GDP-dissociation inhibitor (GDI) for the CDC42Hs protein. J. Biol. Chem. 267, 22860-22868.

Maher, P. A., Pasquale, E. B., Want, J. Y. J. and Singer, S. J. (1985). Phosphotyrsoine-containing proteins are concentrated in focal adhesions and intercellular junctions in normal cells. Proc. Nat. Acad. Sci. USA 82, 6576-6580.

Manser, E., Leung, T., Salihuddin, H., Tan, L. and Lim, L. (1993). A non-receptor tyrosine kinase that inhibits the GTPase activity of p21^{cdc42}. Nature 363, 364-367.

Maru, Y. and Witte, O. N. (1991). The BCR gene encodes a novel serine/threonine kinase activity within a single exon. Cell 67, 459-468.

Matsudaira, P. (1991). Modular organisation of actin crosslinking proteins. Trends Biochem. Sci. 16, 87-92.

Miki, T., Smith, C. L., Long, J. E., Eva, A. and Fleming, T. P. (1993). Oncogene Ect2 is related to regulators of small GTP-binding proteins. Nature 362, 462-465.

Miura, Y., Kikuchi, A., Musha, T., Kuroda, S., Yaku, H., Sasaki, T. and Takai, Y. (1993). Regulation of morphology by rho p21 and its inhibitory GDP/GTP exchange protein (rho GDI) in Swiss 3T3 cells. J. Biol. Chem. 268, 510-515.

Moolenaar, W. H., Jalink, K. and van Corven, E. J. (1992). Lysophosphatidic acid: a bioactive phospholipid with growth factor-like properties. Rev. Physiol. Biochem. Pharmacol. 119, 47-65.

Morel, F., Doussiere, J. and Vignais, P. V. (1991). The superoxide-generating oxidase of phagocytic cells. Eur. J. Biochem. 201, 523-546.

Nobes, C. and Hall, A. (1994). Regulation and function of the Rho subfamily of small GTPases. Curr. Opin. Genetics Dev. 4, 77-81.

Ridley, A. J. and Hall, A. (1992). The small GTP-binding protein rho regulates the assembly of focal adhesions and actin stress fibers in response to growth factors. Cell 70, 389-399.

Ridley, A. J., Paterson, H. F., Johnston, C. L., Diekmann, D. and Hall, A. (1992). The small GTP-binding protein rac regulates growth factor-induced membrane ruffling. Cell 70, 401-410.

Ridley, A. J., Self, A. J., Kasmi, F., Paterson, H. F., Hall, A., Marshall, C. J. and Ellis, C. (1993). rho family GTPase activating proteins p190, bcr and rhoGAP show distinct specificities in vitro and in vivo. EMBO J. 12, 5151-5160.

Ridley, A. J. and Hall, A. (1994). Signal transduction pathways regulating Rho-mediated stress fibre formation: requirement for a tyrosine kinase. EMBO J. 13, 2600-2610.

Schaller, M. D. and Parsons, J. T. (1993). Focal adhesion kinase: an integrin-linked protein tyrosine kinase. Trends Cell. Biol. 3, 258-262.

Segal, A. and Abo, A. (1993). The biochemical basis of the NADPH oxidase of phagocytes. *Trends Biochem. Sci.* **18**, 43-47.

Settleman, J., Narasimhan, V., Forster, L. C. and Weinberg, R. A. (1992). Molecular cloning of cDNAs encoding the GAP-associated protein p190: implications for a signalling pathway from Ras to the nucleus. *Cell* **69**, 539-549.

Stossel, T. P. (1993). On the crawling of mammalian cells. *Science* **260**, 1086-1094.

Tominaga, T., Sugie, K., Hirata, M., Morii, N., Fukata, J., Uchida, A., Imura, H. and Narumiya, S. (1993). Inhibition of PMA-induced, LFA-1-dependent lymphocyte aggregation by ADP-ribosylation of the small molecular weight GTP-binding protein, Rho. *J. Cell Biol.* **111**, 2097-2108.

van der Bend, R. L., Brunner, J., Jalink, K., van Corven, E. J., Moolenaar, W. H. and van Blitterswijk, W. J. (1992). Identification of a putative membrane receptor for the bioactive phospholipid, lysophosphatidic acid. *EMBO J.* **11**, 2495-2501.

Zachary, I., Sinnett-Smith, J. and Rozengurt, E. (1992). Bombesin, vasopressin and endothelin stimulation of tyrosine phosphorylation in Swiss 3T3 cells. *J. Biol. Chem.* **267**, 19031-19034.

Index

Journal of Cell Science Supplements

No. 1   Higher Order Structure in the Nucleus
Edited by P. R. Cook and R. A. Laskey
ISBN: 0 9508709 4 3   234 pp.
Proceedings of 1st BSCB–COB Symposium
£8   U.S.$17   1984

No. 2   The Cell Surface in Plant Growth and Development
Edited by K. Roberts, A. W. B. Johnston, C. W. Lloyd, P. Shaw
and H. W. Woolhouse
ISBN: 0 9508709 7 8   350 pp.
The 6th John Innes Symposium
£11   U.S.$24   1985

No. 3   Growth Factors: Structure and Function
Edited by C. R. Hopkins and R. C. Hughes
ISBN: 0 9508709 9 4   242 pp.
BSCB–COB Symposium
Sold out   1985

No. 4   Prospects in Cell Biology
Edited by A. V. Grimstone, Henry Harris and R. T. Johnson
ISBN: 0 948601 01 9   458 pp.
An essay volume to mark the journal's 20th anniversary
Sold out   1986

No. 5   The Cytoskeleton: Cell Function and Organization
Edited by C. W. Lloyd, J. S. Hyams and R. M. Warn
ISBN: 0 948601 04 3   360 pp.
BSCB–COB Symposium
Sold out   1986

No. 6   The Molecular Biology of DNA Repair
Edited by A. R. S. Collins, R. T. Johnson and J. M. Boyle
ISBN: 0 948601 06 X   353 pp.
£36   U.S.$64   1987

No. 7   Virus Replication and Genome Interactions
Edited by J. W. Davies et al.
ISBN: 0 948601 10 8   350 pp.
The 7th John Innes Symposium
£36   U.S.$64   1987

No. 8   Cell Behaviour: Shape, Adhesion and Motility
Edited by J. Heaysman, A. Middleton and F. Watts
ISBN: 0 948601 12 4   449 pp.
BSCB–COB Symposium
£31   U.S.$54   1987

No. 9   Macrophage Plasma Membrane Receptors: Structure and Function
Edited by S. Gordon
ISBN: 0 948601 13 2   200 pp.
£25   U.S.$44   1988

No. 10   Stem Cells
Edited by Brian I. Lord and T. Michael Dexter
ISBN: 0 948601 16 7   285 pp.
BSCB–COB Symposium
£31   U.S.$59   1988

No. 11   Protein Targeting
Edited by K. F. Chater et al.
ISBN: 0 948601 21 3   261 pp.
The 8th John Innes Symposium
£31   U.S.$59   1989

No. 12   The Cell Cycle
Edited by R. T. Hunt et al.
ISBN: 0 948601 23 X   300 pp.
BSCB–COB Symposium
Sold out   1989

No. 13   Growth Factors in Cell & Developmental Biology
Edited by M. Waterfield
ISBN: 0 948601 27 3   208 pp. + index
£26   U.S.$49   1990

No. 14   Motor Proteins
Edited by R. Cross and J. Kendrick Jones
ISBN: 0 948601 29 9   175 pp.
EMBO techniques workshop
£31   U.S.$54   1991

No. 15   Nerve Cell Biology
Edited by Dennis Bray and A. Lumsden et al.
ISBN: 0 948601 30 2   134 pp.
BSCB–COB Symposium
£34   U.S.$62   1991

No. 16   Transcriptional Regulation in Cell Differentiation and Development
Edited by Peter Rigby, Robb Krumlauf and Frank Grosveld
ISBN: 0 948601 37 X   130 pp.
BSCB–COB Symposium
£34   U.S.$52   1992

No. 17   Epithelial and Neuronal Cell Polarity and Differentiation
Edited by E. Rodriguez Boulan and W. J. Nelson
ISBN: 0 948601 40 X   245 pp.
Keystone Symposium
£49   U.S.$69   1993

This series of supplementary casebound volumes deals with topics of outstanding
interest to cell and molecular biologists

These are provided free to subscribers to *Journal of Cell Science*. They may be purchased separately from:
The Company of Biologists Limited, Bidder Building, 140 Cowley Road, Cambridge CB4 4DL, UK

ORDERING: Add £4 ($6) per book for postage and packaging
24-hour by FAX: Cambridge (01223) 423353/International +44 1223 423353